Natural and Divine Law
Reclaiming the Tradition
for Christian Ethics

Saint Paul University

NOVALIS

William B. Eerdmans Publishing Company
Grand Rapids, Michigan / Cambridge, U.K.

First published 1999 by Novalis, Saint Paul University,
223 Main Street, Ottawa, Ontario K1S 1C4 Canada.

This edition published 1999 by
Wm. B. Eerdmans Publishing Co.
255 Jefferson Avenue SE, Grand Rapids, MI 49503 /
P.O. Box 163, Cambridge CB3 9PU U.K.

Printed in the United States of America.

ISBN-10: 0-8028-4697-1
ISBN-13: 978-0-8028-4697-6

www.eerdmans.com

Natural and Divine Law

Reclaiming the Tradition
for Christian Ethics

For Sister Mary Emil Penet, I.H.M.

Table of Contents

Preface

It is my pleasant task to thank those who have supported my efforts in writing this book. Thanks are due first of all to the administration of the University of Notre Dame, and to my departmental chair, John Cavadini, for granting me a sabbatical during the 1997–1998 academic year, during which this book was completed. My research and writing were supported by generous grants from the Notre Dame Graduate School, the Institute for Scholarship in the Liberal Arts of the College of Arts and Letters at Notre Dame, and by a Henry Luce III Fellowship for 1997–1998 awarded by the Association of Theological Schools in the United States and Canada. During my sabbatical, I also benefited from the hospitality of Christ Church, Oxford, as a temporary Honorary Member of their Senior Common Room. I am deeply appreciative of this institutional and financial support, since without it my work would have been much more difficult.

I also want to express my thanks to those who commented on some portion of the manuscript, including Margaret Farley and Hindy Najman. Joseph Pearson read an early draft of the complete manuscript and offered me a number of invaluable comments and suggestions, as well as preparing an extensive bibliography. In addition, Mark Johnson provided me with a very helpful bibliography on topics related to this project. William Mattison prepared the bibliography for this volume, thus saving me much time and trouble. I am also indebted to two anonymous readers; to my editor at Novalis, Stephen Scharper; and to the copy editor who worked on my manuscript, Curtis Fahey, for many helpful comments and suggestions. Finally, my thanks to Anne Louise Mahoney of Novalis for invaluable assistance in facilitating the process.

Portions of this manuscript were read at a series of lectures sponsored by the Australian Theological Forum and in two lectures sponsored by the Catholic Institute of Sydney during April 20-28, 1998, and I benefited greatly from the discussions afterwards. My husband, Joseph Blenkinsopp, read and commented on a portion of the manuscript, and in addition reviewed many of my translations. He has saved me from many errors; of course any that remain are my responsibility alone. It goes without saying – but I will nonetheless say it – that his support went well beyond this, and I never can adequately express my gratitude to him.

This book is dedicated to a woman whose influence in my life, and in the life of the U.S. Roman Catholic Church, has been incalculable. Sister Mary Emil Penet, a member of the Sisters, Servants of the Immaculate Heart of Mary, introduced me to moral theology while I was a student at Weston School of Theology (now Weston Jesuit School of Theology) from 1976 to 1980, and it is largely due to her influence that I went into this field. For me, she was an inspired and inspiring teacher and mentor, and remains a beloved friend. For the church, she was a challenging leader at a time of transition for women religious, an educator, and a theologian who helped to bring the insights of Vatican II to the Catholic Church in the United States. This book is dedicated to her as a token of my love and gratitude.

Foreword

From its beginnings among the Stoics of antiquity, the natural law tradition of ethical theory has undergone many transformations. The most prominent contemporary spokesmen of the tradition, John Finnis and Joseph Boyle, who see themselves as representing the Aristotelian-Thomistic version of the tradition, offer natural law theory as a mode of ethical inquiry which is independent both of all comprehensive religious and philosophical perspectives, and of all concrete moral communities. In particular, they present it as independent of theology. It is from human nature as such that they propose to derive ethical principles; and it is their claim that these principles are not only knowable, but in good measure actually *known*, by every rational adult human being whatsoever.

These claims have evoked reactions in many quarters – from, among others, those "secular" theorists who insist that ethical theorizing has no other basis than the concrete moral practices of particular communities, and from those theologians who insist that revelation alone gives us reliable access to what it is that is morally required of us. Unaided reason, say these theologians, is not only insufficient; it demonstrably leads us astray.

Jean Porter's book, *Natural and Divine Law: Reclaiming the Tradition for Christian Ethics*, represents an extraordinarily important intervention into this current discussion. It is typical of present-day discussions of natural law to treat Aquinas as representative of the entire medieval scholastic version of the tradition. While by no means neglecting Aquinas,

Professor Porter considers a wide range of natural law thinkers, from the mid-twelfth century to the end of the thirteenth. Aquinas is thus placed in context rather than being treated as a solitary mountain peak.

What emerges is a strikingly different understanding of the scholastic natural law tradition from that which has become familiar to us. What Professor Porter shows, beyond dispute, is that the medieval scholastics, rather than theorizing about natural law independently of theology, embedded such theorizing firmly within their theology. They did indeed see ethics as grounded in the natural givens of human life; but their understanding of those natural givens was forthrightly based in Scripture and shaped by theological reflection. In Professor Porter's own summary of their procedure, the process of ethical reflection "typically involves some reflection on the givens of human nature, yet the moral significance of these givens can never just be read off from observation and experience. Christian reflection on human nature, or human experience or needs or aspirations, always involves an element of selective interpretation in the light of theological commitments."

In developing her thesis, Professor Porter goes beyond demonstrating that the medieval scholastics interpretated natural law in terms of such abstract theological categories as creation, divine wisdom, etc.; in a fascinating discussion she shows how even their understanding of partic-ular ethical principles was shaped by their theological convictions – as well as by a variety of ecclesiastical and civic concerns during a time of drastic and rapid social change. In particular, she devotes one of her chapters to a fascinating discussion of how their understanding of human equality was shaped in this way.

Though her book, at heart, is an essay in intellectual history, Professor Porter is by no means an antiquarian; sprinkled throughout her discussion are imaginative suggestions as to how the medieval scholastic version of the natural law tradition can be appropriated in our own day. The upshot is two-fold. On the one hand, natural law theorizing is reclaimed for Christian theology. Rather than being seen as ineluctably foreign to Christian theological ethics, we now have before our eyes an example of how natural law theory can be embedded within, and shaped by, Christian theology. On the other hand, human nature itself is restored to Christian ethics. Christian ethics need not be treated as reporting the content of a bolt of grace from the transcendent having nothing to do with what we are; Christian ethics speaks to what is required if creatures with natures such as ours are to flourish.

Professor Porter nicely captures this double import for Christian ethics of her discussion when she says, "Christian morality is grounded in a theological interpretation of the natural givens of human life." Christian ethics speaks of *the natural givens of human life*. But in the conviction that a neutral interpretation of those givens is not possible, it offers its own scripturally based *theological interpretations* of those natural givens.

Nicholas Wolterstorff
Noah Porter Professor of Philosophical Theology
Yale University

Introduction

The influence of natural law theories on the formation of modern moral and political thought has long been recognized. Even in contemporary secular society, we do not seem to be able to do without some minimal conception of what is natural or appropriate to human life, particularly in relation to sexuality, family relationships, and medical ethics. As these issues become more pressing and complex, we are seeing a revival of interest in the natural law and related subjects among philosophers and legal scholars.

Yet in spite of recent groundbreaking work on the theological significance of the natural law, theologians still tend to be suspicious of it. This is unfortunate. By rejecting the natural law as a source for moral reflection, theologians are rejecting a potentially fruitful point of contact with the work of scholars in related fields, in an area that has long been considered to be the special province of theologians. Even more importantly, they are overlooking one of the richest resources in our tradition for developing a distinctively Christian account of the moral life.

To a considerable extent, the reluctance to consider a natural law ethic as a viable option for contemporary Christian ethics is based on a conception of the natural law that emerged in the early modern period, and that still dominates contemporary discussions of this topic. However, medieval interpretations of the natural law are significantly different from most later versions, including the influential "new natural law" theory of

Germain Grisez and John Finnis. Once medieval natural law thinking is appreciated on its own terms, it offers an unexpectedly fruitful starting point for distinctively theological reflection on contemporary moral questions.

In this book, I will offer an interpretation of one medieval concept of the natural law, seen on its own terms and in light of its relevance for contemporary Christian ethics. More specifically, I will draw on a representative sample of texts from canonical jurists and theologians from the time of Gratian's *Decretum* (c. 1140) to the latter part of the thirteenth century. My aim in doing so will first of all be to offer an accurate interpretation of these texts, seen in their own intellectual and social context. However, my overall purpose in this project is constructive as well as historical. I will read these authors as an ethicist, with the aim of reconstructing the moral arguments that they present and drawing them into conversation with our own contemporaries. This is likely to strike many readers as an odd or unpromising project; let me say something more about its rationale.

At least part of the reason for the suspicion of the natural law among many theologians lies in the fact that until recently, Roman Catholic thinkers in particular emphasized the purely rational and non-theological status of the natural law. For this very reason, many contemporary theologians, Catholic as well as Protestant, have concluded that a natural law morality is insufficiently grounded in a distinctively Christian world view.

The view of the natural law just described can be traced to the early modern period, when both theologians and secular political thinkers began to emphasize the rational autonomy of the natural law. However, the understanding of the natural law that dominated medieval thought, particularly in the scholastic period, is very different from the modern conception in this regard. As R. W. Southern has brilliantly argued in his recent *Scholastic Humanism and the Unification of Europe*, the scholasticism of the twelfth and thirteenth centuries was intimately connected with the rapid institutional and social development that marked that period; it was shaped by these developments, and served in turn to direct and solidify them.[1] Within this context, the doctrine of the natural law provided a basis for interpreting and legitimating new forms of social life. No purely philosophical or non-Christian theory could have functioned in this way in Western medieval society. Yet it would not have been possible for this society to arrive at social consensus on the basis of an appeal to Scripture or the practices of the church alone. Not only was this period marked by a bewildering variety of new institutions and ways of life, including new forms of vowed religious life, competing understandings of marriage, and the new political and economic practices occasioned by the rapid expansion of urban life, but the advocates of new practices were regularly thrown into conflict with defenders of more traditional customs. In these conflicts, *all* parties claimed that the practices that they were defending were grounded in Scripture and Christian morality.

Contrary to what is commonly assumed, medieval natural law thinkers did not attempt to derive moral principles from a supposedly self-evident and fixed conception of human nature. The concept of nature was a theological and not merely a philosophical notion for them, thanks to the extensive work on the theological significance of the natural world that began early in the twelfth century. Building on this work, taken together with key scriptural texts from Genesis and the Pauline letters, they developed a theological conception of human nature that enabled them to distinguish between those aspects of our nature that are normative, and those that are not. Interpreted on this basis, the natural law in its primary sense was identified either with reason or with the most basic natural principles of action, which were in turn linked to the image of God, that is, the capacity for moral judgment found in all men and women. So understood, the natural law was distinct from specific customs, practices, and laws, which could thus be evaluated by the criterion of their (necessarily imperfect) approximation to the ideals of natural equality and respect for the goodness of creation.

The doctrine of the natural law was valuable to theologians and jurists in this period because it offered a generally acceptable framework for adjudicating these competing claims, by providing a theological interpretation of the most fundamental principles of human action. As we will see, there were other social and moral concepts to which they might have turned: for example, the image of society as a body, or the motif of the three orders of society. However, these other concepts were too closely linked to specific social arrangements to be useful in a situation of far-reaching social change. In contrast, the idea of a natural law, because it focused analysis at the level of the most basic principles of human action, was more readily adapted to the task of explaining and evaluating practices in a rapidly evolving society. At the same time, because the scholastics understood the natural law in theological terms, they were able to develop this idea into a framework for social analysis and justification suited for an overwhelmingly Christian society.

When medieval natural law writings are approached on their own terms, in light of their own agenda and assumptions, they are revealed to be more sophisticated and persuasive on a wide range of topics than we generally realize. Our social context and our theological and philosophical assumptions are too different from those of our medieval predecessors to allow us to adopt their conception of the natural law without considerable reformulation. Nonetheless, just as the very considerable social and intellectual distance between the Greeks and ourselves has not prevented the recent philosophical reappropriation of Aristotle's theory of virtue, so the distance between the medieval world and ourselves need not prevent us from learning from their theological interpretation of morality.

I also want to make a stronger claim for the relevance of medieval natural law reflection for contemporary thought. That is, I believe that the particular concept of the natural law to be examined in this book is fundamentally sound and can still serve as a basis for fruitful moral reflection. Of course, such a contemporary reappropriation of this concept would involve its thoroughgoing revision, as I have already noted. Nonetheless, contemporary Christian ethicists who find the natural law approach congenial need not invent it *de novo*; there is a medieval version of this approach that is both cogent and supple enough to allow for development and appropriation in our own context. That, at least, is my claim.

Furthermore, at the level of discussion of specific topics, medieval reflection on the natural law contains much that is of value. At the very least, it illuminates the often hidden theological assumptions that still govern secular as well as religious thinking on such issues as the moral significance of family relationships, the morality of killing, and the grounds for and limits of equality. Precisely for this reason, a study of medieval natural law writings can offer an unexpected basis for dialogue between theologians and secular thinkers on such issues. And the moral arguments of our medieval forebears on concrete issues are often unexpectedly subtle and cogent, offering insight even when they do not persuade.

In what follows, I will approach the views of selected medieval authors as an ethicist who attempts to draw on the work of historians, rather than as a historian in my own right. I rely extensively (although not exclusively) on two collections of primary texts by Odon Lottin and Rudolf Weigand, and I depend on the scholarship of others to reconstruct the intellectual and social contexts for medieval thought. Whatever claim to distinctiveness this study may have, it lies in my analysis of the moral arguments of medieval authors and in my efforts to draw out the implications of those arguments.

At the same time, the distinction between historical and constructive scholarship is not sharply fixed. Intellectual history, which takes the development of ideas as its proper domain, will almost always be grounded in the interpretation of historical texts. And as Hans-Georg Gadamer has taught us, this process of interpretation necessarily requires an active engagement with the claims and arguments put forth in these texts: "When we try to understand a text, we don't try to transpose ourselves into the author's mind, but, if one wants to use this terminology, we try to transpose ourselves into the perspective within which he has formed his views. But this simply means that we try to understand how what he is saying could be right. If we want to understand, we will try to make his arguments even stronger."[2]

For this reason, any text that speaks to us out of a particular intellectual discipline will necessarily be approached from within the perspective of our own best understanding of that discipline. In order to understand a philosophical, theological, or legal text, the historian must engage in the practice of philosophy, theology, or jurisprudence, at least to some degree. By the same token, a theologian (for example) who wishes to learn from historical texts will necessarily find herself thinking as a historian, inseparably from her critical engagement with those texts.

This does not mean that we are free to ignore the distance between ourselves and authors of the past. One of the commonest sources of misunderstanding of the medieval texts on the natural law has been the widespread assumption that they understand such key concepts as reason and nature in precisely the same way as we do.[3] And yet we can only approach historical texts from within the framework of our own presuppositions and our best understanding of the subject at hand. Through the process of critical engagement with historical texts, the differences between their conceptual framework and our own will progressively emerge, if we are open to seeing these differences. This, in turn, is one reason why the serious study of historical texts is so valuable for scholars in a wide range of disciplines; not only does it offer access to arguments and ideas that would otherwise be forgotten, it can also provide a critical perspective on fundamental assumptions of contemporary thought.

The process of interpreting historical texts will always carry with it the dangers of anachronism and hasty appropriation in the service of one's own concerns. No doubt the trained historian is less likely to fall into these traps than are scholars in other fields, but these dangers are inherent in the process of interpretation itself. Yet it is possible to minimize them by remaining attentive to the social location and the purposes of the text, so far as these can be recovered. In addition, the scrutiny of colleagues and the self-correcting mechanisms of critical reflection will provide additional controls to anachronistic or hasty interpretations. In the last analysis, the best remedy for the errors generated by the interpretative process is a further and more judicious application of the same process.

Because this study represents an attempt to draw on historical texts in the service of moral reflection, it can be read from more than one perspective. Seen in one way, it offers an interpretation of the concept of natural law developed by the first generations of scholastic jurists and theologians. In order to develop this interpretation, I begin by placing these writings in their social and intellectual contexts in Chapter 1. I then go on in Chapters 2 and 3 to explore the understandings of nature, reason, and Scripture that inform scholastic reflections on the natural law, paying particular attention to the emergence of a specifically Christian theological account of the natural law in this period. In Chapter 3, I also take up the relation of the natural law to the eternal law, and consider how far the scholastics considered the natural law to be a legally binding code. Then, in Chapters 4 and 5, I draw out the implications of this concept by examining how it was applied to sexual ethics, including the question of the relation between the sexes, and social ethics, including most fundamentally the problems raised for a natural law morality by the conventional character of most social institutions.

Alternatively, this study can be read from the perspective of the moral questions that it addresses. Chapter 1 surveys recent contemporary theological work on the natural law and the moral significance of human nature, including the work of such Protestant scholars as James Gustafson and Oliver O'Donovan, as well as Catholics such as Stephen Pope. Chapters 2 and 3 offer reflections on the relation of Christian ethics to its basic sources: that is, nature, reason, and Scripture. In Chapter 2, I consider the various senses in which nature and reason can be taken to be morally normative, and address some of the objections to moral appeals to human nature generated by modern social and scientific understandings of the human person. In Chapter 3 I defend the scholastic understanding of the natural law as a scriptural doctrine against those who understand the natural law as a purely rational universal morality, on the one hand, and Barthian defenders of an exclusively Christocentric approach to ethics on the other. Finally, in Chapter 4 I discuss a number of specific questions, including the moral and theological significance of marriage, the status of women, contraception, and homosexuality; similarly, in Chapter 5 I take up such topics as equality, ownership, servitude, the use of force by Christians, and the status of natural rights. In each case, I take my starting points from medieval reflections. However, I also discuss the views of such contemporary authors as James Barr, Lisa Cahill, and Stanley Hauerwas, with the aim of placing their views in a mutually illuminating relationship with the views of their medieval forebears. My aim throughout has been to present these medieval authors as conversation partners from whom we can learn, even as we transform their ideas in the process of appropriating them for our own moral reflections.

These days we are all rightly attentive to the ways in which personal history and social location shape our scholarly efforts. No doubt the fact that I am a Catholic had a great deal to do with my initial interest in medieval moral thought, and it probably helps to account for my rather peculiar enthusiasm for it. Nonetheless, I am convinced that the interest and importance of moral thought in this period cuts across the usual denominational and ideological lines. This book reflects that conviction, and represents my best effort so far to explain and justify it.

Except where otherwise indicated, all translations are my own. I have usually anglicized the spelling of personal and place names, except when to do so would be confusing or produce incongruous results. However, I generally leave the titles of works in Latin, and when a work is referred to by its opening words, I leave those in Latin as well.

In translating the scholastics or describing their views, I use the masculine personal pronoun for general references to human beings, and for references to God. I hope that this is not offensive; it seemed to me that any other usage would modernize these authors in a misleading way. When discussing my own views and those of our contemporaries, I use the feminine pronoun for general references to human beings, and I avoid the use of personal pronouns to refer to God.

Notes to the Introduction

1   R.W. Southern, *Scholastic Humanism and the Unification of Europe, Volume One: Foundations* (Oxford: Blackwell Press, 1995).

2   Hans-Georg Gadamer, *Truth and Method*, 2nd ed., translation revised by Joel Weinsheimer and Donald G. Marshall (New York: Crossroad, 1989), 292.

3   I argue for this claim in more detail in "Contested Categories: Reason, Nature, and Natural Order in Medieval Accounts of the Natural Law," *Journal of Religious Ethics* 24:2 (1996), 207-232.

Chapter 1

Framing the Question

Summary: This chapter places the current investigation of the natural law into two contexts: namely, the contemporary renewal of interest in the natural law, and the social and intellectual milieu that shaped the scholastic concept on which this study is focused. The first section examines traditional theological criticisms of the natural law, and then goes on to look at the considerations that have motivated a growing number of theologians, Protestant as well as Catholic, to reassess natural law approaches to ethics. The second section looks at the "twelfth-century renaissance," which provides the social context for the emergence of the scholastic concept of the natural law, and the third focuses on scholasticism itself as the intellectual context for this concept. At the same time, the parameters of this study are delineated more precisely, as comprising selected canon lawyers and theologians from the time of the canon lawyer Gratian (c. 1140) to the death of both Bonaventure and Aquinas in 1274. Finally, the last section offers a preliminary sketch of the main lines of the scholastic concept of the natural law.

■

The idea that we can remake ourselves indefinitely, without reference to natural boundaries, is widely considered to be one of the hallmarks of modernity. Yet even in contemporary secular society, we do not seem to be able to do without some minimal concept of what is natural or appropriate to human life, particularly in relation to sexuality, family relationships, and medical ethics. As these issues become more pressing and complex, we are seeing a revival of interest in the moral significance of human nature.

Until comparatively recently, this topic would have been ruled out of consideration from the outset. Most educated people believed that evolutionary theory has fatally undermined the belief that we possess any definite human nature at all. Furthermore, most philosophers assumed that David Hume and G.E. Moore had shown the logical impossibility of deriving moral conclusions from the facts of human nature, a mistake that came to be known as the naturalistic fallacy.[1]

Yet today there is a rapidly expanding field of scientific research, known as evolutionary psychology, built on the premise that human behavior can be explained, at least in part, as an expression of species-specific nature that can be interpreted in terms of evolutionary adaptions.[2] This observation is meant to include our moral behavior which, it is said, should be a subject for scientific study rather than philosophical speculation.[3] Philosophers might be excused for being less than enthusiastic about this prospect. Nonetheless, a growing number of philosophers are also exploring the claim that human nature is morally significant. Many of these, including Mary Midgley, Owen Flanagan, and Leon Kass, are motivated by recent developments in science and medicine, while others, for example, Martha Nussbaum, John Casey, and Julia Annas, raise this question in the course of exploring the contemporary significance of classical moral thought.[4]

It would appear that the idea of a morally significant human nature is an idea whose time has come, or has come again. In saying this, I do not mean to suggest that this idea is accepted by everyone. On the contrary, the work of evolutionary psychologists and of the philosophers mentioned above is highly controversial. Nonetheless, owing to their efforts, human nature is once again a mainstream topic for moral philosophy as well as scientific inquiry. As the case for the biological roots of morality becomes more impressive, and as issues of medical and sexual ethics and ecology become more complex and pressing, we can expect to see still more philosophical interest in this topic.

Until recently, most Christian theologians and ethicists have been reluctant to address the question of the moral significance of human nature.[5] At first glance this reluctance is surprising, because there is a rich tradition of specifically theological reflection on the moral significance of human nature: namely, the Christian tradition of natural law morality. In fact, however, Christian ethicists have been slow to enter into discussions about the moral significance of human nature precisely because they associate this topic with pre-modern accounts of the natural law. For many Christian theologians, Catholic as well as Protestant, these accounts are deeply problematic. The widely influential "new natural law" theory developed by Germain Grisez and John Finnis might seem to offer a counterexample to this claim. However, this theory is explicitly distinguished from "old" natural law theories by the fact that it does not attempt to derive moral conclusions from observations about human nature.[6]

Yet so long as Christian theologians avoid talking about the moral significance of human nature, both theological ethics and the wider social discourse will be impoverished. Problems in biomedical and sexual ethics lead the Christian ethicist inevitably to reflect on this question and, as Stephen Pope has recently shown, it is also inextricably connected with the foundational issue of the ordering of our obligations to others.[7] Moreover, this reluctance prevents Christian theologians from bringing a distinctively theological perspective to bear on recent work on the biological roots of morality.

These and similar considerations have led a growing number of Christian ethicists to take up the problem of the moral significance of human nature. By no means has this interest been confined to Catholic scholars. One of the most influential voices in this discussion has been the Reformed theologian James Gustafson, whose insistence on the significance of nature as a theological category has shaped the thought of both Catholic and Protestant ethicists.[8] Similarly, the Anglican theologian Oliver O'Donovan has recently argued that an evangelical theology is not at variance with, but to the contrary implies an attentiveness to the natural order as the basis for Christian ethics.[9] In addition, and partly thanks to, the influence of Gustafson and O'Donovan, a number of other scholars, both Catholic and Protestant, have begun to reconsider the prospects for developing a natural law ethic that acknowledges the moral significance of our shared nature. Among Catholics, these include, in addition to Stephen Pope, Martin Rhonheimer, Ruth Caspar, Thomas Schubeck, and Cynthia Crysdale, and among Protestants, Philip Hefner, Michael Northcott, and Martin Cook.[10]

So far, however, this renewed openness to some version of the natural law has not led to much interest in examining earlier versions of these accounts. The exception to this, of course, is the account of the natural law offered by Thomas Aquinas, which figures centrally in the work of a number of contemporary Christian ethicists. Yet, as noted in the Introduction, no one author – not even Aquinas – can fairly represent the richness of an extended tradition of discussion. And the discussion of the natural law that provides the immediate context for Aquinas' work is one of the richest, and yet most undervalued, traditions to be found in the long history of Christian theological ethics.

In this book, I will examine the concept of the natural law as it emerged in this medieval discussion, with the aim of recovering it as a resource for contemporary Christian ethics. More specifically, I will set out an interpretation of this concept as it was developed through the work of canon lawyers and theologians in the twelfth and thirteenth centuries. (Hereafter, I will refer to this as the scholastic concept of the natural law, for reasons to be explained in more detail below.) In doing so, I am motivated by two convictions. The first is that the concept of the natural law that emerged in this period is interesting and worthy of serious study in its own right. Second, I am convinced that medieval scholastic writings on the natural law include a great deal that is sound and relevant to contemporary moral thought, and more especially to Christian ethics.

What I will offer, then, is an interpretation of the scholastic concept of the natural law that is grounded in an engaged reading of selected texts. In doing so, I hope to present the ideas and arguments of these texts accurately but, at the same time, I intend to evaluate them precisely as ideas and arguments. This will involve both placing these texts in the context of the assumptions and concerns that gave rise to them, and evaluating what we find there in the light of our own best understanding of the issues at stake. My aim in this project is thus constructive as well as historical. By reflecting on certain issues with the authors of these texts, I hope to offer a contribution to contemporary theological ethics, as well as advancing our understanding of those authors' views.

In *Truth and Method,* Hans-Georg Gadamer remarks that in order to interpret a text, we must attempt a fusion of horizons; that is, we must bring together the assumptions, commitments, and concerns that shape our approach to a text, with the possibly quite different assumptions and concerns out of which it was produced.[11] That will be my aim in this chapter. In the first section, I will look more closely at recent work on the natural law among contemporary Christian ethicists, in order to delineate the assumptions and concerns that form our own horizon. The next two sections will be devoted to the social and academic contexts that gave rise to the scholastic concept of the natural law. In the last section, I will offer a first sketch of that concept, with the aim of indicating in a preliminary way how it is significant for theological ethics today.

1. Recent work on the natural law

Appeals to a natural law comprise a long and rich tradition of moral discourse, which includes a number of approaches to morality. Within the context of theological ethics, the natural law has generally been understood in terms of what I will describe as its traditional versions, to distinguish them from the "new natural law" mentioned above.

I speak of traditional versions or accounts of the natural law, rather than of one traditional theory of the natural law, because there have been a number of such accounts.[12] The most familiar of these is the version that emerged in early modern Catholic theology and subsequently was incorporated into official Catholic teachings. According to this version, pre-rational aspects of our nature, particularly those associated with the processes of reproduction, set clear limits on human action in the form of prohibitions against acts that violate the natural teleologies of biological processes. Hence, this version presupposes a definite idea of human nature and offers a natural law comprised of definite, stringent moral precepts. While it would be unfair to characterize it as a sexual ethic only, its norms for sexual behavior comprise its most distinctive feature.

Moreover, the official Catholic version of the natural law implies a strong commitment to moral universalism. Because moral norms are grounded in human nature, which is the same everywhere, they are accessible to all reasonable men and women without the necessity of revelation. It does not follow on this view that the natural law exists independently of God; to the contrary, the natural law is grounded in God's wisdom as creator, and sanctioned by God's authority as supreme lawgiver. Nonetheless, Christian revelation is not necessary in order to arrive at some knowledge of the natural law on this view, although revelation does clarify and confirm our natural law reasoning.

The great appeal of the official Catholic version of the natural law lies in its confidence in the moral capacities of the human race and its optimism about the possibilities for building a moral community among all persons of good will.[13] But these qualities have also given rise to trenchant theological criticisms. Since the time of the Reformation, Protestant theologians have tended to view the doctrine of the natural law as an expression of human pride, an effort to establish human righteousness apart from God's law and God's grace – a line of criticism powerfully expressed in this century by Karl Barth.[14] Similarly, Reinhold Niebuhr forcefully argued for the classical Protestant view that the pervasive reality of human sinfulness has decisively undermined our knowledge of a natural moral order.[15] More recently, Stanley Hauerwas has rejected the doctrine of the natural law on the grounds that it provides an insufficiently theological basis for a Christian ethic.[16]

It would be a mistake, however, to assume that the official Catholic version of the natural law has consistently been attacked by Protestants and defended by Catholics. This would have been roughly true in the early decades of the twentieth century, when Catholic moral theology was still dominated by this version of the natural law. Even then, however, Catholic theologians were themselves beginning to raise questions about the validity of this understanding of the natural law, and after the Second Vatican Council it was subjected to widely accepted criticisms.

What were these criticisms? Most fundamentally, many theologians came to reject the basic claim that there is an unchanging human nature from which moral norms can be derived. A number of factors came together to render this claim unacceptable to many. To mention the most obvious, as the traditional Catholic sexual ethic became increasingly problematic to the laity as well as theologians, the natural law reasoning undergirding that ethic was likewise called into question. Widespread dissatisfaction with Catholic sexual teachings, in turn, both drew on and gave greater credence to more general theological objections to the official

Catholic account of the natural law. Both Karl Rahner and Bernard Lonergan argued that this account of the natural law is inadequate because it represents a "static" or "classical" view of human nature.[17] The more we become conscious of the ways in which the expression of our human nature is historically conditioned, the less we are prepared to draw moral conclusions from our own ideas of the "permanent" structures of that nature; or so the argument goes.

Catholic scholars usually did not go so far as to deny the existence of a universally accessible and binding natural law. Instead, they equated the natural law with the deliverances of moral reason, which can of course be interpreted in any one of a number of ways. In the words of Charles Curran and Richard McCormick, "From the viewpoint of moral theology or Christian ethics anyone who admits human reason as a source of moral wisdom adopts a natural law perspective."[18]

It should be noted that this line of interpretation is not limited to revisionist, or broadly speaking, liberal Catholic moralists. As we have noted above, the "new natural law" developed by Grisez and Finnis is likewise understood as derived from the operations of pure practical reason. They insist that moral conclusions cannot be derived from factual or metaphysical premises; in Finnis' words, "No value can be deduced *or otherwise inferred* from a fact or set of facts."[19] Rather, according to them, the norms of the natural law are derived from rational intuitions of basic human goods, which are self-evidently human goods. Grisez and Finnis defend the moral teachings of the magisterium, including its prohibition against the use of contraceptives, but they do so on the basis of arguments that are very different from those set out by the magisterial documents themselves. For example, although Grisez and Finnis accept the magisterium's teaching that the use of contraceptives is always wrong, they do not consider this practice to be a violation of the innate natural purpose of human sexuality. They argue instead that the use of contraceptives is an attack on life, which they understood as a rationally self-evident good, and thus as an act similar in kind to murder.[20]

Since Vatican II, disagreements over the natural law among Catholic theologians have been tantamount to disputes over the character of moral reasoning. Disputes between Protestant and Catholic scholars over the natural law have focused on its supposed universality, with the former arguing that a universal natural law ethic leaves insufficient room for a distinctively Christian ethic, and the latter replying that without some commitment to a natural law ethic, the Christian community is in danger of becoming sectarian. This is an important issue, but it does not presuppose anything that might be thought of as a distinctively natural law approach to morality; the same arguments could be framed in terms of any version of moral realism. With the debates on Christian ethics cast in these terms, the distinctiveness and the possible contributions of traditional accounts of the natural law have been largely hidden from view.

However, the same factors that precipitated philosophical interest in the moral significance of human nature have now begun to lead theologians to a reconsideration of traditional accounts of the natural law. It is interesting to note that one of the first and most influential of those calling for such a reconsideration was the Reformed theologian James Gustafson.

On Gustafson's view, the Catholic commitment to a natural law ethic preserves the insight that nature is an important theological category: "If God is in any sense controlling or ordering nature — from the creation of the universe to its prospective demise, from the simplest forms of life to the complexity of the human organism — how can theological ethics avoid nature?"[21] This is, of course, a rhetorical question. As he goes on to argue, Protestant theologians have mistakenly attempted to understand all divine and human activity under the rubric of the historical, interpreted in a way that stresses the radical freedom both of God and of the human agent. At the same time, this is at best a partial vindication of Catholic natural law theory, because the fundamental assumptions of this theory cannot be sustained in the light of contemporary science. Hence, for both Protestant and Catholic theologians, "the question to be addressed somewhat systematically is that of the status of nature in theological ethics."[22]

Gustafson's own response to this question, as set forth in his two-volume *Ethics from a Theocentric Perspective* and subsequent works, does not take the form of a retrieval of a classical account of the natural law. Rather, drawing heavily on the work of H. Richard Niebuhr, Gustafson develops an ethic of responsiveness and responsibility in the face of the transpersonal forces that both sustain and threaten human life, including broad cultural forces as well as non-human nature and those aspects of our human nature that are not in our control. He calls on the Christian to respond to these forces with an attitude of piety, through which they are construed as expressions of divine agency. Correlatively, piety is carried into action through a process of discerning how best to respond to divine agency as expressed through these forces.[23]

Other theologians, both Protestant and Catholic, have been more prepared than Gustafson to reconsider the viability of traditional accounts of the natural law. While almost no one has attempted to defend the official Catholic view of the natural law as set forth by the magisterium, there is a growing sense among theologians that this account of the natural law contains insights that are worth preserving. In the words of Martin Cook:

> ...we may well be advised to reflect on the degree to which aspects of human biology and of the traditional socially sanctioned uses of our bodies – things which have traditionally been "givens" – are properly subject to indefinite alteration, manipulation, and technological control. Cumulatively, these technologies bring us back to questions once dismissed as irrelevant to proper ethical reflection: Are there naturally preferred forms of human conduct and social organization which we tamper with at our peril? Can we look to naturally based considerations as a guide, if not a determiner, of morally correct action and judgement? If we believe that richer concepts than individual rights, choice, autonomy, and harms to others are needed to guide our choices and moral judgements, can we develop sufficiently coherent alternative concepts to govern adequately our assessments of the courses of action ópened by these technologies?[24]

At this point, theological reflection on the moral significance of nature remains tentative and exploratory. There have been few attempts to develop full-scale theories of the natural law, and many authors writing on this subject admit that they are not prepared to say in any detail just how "naturally based considerations" should "guide ... morally correct action and judgement."[25]

Nonetheless, the recent revival of interest in traditional accounts of the natural law indicates a point of contact between scholastic reflections on the natural law and our own moral reflections. The scholastic authors, like many of our own contemporaries, appealed to an account of a natural law as a way of reflecting on the moral significance of naturally given conditions and boundaries of human action. This claim may seem surprising, because traditional accounts of the natural law are usually thought to take the form of a deductive system of moral truths based on a definite account of human nature; and for better or for worse, such a system is far more ambitions than anything we find in the writings of most of our contemporaries.

This assumption would be true of some traditional accounts of the natural law, particularly those developed in the early modern period. However, it does not fit the scholastic concept of the natural law that we will be examining.[26] The scholastics did not set out to derive moral truths from fixed starting points provided by reason or by observations of the natural world. Rather, their concept of the natural law took its starting points from traditional definitions drawn from both Christian and classical authorities, and it was developed through reflection on the diverse and unorganized laws, customs, and moral beliefs of their own society.

The scholastic concept of the natural law cannot fully be understood unless it is seen as the result of this intensely practical process of reflection. It is therefore necessary to place it within two contexts, namely, the historical context of European social development and the intellectual context of scholasticism itself. We now turn to a closer examination of the first of these two contexts.

2. The social context:
The consolidation of European society

At the outset of his groundbreaking study, *The Renaissance of the Twelfth Century*, Charles Homer Haskins observes that the European Middle Ages "form a complex and varied as well as a very considerable period of human history."[27] Nonetheless, as he goes on to observe, there are still many persons, including some scholars, for whom "the Middle Ages are synonymous with all that is uniform, static and unprogressive."[28]

Thanks to Haskins' own work, together with that of Marc Bloch, M.-D. Chenu, and other medievalists earlier in this century, historians are no longer tempted to think of the Middle Ages as an unbroken period of social stagnation. Although the details of Haskins' argument, the precise dating of his "renaissance," and even his choice of terminology have been much debated, no historian of this period would deny that Western

European society changed in fundamental ways in the period between the end of the eleventh century and the beginning of the fourteenth century.[29] These far-reaching developments provide the social context for the scholastic concept of the natural law that we will be examining.

Accordingly, in this section I will outline these developments. This sketch will necessarily be drawn with broad strokes, omitting many details and variations within the different regions of Western Europe. Nonetheless, I hope that this brief sketch will serve to place scholastic thought on the natural law in its appropriate context, thus rendering it intelligible on its own terms.[30]

After the fourth-century division of the Roman empire into an eastern empire with Constantinople as its capital, and a western empire still centered on Rome, these two regions of Europe entered upon very different historical trajectories. The eastern empire was to remain intact for over a thousand years, until the fall of Constantinople to Muslim forces in 1453. The western Roman empire, in contrast, began a process of disintegration that was made evident, but probably not much hastened, by the sack of Rome by Alaric the Goth in 410 and the removal of the boy emperor Romulus Augustulus in 476.

Throughout the following six centuries, Western Europe was kept in a state of perpetual turmoil by invasions and raids from northern and central Europe.[31] By and large, European societies in this period were unable to develop reliable and safe routes for communication and travel.[32] Trade was limited, cities were few and small, and the economy was largely rural and agrarian. Under these conditions, national governments were not able consistently to offer their subjects either security from external foes or effective means for safeguarding the public peace. Charlemagne attempted to bring Europe once again under the control of a central government, but his empire scarcely survived him as an effective political force.[33] Moreover, the same conditions that curtailed the effectiveness of national governments in this period also limited the practical authority of the Roman Catholic church, even though the bishop of Rome was considered by most Christians in the West to be the supreme religious authority.

Hence, although national kingdoms continued to exist and to command the allegiance of their subjects, most men and women in this period looked elsewhere for everyday security and stability.[34] The relative weakness of national governments led to the creation of more localized institutional forms, largely although not exclusively through agreements of personal loyalty among individuals. Men and women of the warrior classes allied themselves through marriage and through the reciprocal commitments of protection and military service characteristic of feudalism. Peasants, free born as well as descendants of slaves, placed themselves under the protection of these warriors, thus giving rise to the manor and to serfdom. Within the church, bishops became local lords in their own right, sometimes competing with secular lords, sometimes in alliance with them. As such, they participated in all the claims and obligations of the feudal and manorial systems as lords, vassals, and owners of both landed estates and serfs. Meanwhile, some men and women devoted themselves to study and prayer behind the relative safety of monastery walls, thus promoting the salvation of the whole community, which supported them and for which they interceded before God.

Beginning in the eleventh century, and moving at an increasing pace through the next two centuries, the social conditions of Western Europe began changing, and as a result new institutions and ways of life began to emerge.[35] What were the forces generating these changes? One critical factor was undoubtedly the cessation of the northern invasions in the eleventh century. After that point, Western Europe was almost entirely free from the disruptions of invasions from outside the region, and this "extraordinary immunity," as Marc Bloch describes it, provided European society with the opportunity for continuous development.[36]

Under these conditions of relative peace and stability, the European society of the eleventh century began to expand, both economically and demographically. The cities of Europe grew as the overall population became more urban. At the same time, travel routes became relatively safe and passable, with the result that reliable communication and extensive trade were possible on the European continent for the first time since the fifth century. With the growth of trade, the economy became predominantly money-based, and an increasing number of people made their living outside the traditional structures of warfare and agriculture.

As medieval society became more urban and complex, the feudal and manorial systems became increasingly inadequate as frameworks for social organization. This inadequacy was particularly evident in the newly emerging urban centers, which were too large and too dependent on the impersonal medium of money to be organized through bonds of personal allegiance and servitude. As a result, "the cities lacked fixed stations and personal bondage. There was relative social mobility and juridical equality," as Hendrik Spruyt observes.[37] According to a twelfth-century German legal adage, "City air makes one free after a year and a day," meaning that a serf who managed to escape to a city and avoid capture for that period was henceforth considered free at law.[38] Not only did medieval cities offer freedom and social mobility to individuals, they also offered corporate self-governance in the form of autonomous, self-governing communes or city-states. Hence, the men and women of the cities did not fit neatly into the threefold division that characterized the simpler society of the earlier feudal period. They were not priests or warriors, but neither were they peasants. Many of them earned their living through trade, while others were independent craftsmen or what we would now call professional men and women.[39]

At the same time, the eleventh and twelfth centuries comprised a period of institutional expansion and consolidation.[40] We have already noted that monarchies continued to exist throughout the Middle Ages; now, under more favorable conditions for centralized authority, they began to exercise real power on a consistent basis. Spruyt argues that the first sovereign, territorial state developed in the twelfth century under the Capetian monarchs, a development that in his view involved a "qualitative shift" from "personal rule to public authority."[41]

These efforts at centralization and reform were both necessitated and made possible by the social and economic expansion that began in this period. They were necessary because as society became more mobile and complex, new forms of interaction and more extensive networks of relationships called for more comprehensive institutional frameworks. Furthermore, older ways of life came into conflict with the newer ways of life developing in this period and, similarly, the emergent centers of civil and ecclesiastical authority clashed with one another. These conflicts called for forms of adjudication that could not be provided by the localized authorities of the eleventh century. At the same time, the social and economic expansion of this period made institutional centralization possible by providing reliable routes of travel and communication.

In the case of the church, institutional development and centralization were not just responses to social and economic forces, although they were partly that. They also stemmed from a reform movement that emerged in the late tenth century and continued throughout the medieval period.

Until that point, the nobility and the church were inextricably inter-connected; the nobility exercised what defenses there were against the external and internal violence of the time, while church authorities and monastic establishments safeguarded the spiritual well-being of the nobility and their dependents through prayer, pastoral care, and the cultic life of the church. The nobility, together with many churchmen, took it for granted that the personnel of the church should be counted among their dependents. As one expression of this relationship of dependence, it became customary for the local nobility to invest the bishops in their territories with the insignia of office, a practice known as lay investiture.

By the end of the tenth century, the customary dependence of the church on lay nobility seemed incongruous, or worse, to many reflective laymen and women as well as to clerics and church leaders.[42] Church reformers sought to establish the independence of the institutional church by striving to eliminate the practice of lay investiture, by centralizing the structure of the church itself, and by imposing a mandatory discipline of clerical celibacy, which served to separate the clergy (to some degree) from the family structures of the aristocracy.

These reform movements are sometimes characterized in terms of a struggle between clerics and laity for control of the church, with the former defending the independence of the church from lay control and the supremacy of clerical over lay authority.[43] There is some truth to this view, but matters were more complex than that. The struggles between clerics and laity in this period were predominantly carried out between church authorities and lay members of the aristocracy and royalty, men and women for whom control of the church had been a real option. When we turn our attention to other segments of the laity, particularly the emergent middle class of urban merchants and professionals, the church appears in this period as the ally of the laity; or, to be more exact, important movements within the institutional church arise and flourish as allies of the newly emergent middle class.

In order to appreciate why this was so, we must appreciate the extent to which new forms of social and economic life gave rise to new forms of spirituality and sensibility. Increasingly, laymen and women were no longer content to leave their spiritual lives in the hands of monks and nuns who would pray for them while they immersed themselves in secular affairs. The twelfth century saw the emergence of a new, widespread yearning for personal contact with God and Christ and, correlatively, a new sense of the dignity and Christian value of the everyday life of laymen and women. These aspirations took many forms, some of them heretical. Yet the most far-seeing churchmen recognized that this flowering of lay spirituality was a positive force, and with their support, new forms of religious life were developed to meet the needs of Christians in the cities.

In particular, the mendicant movement, which originated among the laity in the late twelfth century, gave rise in the early thirteenth century to a new kind of clerical order, with a particular apostolate to the emergent lay urban and mercantile classes.[44] These mendicants, including both Franciscans and Dominicans, were not bound by vows of stability to a monastery. They were free to range throughout Europe, preaching and, after the mid-thirteenth century, also serving as confessors. As a result, they were regarded by many monks and secular clergy as a disruptive force – with some justification, since they allied themselves with the urban and mercantile laity, over against an older concept of the monastic life as the only true Christian life.

In summary, the twelfth and thirteenth centuries were a period of rapid social, economic, and institutional development. The growing expansion and complexity of both civil and ecclesiastical life, and the conflicts that inevitably emerged, generated a need for a framework for legitimation, within which competing social claims could be adjudicated and ordinary men and women could find guidance and structure for their day-to-day lives. It might seem that in this period the Christian faith itself would provide all the legitimation that this society needed; in a sense, this was indeed the case. Western European society was predominantly (although not exclusively) Christian, and for this reason claims to social recognition and power were typically grounded in appeals to Christian beliefs or practices.

Nonetheless, Christianity alone could not provide an adequate structure for social legitimation. In the social conflicts of this period, all parties,

whether civic or ecclesiastical, claimed the support of the Scriptures and
Christian tradition. Hence, the practical meaning of Christian doctrines
was precisely the point at issue in these conflicts. What was needed,
therefore, was some theologically grounded framework within which the
competing interpretations of Christian belief could themselves be assessed
and adjudicated. To put the matter in our terms, European society in this
period urgently needed a comprehensive Christian ethic.

Not only did European society at the beginning of the twelfth century
need an intellectual framework, it also needed a legal framework within
which conflicts might be adjudicated. We now take for granted the
elaborate structure of legislatures and courts that characterize modern
industrial society.[45] Yet, until the twelfth century, institutional structures
for legislation and legal adjudication were localized and rudimentary, at
least outside of England. As R.C. van Caenegem observes, from the late
ninth century until the beginning of the twelfth century, "the European
Continent lived without legislation," either civic or ecclesiastical, and
was governed in this period entirely by customary law.[46] Generally, lords
and princes served as judges within their territories, and there were no
agreed-upon forms for procedure or processes for appeal.

Within the church, the situation was much the same as in civil society.
In the Western church it was generally agreed that the pope provided
the ultimate court of appeal from the judgments of individual bishops,
but in the earlier Middle Ages the difficulties attendant on travel and
communication all but precluded such an appeal in practice. More importantly, there was no agreed-upon legal code within the church any more
than within civil society. In theory, everyone agreed that certain decrees
of popes and church councils were binding, but in practice these decrees
seem not to have been consulted with any regularity. Nor is this surprising
when we realize that the relevant material had never been gathered in
any systematic way, but remained scattered in texts that were difficult to
find and hard to use.[47]

In order to move forward, therefore, European society at the end of
the eleventh century needed a legitimating framework, within which the
rapid development of new forms of life and institutions could be understood and directed. Just as urgently, it needed to develop legislative and
legal structures within which these processes could be put into effect.

How were these structures, both intellectual and institutional, to be developed?

The centers of learning that had sustained Europe through the earlier Middle Ages – that is, the monasteries and the cathedral schools – were not able to provide such a framework.[48] The extent and value of the intellectual work supported by these centers should not be minimized; to mention nothing else, they provided the locus for the renewal of natural philosophy, which was foundational for later scholastic reflection on the natural law. Nonetheless, monasteries and cathedral schools tended to be oriented towards local needs and concerns and, correlatively, they did not command a broad base of scholars and students.

In contrast, the newly emergent universities, above all those of Paris and Bologna, provided the necessary milieu within which systematic frameworks of thought and institutional practice might be developed.[49] These universities were genuine international centers of learning, staffed by secular clerics and, after the beginning of the thirteenth century, by growing numbers of the cosmopolitan mendicants. The best of them commanded the talent of the most innovative scholars in Europe, and for this reason they attracted quantities of intelligent and ambitious students. As a result, the universities quickly became one of the leading reservoirs for administrative talent and leadership, both for civil authorities eager to extend themselves and to consolidate their power and for the newly reorganized bureaucracy of the church. When European society developed the intellectual and legal structures that it needed in order to consolidate its development, these structures were largely the products of its great universities. In the period we are considering, that is equivalent to saying that they were the products of scholasticism.

3. The intellectual context: Scholasticism

We are accustomed to think of scholasticism as a dry, academic enterprise, the original product of the ivory tower. For scholasticism in the period we are considering, nothing could be further from the truth. The goals that animated scholastic research in this period were intensely practical, as well as comprehensive in their intellectual scope. In the words of R.W. Southern:

...it was the twelfth century innovators who first introduced systematic order into the mass of intellectual material which they had inherited in a largely uncoordinated form from the ancient world. The general aim of their work was to produce a complete and systematic body of knowledge, clarified by the refinements of criticism, and presented as the consensus of competent judges. Doctrinally the method for achieving this consensus was a progression from commentary to questioning, and from questioning to systematization. And the practical aim of the whole procedure was to stabilize, make accessible and defend an orthodox Christian view of the world against the attacks of heretics within, and unbelievers – or misbelievers – outside the area of organized Christendom.

In principle, they aimed at restoring to fallen mankind, so far as was possible, that perfect system of knowledge which had been in the possession or within the reach of mankind at the moment of creation.[50]

This "perfect system of knowledge" was not achieved, and from our standpoint it appears that it could never have been achieved. Nonetheless, in pursuing their ideal the scholastics produced an impressive body of systematic doctrine. Within this system, the details of social life were argued on the basis of fundamental principles, and the highest and most recondite doctrines of Christianity became intensely practical.

Because they hoped to attain a comprehensive system of knowledge, these theologians drew on every textual source at their disposal.[51] Truth had been scattered throughout the world, and it was the task of the scholar to gather up all its fragments wherever they might be found. First among these texts, of course, was the Bible itself, which was considered to be completely inerrant. But many other texts, both Christian and non-Christian in their origins, were also thought to be authoritative, although not strictly inerrant.

Correlatively, the methods and forms of exposition characteristic of scholasticism were based, directly or indirectly, on the systematic exposition of authoritative texts. As Southern remarks, this exposition moved "from commentary to questioning, and from questioning to systematization." At its simplest level, the exposition of texts took the form of a gloss: that is, a line-by-line commentary on a text. Such a close reading was bound to reveal obscurities, inconsistencies, and seeming errors in even the simplest texts; these difficulties were resolved, as far as possible, through close logical and verbal analysis or, in the case of historical narratives, through reconstruction of the narrator's distinctive viewpoint. These efforts might be incorporated into a gloss, or they could be given a fuller treatment in a more discursive commentary.[52]

In addition to writing glosses and commentaries on key texts, the scholastics also attempted to gather together everything in these texts that was relevant to a given topic and to present the resultant material in a systematic form. One way of doing so was to present a digest of excerpts from commentaries on an authoritative text, particularly on the Bible; this sort of master commentary was known as a catena. Alternatively, the scholar might gather together all of the authoritative sayings on a given subject and arrange them topically, with more or less of an attempt to resolve inconsistencies and to develop the author's own doctrine. This gave rise to the most familiar literary product of this period, the summa, which comprised a systematic exposition of everything that could be known on a given topic. The *Summa theologiae* of Thomas Aquinas is today the best-known example of this genre. A systematic commentary on a legal text (typically, the *Digest* or the *Decretum*) was also referred to as a summa.[53]

The literary genres of scholasticism appear strange and artificial to most contemporary readers. Yet they mirrored the forms of teaching and exposition that were practiced in the universities, just as modern textbooks and scholarly writings reflect the discursive style of our own preferred form of instruction, the classroom lecture. The fundamental form of teaching consisted of reading through an authoritative text and commenting on it line by line. In addition, the masters of a school regularly held disputations. These, as the name suggests, were essentially public debates among the junior faculty of a university, presided over by a master who would conclude the event by resolving the question under consideration. Apparently, they provided not only instruction but also a great deal of the entertainment in the universities of the time.[54]

This practice left its stamp on the literary products of scholasticism, particularly the summa, which was frequently cast in the form of a disputation with summaries of opposing arguments followed by a resolution. Even more significantly, the practice of disputation shaped the methodological procedures of the schools in a decisive way by institutionalizing a preference for Aristotelian dialectic as the preferred mode of argumentation, rather than logical deduction from rationally self-evident premises.[55] At the same time, this mode of argument was particularly well suited to the distinctively scholastic aim of analyzing and harmonizing a heterogeneous textual tradition. Following this mode of argument, the scholastics moved from the starting points provided by an authoritative textual tradition to an articulation of the rationale underlying those claims. They then employed that rationale to extend the tradition, to correct it where necessary, and to resolve its inconsistencies.[56]

The practice of disputation, together with the dialectical approach that it embodied, had a practical as well as a pedagogical function. As we noted above, the aim of the scholastics was to construct a comprehensive system of knowledge, not only so that men and women might contemplate it, but in order that they might live by it. Thus, for practical as well as intellectual reasons, the scholastics took great pains to construct a system that could stand up to the most searching criticisms. Southern observes that Western society was not naturally conformist, and if the intellectual and legal dicta of the schools were to meet with general acceptance, the strongest possible opposing arguments had to be aired and, as far as possible, answered. In this sense, he adds, "the schools were the parliaments of medieval Europe."[57]

In the last section, we saw that the scholastic concept of the natural law emerged out of reflection on existing norms and practices. At the same time, the scholastics approached social and moral questions in the same way as they approached every other question: namely, by attempting to situate and resolve them within a framework of traditional dicta drawn from authoritative texts. In other words, the scholastic concept of the natural law took its starting point from a set of authoritative texts, which were systematized and interpreted in the process of being applied to the problems of the day. Therefore, if we are to set out the scholastic concept of the natural law, we must begin by taking note of the authoritative texts out of which this concept was formed.[58]

These included Scripture itself, the patristic writings, and classical texts from Greek and Roman authors. The key scriptural texts were, first, Paul's references to the natural law in Romans and, second, the account of the creation and fall in Genesis. Many of the relevant patristic writings were mediated through the *Glossa Ordinaria,* or Ordinary Gloss, which was a collation of patristic sayings on scriptural texts. Among these, Origen's comments on Paul were frequently cited; in addition, the influence of Augustine, mediated through multiple sources, was pervasive here as everywhere throughout the medieval period. The influence of Cicero's writings was likewise pervasive: particularly, in this connection, his political and rhetorical writings. Plato's *Timaeus* and its commentaries played a key role in the revival of theological interest in the natural order early in the twelfth century, and so it is no surprise to find frequent references to this text, especially among the more Platonically minded natural law thinkers. Later in the period we are considering, after the recovery of a wider range of Aristotle's philosophical and ethical writings, we find more Aristotelian scholars drawing on his remarks on natural justice as a further way of approaching the natural law.

In addition, the work of Roman jurists from the early centuries of the Common Era apparently survived in some form, although the compilation of Roman legal and jurisprudential texts known as Justinian's *Digest* was largely ignored, or perhaps unknown, until the latter part of the eleventh century.[59] Until that point, much of the surviving Roman legal thought was transmitted in a redacted form by Isidore of Seville in the fifth book of his *Etymologies*; as a result, he became perhaps the most important of the early medieval authors for subsequent legal and political thought.[60] Subsequently, the rediscovery of or renewal of interest in the *Digest* in about 1070 gave rise to a tradition of commentary on secular law, which found its primary institutional home in the great law school of Bologna. The jurists who took secular law as their field of study, and the *Digest* as their textbook, are today collectively known as the civilians.

Scholastic reflection on the natural law in the twelfth and thirteenth centuries was also shaped by early products of scholastic thought. Two texts call for special mention. Peter Lombard's *Liber Sententiarum* (also known as the *Sentiniae in IV Libris distinctae,* or in English as the *Sentences)* written around 1152, quickly became the standard textbook for theology, a status that it was to enjoy for four centuries.[61] While his explicit remarks on the natural law were few and scattered, he provided *loci classi* for subsequent theological reflection of the natural law in his discussions of conscience (II *Sent.* 39) and the so-called "sins of the patriarchs" (IV *Sent.* 33).

From the standpoint of reflection on the natural law, a second product of early scholasticism is still more important, and indeed foundational. In about 1140, Gratian, a legal thinker associated with Bologna, compiled a textbook of canon law known as the *Concordia discordantium canonum* or, more commonly, as the *Decretum Gratiani*.[62] Although there had been other compilations of canons, Gratian is the first, as far as we know, to attempt to bring these canons into a coherent system. His book quickly became the standard textbook for canon law, just as Peter Lombard's *Sentences* was the standard textbook for theology and, like the latter, it was the subject of extensive commentaries and glosses.

The scholastic concept of the natural law emerged out of a process of shared reflection in which secular and canon lawyers and theologians all played a part. It would be a mistake to project our assumptions and prejudices about legal thought into this discussion. The canonists and theologians were reading each other throughout this period, sometimes commenting explicitly on one another; to a lesser extent, the secular jurists also influenced and were influenced by both canonists and theologians. Among theologians, the level of interest in the natural law varied considerably. Although they discussed it in connection with other issues, scholastic theologians did not take the natural law as a distinct object of attention until after the beginning of the thirteenth century.[63] Even after that point, some of them, following the lead of Peter Lombard, referred to it only in connection with specific theological problems.[64] Others, however, devoted considerable attention to the topic, whether in the context of a consideration of other issues, such as we find in Bonaventure's writings, or through more extended systematic discussions, such as we find in the *Summa* of Alexander of Hales as well as in the works of both Albert and Aquinas.[65]

In what follows, we will examine the medieval doctrine of the natural law as it developed in the period between the publication of the *Decretum* and the latter part of the thirteenth century. Within this period, we will focus on two sets of texts. The first includes Gratian's *Decretum* itself and the commentaries, glosses, and summae that it generated.[66] The second includes the writings of selected scholastic theologians, beginning with

William of Auxerre, whose *Summa aurea* was written around 1220, and ending with Bonaventure and Aquinas, both of whom died in 1274.

These parameters have been chosen primarily to keep this study within manageable bounds. Nonetheless, they are not arbitrary. While there is a rich tradition of Christian natural law reflection prior to Gratian, the appearance of the *Decretum* nonetheless marks a turning point, if only because of its subsequent importance for the study of canon law and its significance for theologians as well as canonists. The year of the death of both Aquinas and Bonaventure does not represent a similarly clear terminus. Nonetheless, the new theological developments of the later thirteenth and fourteenth centuries, and even more important, the far-reaching social changes of the fourteenth century, suggest 1274 as a reasonable stopping point.

The secular jurists understand the natural law in terms of the definition given by the Roman jurist Ulpian, as recorded in the *Digest,* as that which nature teaches to all animals, and they distinguish clearly between the natural law, so defined, and the distinctively human and rational law of nations.[67] They are accordingly less interested in the natural law than the canonists and theologians, for whom the natural law includes distinctively human as well as more universal principles of action. As a result, the civilians, in contrast to the canonists and theologians, do not develop a theoretically sophisticated concept of the natural law. For this reason, I have focused on the canonists and theologians in this study, and when I speak of the scholastic concept of the natural law, what I have in mind is the theological concept that they developed.

At the same time, the civilians do influence both the canonists and theologians, and draw on them in turn. We find efforts to reconcile the different approaches to the natural law among representatives of all three, and there are suggestive parallels between civilian concepts of equity and the law of nations, on the one hand, and the theological concept of the natural law developed by the canonists and theologians, on the other. Accordingly, while I focus primarily on the canonists and theologians in what follows, I also draw on the writings of the civilians, both for the sake of comparing the two approaches, and also to illuminate certain aspects of the theological concept of the natural law.

Finally, in order to prevent confusion, I should add that my investigation is limited to those authors who worked extensively in a university setting or exercised a formative influence in the universities. I have not attempted to deal in any systematic way with those political thinkers, such as John of Salisbury, who received a scholastic education but pursued careers in public or ecclesiastical service. Thus, when I refer to scholastic natural law thinkers, I am referring to those canon lawyers and theologians who spent much or all of their adult lives as academics and whose work was intended primarily for an academic audience.[68]

4. The scholastic concept of the natural law

Scholastic reflection was a practical as well as a theoretical enterprise, insofar as it was intended to provide a rationale for the institutions and practices of European society. At the same time, some aspects of scholastic thought were more immediately practical than others. The emerging disciplines of secular and canonical jurisprudence were explicitly directed towards the reform and direction of legal procedures, and theological reflection on moral and social questions was intended to have, and did have, direct practical application in a number of contexts. Within these contexts of thought and practice, the emerging concept of the natural law offered a framework within which social practices and institutions could be interpreted and, where necessary, criticized.

Why did the canonists and theologians in this period develop a concept of the natural law to provide them with such a framework? It might seem that this is sufficiently explained by the fact that they found references to the natural law in sources that they considered to be authoritative. However, this cannot be the whole answer. The idea of a natural law was only one among a number of themes contained in authoritative sources that could have served as an organizing principle for moral and social reflection.[69] The metaphor of society as a body figures prominently in Paul as well as in classical sources and, as we shall see in the next chapter, it also played a central role in the theology of the first half of the twelfth century. The motif of the three orders of society, usually given as priests, knights, and peasants, played a prominent role in the social thought of the tenth and eleventh centuries, and it was revived late in the thirteenth century in the context of royal courts.

These images of society appear in the writings of the scholastics as well, but they do not figure centrally in scholastic discourse as organizing concepts for moral and social reflection. Moreover, as we noted above, the concept of the natural law is not of equal importance for all the scholastics; it receives far more attention from the canonists and theologians than from the secular jurists. Hence, the concept of the natural law developed by the canonists and theologians represents a selective appropriation and reinterpretation of received traditions of thought.

There are at least three reasons why the concept of the natural law was so significant for canonists and theologians in the period we are considering. In the first place, earlier traditions of natural law were given saliency by the intense interest in and reverence for nature, which was central to the intellectual renewal of the twelfth century. As we will see in the next chapter, this "rediscovery of nature" was motivated by theological commitments, which were in turn incorporated in twelfth-century natural philosophy. This natural philosophy, in turn, provided a framework within which to reflect on the moral significance of the pre-rational components of human nature, those aspects that we share with the animals or with creatures more generally. As a result, the concept of the natural law that emerged out of these reflections emphasized the complexity of human nature and its continuities with the rest of creation. It was accordingly more useful as a theological framework for social thought than the narrower civilian notions of reason or equity, and in addition, it provided more adequate resources for addressing some specific moral questions, particularly those pertaining to sexual ethics.

Second, the idea of the natural law as the scholastics received it was by this point thoroughly imbedded in a framework of scriptural and theological reflection. It is difficult for us to appreciate the significance of this fact, since we tend to associate the natural law with a kind of moral rationalism that excludes any appeal to specific religious claims. For the scholastics, however, the natural law was a scriptural doctrine; it had been understood as such both by the church fathers and by some of the most respected theologians of the earlier twelfth century. Hence, the idea of the natural law was congenial to the canonists, who sought to place church law within a theological framework, as well as the theologians.

There is a further and more fundamental reason why these scholastics focused on the natural law, as opposed to (for example) the image of society as a body or the idea of the three orders as a key moral concept.[70] These other images were traditionally associated with the defense of particular social arrangements, particularly the stratified arrangement of the social classes. As such, they did not fit the new social arrangements of the more urban and mobile society of this period. Even more important, they offered few resources for understanding and evaluating social change and the claims of competing practices and moral ideals.

In contrast, the concept of the natural law, because it was closely tied to the more general idea of the intelligibility of nature, was more readily adapted to the task of explaining and evaluating practices in a rapidly evolving society. The authoritative texts that formed the starting point for the development of this context were patient of this interpretation, because they tended to identify the natural law with fundamental principles of action, as opposed to specific norms or social arrangements. At the same time, because the concept of the natural law was theological and not merely philosophical, it provided a framework for social analysis and justification that was acceptable in a society that was overwhelmingly Christian. As such, it was particularly well suited to defend innovations in religious practices, and this further reinforced its value for canonists and theologians.

It would be a mistake to look for a highly developed theory of the natural law that the canonists and theologians held in common, if only because the characteristic scholastic genres of commentary and gloss did not lend themselves to the elaboration of systematic theories. Some of the theologians whom we are considering do offer systematic theories of the natural law, but these are distinctive theories, not representations of one commonly held view.

Yet if the texts that we are considering do not share one systematically developed theory of the natural law, neither do they present a series of ad hoc appeals to nature or fragments drawn from earlier literature. Rather, what we find in these writings is a distinctive concept of the natural law, less comprehensive than a systematic theory but more coherent than a set of ad hoc and fragmentary remarks. In the earlier writings, this concept is naturally less developed, since it emerges through the cumulative reflection of authors who are reading and responding to one another as well as commenting on shared authoritative sources. But throughout this period, the concept of the natural law is unified by shared aims and procedures, by general agreement on which texts are centrally important and which questions are particularly salient, and by shared assumptions about nature, reason, and the social order.

What is this concept of the natural law? The full answer to this question will be developed in the remainder of this book. In the rest of this section, I will offer an outline of the scholastic concept of the natural law in order both to provide an overview of what follows and to indicate in a preliminary way how this concept is relevant to contemporary Christian theological ethics.

The scholastic concept of the natural law brings together three traditional loci for moral reflection: nature, reason, and Scripture. Although each of these was a familiar idea (or text, in the case of Scripture) with a long tradition of reflection behind it, or perhaps because of that fact, the meaning of these loci was far from clear, and their proper interrelationships were even less clear. Reflection on these issues set the agenda for scholastic reflection on the natural law.

In sorting through the variety of traditional definitions of the natural law, the scholastics make use of the well-established distinction between the natural and the conventional to bring order to this variety. They do not interpret this distinction in a way that equates the natural with the morally good *tout court,* or the conventional with what is morally bad or suspect. Not only do they recognize that the institutions of society are largely the products of human custom and positive law, but some of them at least recognize that much sinful behavior is in some sense natural. Rather, they use the distinction between the natural and the conventional as a warrant for interpreting human action in the light of the diverse forces that ground and limit it. These pre-conventional givens include the exigencies of our biological nature as well as reason, which is seen as setting both normative and practical constraints on human freedom, and Scripture, seen as a revelation of divine wisdom and will.

Understood in this way, the natural law is said to be natural in the sense of being pre-conventional, and law in the sense that it is comprised of intrinsic, normative principles by which action should be regulated. Because it is grounded in nature comprehensively considered, the natural law is also said to be primal and supremely authoritative. At the same time, it also allows considerable room for diversity and adaptation to circumstances at the level of specific precepts.

As I will attempt to show in Chapters 2 and 3, there are a number of points of contact between the scholastic conception of the natural law and contemporary thought. For example, when we examine scholastic writings on the relationship between the pre-rational aspects of our nature and rationality, we find striking resemblances to recent scientific and philosophical attempts to come to terms with the continuities between animal behavior and human morality.[71] The scholastics do not attempt to derive moral norms directly from observations of animal behavior, as they are often accused of doing, but they do interpret human morality as the distinctively rational expression of needs and ways of behaving that are found more generally throughout the animal kingdom.

If this were the only point of contact between the scholastics and ourselves, it would represent an interesting and unsuspected continuity between our forebears and ourselves, but it would not suggest that the scholastic concept of the natural law has anything distinctive to contribute to contemporary theological reflection. However, there is a second point of contact between these authors and those of us who work in the field of theological ethics. That is, the scholastic concept of the natural law is a theological concept, not a purely philosophical construct such as we associate with later versions of the natural law. It is theological, first of all, because it is formulated with a view to affirming the goodness of creation and drawing out the social implications of that affirmation, in response to those such as the Cathars who denied the goodness of the material world. Second, the canonists and theologians draw on and extend the scriptural aspects of earlier natural law thought.

Most contemporary theologians are familiar with the claim that the natural law and Scripture should be seen as two mutually complementary sources of moral knowledge, each of which can serve to supplement and correct the other. But the connection between the scholastic concept of the natural law and Scripture is more substantive than this claim would suggest. For the scholastics, the scriptural grounding of the natural law provides a way of identifying those aspects of human nature that are normative. Hence, the scholastic concept of the natural law offers us a way of addressing the problem set for theological ethics by the moral ambiguity of human nature, even though the scholastics themselves do not seem to have formulated this problem explicitly.

The test of any moral concept lies in its application, and in Chapters 4 and 5, I will examine the ways in which the scholastics applied their concept of the natural law to questions of sexual and social ethics. Here we will find some of the most problematic aspects of the scholastic concept of the natural law. Nonetheless, a careful reading of the scholastic views on these questions reveals them to be more sophisticated than is usually recognized. That does not mean their views are always persuasive, but they do offer us unexpected insights into our own questions of sexual and social morality.

Finally, in the last chapter I will consider the contemporary significance of the scholastic concept of the natural law. Precisely because of its theological character, this concept does not offer a universal moral code that can be discerned by all rational men and women. Yet it offers us other advantages, which are arguably more important for contemporary theological ethics. It offers a theology of morality that preserves central theological commitments and can be developed into a moral theology with specific content. It suggests a theological framework within which to interpret the phenomenon of human morality and to account for the variability of different moral codes. Even more important, it offers us a way to understand Christian morality as one distinctive expression of human nature, which is therefore not wholly discontinuous with other moral systems, and yet retains its distinctiveness as one possible development, out of many, of natural human inclinations.

It would call for another book to reformulate the scholastic concept of the natural law into a fully adequate theological ethic, informed by and responsive to our own insights and concerns. Yet this task of reformulation presupposes that we are familiar with the scholastic concept of the natural law and, more important, have some sense of its value for us today. My aim in what follows is to recover a tradition of Christian ethics that has long been neglected by setting forth the main lines of this concept and drawing out some of its implications for contemporary theology and moral reflection.

Notes to Chapter 1

1   The relevant texts are David Hume, *A Treatise of Human Nature*, L.A. Selby-Bigge, ed. (Oxford: Oxford University Press, 1888), 469, and G.E. Moore, *Principia Ethica* (Cambridge: Cambridge University Press, 1903, repr. 1948), 46-58.

2   For a good summary and critical assessment of the relevant literature, see Stephen J. Pope, *The Evolution of Altruism and the Ordering of Love* (Washington, D.C.: Georgetown University Press, 1994), 99-127; for a survey of more recent work, see Galen Strawson, "In Deepest Sympathy: Towards a Natural History of Virtue," *Times Literary Supplement,* November 29, 1996, 3-4.

3   This claim is made by, among others, Edward Wilson in his widely influential *On Human Nature* (Cambridge, MA: Harvard University Press, 1978), 5, and more recently by Frans de Waal, *Good Natured: The Origins of Right and Wrong in Human and Other Animals* (Cambridge, MA: Harvard University Press, 1996), 218.

4   See Mary Midgley, *Beast and Man: The Roots of Human Nature* (New York: Meridian, 1978), and more recently, *The Ethical Primate: Humans, Freedom and Morality* (London: Routledge, 1994); Owen J. Flanagan, Jr., "Quinean Ethics," *Ethics* 93 (1982), 56-74 and *Varieties of Moral Personality: Ethics and Psychological Realism* (Cambridge, MA: Harvard University Press, 1991); Leon Kass, *Toward a More Natural Science: Biology and Human Affairs* (New York: Macmillan, 1985); Martha Nussbaum, "Non-Relative Virtues: An Aristotelian Approach," 32-53 in *Midwest Studies in Philosophy XIII: Ethical Theory: Character and Virtue,* Peter French, Theodore E. Uehling, Jr., and Howard K. Wettstein, eds. (Notre Dame, IN: The University of Notre Dame Press, 1988), and *The Therapy of Desire: Theory and Practice in Hellenistic Ethics* (Princeton: Princeton University Press, 1994); John Casey, *Pagan Virtue: An Essay in Ethics* (Oxford: Clarendon Press, 1990); and Julia Annas, *The Morality of Happiness* (Oxford: Oxford University Press, 1993).

5   There have, of course, been notable exceptions to this rule, including John Courtney Murray and Jacques Maritain; see John Courtney Murray, *We Hold These Truths* (New York: Sheed and Ward, 1960), and (for example) Jacques Maritain, *The Person and the Common Good,* John J. Fitzgerald, trans. (Notre Dame, IN: University of Notre Dame Press, 1947), and *Man and the State* (Chicago: University of Chicago Press, 1951). However, Murray's retrieval was focused specifically on the question of church-state relationships, and did not readily lend itself to a consideration of other questions. Maritain's work, while much admired, does not appear to have had a widespread and lasting influence, perhaps because it appeared just as the critiques of Karl Rahner and Bernard Lonergan were leading most Catholic scholars to reject so-called classical natural law theories. For a good sampling of discussions of the natural law within Catholic theology earlier in this century, see Charles E. Curran and Richard A. McCormick, eds., *Readings in Moral Theology No. 7: Natural Law and Theology* (Mahwah, NJ: Paulist Press, 1991).

6   See Germain Grisez, Joseph Boyle, and John Finnis, "Practical Principles, Moral Truth, and Ultimate Ends," *American Journal of Jurisprudence* 32 (1987), 99-151, for a summary of their theory of the natural law, including a detailed commentary on their earlier works and responses to critics. This is the definitive statement of the theory as it was formulated up until 1987. Since then, Grisez has offered a detailed exposition of his moral theory in *The Way of the Lord Jesus 1: Christian Moral Principles* (Chicago: Franciscan Herald Press, 1983) and *The Way of the Lord Jesus 2: Living a Christian Life* (Chicago: Franciscan Herald Press, 1993). But as far as I can determine, these books do not add major theoretical revisions, although they expand the basic theory a great deal. John Finnis' *Aquinas: Moral, Political, and Legal Theory* (Oxford: Oxford University Press, 1998) appeared too late for me to consider it in detail in preparing this manuscript. However, it does not appear that Finnis departs radically from his earlier interpretation of Aquinas as developed in *Natural Law and Natural Rights* (Oxford: Clarendon Press, 1980), at least with respect to the point at issue here; compare *Aquinas*, 20-55 with *Natural Law and Natural Rights*, 59-99.

7   Pope, *The Evolution of Altruism and the Ordering of Love*, passim.

8   Gustafson has written extensively on this subject; for a good example, see "Nature: Its Status in Theological Ethics," *Logos* vol. E (1982), 5-23. He develops his own views most extensively in his two-volume *Ethics from a Theocentric Perspective, Volume One: Theology and Ethics* (Chicago: University of Chicago Press, 1981), and *Volume Two: Ethics and Theology* (Chicago: University of Chicago Press, 1984).

9   Oliver O'Donovan, *Resurrection and Moral Order: An Outline for Evangelical Ethics* (Grand Rapids, MI: Eerdmans, 1986), 31-52. At the same time, however, he insists that he is not advocating a return to a "natural ethic"; see *The Desire of the Nations: Rediscovering the Roots of Political Theology* (Cambridge: Cambridge University Press, 1996), 19-20.

10   Pope, *The Evolution of Altruism and the Ordering of Love*, Martin Rhonheimer, *Natur als Grundlage der Moral* (Innsbruck-Wein: Tyrolia Verlag, 1987); Ruth Caspar, "Natural Law: Before and Beyond Bifurcation," *Thought* 60: 236 (1985), 58-72; Thomas L. Schubeck, "The Reconstruction of Natural Law Reasoning: Liberation Theology as a Case Study," *The Journal of Religious Ethics* 20:1 (1992), 149-178; Cynthia S. W. Crysdale, "Revisioning Natural Law: From the Classicist Paradigm to Emergent Probability," *Theological Studies* 56 (1995), 464-484; Philip Hefner, *The Human Factor: Evolution, Culture, and Religion* (Minneapolis: Fortress Press, 1993); Michael S. Northcott, *The Environment and Christian Ethics* (Cambridge: Cambridge University Press, 1996), 257-327; and Martin Cook, "Ways of Thinking Naturally," *The Annual of the Society of Christian Ethics* 1988, 161-178.

11   Hans-Georg Gadamer, *Truth and Method*, second revised edition; translation revised by Joel Weinsheimer and Donald G. Marshall (New York: Crossroad, 1989), 305-306.

12   For a standard, and very useful survey of the history of natural law thought, see A.P.
     d'Entreves, *Natural Law: An Introduction to Legal Philosophy*, second revised edition
     (London: Hutchinson, 1970).

13   At least, this would have been the case until recently. However, the encyclical *Ver-
     itatis Splendor* implies a more pessimistic view of the capacities of human reason
     unaided by revelation; see *Veritatis Splendor*, *Origins: CNS Documentary Service* 23 (14
     October 1993), para. 44, 53, 117 in particular.

14   Karl Barth, *Church Dogmatics,* vol. II, pt. 2, G. W. Bromiley, *et al*, trans. (Edinburgh:
     T. and T. Clark, 1957), 528-535.

15   Reinhold Niebuhr, "Christian Faith and Natural Law," originally published in
     1940, reprinted in *Love and Justice: Selections from the Shorter Writings of Reinhold Nie-
     buhr* (Louisville, KY: Westminster/ John Knox Press, 1957), 46-54.

16   Stanley Hauerwas, *The Peaceable Kingdom: A Primer in Christian Ethics* (Notre Dame,
     IN: University of Notre Dame Press, 1983), 50-71.

17   For a helpful discussion of Rahner's reformulation of the natural law, with an exten-
     sive bibliographic note, see James F. Bresnahan, "An Ethics of Faith," in Leo J.
     O'Donovan, ed., *A World of Grace: An Introduction to the Themes and Foundations of
     Karl Rahner's Theology* (New York: Crossroad, 1981), 169-184. Michael J. Himes
     offers a good overview and assessment of Lonergan's work on the natural law in
     "The Human Person in Contemporary Theology: From Human Nature to
     Authentic Subjectivity," originally published in 1983, reprinted in Ronald R.
     Hamel and Kenneth R. Himes, O.F.M., eds., *Introduction to Christian Ethics: A
     Reader* (New York: Paulist Press, 1989), 49-62. Charles Curran offers a critique of
     "classical" natural law theory which incorporates the insights of both authors in his
     "Natural Law in Moral Theology," originally published in 1970, reprinted in
     Charles E. Curran and Richard A. McCormick, eds., *Readings in Moral Theology
     No.7: Natural Law and Theology* (New York: Paulist Press, 1991), 247-295.

18   Curran and McCormick, *Natural Law and Theology*, 1.

19   John Finnis, *Natural Law and Natural Rights*, 66; emphasis added.

20   See, for example, Grisez, *Living a Christian Life,* 509-10, and Germain Grisez, Joseph
     Boyle, John Finnis, and William May, "Every Marital Act Ought to Be Open to
     New Life: Towards a Clearer Understanding," *The Thomist* 52.3 (July, 1988), 365-
     426.

21   Gustafson, "Nature: Its Status in Theological Ethics," 8.

22   *Ibid.*, 6.

23   This basic program is set forth in Gustafson, *Ethics from a Theocentric Perspective,* vol. 1,
     195-280.

24   Cook, "Ways of Thinking Naturally," 163-164.

25   *Ibid.*

26 For a more detailed comparison of medieval and modern versions of the natural law, see Michael Crowe, *The Changing Profile of the Natural Law* (The Hague: Martinus Nijhoff, 1977), 192-245.

27 Charles Homer Haskins, *The Renaissance of the Twelfth Century* (Cambridge, MA: Harvard University Press, 1927; repr. by Cleveland, Ohio: Meridian, 1957), 1. All citations are from the 1957 Meridian edition.

28 *Ibid.*, 1, 2.

29 For a survey of the scholarly discussion of Haskins' thesis since his book appeared, and a review of the main issues generated by that thesis, see the "Introduction" to Robert L. Benson and Giles Constable, eds., with Carol D. Lahnam, *Renaissance and Renewal in the Twelfth Century* (Cambridge, MA: Harvard University Press, 1982; repr. by Toronto: University of Toronto Press, 1991), xvii-xxx; and in the same volume Gerhart B. Ladner, "Terms and Ideas of Renewal," 1-36.

30 In this section, I have relied primarily on the following sources: Marc Bloch, *Feudal Society*, 2 vols., L. A. Manyon, trans. (Chicago: University of Chicago Press, 1961); James A. Brundage, *Medieval Canon Law* (London: Longman, 1995); M.D. Chenu, *Nature, Man, and Society in the Twelfth Century*, Jerome Taylor and Lester K. Little, eds. and trans. (Chicago: University of Chicago Press, 1968); Georges Duby, *The Three Orders: Feudal Society Imagined*, Arthur Goldhammer, ed. (Chicago: Chicago University Press, 1980); Judith Herrin, *The Formation of Christendom* (Princeton, NJ: Princeton University Press, 1987); C.H. Lawrence, *The Friars: The Impact of the Early Medicant Movement on Western Society* (London: Longman, 1994); Lester K. Little, *Religious Poverty and the Profit Economy in Medieval Europe* (Ithaca, NY: Cornell University Press, 1978); Barbara Reynolds, *Fiefs and Vassals: The Medieval Evidence Reinterpreted* (Oxford: Oxford University Press, 1994); R. W. Southern, *Scholastic Humanism and the Unification of Europe, Vol. I: Foundations* (Oxford: Blackwell, 1995); Hendrik Spruyt, *The Sovereign State and Its Competitors* (Princeton, NJ: Princeton University Press, 1994), 59-150; R. C. van Caenegem, "Government, Law and Society," 174-210 in J.H. Burns, ed., *The Cambridge History of Medieval Political Thought: c.350-c.1450* (Cambridge: Cambridge University Press, 1988); and André Vauchez, *Les laïcs au Moyen Age: Pratiques et expériences religieuses* (Paris: Cerf, 1987).

I am aware that Bloch's interpretation of feudal society has been challenged, most sharply by Reynolds. However, it does not seem to me that Reynolds' critique invalidates those aspects of Bloch's analysis that are most pertinent to this study. Her main point is that historians (including Bloch) have over-read the evidence pertinent to the institutional structure of feudalism; in her view, we simply do not have sufficient evidence for the existence of feudalism as a determinate institution, at least before the twelfth century. Nothing in this study turns on the resolution of this debate. Her second claim is that the nation continued to function as a social force throughout the (so-called) feudal age, but Bloch does not deny this; see below, note 34.

31 On the impact of these raids, see Herrin, *The Formation of Christendom*, 133-144 and Bloch, *Feudal Society*, 3-56. In general, Bloch places more weight on the effect of these raids than does Herrin.

32 England was a partial exception to this generalization; see Bloch, *Feudal Society*, 430 and van Caenegem, "Government, Law and Society," 183-185.

33 See van Caenegem, "Government, Law and Society," 174-183, for further details on the disintegration of the Frankish empire and its aftermath.

34 Reynolds argues that national governments continued to exist and to function as forces for social cohesion throughout the medieval period; see *Fiefs and Vassals*, 34-46. However, Bloch does not deny this; see *Feudal Society*, 375-393, 408-409. His point is rather that the most *effective* and sometimes the only functioning institutions took the form of alliances of personal allegiance, mutual aid, and protection among individuals. Spruyt makes a similar point in *The Sovereign State and Its Competitors*, 79. Reynolds also acknowledges the practical ineffectiveness of state governments before the twelfth century; see *Fiefs and Vassals*, 26-27, 46-47.

35 For discussions of the social changes of the later eleventh and twelfth centuries, and different perspectives on the forces underlying them, see Bloch, *Feudal Society*, 421-437; Duby, *The Three Orders*, 174-177, 206-217; Little, *Religious Poverty and the Profit Economy in Medieval Europe, passim*; Reynolds, *Fiefs and Vassals*, 42-47, 64-74; and Southern, *Scholastic Humanism and the Unification of Europe*, 134-141.

36 Bloch, *Feudal Society*, 56.

37 Spruyt, *The Sovereign State and Its Competitors*, 93.

38 Quoted and explained in Little, *Religious Poverty and the Profit Economy in Medieval Europe*, 25; this is Little's translation. Spruyt describes this as a "standard practice" in *The Sovereign State and Its Competitors*, 90.

39 On the emergence of the new bourgeoisie, and its relation to older ideologies of social organization, see Duby, *The Three Orders*, 206-217.

40 For the remainder of this section, I am especially indebted to Southern, *Scholastic Humanism and the Unification of Europe*. With respect to the civic and ecclesiastical reforms of the late eleventh and early twelfth centuries, see in particular *ibid.*, 134-162; additionally, see Bloch, *Feudal Society*, 421-437, Brundage, *Medieval Canon Law*, 18-43, and R.W. Southern, *The Making of the Middle Ages* (New Haven, CT: Yale University Press, 1953), 134-154.

41 Spruyt, *The Sovereign State and Its Competitors*, 81 and, more generally, 77-108.

42 In part, this represented a reaction to genuine abuses, as Brundage emphasizes in *Medieval Canon Law*, 34-36. However, it also reflected changing perceptions of practices that had once seemed unexceptional. As Little notes, so long as European society was dominated by a system of exchanges in which mutual gifts played a central role, the exchange of material for spiritual wealth, in the form of a payment for the bestowal of church office or entrance into a monastery, was likely to appear

as an unproblematic exchange. Once Europe had shifted to a predominantly monetary economy, however, such transactions became stigmatized as simony. See Little, *Religious Poverty and the Profit Economy*, 31.

43 See, for example, Gerd Tellenbach, *Church, State and Christian Society at the Time of the Investiture Contest*, R.F. Bennett, trans. (1940; repr. Toronto: University of Toronto Press, 1991), or whom the proper relationship between clergy and laity in the church appears to be *the* issue at stake in the church reforms of this period.

44 On the emergence of the mendicant movement, see Lawrence, *The Friars, passim*; for a discussion of the alliance between the mendicants and the "new laity," see in particular *ibid.*, 102-126, and cf. Duby, *The Three Orders*, 129-146, 206-217.

45 On the limits of the legal system until the twelfth century, see Bloch, *Feudal Society*, 109-122, 359-374; Brundage, *Medieval Canon Law*, 18-43; Southern, *Scholastic Humanism and the Unification of Europe*, 145-158, 237-244, 264-274; R.C. van Caenegem, *An Historical Introduction to Private Law*, D.E.L. Johnston, trans. (Cambridge: Cambridge University Press, 1992), 16-29 and "Government, Law and Society," 180-183; and Paul Vinogradoff, *Roman Law in Medieval Europe*, second edition (Oxford: Clarendon, 1929), 11-42. In addition, see Stephan Kuttner, "The Revival of Jurisprudence," and Kurt Wolfgang Norr, "Institutional Foundations of the New Jurisprudence," in Benson and Constable, *Renaissance and Renewal in the Twelfth Century*, 299-323 and 324-338, respectively, for background on the intellectual (Kuttner) and institutional (Norr) contexts of the revival of jurisprudence in the twelfth century.

46 Van Caenegem, "Government, Law and Society," 181.

47 In this connection, it is important to realize that a workable scholarly apparatus was not developed until the twelfth century; see Richard H. Rouse and Mary A. Rouse, "*Statim invenire*: Schools, Preachers, and New Attitudes to the Page," Benson and Constable, *Renaissance and Renewal in the Twelfth Century*, 210-225.

48 On this point, see Jean Leclercq, "The Renewal of Theology," in *Renaissance and Renewal in the Twelfth Century*, 68-87 and Giles Constable, *The Reformation of the Twelfth Century* (Cambridge: Cambridge University Press, 1996), *passim*.

49 See Southern, *Scholastic Humanism and the Unification of Europe, passim* and particularly 141-162, 198-231.

50 *Ibid.*, 4-5.

51 Throughout this section, I rely primarily on Southern, *Scholastic Humanism and the Unification of Europe*, especially 1-57 and 102-133, and M.-D. Chenu, *Toward Understanding St. Thomas*, Albert M. Landry and Dominic Hughes, trans. (Chicago: Henry Regnery, 1964), 79-95, 126-202.

52 More exactly, a gloss refers to a particular interlinear comment or query, and a collection of such glosses by a particular master is referred to as a gloss apparatus; see Brundage, *Medieval Canon Law*, 49.

53   *Ibid.*, 49.

54   For a fuller description of the disputation, including an account of variant forms, see *Toward Understanding St. Thomas*, 88-93.

55   The scholastics did of course employ the methodologies of strict deduction, either in the course of a disputation, or (more rarely) as the structure of a whole treatise. An example of the latter is provided by Alan of Lille, who attempts in his *Regulae de Sacra Theologia* to find common ground with the Cathars through an appeal to self-evident reason. For a discussion of this work, see Roger French and Andrew Cunningham, *Before Science: The Invention of the Friars' Natural Philosophy* (Aldershot, U.K.: Scolar Press, 1996), 107-108.

56   For a discussion of dialectic and its relation to the practice of disputation, see Anthony Kenny and Jan Pinborg, "Medieval Philosophical Literature," 11-42 in *The Cambridge History of Later Medieval Philosophy*, Norman Kretzmann, Anthony Kenny, and Jan Pinborg, eds. (Cambridge: Cambridge University Press, 1982), 24-26.

57   Southern, *Scholastic Humanism and the Unification of Europe*, 144.

58   For a fuller accounts of the sources for the scholastic concept of the natural law, see Crowe, *The Changing Profile of the Natural Law*, 1-71.

59   It is sometimes said that the *Digest* was rediscovered in 1070, but Southern questions whether it was ever really lost; see *Scholastic Humanism and the Unification of Europe*, 274-282.

60   On this point, see Crowe, *The Changing Profile of the Natural Law*, 68-70.

61   See *ibid.*, 114-115, on Lombard's significance.

62   On the emergence of civil jurisprudence, and the achievement of Gratian, see Southern, *Scholastic Humanism and the Unification of Europe*, 274-318. Brundage, *Medieval Canon Law* also offers a helpful discussion of the emergence of canon law, seen in the context of early secular jurisprudence, at 44-69. In addition, see Kuttner, "The Revival of Jurisprudence" and, with special reference to civil jurisprudence, Vinogradoff, *Roman Law in Medieval Europe*, 43-70.

63   See M. Grabmann, "Das Naturrecht der Scholastik von Gratian bis Thomas von Aquin," in vol. I of *Mittelalterliches Geistesleben: Abhandlungen zur Geschichte der Scholastic und Mystik* (three volumes) (München: Hueber, 1926), 65-103 at 67.

64   Crowe, *The Changing Profile of the Natural Law*, 114-115.

65   It should be noted that the *Summa* of Alexander of Hales is actually a compilation of writings drawn primarily from his own writings and those of his collaborator John of La Rochelle, which was completed only after the death of the former in 1245. See Crowe, *The Changing Profile of the Natural Law*, 117-118, for further information.

66 Among the canon lawyers, I limit myself to considering Gratian and his commentators, who are known technically as the decretists to distinguish them from commentators on the new papal legislation appearing in the twelfth and thirteenth centuries; these latter are known as decretalists. In practice, the later decretists and the decretalists were often the same persons. In the century following Gratian's death, Pope Gregory IX (d. 1241) commissioned a new collection of canons, which came to be known as the *Liber extra,* but according to Grabmann, this latter collection generated little discussion of the natural law; see *Mittelalterliches Geistesleben,* 70. I have also not attempted to trace the emergence of the different schools of canon law in any detail. Further information on these matters may be found in Crowe, *The Changing Profile of the Natural Law,* 72-110, and Brundage, *Medieval Canon Law,* 44-69.

67 Crowe makes this point in *The Changing Profile of the Natural Law,* 110.

68 Gratian himself may be an exception. Southern argues that he seems to have been a practicing lawyer, at least at some point in his career; see *Scholastic Humanism and the Unification of Europe,* 286-288. It is also the case that Bonaventure's actual academic career was relatively brief, extending only from 1248 to his election as minister general of the Franciscan order in 1257. However, he continued to live in and work primarily in Paris and remained active in the intellectual life sustained by the university there. At any rate, to exclude him from the ranks of the scholastics would be captious in the extreme.

69 On the metaphor of society as a body in John of Salisbury and others, see Duby, *The Three Orders,* 263-268, 315-317; on the revival of the image of the three orders in royal courts, see *ibid.,* 337-353.

70 Significantly, the image of society as a body and the motif of the three orders apparently were not central for the civilians, either. For them, the concept of equity functioned in a way similar to the function of the concept of the natural law for the canonists and theologians.

71 In addition to the work of the evolutionary psychologists discussed above, and Mary Midgley's writings (see above, notes 2-4), see Stephen R.L. Clark, *Animals and Their Moral Standing* (London: Routledge, 1997).

Chapter 2

Nature and Reason

Summary: The scholastic concept of the natural law incorporates three traditional loci for Christian moral reflection – namely, nature, reason, and Scripture – each of which was already the subject of extensive discussion by the medieval period. This chapter takes up the interpretations of nature and reason that informed the scholastic concept of the natural law, leaving a consideration of the scriptural roots of the concept for the next chapter. Accordingly, it begins with an examination of the accounts of nature and reason which the scholastics inherited from their classical sources and from the early twelfth-century "discovery of nature," and then moves on to examine the accounts of nature and reason that informed the scholastic concept of the natural law itself. Because this concept focuses on the natural roots of the conventions that structure society, it can accommodate almost any view according to which nature is structured in accordance with general, intelligible purposes. Correlatively, the scholastic concept of the natural law is first a legitimating concept, through which innovative practices can be justified as intelligible expressions of some natural purpose. The scholastic concept of reason identifies rationality as the distinctive aspect of human nature, and emphasizes the importance of rational discernment in drawing moral conclusions from reflection on human nature; however, the scholastics never interpret reason in a way that drives a wedge between reason and the pre-rational aspects of human nature, as some later natural law theorists have done. Finally, this chapter concludes with an examination of the contemporary signif-icance of the naturalism of the scholastic concept, and addresses some common criticisms of natural law approaches from this perspective. The scholastic concept of the natural law offers a natu-ralistic view of morality as a human phenomenon, which is not a locus for transcendence but which does share in the goodness of human nature as an expression of God's creative wisdom and love. It does not require us to deny the theory of evolution, and it does not presuppose arguments from design or other problematic inter-pretations of natural purpose, although it does presuppose that there are natural purposes in some sense. Similarly, it does not run afoul of the so-called naturalistic fallacy argument. However, it does raise other questions; these are deferred to the next chapter.

■

The idea that we should live in accordance with nature is one of the most ancient and pervasive moral ideas. We find it in some version in most traditional societies, and it retains its hold even in the industrialized West. Yet the very familiarity of the general idea can pose an obstacle to understanding it in its specific applications. To turn to the case at hand, it is easy to assume that when the scholastics refer to a natural law, they mean just what Plato meant by natural justice, or what the Stoics meant by living in accordance with nature, or what a late-twentieth-century papal letter means by the natural law. Or else, we assume that they mean what we would by an appeal to naturalness, or to the ideal of acting out of one's own individual nature. Such assumptions can be helpful as a way of framing a first approach to scholastic writings on the natural law, but they must then be tested by a careful examination of the texts themselves.

For example, some contemporary interpreters have assumed that scholastic theologians simply read off moral conclusions from their obser-vations of the natural world. Approached in this way, the specific argu-ments that these authors develop are bound to seem naive at best, or else ideologically driven. Vern Bullough expresses a common reaction when he remarks, "In effect, the appeal to nature was a teaching device used to reinforce theoretical assumptions. It was not really based upon obser-

vations of what took place in nature, since anything contrary to precon-
ceived notions was ignored."[1]

James Gustafson, who is a more sympathetic critic of traditional
natural law theories, expresses a second common assumption when he
writes, "Roman Catholic moral theology has been able to provide great
certitude in its judgements about biomedical matters because of its confidence that there is a telos in nature, and that various entities, including
man, have essences that form their matter, and that fit their functions in
the larger scheme of things."[2] Similarly, the Catholic theologian Charles
Curran claims that "The classicist methodology tends to be abstract, *a
priori*, and deductive. It wants to cut through the concrete circumstances
to arrive at the abstract essence which is always true, and then works with
these abstract and universal essences. In the area of moral theology, for
example, the first principles of morality are established, and then other
universal norms of conduct are deduced from these."[3] Understood in this
way, appeals to a natural law need not be naive or ideological, but they
do presuppose an untenable view of human nature as determinate, fixed,
and clearly knowable.

Perhaps in reaction to such critiques, some scholars have recently
attempted to recast the whole of the historical natural law tradition in
terms of the "new natural law" proposed by Germain Grisez, John Finnis,
and their collaborators. For example, Robert George declares without
qualification that "The most basic precepts of the natural law direct people
to choose and act for *intelligible* ends and purposes."[4] As he goes on to
explain, the precepts of the natural law thus refer to the range of "basic"
(i.e., non-instrumental or not-merely-instrumental) human goods for the
sake of which people can intelligently act" — the rationally self-evident
basic goods, that is, that provide the foundation for the natural law theory
of Grisez and Finnis.[5]

Bullough's reading of the scholastic concept of the natural law does
not withstand a careful examination of the texts, as we will see. A better
case can be made for the interpretations of both Gustafson and George.
The scholastics do assume that human beings have a species-specific nature
that is both knowable and morally significant; moreover, they do
frequently speak of the natural law as being tantamount to reason, or to
human rationality considered as conscience or practical reason.

Nonetheless, if we are to understand the scholastic concept of the natural law, we cannot assume too quickly that the scholastics would have taken either human nature or reason to mean just what they mean to Gustafson or George, or to most of our contemporaries. Indeed, a preliminary examination of scholastic writings on the natural law suggests that they did not. For most of our contemporaries, Gustafson's interpretation of the natural law as presupposing a substantive account of human nature, and George's insistence that it be understood as a function of pure practical reason, would be seen as two disparate interpretations of the natural law, which stand in tension if not outright contradiction to one another. For the scholastics, on the other hand, appeals to the pre-rational aspects of human nature and to reason are seen as complementary and mutually interpreting. At the very least, this fact suggests that reason as the scholastics understood it is not equivalent to the autonomous, self-legislating practical reason of Kant, or to the purely rational grasp of self-evident basic goods proposed by the "new natural law." It further suggests that human nature as they understood it is not something that is completely fixed prior to the operations of reasonable judgment and the emergence of culture.

If we are to understand and learn from the scholastic concept of the natural law, we should begin by asking how the scholastics developed the mutually interpreting ideas of nature and reason. In order to do so, we must first have some sense of the presuppositions that shaped their own approach to these ideas. These presuppositions were mediated to them through the tradition of reflection on the natural law as they received it, on the one hand, and through the newly ascendent discipline of natural philosophy, on the other.[6]

1. The scholastic concept of the natural law: Sources and context

Until thirty years ago, it was widely assumed that the classical Christian theory of the natural law is essentially Stoic in its origins and its main lines. However, in 1968 this assumption was challenged in an influential article by Helmut Koester, who pointed out that the explicit phrase "law of nature" is rare in the surviving writings of Stoic authors prior to the first century BCE.[7] On the other hand, the phrase itself and the idea that it expresses frequently occur in the writings of the Jewish philosopher Philo. Hence, Koester concludes that the idea of a law of nature originated with Philo himself.

More recently, Koester's thesis has been challenged by Richard Horsley, who argues that it is unlikely that Philo originated the idea of the natural law, since we find the same idea in the writings of Cicero, who wrote some two generations before Philo.[8] On Horsley's view, the accounts of the natural law offered by Cicero and Philo reflect their common participation in "a broader movement of eclectic social-political philosophy in the first century B.C.E."[9] Indeed, the close parallels between them suggest that they shared a common source, whom Horsley identifies with the early-first-century BCE philosopher Antiochus of Ascalon. Horsley goes on to argue that the account of the natural law expressed by both Cicero and Philo is derived from a Stoic tradition on universal law and right reason, but "this Stoic tradition had been reinterpreted by a revived and eclectic Platonism upon which both Cicero and Philo drew."[10] This eclectic philosophy included an account of the natural law that was "standard and widespread" and that Horsley locates in subsequent authors as diverse as the Stoic Marcus Aurelius, the Platonist Maximus of Tyre, and the Christian Origen.[11]

This does not mean that Philo contributed nothing distinctive to the development of the natural law tradition. Recently, Hindy Najman has argued that Philo's treatment of the natural law is distinctive in one respect; that is, he identifies the natural law with the written law of Scripture, in contrast to classical and Hellenistic philosophers who underscored the contrast between natural and written law.[12] In view of the close connection that the scholastics were later to draw between natural and divine – that is, scriptural law – this is suggestive, and the scholastics may well have been aware of Philo's views either directly, or through those patristic authorities, primarily Origen and Ambrose, who drew heavily on the Jewish philosopher.

At any rate, Horsley's analysis is of the first importance for understanding the account of the natural law mediated to the scholastics by their sources. Cicero himself is arguably the single most important pre-Christian author for the subsequent development of a Christian natural law tradition; only the Roman jurists collected under Justinian had a comparable influence.[13] In addition, the thought of these Roman jurists was itself shaped by this same eclectic political philosophy, and the same is true for the most important Christian sources for subsequent reflection on the natural law, including Paul's letters and the writings of Origen, Lactantius, Ambrose, and Augustine.

What, then, are the main lines of this eclectic account of the natural law? In Horsley's view, it is almost certainly grounded in Stoic thought, with additional influences from Aristotle and the Cynics.[14] Even though we do not have a complete account of the natural law in any author before Cicero, the key elements of this account are standard Stoic ideas. In particular, the idea of a universal reason that is equivalent to universal nature, the law of nature, fate, and even to God, is Stoic in origin. Correlatively, the Stoics taught that men and women ought to live in accordance with nature, or equivalently with right reason or the universal law. The Stoics were also responsible for the claim, prominent in the writings of both Cicero and Philo, to the effect that the whole human race comprises one commonwealth under one universal law of justice. Indeed, in Horsley's view, "This concern about the unity of mankind provides the context and the point of the Stoic argument regarding the reason or law of nature."[15] Moreover, in contrast to Aristotle they taught the natural equality of all persons, which they understood in terms of an equality of capacity for virtue.[16]

To anyone who is acquainted with traditional theories of the natural law, these claims will have the sound of truisms. However, it would be a mistake to assume that they always carried the same connotations for the Stoics as they did for later natural law thinkers. There was no room for a transcendent deity in the materialistic Stoic universe, and very little room, if any, for human freedom. The injunction to live in accordance with nature, or with reason, could be understood as equivalent to willing acceptance of fate or providence, of whatever happens, seen as an expression of the immanent reasonableness of the universe. There is perhaps an echo of this view in Isidore's remark that the natural law is equivalent to what is licit or permitted, *fas*, which can also be translated as fate or chance (*Etymologies* V.2). Nonetheless, neither Cicero and most of his contemporaries nor later Christian authors were prepared to accept the complete immanence of the natural law or its equivalence with fate.

It is at this point that the Platonic influence on the account of the natural law was most important. Under the influence of Platonic conceptions of a transcendent deity, the eclectic philosophers who shaped this account reinterpreted Stoic conceptions of reason and nature in a way that introduced the idea of a divine legislator, separate from and transcendent to the world. In Horsley's words,

> The Stoics apparently understood the right reason of nature as the divine structure immanent in the cosmos, inherent in the (empirical) order of things. In the versions of the law of nature argument in Cicero, Philo, and others analyzed above, the presence of terms such as "mind of God," "ordinance," and God as the "legislator" of the universal natural law, signals a significant shift in meaning. These are Platonic terms, but more importantly, they are terms used by Platonic philosophy to express the transcendence of God and the divine mind over the cosmos which it "orders." The right reason or law is a transcendent *noetic* reality. Even *nature* must be understood in a metaphysical sense as "Being," almost in the sense of "divine existence" (or even "God").[17]

On this view, nature is still seen as reasonable and reason is likewise seen as natural, as the Stoics taught. However, neither reason nor nature can be understood as equivalent to the innate order of a self-contained, materialistic universe, or equated straightforwardly with the actual course of events. Rather, on this view both nature and reason are grounded in and reflective of a transcendent reality, and for this reason, the laws of nature can also be understood as expressions of the will of a divine legislator.

As we will see, the scholastic concept of the natural law preserved these general ideas of nature, reason, and the relation of both to the will or law of God. At the same time, they brought specificity to these general ideas, in part because they interpreted them through the sophisticated apparatus of twelfth- and thirteenth-century philosophies of nature. Before turning to an examination of medieval natural philosophy, however, there are two further points about the sources for the scholastic concept of the natural law to be noted.

We have not yet considered the writings of the Roman jurists collected at the behest of the Christian emperor Justinian in the *Institutes* and the *Digest*. Yet these were fundamentally important, not only for the secular jurists who took the *Digest* as their primary authority, but also for the canonists and theologians. In particular, Ulpian's definition of the natural law as a law that is shared by all animals, human beings included, helped to ensure that the scholastic concept of the natural law did not base itself on reason, narrowly understood. This highly influential definition is worth quoting: "The law of nature is that which nature teaches all animals. For that law is not proper to the human race, but it is common to all animals which are born on the earth and in the sea, and to the birds also."[18]

It is sometimes said that Ulpian's definition of the natural law is Stoic in origin, with the implication that this accounts for its influence.[19] But as Marcia Colish points out, this is a mistake. The Stoics emphasized the discontinuity between human rational action and animal behavior and, correlatively, denied that human morality could be derived from a consideration of animal behavior.[20] Ulpian's definition thus represents a break with Stoicism, and to the extent that the scholastics build this definition into their understanding of the natural law, they too move away from Stoicism.

Second, some readers may have been surprised by the omission of Plato and especially Aristotle as sources for the scholastic concept of the natural law. However, the writings of Plato and Aristotle are more significant as foundational texts for the natural philosophy of the twelfth and thirteenth centuries than as direct sources for the scholastic concept of the natural law. Plato's idea of natural justice is important for the cathedral scholars who lay the foundations for this natural philosophy, yet it is not central for the scholastic authors on whom this study is focused. As for Aristotle, his distinction between natural and conventional justice does find a place in the thought of those scholastics who are particularly indebted to him, including both Aquinas and his teacher, Albert the Great. However, by the time Albert and Aquinas were developing their theories of the natural law, the distinction between natural and conventional had long been a commonplace among the scholastics. Indeed, this distinction was fundamental to the eclectic account of the natural law that provided the starting point for scholastic reflection, and for this reason, the scholastics did not need to take it directly from Aristotle, even though it may have originated with him.

By the same token, Aristotle's *direct* influence on the political thought of the later Middle Ages should not be exaggerated. Certainly, Aristotle exercised a considerable influence on scholastic moral and political thought. But much of that influence was indirect, mediated through Aristotle's influence on later classical and patristic authors who shaped the scholastic discussion. As Cary Nederman points out, key ideas from Aristotelian ethics were in general circulation for at least 150 years before the full text of the *Nicomachean Ethics* became available in Latin.[21]

At this point, let us turn to the natural philosophies that provided the context for the scholastic appropriation of natural law thinking. As Charles Haskins argued, and as a number of scholars have since confirmed, one of the hallmarks of the twelfth-century renaissance was a resurgence of interest in the natural world, together with a new understanding of the religious significance of the natural.[22] In the words of Andreas Speer, "The older understanding was a symbolic-speculative interpretation of nature using a hermeneutic parallel to the book of Scripture with a reference to the Author of both books, by which man could come to know the creator. This view is increasingly replaced by an original interest in the structure, constitution and autonomy of the physical world, which, without reverting to traditional frames of reference, can be rationally grasped as in itself meaningful."[23]

This "discovery of nature," as Haskins called it, gave rise to the development of a discipline of natural philosophy comprised of rational reflection on the nature of particular things and of the universe as a whole. Interest in natural philosophy continued into the thirteenth century, now transformed by the appropriation of Aristotle's naturalistic and scientific works, read both on their own terms and through the lens of Islamic philosophy. By now, natural philosophy was central to the university curriculum, and all students, including those preparing for theological studies, were expected to study it. At this point, too, the newly emergent mendicant orders began to emphasize the importance of natural philosophy as a basis for responding to the heretical movements flourishing in southern France and parts of Italy.[24]

A heightened interest in nature seems to have been in the air, so to speak, from the earliest decades of the twelfth century. However, twelfth-century natural philosophy is especially associated with the work of a number of teachers and administrators connected to the cathedral school of Chartres between 1115 and 1160, including Bernardus Silvestris, Gilbert of Poitiers, Bernard and Thierry of Chartres, and William of Conches, together with their two most influential students, John of Salisbury (d. 1180) and Alan of Lille (d. 1202/3).[25]

These scholars are characterized, first, by their commitment to Platonic philosophy, particularly as it was mediated to them through Plato's *Timaeus* (the only Platonic dialogue available in Latin translation at this time), Augustine, pseudo-Dionysius, Macrobius, and Boethius.[26] As Winthrop Weatherbee says, for these scholars "to study nature was in effect to decode the *Timaeus*,"[27] and they were particularly concerned to reconcile Plato's account of the fabrication of the world with the creation story given in Genesis. Their devotion to Plato and his commentators generated views that seem strange to us, including (for some) a belief in a world-soul that exists apart from both God and the visible universe, an openness to the use of mythical and figurative language as a tool for philosophical speculation, and perhaps as a result of that openness, a tendency to personify Nature, speaking as if she were an entity in her own right.

These unfamiliar views should not be allowed to obscure just how innovative these scholars were. The twelfth century marks the first point at which Christian scholars made a systematic attempt to reconcile Scripture with philosophical efforts to explain the beginning of the world in terms of natural causes. Given the subsequent history of conflict between scientists and defenders of Scripture, it is startling to read William of Conches coolly announcing that the Genesis story of the creation of Adam and Eve "must not be believed literally."[28] More generally, they insisted on the intelligibility of natural processes, which should be understood in terms of the unfolding of intrinsic principles through natural causes. They did not deny the doctrine of the creation, but they insisted that God created the world as an integral whole, with internal principles of action sufficient to generate the processes of growth and decay that sustain the created order. Hence, they emphasized God's creative wisdom, while de-emphasizing the role played by miraculous interventions into the cosmic order.

The Platonic natural philosophy of the early twelfth century was motivated by moral as well as theoretical concerns. The scholars of Chartres appropriated Plato's concept of natural justice – that is, the proper interrelationships of creatures arrayed in a hierarchy of being, from the highest intelligences to the lowest forms of material existence. In the words of William of Conches, "Since natural justice is most apparent in the creation of things and the government of creatures – for whatever is created by God is right and just and is not invented by man – [Plato] moves on to discuss this, in order to show the nature and extent of the justice observed by the creator."[29] So understood, natural justice finds its counterpart in a social hierarchy, expressed in the harmonious interrelationships between those who hold a dominant position in society and those who occupy more humble stations. This interpretation of the social order, in turn, has obvious affinities with the Pauline image of society as a body, in which the different parts function together for the mutual benefit of each of them and for the whole society.

The interrelated ideas of Platonic natural justice, the naturalness of a social hierarchy, and the corresponding metaphor of society as a body are taken by many to be the quintessence of the natural law theory of society. Certainly, these ideas were central for the scholars associated with Chartres as well as for two of their most distinguished students, John of Salisbury and Alan of Lille. And there is no question that they continued to be influential in some strands of late medieval and modern thought, culminating in the papal encyclical *Rerum novarum*, which presents the organic ideal of society as *the* Catholic natural law account of the social order.[30]

The question is, how central were the ideas of social hierarchy and society as a body for the scholastic concept of natural law that we are examining? The scholastics would have agreed that God's wisdom as expressed in creation and providence is the fundamental form of justice, and a number of them explicitly include Platonic natural justice among the different possible senses of the natural law.[31] Yet the more distinctive Platonic ideas of a natural social hierarchy, and of society as a body, play at most a secondary role in their reflections on the natural law. It is worth noting that Aquinas, who does make use of a Platonic idea of natural justice in his commentary on *The Divine Names* of pseudo-Dionysius (*De Divinis Nominibus* X.1, 857), nonetheless repudiates the view that social inequalities reflect a natural hierarchy among human beings, comparable to the angelic hierarchy (*Summa theologiae* I 109.2 *ad* 3).

By the middle of the twelfth century, the neo-Platonic natural philosophy developed by the scholars of Chartres and their pupils began to be supplanted by the philosophical works of Aristotle and his Greek and Arabic commentators, which were increasingly being made available in Latin translations. These treatises formed the basis for the discipline of natural philosophy as it was institutionalized in the university curriculum. This was doubly significant. Because natural philosophy was a part of the arts curriculum, its scholars demanded and won independence for it as a discipline as a part of their efforts to secure their independence as a faculty. At the same time, every scholar in the medieval university had to receive a degree from the faculty of arts in order to pass on to further studies. This meant that the scholastic jurists and theologians were all trained in Aristotelian natural philosophy.

At the beginning of the thirteenth century, the study of natural philosophy was given further impetus by the growing strength of the Cathar movement in southern France and Italy.[32] In the view of the Cathars, the world is so manifestly evil that it cannot be the result of a good God; it can be explained only as the product of fallen angels who have escaped from God's control and are now acting contrary to God's will. Some of them went so far as to assert the existence of two primal creative forces, one good, the other evil. Hence, they viewed the material world, the body, and the processes of reproduction as evil, and held that the Christian can be saved only by breaking with the material world as far as possible. As their contemporaries quickly recognized, the views of the Cathars were similar to those of the Manicheans who so attracted the young Augustine, although they were almost certainly not directly derived from the Manichee movement, which had died out long ago. Like the Manichees, they also rejected the authority of much of Scripture, including the Old Testament and parts of the New Testament.

As is well known, the Catholic church attempted to suppress the Cathar movement by all the means at its disposal, including violence.[33] However, beginning in the mid-twelfth century, efforts were also made to respond to the Cathars through theological argument and persuasion, and early in the thirteenth century the newly emergent mendicant orders took this task on as one of their distinctive vocations. For the Dominicans in particular, the natural philosophy of Aristotle provided a basis for arguing that the physical world is good and can be understood as the creation of God alone, acting without any secondary principle. This appropriation, in turn, provided further impetus for the study of natural philosophy in the twelfth century.

Aristotelian natural philosophy in the thirteenth century and beyond proved to be remarkably fruitful in providing ways of thinking about the natural world. It would take us beyond the scope of this book to examine the details of this world-view, but certain points should be noted. The proponents of Aristotelian natural philosophy typically understood "nature" in terms of the nature of particular creatures: that is, as the complex of intrinsic principles that are expressed in the mode of activity proper to a creature of a given kind. This set them apart from their more Platonically minded predecessors, who were more inclined to speak of nature as an autonomous generative and directive force, which can be said to direct or instruct individual creatures from without.[34] For this reason, many of the characteristic motifs of twelfth-century natural philosophy, including the idea of a world soul and the image of Nature as a personified being, more or less disappeared in this period. Thirteenth-century thinkers did sometimes speak of nature as the whole complex of existing beings, but they tended to identify nature so understood with creation: that is, as the term of God's creative activity. Alternatively, they identified nature understood as a creative force with God, designated as *natura naturans*, seen in contrast to nature as creation, that is, *natura naturata*.

At the same time, thirteenth-century natural philosophy preserved much of the spirit of its twelfth-century antecedents. If scholars in this period were more hesitant than their predecessors to speak of nature as an autonomous principle of action, nonetheless they did affirm the relative independence of nature. They continued to look for explanations of natural phenomena in terms of intrinsic principles, rather than appealing to God's inscrutable will or focusing on possible symbolic or allegorical interpretations. Correlatively, they insisted on the intelligibility and goodness of natural phenomena, seen on their own terms and as expressions of the wisdom and love of God as creator.

These commitments to the intelligibility and the goodness of nature proved to be central to the development of scholastic thinking on the natural law. They provided a basis for drawing a connection between nature and reason which, as we will see, was central to the scholastic concept of the natural law.

2. The starting point: Nature and convention

The authoritative texts that provided the starting points for scholastic reflection on the natural law contained diverse and not always harmonious accounts of what the natural law is. Moreover, these texts were interpreted in the light of the rapidly developing discipline of natural philosophy, which added its own complexities to the interpreter's task. Given all this, it is not surprising that definitions of the natural law proliferated among the scholastics themselves. The canonist Stephen of Tournai, writing in about 1160, offers a summary of the most common definitions:

> And it should be noted that the natural law is spoken of in four senses. For we speak of a natural law which is introduced by nature itself, and is not placed only in the human person, but also in other animals, from which derive the union of male and female and the procreation and education of children. The law of nations, which takes its origin from human nature alone, as it were beginning with it, is also said to be a natural law. The divine law, which our highest nature, that is, God, taught us, and placed before us through the law and the prophets and the gospel, is also said to be natural law. We also speak of a natural law which includes at once both human and divine law, and also that law which is placed in all animals by nature. And according to this last understanding, something is established "by natural law, that is, by divine, and that other primitive law." Or, if you can stand a fifth understanding of the natural law, understand, that is said to be the natural law which is placed by nature in the human person alone, and not the other animals, namely, [a faculty directed towards] doing good and avoiding evil. This is, as it were, a part of the divine law (Weigand no. 244-46).

Stephen of Tournai was the first, but he was scarcely the last, to offer this kind of listing of the various possible senses of the term "natural law."[35]

There are yet other interpretations of the natural law that could be added to these. As was noted above, some theologians and canonists added Plato's natural justice, by which all creatures take their place in the hierarchy of being, to the senses of the natural law. A few canonists, for example, Odo of Dover (Weigand no. 271), associate the natural law with the civilian concept of equity, considered an objective standard of fairness. Later, with the rediscovery of Aristotle's ethical writings, efforts are made to identify his concept of natural justice with the natural law, seen in contrast to his concept of legal justice, which is associated with the laws of particular communities.[36]

It might seem that this multiplicity of definitions would resist any systematic treatment. Yet the scholastics attempt to bring order to this diversity. In order to do so, they rely on a traditional distinction between what is natural in the sense of existing prior to human customs and legal enactments, and what is conventional or established by human design.[37]

Hence, anything that can be said to exist prior to human customs and enactments, and that somehow gives rise to or structures those customs and enactments, can be included in the concept of the natural, as the scholastics understand it. Interpreted in this way, the concept of the natural can encompass "nature" understood in both of the primary senses discussed above: that is, nature seen as the ordered totality of all creatures, and nature seen as the intrinsic characteristics of a given kind of creature. It can also refer to the human capacity for rational judgment, which gives rise to moral norms, or to God's will as revealed in Scripture, since the divine will certainly exists prior to all human enactments and provides their ultimate norm.

At the same time, while this interpretation of the natural can be extended widely, it does not encompass every possible sense in which nature can be understood. In order to be incorporated into the concept of the natural law, a given idea of nature has to carry connotations of order and intelligibility. Nature in the sense of sheer facticity is not incorporated into the scholastic concept of the natural law, because nature taken in this sense cannot offer a basis for understanding the regularities of the non-human or social world. We observed above that Isidore of Seville includes the idea of *fas*, or fate, as a possible meaning of the natural law, perhaps under Stoic influence, but he interprets the natural law in this sense to mean that which is permissible, playing on another meaning of *fas* as licit. Similarly, the natural so understood does not encompass the nature of a particular individual, understood in the sense of an individual person's constitution and personality, because nature in this sense is not general enough to provide a basis for interpreting social regularities. (For an example of this distinction, see Aquinas, *Summa theologiae* I–II 31.7.)

Finally, the scholastic concept of the natural law presupposes a sense of nature that carries connotations of goodness as well as intelligibility. Occasionally we find Paul's "law of sin" mentioned as a form of natural law, but this usage appears to have been rare.[38]

It is clear that the contrast between the natural and the conventional is central to scholastic moral thought. But what is the point of this contrast? How does it serve to establish normative judgments on the conventions of their society?

It is important to realize, in the first place, that the contrast between the natural and the conventional does not in itself imply a moral judgment. It is obvious to the scholastics that most conventional practices are morally acceptable, and furthermore, they are not prepared to say without qualification that what is natural is morally praiseworthy. Rather, the contrast between natural and conventional provides them with a framework for analyzing the practices of society, with the aim of establishing their foundation in natural principles. The scholastics attempt first of all to explain the practices that they see around them by interpreting these as the expressions of nature in one of its many possible senses, and therefore, arguably, as expressions of natural law in some sense or other.

This kind of analysis is ubiquitous among scholastic natural law thinkers. We find it in the canonists' analysis of the senses in which divine (that is, scriptural) and canon law are forms of natural law, and it also appears in the civilian jurists' explanations of the way the law of nations may be said to be a kind of natural law.[39] To take more specific examples, the anonymous canonical *Summa reginensis* sets forth an explanation of the way in which the laws of inheritance can be understood as originating from the evangelical law, or reason, or inclinations grounded in that sensuality that we share with other animals (Weigand no. 385), and the secular theologian Philip the Chancellor (d. 1236) explains that the precept against killing originates in pre-rational nature and is then specified by reason (Lottin 114). In subsequent chapters, we will see many more examples of this sort of analysis applied to marriage, servitude, and property.

In a sense, Gustafson is correct to claim that the concept of the natural law presupposes that "various entities, including man, have essences that form their nature."[40] To be more exact, the scholastic concept of the natural law, in many of its interpretations at least, presupposes that the human person is a substance with an intelligible, specific nature, in terms of which human behavior can be understood and evaluated. Yet, as the examples just cited illustrate, the scholastics do not begin with a fully determinate account of human nature, on the basis of which they deduce moral conclusions. They presuppose that the practices that they observe are expressions of some aspect of human nature, and are intelligible as such, but this presupposition leaves room for some agnosticism about what human nature actually includes. Furthermore, they arrive at moral conclusions through a process of dialectical reflection that moves between their understanding of human nature, and the specific norms and practices said to express this nature, and not through a process of deduction from a fixed idea of what is natural, as Curran claims. As we will see in what follows, this process allows for the recognition that there can be more than one legitimate practical expression of human nature.

Once the scholastics establish that a particular practice or custom is an expression of the natural law, in one of its many possible senses, this in turn provides them with a basis for normative judgments. The question still remains, how are these normative judgments derived? Or to put it another way, what is at stake in establishing that a particular practice is an expression of the natural law? These questions are answered, in the first instance, by appealing to traditional dicta concerning the natural law: "The natural law precedes others in dignity, as it [precedes them] in time; with respect to time, because it began with human nature; with respect to dignity, because while other laws may be changed, it remains immutable" (*Cologne Summa,* Lottin, 106).[41] Some of them also appeal to the innate goodness of nature; thus, it is sometimes said that the natural law does not prescribe anything injurious, or anything sinful (for example, see Albert, *De bono* V 1.2). Hence, if a particular practice can be interpreted as an expression of nature, in one of the many senses in which nature is understood, that provides a *prima facie* justification for the practice in question. On this basis, the scholastics offer a defense of marriage, in terms of which the normal mode of lay life could be defended against the suspicions of monastic thinkers and the outright condemnation of the Cathars. For example, Aquinas defends the moral legitimacy of sexual intercourse within marriage with the argument (among others) that "It is impossible that the natural inclination of a species should be directed towards that which is evil in itself" (*Summa contra gentiles* III. 126). It is interesting to note that he goes on immediately to argue on natural law grounds that no kind of food is evil in itself, an argument that appears to be directed against Cathar prohibitions against eating meat (*SCG* III.127).[42]

This line of argument is particularly effective in defense of practices that are considered by some to be dangerously innovative or otherwise problematic from the standpoint of long-standing custom. We find a remarkable example in Bonaventure's treatise, *De perfectione evangelium*, written in defense of the Franciscan way of life. While Bonaventure does not draw on natural law arguments alone, we find them at key points throughout the treatise.[43] He defends the Franciscan ideal of radical poverty by arguing that someone who is poor attains the greatest possible approximation to the natural state of the human person (*De Per. Evan.* II. 1). Similarly, he sorts out different senses of nature in order to show that virginity is not contrary to the natural law (*De Per. Evan.* III.3, ad 8, 10, 11), and he appeals to a further, scripturally-based interpretation of the natural law both to justify the practice of religious obedience and to place limits on its scope (*De Per. Evan.* IV.1, 2).[44]

The presupposition that natural processes are *prima facie* good is closely connected to another aspect of the scholastic concept of the natural law. That is, the scholastics readily ascribe intrinsic value to those aspects of existence and life that we share with other animals, and even with other creatures *tout court*. The scholastics differ over whether animals may properly be said to follow a natural law. For the secular jurists, following Ulpian, the natural law in its primary sense is common to humans and other animals, as we have seen. The canonists and theologians do not generally take Ulpian's to be the primary definition of the natural law, but many of them do nonetheless admit that non-rational animals may be said to follow a natural law. Others deny this, on the grounds that following a law presupposes an ability to act in accordance with a rational grasp of the principles that one is following.[45] Nonetheless, this disagreement should not be allowed to obscure a more fundamental consensus: for all the scholastics, those natural processes that we share with the animals are intrinsically valuable and form the basis for an important aspect of distinctively human forms of the natural law.[46]

As is well known, the scholastics hold that the natural structures of sexuality, which we share with other animals, place moral constraints on human sexual activity. However, the moral significance of those aspects of our nature that we share with other animals goes beyond their implications for sexual ethics. For at least some of the scholastics, the most basic precepts of morality, including injunctions against killing, are also grounded in those aspects of our nature that we share with other animals.[47] The civilian jurist Azo finds it necessary to explain the fact that some animals do in fact naturally harm others (perhaps, he suggests, they do not harm their own kind), precisely because he holds that the injunction to do no harm stems from that natural law that we share with sub-rational animals (Weigand no. 85). And in an anonymous canonical text, we read that the most basic principles of human morality, including the fundamental injunction against doing harm, are grounded in that form of the natural law that we share with the animals:

> The natural law of the first division [that is, the natural law that we share with other animals] consists in:
>
> Precepts: that each animal should unite bodily with another, male and female. This law directs, "do not kill," but it does not direct, "do not commit adultery," although it does direct, "do no injury."
>
> Prohibitions: That animals should not unite contrary to nature, male with male ... "Increase and multiply" is a precept of nature and of the natural law ... Also, this law prescribes, "love thy neighbor." (Distinctio, Lex naturalis, Weigand no. 361)

This is the sort of passage that leads many contemporary readers to dismiss scholastic thought as primitive and confused. We tend to assume that moral considerations must be grounded in our freely chosen commitments, or at least in rational judgments. Yet it is important not to exaggerate the difference between the scholastics and ourselves on this point. Like us, the scholastics believe that rational judgment is a prerequisite for responsibility and therefore for moral accountability. Hence, they do not consider animal behavior to be subject to moral appraisal, any more than the behavior of young children or the insane should be.[48] Nonetheless, it is true that their concept of morality is different from ours at this point. Unlike us, they are prepared to ascribe intrinsic value to the

integrity displayed by animal behavior. While this does not imply that
animals are morally accountable for their behavior, it does mean that the
lives of animals display an intrinsic goodness. Even more importantly,
human morality is to a large degree the distinctively human expression
of the goodness that we share with the other animals.

At any rate, these would have been points of difference between us
and the scholastics until recently. However, the recent upsurge of interest
in the biological roots of human behavior, and in the related question of
the moral standing of animals, has led a growing number of philosophers
and scientists to question the sharp division between a human morality
supposedly grounded in autonomy and reason, and instinctual, non-
rational animal behavior.

In the first place, there is a growing body of research confirming the
scholastics' basic claim that there are considerable continuities between
what we think of as moral practices and the behavior of at least the higher
animals. In the words of the ethologist Frans de Waal, "The question of
whether animals have morality is a bit like the question of whether they
have culture, politics, or language. If we take the full-blown human
phenomenon as a yardstick, they most definitely do not. On the other
hand, if we break the relevant human abilities into their component parts,
some are recognizable in other animals."[49] He then goes on to list these
component parts, including attachment, empathy, adjustment to and
special care for the disabled, internalization of "prescriptive social rules,"
concepts of giving, trading, and revenge, tendencies towards peacemaking
and social maintenance, and the practice of negotiation.[50]

Observations such as these have led, secondly, to a willingness to
reconsider the sharp line that we have drawn between human morality
and animal behavior. If animals do indeed exhibit many analogues to
human morality, then at the very least it is difficult to avoid every trace
of moral judgments in our attitudes toward them.[51] Those who have
worked extensively with animals have often noted this; the more their
familiarity grows, the more they find themselves responding with approval
or disapproval, admiration or dismay, to those they are observing. If our
moral sentiments can be aroused through interaction with non-rational
animals, this suggests that our moral responses to other people are not
fully dependent on assessments of their rational attitudes, either.[52] It would
be a mistake to go to the opposite extreme, to conclude that freedom

and rational judgment have no place in morality. However, there does seem to be an organic continuity between our pre-rational attitudes and responses and our fully developed moral judgments. The pre-rational roots of human morality, in turn, can be illuminated by comparisons between human and animal behavior.

This brings us to another point in Gustafson's characterization of the natural law. Gustafson's main critique of the traditional account of the natural law is that it presupposes that human persons are the apex of creation and that everything else exists for our benefit.[53] There are indeed reflections of these attitudes in some of the authors we are studying. But these attitudes must be balanced against the pervasive scholastic sense of the continuity between us, considered precisely as moral agents, and the other animals. This sense of continuity, in turn, presupposes that there is a kind of goodness that is more fundamental than human moral rectitude: namely, the goodness displayed in any life that unfolds in accordance with its intrinsic principles of operation. Furthermore, this goodness is an expression of the still more basic goodness that each creature enjoys simply by virtue of being the creature of a good Creator.

So far, we have seen that the understanding of nature implied by the scholastic concept of the natural law takes its starting point from the ancient distinction between the natural and the conventional. It is then developed in a way that emphasizs the intelligibility and goodness of natural processes, such that the naturalness of a practice counts as a *prima facie* justification for it.

At the same time, the scholastics recognize that there are problems in appealing to what is natural without further qualification as a basis for moral justification. It is widely assumed that they attempt to derive moral conclusions directly from an observation of animal behavior, and their emphasis on the continuities between animal and human behavior might seem to support this assumption. But, in fact, they are well aware of the dangers of this approach. As the Dominican theologian Roland of Cremona, writing between 1229 and 1230, observes:

> If it is objected, concerning the beasts which do not have reason in themselves, but nature only, and which are not content with one mate only, that the fact that they are not content with one mate only is of the natural law; we say that this is true, because

there are multiple senses in the law, such that there is one law
for this kind of creature, and another law for that kind. I say that
marriage is derived from the same law, because synderesis directs
that marriage should be contracted, and there should be no
running around to this female and that female, as the beasts do.
For synderesis prescribes that the human person should not live
as a beast does. And that is the law which always agrees with the
divine will, because synderesis always wills the good and protests
against what is evil. (Lottin 115; 'Synderesis' refers to the higher
or superior component of reason; for a fuller explanation, see
below, p. 89.)

Furthermore, the scholastics recognize that the supposedly
unchanging and definitive natural law has been changed and altered by
human custom in a variety of ways, not all of them obviously sinful. As
we will see in more detail in Chapter 5, they consider property and
servitude to be conventional rather than natural, and yet they defend the
legitimacy of at least some forms of these institutions. Moreover, just as
there are some practices which contravene nature in some sense, and yet
are morally licit, so there are other practices which are natural, at least in
some plausible sense, and yet are sinful. This latter difficulty was, if
anything, more serious than the first.

Some of the scholastics deal with this problem simply by appealing
to the dictum "The natural law does not establish sin" to rule out
fornication and other sexual sins as expressions of the natural law. Nonetheless, these forms of behavior are obviously expressions of human nature,
at least in the sense of expressing tendencies that are fundamental to that
aspect of our nature which we share with other animals. Hence, a few
of the scholastics are prepared to say that, in some sense, sexual sins do
stem from the natural law. For example, the anonymous author of the
Leipzig Summa observes:

> It is customary to inquire about what is said, that the union of
> husband and wife is derived from the natural law. Therefore:
> either it is natural, or it is not. If it is natural, then so is the [union]
> of brute animals, and similarly, so is a fornicating union. But that
> is a mortal sin, and thus sin would be derived from the natural
> law, which is false. Yet if it should be said that no union is derived

from the natural law, this would seem to be false.... Some say, however, that only a legitimate union, and principally that which is brought about through matrimony, is derived from the natural law. But it is better to say that any natural union, whether with brother or sister or even with the mother is derived from the natural law, but not considered as this kind of union [that is to say, a sinful union], just as any act is from God, insofar as it is an act, but not considered as a sinful act (Lottin 108-109).[54]

The anonymous author of this passage offers a useful way out of the dilemma raised by the seeming naturalness of sexual sins; that is, he distinguishes between the naturalness of these acts, in virtue of which they are good in a sense, and their conformity to the rational standards appropriate to human nature. By doing so, he points the way to the resolution of this difficulty and takes us to the next level of reflection on the meaning of "natural" for these exponents of the natural law.

3. Nature and reason

It is one of the legacies of modern romanticism that we tend to think of nature and reason as contrasts. The scholastics were not unaware of such a contrast. For example, the theologian William of Meliton argues that, in one sense, marriage is not derived from the natural law, because it requires the free (and therefore reasonable) consent of the two parties (Lottin 121); and in his early commentary on the *Sentences*, Aquinas remarks that understood in one sense, nature is contrasted with reason (*In IV Sent.* 33.1.1 *ad* 4). Nonetheless, the understandings of nature that were mediated to them, both through their authoritative sources and the natural philosophy of their own time, generally emphasized the continuities between nature and reason. Indeed, as D.E. Luscombe observes, theologians in the first half of the twelfth century frequently equated nature and reason, since they saw the orderly processes of nature as expressions of the reason of God.[55] Nature seen as a personified force is depicted as arranging the creatures of the universe and governing them in accordance with an orderly plan; nature seen as the cosmos, or the whole of material creation, is understood as a self-contained and orderly unity, and nature seen as the nature of a specific kind of creature is understood as the intrinsic principle for the operations specific to that kind of creature. In all of these interpretations of nature, the intelligibility, and hence the reasonableness of natural processes, is underscored.

The scholastics do distinguish between nature, understood specifically as pre-rational, and the characteristically human ability to reason.[56] Nonetheless, they see no inconsistency in claiming that the human person is characteristically rational, while at the same time insisting on the fundamental continuity between ourselves and the rest of creation. Nor, correlatively, does their emphasis on reason lead them to deny the moral significance of those aspects of our nature that we share with the other animals. On the contrary, if the natural world taken as a whole is informed by reason, then human reasonableness is itself an expression of our continuity with the natural world.

We have already seen one example of this attitude in Roland of Cremona's explanation of how it is that the natural law prescribes different forms of behavior for human beings and non-rational animals. There, the diversity between appropriate forms of human and animal behavior is not taken as a sign of any radical discontinuity, but simply as an indication that the natural law makes provisions for the differences among various kinds of creatures. We find a still more striking illustration of this attitude in an earlier canonical summa, written around 1184:

> Thus according to a less precise understanding, the natural law is said to be that which the highest nature has placed universally in the animal, insofar as it naturally directs [the animal] to act or to refrain from acting. I say naturally, not in accordance with the illicit things of the natural senses, but in accordance with what is better and more excellent in animal nature. For example, reason is the better part in the human person, and the image of reason, that is, imagination, is the better part in the brute animal. Reason directs the human person alone, and the imagination directs the brute animal, to resist force by force; this is vengeance, which is a kind of natural law, according to what Tully [Cicero] says in his *Rhetoric*. Also, just as reason directs the human person, so imagination directs the brute animal to bring forth offspring and to educate and care for what is brought forth. Considering this, one who is learned in civil law [Ulpian] says: "We see that other

living creatures are thought to be learned in this law." It is said
therefore to be law, because that which naturally directs [the
animal] was put in office by the highest nature, that is, God.
Hence also natural justice is said to be, as it were, the office of
that which naturally directs [us]. More strictly, the natural law is
said to be that law which is understood to extend only to the
human person and not to all animals, and to be brought forth
with the human person from the beginning ... (*Summa "Reverentia
sacrorum canonum,"* Weigand no. 324-327).[57]

At the same time, rationality is considered to be the human characteristic *par excellence*. This fits well with the understanding of nature as
equivalent to the essential or proper characteristics of a specific kind of
being; if the natural law is understood as an expression of the principles
of action intrinsic to a given kind of nature, then it makes sense to say
that the properly human expression of the natural law involves acting in
accordance with reason, because the characteristic expression of human
nature *is* to act in accordance with reason. Among the later scholastics,
this continuity is expressed by the phrase, "reason as nature," which
appears to have been first used by Philip the Chancellor.[58] This expression
points to the distinctively rational character of human nature, but at the
same time it also keeps the continuities between human and animal nature
in view:

...since the natural law is so called from nature, that is, it is that
which natural reason directs and that which is written in the
natural reason, since according to this way of speaking, reason is
itself nature, so in the same way, it is possible to take nature as
nature, or nature as reason. Nature, insofar as it is nature, directs
the rational creature, that is, the human person, to have sexual
relations with another, that is, for the well-being of the species,
that is, for the preservation of the well-being of the species itself;
and for this purpose, there is the command, "do not commit
adultery," and so on; just as for the preservation of the individual
there is the command, "do not kill." Nature as reason directs
that one have sexual relations with one and not many; but reason
as reason directs that this be one who is united to oneself. For I

say "united" as regards nature, insofar as it is reason (Philip the Chancellor, Lottin 112-113).

If nature as a whole is thought to be reasonable in its operations, then how can reason be said to be distinctive to the human person? So far as I have been able to determine, the scholastics do not explicitly raise this question, but their answer to it may be gathered from Aquinas' statement that what is distinctive about the human person is the capacity for rational self-direction (see, for example, *Summa theologiae* I-II 1.6). In other words, while all of creation acts *in accordance with* rational principles, only rational creatures (angels as well as human beings) are capable of consciously *following* rational principles (*ST* I-II 91.2 *ad* 3). Hence, as Albert observes, only a rational creature can be said, properly speaking, to be under an obligation (*De bono* V 1.2 *ad* 12).

We have already observed that the civilians distinguish between the natural law and the rational and distinctively human law of nations. The canonists and theologians, on the contrary, understand natural law in a more comprehensive sense. For that very reason, they are at pains to develop a concept of a distinctively human – that is, a rational – form of the natural law. Such a concept is implicit in Gratian's definition of the natural law as that which is contained in both law and gospel, that is to say (he adds), the Golden Rule (*Decretum* D. 1.1). One of his first commentators, the canonist Rufin (whose *Summa* was written between 1157 and 1159), goes further along these lines than Gratian himself. According to Rufin, Ulpian's definition of the natural law is not relevant to canon law, although he does not say that it is mistaken or illegitimate. From the canonist's standpoint, the natural law should be understood in a distinctively human sense: "The law of nature is thus a certain power, placed in the human creature by nature, directed towards doing what is good and avoiding what is contrary" (Weigand no. 237).[59]

A little later, the distinguished canonist Huguccio of Ferrara, writing about 1188, offers a second understanding of the natural law as equivalent to reason itself:

The natural law is said to be reason, that is to say, a natural power of the soul by which the human person distinguishes between good and evil, choosing good and rejecting evil. And reason is said to be a law [*jus*] because it commands [*jubet*]; [also, it is said to be] law [*lex*] because it binds [*ligat*] or because it compels [one] to act rightly [*legitime*]; [it is said to be] natural, because reason is one of the natural goods, or because it agrees with the highest nature, and does not dissent from it ... Now in the second place, the natural law is said to be a judgment of reason, that is to say, a motion proceeding from reason, directly or indirectly; that is, any work or operation to which one is obliged by reason, as to discern, to choose, and to do good, to give alms, to love God, and other things of this kind ... But understood in this way, it is said to be natural law improperly; because any of the things which we have said to be contained in this understanding [of the natural law] should rather be [said to be] an effect of the natural law, or should be [said to] derive from it, or to be something that one is bound to do by [the natural law], rather than [taking it as] the natural law itself (Lottin 109).[60]

After the beginning of the thirteenth century, some canonists and theologians understand the natural law to be equivalent to synderesis, which is taken to be the higher or superior component of reason. Among the canonists, Simon of Bisignano is the first to make this identification (Lottin 106-107), and we also find it in the Dominican theologian Roland of Cremona (Lottin 115).[61]

In contrast to Roland, most of the theologians whom we are considering take the natural law in its primary sense to be comprised of precepts.[62] However, these are not specific moral rules but basic axioms of practical reason, analogous to such fundamental axioms of speculative reason as the law of non-contradiction. According to the secular theologian William of Auxerre (d. 1231), the precepts of the natural law are known through the direct perception of God which, in his view, is innate to every human soul, in virtue of the fact that God is supreme truth, goodness, and justice (*Summa aurea* III 18.4).[63] None of the other scholastics is prepared to go quite so far in the direction of sheer Platonic exemplarism. The *Summa* of Alexander associates the natural law with free judgment, and thus with reason and will working in concert (*SFA* III-II Inq.2, Q. 1.2).[64] On the other hand, Albert, Aquinas, and Bonaventure all consider the natural law to be habitually known through the reason, more specifically through synderesis, in the case of the former two, or conscience in Bonaventure's case.[65]

The theologians (with a few exceptions, such as Roland of Cremona) thus differ from the canonists in that they understand the natural law, taken in its proper sense, to consist of precepts rather than a capacity for judgment. Yet this difference should not be exaggerated. For the canonists, the natural law is understood primarily as a capacity for moral judgment, while the theologians take it to be, properly speaking, a set of basic axioms that serve as the starting points for moral judgment. In other words, for the latter, the natural law in its primary sense is understood as comprised of the fundamental norms by which the power of moral discernment operates, rather than as the power itself; but neither they nor the canonists consider the natural law in its primary sense to be comprised of specific moral rules.

This way of interpreting the natural law is likely to seem strange to us, because we usually think of a law as an explicitly formulated rule or a set of such rules, which may or may not express an underlying rationale. This conception of law is by no means unknown to the scholastics, but they are more inclined to speak of law as an intrinsic principle of order, which is expressed in judgments and actions without being reduced to them.[66] Correlatively, they prefer to speak of the natural law as a principle of judgment or action rather than a collection of specific moral rules. One exception to this general tendency is found in the anonymous canonical summa *"Tractaturus magister,"* written about 1185, according to which "it seems rather that reason uses the natural law, than that it is itself the natural law, all the more so since according to some, reason is nothing other than free judgement. Hence, it should be said that according to this understanding, the natural law is a collection of precepts, prohibitions and indications placed in the human mind by God" (Weigand no. 319). Nonetheless, a later gloss that is found immediately after this passage reflects uneasiness with such straightforward identification: "I do not say [that it is] the collection itself, but a certain quality arising in the soul from these things collected, just as knowledge is not said to be the things known themselves, but a quality arising from them" (Weigand no. 320).

This does not mean that, for the scholastics, the natural law cannot be said in any sense to contain or generate more specific moral rules. They do not take the line, sometimes attributed (mistakenly) to Aquinas, that the natural law offers no concrete moral guidance.[67] On the contrary, they accept the traditional view that the precepts of the Decalogue express fundamental tenets of the natural law, and that other scriptural precepts, or even human laws and customs, can also be said to be part of the natural law in some sense. Nonetheless, these precepts are widely seen as grounded in, or as expressions of, the natural law understood as reason, conscience, or more basic axioms of practical reason.

This raises a further question. What is the relationship between the natural law, understood in its primary sense as a rational capacity or as a set of first principles, and the more specific moral judgments that can also be said to belong to the natural law? Albert, perhaps influenced by an assumption that the natural law cannot be taught, answers in this way:

> ...there is a knowledge of the law which is a first potency with respect to the general matters of the law, concerning which it is only necessary to know the terms of the commandment, that is to say, what is stealing and what is adultery, and then through knowledge of these terms, it is evident that one should not steal or commit adultery. Hence, the knowledge of these principles is not acquired except in an accidental sense, namely, through the knowledge of the terms, and not through anything that is prior [to these principles] themselves, as the knowledge of conclusions is acquired. Thus, the knowledge of such principles is placed in us by nature, simply speaking, and is acquired in an accidental sense through knowledge of the terms...(De bono V 1.1).[68]

However, the claim that the laws of the Decalogue are self-evident was not convincing to everyone:

> The law of Moses or Aeschylus does not concern the common conceptions of the soul. For it is not the case that as soon as someone hears, "do not steal," he understands that he is not to steal, and so with respect to the other commandments. Thus, many doubt whether fornication is a mortal sin. But the natural law is concerned with the common conceptions of the soul, as for example, "do not do to another what you do not wish to have done to yourself"; hence, it is by means of the natural law that we understand and are conscious, that is, as soon as we apprehend something, we understand that so it must be done; for "to know with" [conscire] is conscience... (Anonymous text, cited by Lottin 125).[69]

Albert's pupil Aquinas harmonizes these two views. He identifies Jesus' commandments to love God and neighbor (Mt. 22: 37-39) as self-evident principles of the natural law, which are known to all persons, but he then goes on to say that the precepts of the Decalogue can be derived from these principles with only a minimum of reflection (*Summa theologiae* I-II 100.3 *ad* 1; cf. I-II 95.1). Hence, they are readily knowable to all persons, even though they are not self-evident, and as such they may be said to belong to the natural law absolutely (*ST* I-II 100.1). This line of analysis, in turn, is similar to Bonaventure's position (*In II Sent.* 39.2), and it may be said to be a more consistent application of Albert's own principle that the more general a precept is, the more properly it may be said to belong to the natural law (*De bono* V 1.1).

For many readers, the scholastic emphasis on the rational character of the natural law will be reminiscent of the "new natural law" proposed by Grisez and Finnis.[70] There is indeed some similarity between Albert's view in particular, and the Grisez/ Finnis theory since, according to both, the natural law is in some sense self-evident. At the same time, we must be careful not to press this similarity too far. According to Grisez, Finnis, and their collaborators, the natural law rests on a self-evident first principle of practical reason, "The good is to be done and pursued; the bad is to be avoided," interpreted in the light of basic goods, which in turn give rise to self-evident principles of the form, "Such-and-such a basic human good is to be done and/or pursued, protected, and promoted."[71] This is not what Albert says, however. Rather, he claims that the wrongness of certain kinds of actions (for example, stealing or adultery) is self-evident to us as soon as we learn the meaning of the terms designating them.

Similarly, when the anonymous author cited above and Aquinas refer to a self-evident principle, the principle that they cite is the Golden Rule (in the former case; again see Lottin 125) or the two great love commandments. It is true that Aquinas does refer elsewhere to a first principle of practical reason, "Good is to be done and pursued, and evil is to be avoided," which is said to be self-evident and to be the most fundamental precept of the natural law (*ST* I-II 94.2). However, he does not say that the precepts of the natural law that stem from this precept are self-evident to all persons.[72] The inclinations to which he refers in this article indicate human goods that are naturally apprehended as such by practical reason, but this does not mean that we can move directly from an apprehension of these goods to self-evident principles of action (*ibid.*).[73] Rather, the precepts of the natural law are said to pertain to the natural law, and correlatively, the inclinations bring order to these precepts, thus guaranteeing the order and unity of the natural law (*ST* 94.2 *ad* 1). This leaves open the question of just how specific precepts of the natural law are grounded in the inclinations. In any case, the moral significance of the inclinations cannot be established apart from some reflection on the virtues, since as Aquinas explains elsewhere, "the virtues perfect us to follow natural inclinations in an appropriate way, which inclinations pertain to the law of nature. And therefore to the determination of each natural inclination there is ordered a particular virtue" (*ST* II-II 108.2).[74]

There is a more fundamental difference between the "new natural law" of Grisez and Finnis and the scholastic concept of the natural law that cannot be brought out simply by a comparison of relevant texts on the natural law and reason. That is, Grisez and Finnis share in the modern view that nature, understood in terms of whatever is pre- or non-rational, stands in contrast to reason. This is implied by their insistence that moral norms must be derived from reason alone: that is, from pure rational intuitions that are in no way dependent on empirical or metaphysical claims about the world. They insist on this point because they are persuaded by Hume's argument that moral claims cannot be derived from factual premises but, as a result, they are forced to deny the moral relevance of all those aspects of our humanity that we share with other animals. Even the traditional Catholic prohibition of the use of contraceptives is interpreted by them as a sin against life, which represents the same stance of will as is present in murder, rather than as a violation of the natural processes of sexuality.[75]

No scholastic would interpret reason in such a way as to drive a wedge between the pre-rational aspects of our nature and rationality. As we have already seen, they always presuppose an essential continuity between what is natural and what is rational, since on their view nature is itself an intelligible expression of divine reason. In particular, the pre-rational components of human nature have their own intelligible structures, in virtue of which they provide starting points and parameters for the exercise of practical reason.[76] As for Aquinas, he also makes use of the expression "nature as reason" in his earlier writings, but not in his later writings (specifically, see *De Veritate* 16). However, this does not mean that he ever denies the continuity between human beings and other animals. To the contrary, in the *Summa theologiae* he states that reflection on animal behavior can help to establish which, out of the spectrum of human desires and inclinations, should be considered to be inclinations characteristic of the human species: "The natural inclination in those things devoid of reason indicates the natural inclination belonging to the will of an intellectual nature" (*ST* I 60.5).

In fact, Aquinas is noteworthy among the scholastics for his readiness to appeal explicitly to aspects of pre-rational nature in support of moral conclusions. Even limiting ourselves to the *Summa theologiae*, we find a number of examples of this readiness. In the article just cited, Aquinas observes that because reason imitates pre-rational nature, it is natural for rational creatures to love both the good of the universe and the divine goodness of God more than themselves as individuals; otherwise, charity would be a perversion, rather than a perfection of nature (I 60.5). Further on, he defends the legitimacy and even the obligatory character of giving preference to one's kin and close associates in acting out of charity, on the grounds that such preferences stem from natural inclinations, and "the disposition [*affectus*] of charity, which is the inclination of grace, is not less ordered than the natural appetite, which is the inclination of nature, because each of these inclinations comes forth from the divine wisdom" (II-II 26.6).[77] He condemns suicide because it violates the natural inclination of all living creatures to stay alive (II-II 64.5). By the same token, he defends killing in self-defense on the grounds that such an act is a legitimate expression of the inclination towards self-preservation (II-II 64.7). Self-mutilation is permitted in order to preserve the health of the body, since the health of the organism is naturally preferable to its physical integrity (II-II 65.1). Vengeance, understood as the infliction of penal suffering for some good cause, is an expression of the natural inclination to resist evil (II-II 108.1,2). The obligations of obedience are limited by the natural tendencies and needs of the body, since with respect to such matters we are all equal (II-II 104.5). The virtue of temperance takes its norms from the natural necessities of human life (II-II 141.6); hence, fasting is an act of virtue when done for appropriate reasons, but it becomes vicious when taken to the extreme of actual harm (II-II 147.1 *ad* 2). And as is well known, Aquinas draws his norms for sexual behavior in part from a consideration of the natural purpose of human sexuality (II–II 154.11).

Let us turn now to a further question. How do we move from the first principles of practical reason, or the immediate conclusions expressed in the Decalogue, to more specific moral judgments? The summary answer to this question would be that these more specific moral judgments are derived through rational reflection, starting from first principles and taking account of the intelligible ordering of human nature and the needs of human life. However, it would be a mistake to attempt to translate this into a formula for arriving at moral conclusions in any and all circumstances. The kind of reflection that is needed, and the generality and certainty of the conclusions, will legitimately reflect the kind of issue being addressed. So understood, the natural law can be extended to include all the judgments, laws, and practices that arise out of rational reflection on the exigencies of human life. [78]

This line of analysis is particularly well developed in Albert, who offers a detailed analysis of the ways in which reason and nature may be said to be connected in the natural law:

The natural law is nothing other than the law of reason or obligation, insofar as nature is reason. When, however, I say that nature is reason, it is possible to understand it more as nature, or more as reason, or equally as nature and reason. If however it is taken as nature, then it would be the principle of actions pertaining to the continuance and well-being of the one in whom it is, and of the rational consideration of those things which pertain to the well-being of the individual, as for example, food, clothing, a house, a bed, the care of health and the procuring of medicine, and other things of this sort which we seek for ourselves through rational consideration. Similar to these are those things pertaining to the well-being of the species, such as a wife and children, and care and provision for each of them. For when reason is said to be nature, and more nature than reason, I do not exclude reason. And because the law does not establish injury, I always assume right reason with regard to these things. On this account, the desire of gluttony and adultery and stealing would not be in accordance with the natural law nor according to nature spoken of in this way, because right reason is that which is rationally discerned about natural things, that is to say, things pertaining to nature, through the natural law (*De bono* V 1.2).

In other words, the human person must fulfill those inclinations that we share with other animals in the way natural to a rational animal: that is, through reasoned reflection, foresight, and judgment.

In addition to those inclinations that we share with the animals, there are of course other inclinations that are proper to the human person. These would include our tendency to form communities that extend beyond the family unit and are structured on the basis of rational agreements, and our spontaneous reverence for a divine being. Albert interprets these in terms of "reason [considered] as reason":

> If however [nature] is understood more as reason, it concerns those things which pertain to religion and justice and human decency, in oneself and in relation to others, in such a way, however, that it should have something from nature, and that it not be [taken] entirely from reason. But then nature is understood as being in good order through the seedbeds of good as it pertains to life. Those seedbeds are the natural law, and thus, the commandments of each table [of the Decalogue], as they are generally and indeterminately understood, are of the natural law. And more briefly, whatever is decent after its fashion is of the natural law (*ibid.*).

Significantly, for Albert even distinctively rational goods such as justice and religion are partly grounded in pre-rational aspects of our nature.

Finally, reason serves to establish norms for social living, and as such it looks primarily to expediency, although always within the parameters set by more basic norms:

> In the third sense, natural reason is equally reason and nature, and accordingly, that which is provided from right reason for the convenience and the usefulness of the human person pertains to the natural law (always in general principles, in accordance with the universal seeds of law, and not in accordance with a case or a particular determination), as for example, to provide for a

dwelling, to regulate a household, to choose magistrates for the purpose of punishing wrongdoers and praising the good, to care for what is one's own, and other things of this sort (*ibid.*).

Understood in this way, specific laws and regulations can be seen as expressions of the natural law, although the laws of particular communities are always considered to be natural law only in a derivative sense.

This is the context within which to understand the civilian distinction between the natural law and the law of nations. Recall that for the civilians, the natural law in its primary sense is understood in accordance with Ulpian's definition, and is thus contrasted with the law of nations, which is distinctive to the human person. Yet many of the civilians also acknowledge that the law of nations can itself be considered to be a form of natural law, or to be derived from the natural law or from natural reason.[79] Even though the law of nations is a product of human reflection, and thus not, strictly speaking, pre-conventional, it is nonetheless a reflection of human reason operating at the most general level of human affairs. It deals with matters that arise perennially in the interaction of nations and of individuals who relate to one another outside the boundaries of their local communities. Thus, it is both universal, in the sense of enjoying widespread recognition, and general, in the sense that it is not closely specified. For these reasons, it can plausibly be considered to be a form of the natural law, more so than the laws and decrees that are specific to particular communities.

We observed in the last section that, for the scholastics, anything that can be said to be natural is *prima facie* good. This must be understood, however, in the context of their assumption that natural processes are directed toward good ends and are intelligible in terms of those ends. This assumption enables them to hold together two approaches to the natural law: one that emphasizes the intrinsic value of the pre-rational, and another that places more stress on the law-giving character of reason. Because the pre-rational components of human nature are intelligible, they are amenable to rational analysis and prudential reflection, on the basis of which the human person is able rationally to pursue the same ends that other animals pursue through instinct. At the same time, reason itself also creates possibilities and generates aims that are distinctively human, and it also belongs to practical reason to pursue these aims, and furthermore to bring order and coherence to the various ends of human life.

4. Medieval naturalism and its implications today

The scholastic concept of the natural law as it has emerged so far is grounded in the traditional distinction between the natural, seen as the ground of human action, and those conventional practices and institutions that build upon nature. Within the broad parameters of this concept, "nature" can be understood in a number of different ways, although it cannot encompass every possible meaning of the term: for example, nature understood as the peculiar characteristics of an individual. At the same time, the scholastics are particularly interested in both those aspects of our nature that we share with other animals and the distinctively human characteristic of reason, and they devote considerable attention to the interrelationships among these aspects of human nature. In the first instance, this concept provides the scholastics with a basis for analyzing existing practices and institutions in terms of their natural origins. Second, because the scholastics start from the assumption that nature (in most of its possible senses) is intelligible and good, their concept of the natural law provides them with a framework for evaluating and revising those institutions.

When we examine the scholastic concept of the natural law, one of its most striking features is its naturalism, understood (following Nederman) as the view that morality arises out of the requirements of human nature rather than divine mandate or sheer convention.[80] In scholastic writings on the natural law, we see the same attitudes that gave rise to the natural philosophies of the twelfth and thirteenth centuries: a new appreciation for the value and integrity of the visible world, a concern to explain phenomena as far as possible through intrinsic principles of operation, and a commitment to analyze those phenomena in terms of their immanent causes. As a result of these attitudes, the scholastic concept of the natural law emphasizes the immanent intelligibility and moral value of human life. Correlatively, the scholastics tend to rationalize moral beliefs and social customs by analyzing them in the light of the exigencies of human life, a tendency that we find particularly pronounced in Albert but that is shared to some degree by nearly all the scholastics. The concept of the natural law that emerges out of scholastic reflection affirms the reasonableness of human morality while at the same time emphasizing the continuity between the human person, considered precisely as a moral agent, and the rest of creation.

The naturalism of scholastic moral thought is perhaps more striking to us than it would have been to the scholastics. Western societies have been deeply shaped by Kant's powerful argument that the experience of moral obligation represents a discontinuity with the phenomenal world of nature and ordinary human experience, with its implication that morality is our only point of access to transcendence. (Of course, Kant is not the only source of this attitude; it is perhaps nearer the mark to say that he offers the most powerful and cogent expression we have of a general sentiment.) In addition, we are the heirs of what Mary Douglas describes as "that still-continuing process of whittling away the revealed elements of Christian doctrine, and the elevating in its place of ethical principles as the central core of true religion."[81] For more than two centuries, there has been a widespread tendency among both Christians and non-believers to take morality as a substitute for older forms of orthodox Christianity, and as a result morality itself has become sacralized.

This view of morality as transcendent or sacred has been challenged many times, yet it has proven to be remarkably resilient. For this reason, defenders of a naturalistic view of morality still find it necessary to apologize for their work. For example, Mary Midgley begins one of her most recent books as follows: "Human morality is not a brute anomaly in the world. Our moral freedom is not something biologically bizarre. No denial of the reality of ethics, nothing offensive to its dignity, follows from accepting our evolutionary origin."[82] Indeed not; yet even now, we do not seem to be able to avoid a sense of humiliation at finding ourselves so much like the other animals, precisely with respect to that aspect of our humanity, our moral sense, which once seemed so godlike.

From the Christian standpoint, this is surely salutary. Anything that challenges our pride and reminds us of our limitations as creatures deserves at least a hearing among Christian theologians. Yet, with only a few exceptions, theologians have not yet attempted to come to terms with the work of evolutionary psychologists and those philosophers influenced by them.[83]

Here we come to a point at which the scholastic concept of the natural law can be relevant for contemporary theological ethics. That is, the scholastics show us that it is possible to interpret a naturalistic account of morality in a theologically satisfactory way. To put it another way, the scholastic concept of the natural law implies a theological loss, at least from one standpoint, but it also brings a compensating theological gain. The loss is that, for the scholastics, morality is desacralized; it is seen as a natural phenomenon, as an expression of the human person's continuity with the rest of the natural world, and not as in itself a medium for transcendence. In compensation, however, the scholastics offer a theological interpretation of this naturalistic morality, precisely because they interpret the natural world itself theologically. Just as the visible, natural world is an expression of God's wisdom and goodness for them, so human morality, considered as a part of that natural world, is also an expression of divine wisdom and goodness. This does not imply for them that the moral life in itself offers a way to salvation; on the contrary, they insist that it does not.[84] Nor would they deny that the actual beliefs and practices of men and women are often inadequate or corrupt. Nonetheless, precisely because they affirm the inherent, immanent goodness of the natural world, they can affirm the value of human morality, with all its limitations and imperfections, because they see it as an expression of the goodness of the created order.

This is a more satisfactory theological approach to the moral life than the currently prevalent view, which sees it as a locus for transcendence. In the first place, it appears to me that the account of human morality provided by the evolutionary psychologists is broadly correct. That is, they are right to insist that morality stems from species-specific behavioral patterns that can be partially explained through evolutionary theory and that are further illuminated by comparison with the characteristic behaviors of other primates. This need not imply the view that morality can be understood reductively in such terms, nor more specifically that our moral behavior can be explained by our common human nature alone, without reference to the ways in which our history and our diverse cultures have shaped diverse expressions of that nature. All this being said, the case for understanding our moral life as being *in part* (not wholly) an expression of our species-specific behavioral patterns, and thus as being in continuity with patterns of behavior exhibited by other animals, is now very strong indeed.

More fundamentally, those who defend the sacralization of morality are forced into an untenable position with respect to the moral life as we actually experience it, even if we bracket any questions about its origins. If morality is itself sacred, or at least a means of transcendence, then how are we to understand the ambiguities, limitations, diversity and, yes, outright corruption that we find among the actual moral beliefs and practices of the human race? It is necessary either to cover these over by speaking at the highest possible level of generality about universal values, or to argue that these problematic aspects could be eliminated if men and women were better educated and more reasonable, or else to reject human societies as altogether corrupt, seen from the perspective of impossibly high moral ideals.

The scholastic concept of the natural law has the great merit of allowing us to avoid both of these extremes. Because human morality is seen as an expression of an immanent nature, and a nature wounded by sin, at that, it is not expected to be unambiguous, perfect, and transparently open to the divine. Yet because it is one expression of a nature that God has created, and that bears the evidences of God's wisdom, albeit in a distorted form, it is nonetheless fundamentally good and worthy of respect. This implies that morality deserves to be respected and cherished, not as an ultimate value, to be sure, but as a genuine penultimate human good.

We have already observed that the scholastic concept of the natural law can accommodate more than one understanding of nature. For this reason, it is not tied to any one of the accounts of nature that emerged in the medieval period and, by the same token, it can be extended to include contemporary understandings of nature. But this concept cannot be stretched so far as to accommodate any and every possible account of nature, as we have already seen. At the least, this concept presupposes an account of nature, and more specifically of human nature, according to which it is stable, intelligible, and intrinsically good. Is such an account of human nature credible, given our best scientific and philosophical accounts of ourselves and the world in which we live?

It is sometimes said that modern science, and more particularly the theory of evolution, has undermined the Christian doctrine of creation. We cannot believe, as our ancestors did, that the intricate marvels of life are products of conscious design, because they can adequately be explained by a process of natural selection. More fundamentally, we cannot accept the view that living creatures, ourselves included, have an essential nature that was bestowed on them at the beginning of time by a creator God. These objections would seem to be fatal to any traditional theory of the natural law.

Consider, first, the claim that modern evolutionary theory has undermined the belief that biological organs and processes are the products of God's design. In this context, the argument from design is understood in the sense made familiar by modern debates over evolution. On this view, the intricacies of living creatures and the amazing ways in which organs are suited to their purposes cannot be adequately explained by Darwinian processes of natural selection alone. They can be the result only of conscious design, together with, as it were, deliberate engineering. In response, defenders of evolutionary theory appeal to a combination of analysis and observation to show that the processes of random selection are fully adequate to generate all the observed complexities of the modern world.

Although this has been a long, complex debate, the overwhelming preponderance of evidence now supports the defenders of evolutionary theory. However, it does not follow that the scholastic concept of the natural law is therefore invalidated. This would follow only if that concept depended fundamentally on the modern argument from design. However, this is not the case. The scholastics do believe that the structures and processes of life at every level reflect God's creative wisdom, but that does not mean that those structures and processes are the result of direct divine intervention. To the contrary, as we have seen, medieval natural philosophy in the twelfth and thirteenth centuries emphasized the relative autonomy of nature and the sufficiency of secondary causes to explain the particular features of the world around us. For them, God's creative wisdom is expressed in the orderly unfolding of created natures that contain within them their own intelligible principles of action. While they did not espouse a Darwinian theory of evolution, they did acknowledge that the world as we know it might have emerged out of the interplay of secondary causes, rather than being the product of a fixed creation. The preoccupation with defending the literal truth of Genesis is a modern, not a medieval, preoccupation.

This brings us to a more basic point at which modern evolutionary theory might be thought to be inconsistent with the scholastic concept of the natural law. The latter concept presupposes that human beings have a definite specific nature, in terms of which our actions can be both interpreted and evaluated. Yet it is often said that evolutionary theory has undermined the claim that living creatures, ourselves included, have specific essences.

This is not obvious, however. Biologists themselves defend the fundamental claim that living creatures are arranged into distinct species. In the words of the biologist and philosopher Ernst Mayr,

> As the naturalists, beginning with the seventeenth century, began to make increasingly careful studies of species of organisms in nature, evidence began to accumulate that these species were something different from so-called species of inanimate objects. These naturalists showed quite conclusively that biological species not only had reality in nature, but also that in many, if not most cases, they were sharply distinguishable from each other by a natural discontinuity.[85]

He goes on to argue that biological species should be defined as "groups of interbreeding natural populations that are reproductively isolated from other such groups," and to draw out the implications of the fact that "every species is the product of evolution," which include the following: "A new species must have acquired reproductive isolation as a result of the process of speciation; it must also have acquired a new, stabilized, well-integrated genotype, and it will, in most cases, have acquired a species-specific niche."[86] Clearly, this is not what the scholastics had in mind when they referred to the specific nature of human beings and other animals, but it is not incompatible with the scholastic idea of specific natures, either.

Or is it? At the very least, the scholastic concept of the natural law presupposes that there are certain qualities or traits that are characteristic of human beings, in the strong sense that these characteristics must be incorporated into any adequate account of what it is to be human. (This does not imply that every human must possess all of these characteristic features, however; an immature or defective person may lack one or more of them while still remaining a human being.) In other words, it presupposes that there is such a thing as the essence of humanity. Is this compatible with evolutionary theory?

In Mayr's view, it is not. While he grants that all the members of a species have properties in common, he denies that this is tantamount to saying that a biological species has an essence: "A property in common and an essence are two entirely different things. To be sure, every essence is characterized by properties in common, but a group sharing properties in common does not need to have an essence. The outstanding characteristic of an essence is its permanence, its immutability. By contrast, the properties that a biological group have in common may be variable and have the propensity for evolutionary change."[87]

But this confuses the unchangeability proper to a concept with the supposed unchangeability of those entities that instantiate the concept. If we do in fact have an adequate concept of a human being, such that we can identify those traits that are characteristic of human beings as such, then the *concept* will be timeless in two distinct senses: it will not need revision (on the supposition that it is adequate to its object), and it will not include within itself any intrinsic reference to time (hence, it can be applied to any human being existing at any time). This does not mean that the reality to which the concept applies is unchanging. It is almost certainly the case that human beings evolved gradually over a considerable period of time, and it may be the case that we will either evolve into something else or (more likely) cease to exist altogether. Therefore, there was a time when the concept of humanity had no application, and there may well be a time when it once again ceases to have application. Nonetheless, it does not follow that the concept itself is subject to time in the same way.

The interesting question, of course, is this: Is there some reality that corresponds to the concept of humanity? Or is this concept a mental construct that hides the fact that "human being" names a collection of heterogeneous entities we have created? This is properly a philosophical rather than an empirical question, a variant of one of the oldest and most intractable of philosophical problems, and it cannot be settled by an appeal to evolutionary theory alone. The fact that humanity evolved over time and may cease to exist does not necessarily imply that there is no such thing as a stable human nature; it simply means that human nature came into existence with human beings and will cease to exist if and when we cease to exist.

What is implied by a belief in the reality (as opposed to the purely notional status) of human nature? The issue at stake is well formulated by John Kekes:

> According to naturalists, there are universal and substantive human characteristics and it is their existence that allows us to speak of human nature. In contrast, historicists maintain that all substantive characteristics are variable, and if there are universal characteristics, they are formal; consequently, conceptions of human nature are bound to be so general, so devoid of content as to be vacuous. In other words, naturalists assert that there are concrete and particular characteristics that all human beings have and historicists deny it.[88]

On Kekes' terms, the scholastics are naturalists, insofar as they believe that there are "universal and substantive human characteristics." So is Kekes himself, and so are a number of other contemporary philosophers who have no stake in defending any traditional version of the natural law. Without attempting to resolve the complex issues raised by philosophical realism, we can at least say that a belief in the reality of human nature, understood in Kekes' terms, is plausible and defensible in terms of presuppositions that are widely, albeit not universally, shared among contemporary philosophers. Taken by itself, this belief does not relegate the scholastics to irrelevance for contemporary thought. On the contrary, it offers a point of contact between the scholastics and ourselves, as H.L.A. Hart long ago recognized.[89]

Nor is the content of the scholastic idea of human nature particularly controversial. The scholastics tend to describe human nature in terms of standing tendencies, including tendencies toward self-preservation, reproduction, and concern for others that we share with other animals, and the distinctively human tendencies toward institutional social life and toward worship, which presuppose rationality. In contrast, contemporary philosophers tend to focus on what Kekes describes as facts of the body, facts of the self, and facts of social life, which comprise all those capacities and needs rooted in our physical, psychological, and social makeup. On closer examination, however, this contrast would seem to be rooted in differences of emphasis rather than in substantive disagreement. Few contemporary philosophers would deny that most human beings desire life, sexual activity and reproduction, participation in social life, and some kind of contact with a transcendent reality (although they might consider the latter desire to be confused, or incapable of fulfillment). Nor would the scholastics deny that human beings have characteristic capabilities, needs, and vulnerabilities.

Yet, even granting that there is a stable human nature and this general account of it is plausible, it may seem that the scholastic concept of the natural law is invalidated by the logical impossibility of moving from statements of fact or, more generally, from any kind of claim about what ought to be the case to conclusions about what should be the case. Earlier in this century, it was a truism among moral philosophers that one cannot derive "ought" from "is." This claim, in turn, rested on two different arguments. The earlier of these is David Hume's famous argument that no moral conclusion can be derived from premises that lack any moral terms, on the grounds (it is assumed) that a deductive argument cannot contain anything in the conclusion that is not implicitly present in the premises. The more recent is G.E. Moore's argument that moral goodness cannot be defined in terms of non-moral qualities.[90]

Once again, if the scholastics are guilty of a fallacy, they have considerable company among our own contemporaries. As we noted in Chapter 1, a number of philosophers today argue for the moral significance of human nature. As for the so-called naturalistic fallacy, the force of Hume's and Moore's arguments began to be questioned over thirty years ago, when philosophers started to question whether an inference from factual premises to moral conclusions can be ruled out on strictly logical grounds.[91] Subsequent arguments over the naturalistic fallacy have been extensive and complex, but I think it is fair to say that few philosophers today would claim that the arguments of Hume and Moore are both valid, and general in scope.

It is particularly difficult to keep fact and value separate when we ourselves are the subject of investigation. As John Kekes says, "Conceptions of human nature are evaluative through and through. In them, fact and value are inextricably mixed. This is so, because we, that is human beings, form these conceptions and we care about ourselves. Morality would not be possible without it."[92] Similarly, in *Ethics and the Limits of Philosophy*, Bernard Williams draws a contrast between scientific thought, which aims to understand a world in which we have no necessary place, and ethical thought in the following terms: "The aim of ethical thought, however, is to help us to construct a world that will be our world, one in which we have a social, cultural, and personal life."[93]

The question is, of course, just how the relevance of human nature to morality is to be spelled out. When we examine the work of contemporary philosophers who defend the moral significance of human nature, we find three different accounts of this significance, although frequently two or even all three are brought together in the work of a particular philosopher. The first and most basic relationship is one of presupposition. If we assume, as nearly everyone does, that morality is centrally concerned with human well-being and harm, then facts about human nature are morally relevant because we must take them into account in deciding what counts as either well-being or harm. A second relationship is that of originating principle. Morality is grounded in our nature as social animals and should be interpreted with its natural origins in mind. Defenders of both of these relationships frequently add that the givens of human nature constrain the development of moral systems or moral theories in a variety of ways. The third might be described as perfectionism. Certain natural capacities or tendencies are normative, in the sense that we ought to strive to fulfill them or to develop them to the greatest extent possible.[94]

Only the first two ways of construing the relationship between human nature and morality are clearly presupposed by the scholastic concept of the natural law. They believe that moral laws and social practices both presuppose and express components of human nature, and may be explained accordingly. However, they do not generally offer strong arguments to the effect that human happiness or perfection requires the fulfillment of natural tendencies or capacities. This may seem surprising, since we are accustomed to associate traditional natural law theories with just this sort of perfectionism. However, there were two factors that kept the scholastic concept of the natural law from developing in a strongly perfectionist direction. First, this concept was first developed in the context of efforts by canon lawyers (and, to a lesser extent, secular jurists) to bring coherence to inherited legal traditions. Legal scholars are concerned to interpret and apply laws, but they do not have any particular stake in showing how these laws are fulfilling for those who observe them. Scholastic jurists were content to leave such questions to the theologians. Second, the scholastics take it for granted that human happiness and fulfillment cannot be attained fully (if at all) in this life. For this reason, the theologians themselves were not particularly concerned to offer accounts of this-worldly fulfillment, or to show how observance of the natural law might promote temporal happiness.

Nonetheless, the scholastic concept of the natural law does include elements of perfectionism. While they do not offer any definite account of those human potentialities that we are obliged to pursue, they do presuppose that the natural processes and tendencies of human life demand respect. This is not perfectionism, but it does imply that these processes and tendencies have intrinsic value. As we have already seen, they consider the naturalness of a practice to be a *prima facie* justification for it, and this of course presupposes that human nature has a positive value. More importantly, the scholastics hold that some aspects of human nature are more good or desirable than others. In other words, their concept of the natural law embodies a selective interpretation of human nature, in accordance with which certain aspects are given primary moral significance and others are given lesser weight.

The difficulty with this way of proceeding is not that it is logically invalid, but that it seems insufficiently grounded in the realities of human nature as they present themselves to us. As Kekes argues, the realities of human nature put constraints on what can count as an acceptable morality, but they do not determine one and only one adequate "natural" ethic.[95]

The scholastics did not formulate this problem explicitly, and yet their concept of the natural law implicitly offers a solution. That is, the scholastics base their concept of the natural law on a particular construal of human nature that is shaped by, and justified in terms of, their theological concerns and convictions. This does not mean that their construal of human nature is wholly determined by their theology. It is not derived from theological premises or scriptural narratives alone, but reflects a theologically informed interpretation of the scholastics' own history and society. Nonetheless, the scholastic concept of the natural law does presuppose a distinctive theology; it is not the product of the pure universal reason that is so important for late natural law thinkers.

The theological character of the scholastic concept of the natural law raises further questions. Yet it also provides a further point of contact between the scholastics and ourselves, particularly those of us working in the field of theological ethics. We now turn to an examination of the scholastic concept of the natural law as a theological concept.

Notes to Chapter 2

1   Vern L. Bullough, "The Sin against Nature and Homosexuality," in Vern L. Bullough and James Brundage, eds., *Sexual Practices and the Medieval Church* (Buffalo, NY: Prometheus Books, 1982), 55-71 at 57.

2   James M. Gustafson, "Nature: Its Status in Theological Ethics," *Logos: Philosophical Issues in Christian Perspective* 3 (1982), 5-23 at 5.

3   Charles Curran, "Natural Law in Moral Theology," in Charles E. Curran and Richard A. McCormick, S.J., eds., *Readings in Moral Theology No. 7: Natural Law and Theology* (Mahwah, NJ: Paulist Press, 1991), 247-295 at 265.

4   Robert P. George, "Natural Law Ethics," in Philip L. Quinn and Charles Taliaferro, eds., *A Companion to Philosophy of Religion* (Oxford: Blackwell, 1997), 460-465 at 460; emphasis in the original.

5   *Ibid.*

6   Throughout this book, I draw extensively on the texts collected by Odon Lottin, *Le droit naturel chez saint Thomas d'Aquin et ses prédécesseurs,* second edition (Bruges: Beyart, 1931), 105-125, and Rudolf Weigand, *Die Naturrechtslehre der Legisten und Dekretisten von Irnerius bis Accursius und von Gratian bis Johannes Teutonicus* (Munich: Max Hueber, 1967), 17-63 (the civilians) and 140-258 (the canonists). References to these texts are given by name and page number, in the case of Lottin, or name and paragraph number, in the case of Weigand. All translations from both collections are my own. I have relied primarily on Lottin and Weigand, together with Michael Crowe, *The Changing Profile of the Natural Law* (The Hague: Martinus Nijhoff, 1977), for basic information on the authors and texts cited. In addition, I consulted Stephan Kuttner's *Repertorium der Kanonistk (1140-1234): Prodromus Corporis Glossarum I (Studi e Testi* 71) (Vatican City, 1937) for further details on the texts cited.

7   Helmut Koester, "NOMOS PHYSEOS: The Concept of Natural Law in Greek Thought," in Jacob Neusner, ed., *Religions in Antiquity* (Leiden: Brill, 1968), 521-541.

8   Richard A. Horsley, "The Law of Nature in Philo and Cicero," *Harvard Theological Review* 71 (1978), 35-59.

9   *Ibid.,* 36.

10 *Ibid.*

11 *Ibid.,* 38-39.

12 Hindy Najman, "The Law of Nature and the Authority of Mosaic Law," *Studia Philonica Annual* 11, 1999. In conversation, Najman kindly provided information on Philo's subsequent influence, on which I draw in the remainder of this paragraph. In addition, see David T. Runia, *Philo in Early Christian Literature: A Survey* (Assen, the Netherlands: Van Gorcum, 1993), particularly 157-183 and 291-311.

13   Cicero's significance is forcefully defended by Gerard Watson, "Natural Law and
      Stoicism," in A.A. Long, ed., *Problems in Stoicism* (London: Athlone, 1971), 216-38,
      and reiterated by Crowe, *The Changing Profile of the Natural Law*, 37. In my view,
      Cicero's direct influence on the scholastic concept of the natural law is also greater
      than Aristotle's; on this point, see below.

14   My account of this eclectic understanding of the natural law is largely dependent on
      Horsley, "The Law of Nature in Philo and Cicero"; however, the possibility of
      Cynic origins for this understanding is raised by Watson, "The Natural Law and
      Stoicism," 219. In addition, I draw on Michael Lapidge, "The Stoic Inheritance,"
      in Peter Dronke, ed., *A History of Twelfth-Century Western Philosophy* (Cambridge:
      Cambridge University Press, 1988), 81-112.

15   Horsley, "The Law of Nature in Philo and Cicero," 39.

16   This point is emphasized by Carlyle, who sees the Stoics' position as the decisive
      break between Aristotelian political thought and the natural law tradition; see R.W.
      and A.J. Carlyle, *A History of Medieval Political Theory in the West*, 6 vols. (Blackwood
      and Sons, 1903-36; repr. 1970), vol. 1, 2.

17   Horsley, "The Law of Nature in Philo and Cicero," 52-53; emphasis in the original.

18   *The Digest*, I 1.1.3; the parallel in Justinian's *Institutes* is I 1.2. The interpretation of
      this passage is complicated for the present-day scholar by the fact that we have it
      only in Justinian's compilations, which are heavily edited to reflect the latter's the-
      ological views. For a discussion of what Ulpian himself might have meant, see Mar-
      cia L. Colish, *The Stoic Tradition from Antiquity to the Early Middle Ages, Vol. I:
      Stoicism in Classical Latin Literature* (Leiden, Germany: Brill, 1990), 358-359.

19   For example, see John Finnis, *Natural Law and Natural Rights* (Oxford: Clarendon
      Press, 1980), 35.

20   As Colish points out in *The Stoic Tradition*, 358-359.

21   Cary J. Nederman, "Aristotelianism and the Origins of 'Political Science' in the
      Twelfth Century," *Journal of the History of Ideas* 52 (1991), 179-94 at 180-1.

22   For Haskin's own views, see Charles Homer Haskins, *The Renaissance of the Twelfth
      Century* (Cambridge, MA: Harvard University Press, 1927; repr. 1957), 303-340.
      There has been a considerable amount of work on this subject since Haskins wrote.
      In the remainder of this section, I rely especially on the following: M.D. Chenu,
      Nature, Man, and Society in the Twelfth Century, Jerome Taylor and Lester Little, eds.
      and trans. (Chicago: University of Chicago Press, 1968; repr. 1997), 1-48; G. R.
      Evans, *Alan of Lille: The Frontiers of Theology in the Later Twelfth Century* (Cambridge:
      Cambridge University Press, 1983), 133-165; Roger French and Andrew Cunning-
      ham, *Before Science: The Invention of the Friars' Natural Philosophy* (Aldershot, U.K.:
      Scolar Press, 1996); Etienne Gilson, *L'Esprit de la Philosophie Medievale* (Paris: Vrin,
      1948), 345-364: Edward Grant, *The Foundations of Modern Science in the Middle Ages:
      Their Religious, Institutional, and Intellectual Contexts* (Cambridge: Cambridge Uni-
      versity Press, 1996); Stephen Gersh, "Platonism – Neoplatonism – Aristotelianism:

A Twelfth Century Metaphysical System and Its Sources," Robert L. Benson and Giles Constable, eds., *Renaissance and Renewal in the Twelfth Century,* (Cambridge, MA: Harvard University Press, 1882, repr. 1991), 512-537; D.E. Luscombe and G.R. Evans, "The Twelfth-Century Renaissance," J.H. Burns, ed., *The Cambridge History of Medieval Political Thought: c.350-c.1450* (Cambridge: Cambridge University Press, 1988), 306-340; R.W. Southern, *Scholastic Humanism and the Unification of Europe: Vol. I: Foundations* (Oxford: Blackwell, 1995), 22-25, 35-39; Andreas Speer, "Reception – Mediation – Innovation: Philosophy and Theology in the Twelfth Century," J. Mamesse, ed., *Bilan et perspectives des études médiévales: Actes du premier congrès européen des études médiévales* (Louvain: La Nevve, 1994), 129-149; Brian Tierney, "*Natura id est Deus*: A Case of Juristic Pantheism?" *Journal of the History of Ideas* 24 (1963), 307-322; and Winthrop Wetherbee, "Philosophy, Cosmology, and the Twelfth-Century Renaissance," in Peter Dronke, ed., *A History of Twelfth-Century Philosophy* (Cambridge: Cambridge University Press, 1988), 21-53. In addition, I have greatly benefited from notes on natural philosophy in the twelfth century prepared for me by Joseph Pearson.

23 Speer, "Reception – Mediation – Innovation," 135.

24 This is particularly emphasized by French and Cunningham in *Before Science,* 99-126. For the wider context of this development, see C.H. Lawrence, *The Friars: The Impact of the Early Mendicant Movement on Western Society* (Essex, U.K.: Longman, 1994), 1-25, and Malcolm Lambert, *Medieval Heresy: Popular Movements from the Gregorian Reform to the Reformation,* second edition (Oxford: Blackwell, 1992), 91-104.

25 Chartres was a cathedral school, that is to say, a school originally established by a bishop for the training of the clergy of his diocese. Hence most of these scholars (with the notable exception of Alan of Lille, who taught at Paris) were not scholastics in the sense that I am using the term – they were not connected with a university.

These scholars are usually referred to as the school of Chartres. Southern argues that it is misleading to describe these scholars as a "school"; see *Scholastic Humanism and the Unification of Europe,* 58-101. However, he does not question their importance for the emergence of natural philosophy in the twelfth century.

26 "Platonism" carries a number of different meanings in the medieval period, not all of them consistent with one another. In addition to Gersh, "Platonism – Neoplatonism – Aristotelianism," see Chenu, "The Platonisms of the Twelfth Century", in Taylor and Little, *Nature, Man and Society in the Twelfth Century,* 49-98, and Tulio Gregory, "The Platonic Inheritance," in Dronke, *A History of Twelfth Century Philosophy,* 54-80, for helpful guides to the different understandings of this term.

27 Wetherbee, "Philosophy, Cosmology, and the Twelfth-Century Renaissance," 34.

28 *Glosae super Platonem,* E. Jeauneau, ed., (Paris, 1965), quoted (in English) in Gregory, "The Platonic Inheritance," 65; I quote Gregory's translation here. At the same time, the twelfth century also saw the emergence of a naturalistic approach to scriptural exegesis; see Beryl Smalley, *The Study of the Bible in the Middle Ages*

(Oxford: Blackwell, 1952; paperback ed., Notre Dame, IN: University of Notre Dame Press, 1964), 112-195, for a discussion of this point.

29   *Glosae super Platonem*, quoted (in English) in Gregory, "The Platonic Inheritance," 61; again, the translation is Gregory's.

30   See *Rerum Novarum* (an encyclical letter of Leo XIII, May 15, 1891), paras. 19-20.

31   The theologian William of Auxerre takes this approach in his *Summa aurea*; see *SA* IV 17, 3.2. The first two Dominican masters at Paris, Roland of Cremona, writing between 1229 and 1230, and Hugh of St. Cher, writing between 1230 and 1235, take a similar line (both in Lottin 115-116), as do the canonists Alan (Weigand no. 386-388) and especially William of Gascony (Weigand no. 399-402).

32   On the main lines of the Cathar heresy, see Lambert, *Medieval Heresy,* 105-146 and, with reservations, French and Cunningham, *Before Science,* 127-145.

33   For a brief discussion of the range of church responses to heretical movements, see Lambert, *Medieval Heresy,* 91-104; for a different, more pessimistic assessment, see R.I. Moore, *The Formation of a Persecuting Society: Power and Deviance in Western Europe, 950-1250* (Oxford: Blackwell, 1987), particularly 11-26.

34   This contrast is particularly emphasized by French and Cunningham; see *Before Science,* 70- 93. In my view, however, they overstate this contrast. Twelfth-century scholars were also aware that nature can be understood in terms of the intrinsic nature of a given creature, although they do not appear to have emphasized this interpretation to the same extent as did later scholars.

35   On this point, see *Das Naturrechtslehre* 148. John the Teuton (Johannes Teutonicus, c. 1215), the probable author of the Ordinary Gloss on Gratian's *Decretum*, gave authoritative status to the hierarchical arrangement of senses of the natural law; see the gloss on D.1, CC.6-7. Other examples include the *Cologne Summa* and the *Leipzig Summa*, both from the latter part of the twelfth century, cited in Lottin, 105-106 and 108 respectively.

36   Most notably, Albert, who tries to reconcile Aristotle's natural justice with Cicero's definition of the natural law in the *Super ethica* Lec.9, 419.35ff, and Aquinas, who identifies Aristotle's natural justice with both the natural law and the law of nations, as these are understood by the civilians in his *In libros ethicorum expositio* V.12, 1019.

37   This distinction was ubiquitous. The most frequently cited texts include Cicero's *De Inventione* I.2 c.53 and Isidore of Seville's *Etymologies* V.2.

38   See, for example, the canonical *Est jus naturale*, Weigand no. 353.

39   The scholastic understanding of divine law, seen in relation to the natural law, will be further discussed in the next chapter. As we noted in Chapter 1, the civilians tend to identify the natural law in its primary sense with Ulpian's definition, "that which nature teaches all animals," but they also considered the law of nations to be in some sense a natural law; see, for example, the *Summa institutionum vindobonensis* Weigand no. 28-32, Martin, no. 38-40, John Bassianus, no. 73, Azo, no. 78, and Accursius,

no. 94. Some of the canonists also mention the law of nations as one of the forms
of natural law; for instance, the *Muenster Summa* (Lottin 107-108) and Stephen of
Tournai (Weigand no. 244).

40   Gustafson, "Nature: Its Status in Theological Ethics," 5.

41   These are standard formulae; for other examples, see among the canonists the *Leipzig*
Summa and Huguccio, cited in Lottin 109 and 111, and the *Paris Summa*, Weigand
no. 255- 257; among the civilians, see the tractate, *Divinam voluntatem vocamus justi-*
tiam, Weigand no. 49-50, and Placentin, no. 64.

42   For a discussion of the moral beliefs and practices of the Cathars, see Lambert, *Medi-*
eval Heresy, 106-148.

43   In this treatise, Bonaventure often refers to what is natural, rather than appealing
explicitly to the natural law; but as Grabmann points out, Bonaventure uses several
expressions to refer to the natural law, including "nature" taken by itself. See M.
Grabmann, "Das Naturrecht der Scholastik von Gratian bis Thomas von Aquin,"
Vol. I of *Mittelalterliches Geistesleben: Abhandlungen zur Geschichte der Scholastic und*
Mystik, three volumes, (Munchen: Hueber, 1926), 65-103 at 77.

44   Aquinas offers a defense of evangelical poverty and celibacy along similar lines in the
Summa contra gentiles III, 131-137.

45   Because the civilians contrast the natural law, which "nature teaches all animals,"
with the law of nations, which is rational and therefore distinctively human, they
generally assume that other animals do follow a natural law; for an exception, see
Martin, Weigand no. 37. On the other hand, the canonists and most of the theologians identify the natural law in its primary sense with human rationality, while also
acknowledging that animals may be said to follow a natural law in a derivative sense.
However, the canonist Simon of Bisiniano (Lottin 106-107) denies that there is any
proper sense in which sub-rational animals may be said to follow a natural law, as
do both Albert (*De bono* V 1.1 *ad* 12) and, in his mature work, Aquinas (*Summa*
theologiae I-II 91.2 *ad* 3).

46   This may seem surprising, in light of the negative views toward animals in the medieval period. However, as Joyce Salisbury shows in *The Beast Within: Animals in the*
Middle Ages (London: Routledge, 1994), more positive attitudes began to emerge in
the twelfth century, as men and women became more conscious of the similarities
between humans and other animals; see especially 103-166.

47   See, for example, Philip the Chancellor, Lottin 112-114.

48   Animals who were involved in human acts of bestiality were sometimes destroyed,
but among the intelligentsia, this custom was interpreted as a way of removing such
acts from human memory; see Salisbury, *The Beast Within*, 92-4. Even today, we
customarily destroy animals that have injured or killed human beings even if they
pose no further threat to human life (for example, animals in zoos), without thereby
ascribing moral responsibility to them.

49 Frans de Waal, *Good Natured: The Origins of Right and Wrong in Humans and Other Animals* (Cambridge, MA: Harvard University Press, 1996), 210.

50 *Ibid.*

51 In this paragraph, I am particularly indebted to the essays by Stephen R.L. Clark collected in *Animals and Their Moral Standing* (London: Routledge, 1997), particularly "The Description and Evaluation of Animal Emotion," 87-96, and "The Reality of Shared Emotion," 121-138.

52 This line of thought is powerfully developed by John Casey in his *Pagan Virtue: An Essay in Ethics* (Oxford: Clarendon Press, 1990); in particular, see 51-103.

53 Gustafson, "Nature: Its Status in Theological Ethics," 12-14.

54 Others who acknowledge the naturalness (in some sense) of sinful acts include the canonist Rufin, Weigand no. 242, and Bonaventure, *In IV Sent.* 33.1.

55 D.E. Luscombe, "Natural Morality and Natural Law," in Norman Kretzmann, Anthony Kenny, and Jan Pinborg, eds., *The Cambridge History of Later Medieval Philosophy* (Cambridge: Cambridge University Press, 1982), 705-719 at 706.

56 In addition to the texts from William of Meliton and Aquinas cited above, see Albert, *Super ethica* V, 419, and Aquinas, *Ad Romanos* I 8, para. 149, and the *Summa theologiae* I-II 31.7, II- II 154. 11. It is worth noting that, in these passages, Aquinas does not identify the irrational as the most proper sense of what is natural, as he did in his *Sentences* commentary.

57 For examples of similar arguments, see among the canonists, John Faventius, Weigand no. 251-254; the apparatus *"Animal est substantia ..."* Weigand no. 421-425; and the *Muenster Summa* , Lottin 107-108. Among theologians in this period, similar arguments are offered by Philip the Chancellor, Lottin 112-113; Roland of Cremona, Lottin 115; and John of La Rochelle, Lottin 120-121.

58 According to Lottin; see *Le Droit Naturel*, 39-40.

59 Apparently, Rufin is the first to define the natural law in this way; see *Le droit naturel* 13 and *Das Naturrechtslehre*, 144-148.

60 There are many other examples of scholastic authors, predominantly among the canonists, who equate the natural law with reason, although it should be noted that all of them (including Huguccio) also acknowledge the legitimacy of other senses of "natural law." Examples include the *Munester Summa* and the *Leipzig Summa*, both cited in Lottin 107-109, the *Summa "Et est sciendum"* (Weigand no. 333, 338), the *"Queritur utrum"* (Weigand no. 380), the *Summa Reginenis* (Weigand no. 382), and the gloss apparatus, *"Ecce vicit leo"* (Weigand no. 413).

61 The terms "conscience" and "synderesis" have a long and complex history. The standard account of the medieval understanding of these terms remains Odon Lottin, "Syndérèse et conscience aux XII et XIII siècles," in *Psychologie et Morale aux XII et XIII Siècles, Vol. 2: Problemes de Morale, Premiere Part* (Louvain: Abbaye du Mont César, 1948; six volumes published between 1942-1960), 103-109; for more

recent discussions, see Crowe, *The Changing Profile of the Natural Law*, 123-135, and Timothy C. Potts, "Conscience," in Kretzmenn et al., *The Cambridge History of Later Medieval Philosophy*, 687-704. In addition, J.F. Quinn provides a detailed account of Bonaventure's treatment of the term in "St. Bonaventure's Fundamental Conception of Natural Law," in *S. Bonaventura 1274-1974*, Vol. 3 (Rome: College of St. Bonaventure, 1974), 517-98.

62   The relevant texts include William of Auxerre, *Summa aurea* III 18 introduction; the *Summa fratris Alexandri* III.II Inq. 2, Q.1.1, Q. 2.1; Albert, *Summa de creaturis* II, 71, and *De bono* V 1.1; Bonaventure, *II Sent.* 39.1,2; and Aquinas, *Summa theologiae* I-II 90.1 *ad* 2, I-II 94.2.

63   William here appeals to Augustine, but as Martin Grabmann points out, William goes beyond Augustine on this point; see "Das Naturhrecht der Scholastik," 73-74, and in addition, see Lottin, *Le droit naturel*, 33-35.

64   Free judgment, that is, *libero arbitrio*, was traditionally defined as "a faculty of reason and will" *(facultas rationis et voluntatis)*, and the *Summa fratris Alexandri* associates knowledge of the natural law with the *facultas*, hence with reason and will working in concert. It should be noted, however, that elsewhere in this composite summa we find another account of synderesis and conscience. See Lottin, "Syndérèse et conscience," 174-187.

65   The relevant texts include Albert, *De bono* V 1.1; Aquinas, *Summa theologiae* I-II 90.1 *ad* 2, I-II 91.2; and Bonaventure, *In II Sent.* 39.1.2. According to Bonaventure, conscience is a cognitive faculty, whereas synderesis is a component of the will; see "Syndérèse et conscience," 203-210.

66   As Lottin observes; see *Le droit naturel*, 75, 98. Typically, the scholastics distinguish between law (*jus*) considered as a legal or normative system, or the principles underlying it, and ordinance (*lex*), which is a written law; see for example Gratian's *Decretum*, D.1, C.2. This usage, however, is not found in either the *Summa fratris Alexandri* or in Aquinas' writings, both of which use *lex* for a normative system or the principles underlying it.

67   For a recent, influential example, see Daniel Mark Nelson, *The Priority of Prudence: Virtue and Natural Law in Thomas Aquinas and Its Implications for Modern Ethics* (University Park, PA: Pennsylvania State University Press, 1992). However, Nelson does acknowledge that, for Aquinas, the natural law does at least give rise to the precepts of the Decalogue; see 112.

68   See, for example, the anonymous canonical *Summa Reginensis*, Weigand no.383, and the *Leipzig Summa*, Lottin 108-109. Similarly, the author of the canonical *Summa Duacensis*, Weigand no. 407, attempts to explain how something can be said to be a part of the natural law even if it is taught.

69   The reference to Aeschylus (*eschylii*), the Greek tragedian (died c. 456 BCE), is somewhat puzzling, but Cicero does mention him and the scholastics may therefore have been aware that his plays deal with the universal demands of justice. I am

grateful to my colleague Brian Daley for identifying the reference and suggesting what its rationale may have been.

70   See Germain Grisez, "The First Principle of Practical Reason: A Commentary on the *Summa theologiae*, 1-2, Question 94, Article 2," in *Natural Law Forum* 10 (1965), 168-201, for Grisez's interpretation of Aquinas, and Germain Grisez, Joseph Boyle, and John Finnis, "Practical Principles, Moral Truth, and Ultimate Ends," *American Journal of Jurisprudence* 32 (1987), 99-151, for a summary statement of the theory considered in itself.

71   This formulation of the first principle of practical reason is taken from Germain Grisez, *The Way of the Lord Jesus 1: Christian Moral Principles* (Chicago: Franciscan Herald Press, 1983), 178, and the formulation of the general form for the determination of this principle is taken from *ibid.* 180; in general, see 173-228.

72   As Grisez apparently thinks he does; see "The First Principle of Practical Reason," 171-172. He bases this view on Aquinas' claim at *ST* I-II 94.2 that "a certain order is found in those things which fall under the apprehension of all things/all persons," reading *in his autem quae in apprehensione omnium cadunt* as referring to things that fall under the apprehension of all persons, that is, the specific precepts derived from the inclinations to which Aquinas later refers. However, *omnium* can mean "of all things" as well as "of all persons," and in either case, what Aquinas has in mind are trans-categorical concepts such as being and goodness, as his immediately following remarks make clear.

73   He does not say that these human goods are self-evident, but rather that they are naturally known, because they are not propositions which could be *per se nota*, that is to say, known through the very meaning of the terms. To say that they are objects of a natural inclination, or naturally known, is not tantamount to saying that they necessarily compel the will; see the *Summa theologiae* I-II 10.1 *ad* 2,3.

74   This does not mean that the natural law, considered as stemming in some way from the inclinations, does not give rise to moral rules; Aquinas does not draw our sharp dichotomy between virtue and rule ethics. I discuss the relation between natural law and virtue in Aquinas in more detail in "What the Wise Person Knows: Natural Law and Virtue in Aquinas' *Summa Theologiae*," 57-69 in *Studies in Christian Ethics* 12.1 (1999).

75   See Germain Grisez, Joseph Boyle, John Finnis, and William May, "Every Marital Act Ought to Be Open to New Life: Towards a Clearer Understanding," *The Thomist* 52 (3) (July, 1988), 365-426.

76   Martin Rhonheimer makes this point with respect to Aquinas in particular; see *Natur als Grundlage der Moral* (Innsbruck-Wein: Tyrolia Verlag, 1987), 82-82. In general, I found his discussion of Aquinas' account of our knowledge of the natural law to be illuminating, although I did not agree with him in every particular; see *ibid.*, 63-84.

77   The word *affectus* can allow a wide range of meanings; I was guided here by Giles
     Constable, *The Reformation of the Twelfth Century* (Cambridge: Cambridge Univer-
     sity Press, 1996), 16.

78   This point is well brought out by Ewart Lewis, "Natural Law and Expediency in
     Medieval Political Theory," in *Ethics* 50 (1940), 144-163.

79   See note 39 above for references.

80   Nederman, "Aristotelianism and the 'Origins of Political Science,'" 180.

81   Mary Douglas, *Purity and Danger: An Analysis of the Concepts of Pollution and Taboo*
     (London: Routledge, 1966), 14.

82   Mary Midgley, *The Ethical Primate: Humans, Freedom and Morality* (London:
     Routledge, 1994), 3.

83   Stephen Pope's work is perhaps the most influential such exception; see *The Evolu-
     tion of Altruism and the Ordering of Love* (Washington, D.C.: Georgetown University
     Press, 1994).

84   This view is reflected in the widespread distinction between the political virtues,
     which fit the human person for life in society, and the theological virtues, which
     bring about final happiness in union with God; see Lottin, *Psychologie et morale* Vol.
     3 (Louvain: Abbaye du Mont Cesar, 1949; six volumes published between 1942 and
     1960), 99-150 for a full discussion of this distinction. Aquinas specifically denies that
     observance of the precepts of the natural law is sufficient, by itself, to lead to salva-
     tion; see the *Summa theologiae* I-II 91.4 *ad* 1.

85   Ernst Mayr, *Toward a New Philosophy of Biology: Observations of an Evolutionist* (Cam-
     bridge, MA: Harvard University Press, 1988), 317-8.

86   *Ibid.,* 318.

87   *Ibid.,* 345.

88   John Kekes, "Human Nature and Moral Theories," *Inquiry* 28 (1985), 231-45, 236.

89   H.L.A. Hart, *The Concept of Law* (Oxford: Clarendon Press, 1961), 182-187; A.P.
     d'Entreves offers an illuminating discussion of Hart's minimal natural law in *Natural
     Law: An Introduction to Legal Philosophy*, revised second edition (London: Hutchin-
     son, 1970), 185-203.

90   For references, see Chapter 1, note one.

91   The landmarks include the essays collected by W.D. Hudson in *The Is/Ought Ques-
     tion* (London: Macmillan, 1969), Julius Kovesi, *Moral Notions* (London: Routledge
     and Kegan Paul, 1967), and Philippa Foot, *Virtues and Vices* (Oxford: Blackwell,
     1978). Foot in particular was greatly influenced by A.N. Prior, *Logic and the Basis of
     Ethics* (Oxford: Oxford University Press, 1949), as was Mary Midgley; see *Beast and
     Man: The Roots of Human Nature* (New York: Meridian, 1978), 156fn. However, as
     Charles Pigden points out, Prior actually defends Hume in that monograph,
     although he later came to change his mind; see "Logic and the Autonomy of Eth-

ics," *Australian Journal of Philosophy* 67, 2 (1989), 127-151, 127-8. For a good summary of recent work on this question, see Charles Pigden's "Naturalism," in Peter Singer, ed. *A Companion to Ethics* (Oxford: Blackwell Press, 1993), 421-431. Pigden himself takes the line that the Hume/Moore argument is valid but limited in scope in his "Logic and the Autonomy of Ethics."

92   Kekes, "Human Nature and Moral Theories," 244.

93   Bernard Williams, *Ethics and the Limits of Philosophy* (Cambridge, MA: Harvard University Press, 1985), 111.

94   Kekes and Williams, together with Hart in *A Concept of Law* provide examples of the first way of construing this relationship, whereas Midgley and Flanagan emphasize the second approach; see Midgley, *Beast and Man* (New York: Meridian, 1978), and more recently, *The Ethical Primate*; and Owen J. Flanagan, Jr., "Quinean Ethics," *Ethics* 93 (1982), 56-47, and *Varieties of Moral Personality: Ethics and Psychological Realism* (Cambridge, MA: Harvard University Press, 1991). Flanagan, it should be noted, places more stress on the fact that natural givens constrain the development of moral systems than does Midgley. There are relatively few contemporary defenders of perfectionism; one such is Thomas Hurka, *Perfectionism* (Oxford: Oxford University Press, 1993).

95   Kekes, "Human Nature and Moral Theories," 242-4. This point is frequently made; for other examples, see Flanagan, *Varieties of Moral Personality*, 49-55 and Williams, *Ethics and the Limits of Philosophy*, 152-155.

Chapter 3

Scripture
and the Natural Law

Summary: The natural law is not commonly associated with a scriptural ethic. Yet as this chapter will show, the scholastic concept of the natural law is a scriptural concept in three related senses: the scholastics justify appeals to the natural law on scriptural grounds; they derive much of the concrete moral content of the natural law from Scripture; and at the same time, they employ their overall concept of the natural law as a framework for interpreting Scripture as a moral document. In this way, the scholastics treat nature, reason, and Scripture as three mutually interpreting sources for moral norms. They begin with assumptions about nature and the moral order which are derived from many sources, including both Scripture and traditions of philosophical reflection. In the process of articulating those assumptions and subjecting them to rational critique, they find themselves confronted with inconsistencies or difficulties, which are sometimes corrected by adjusting their constructive arguments, and sometimes by revising their interpretation of Scripture. After examining the patristic and early medieval roots of the scholastic appropriation of the natural law as a scriptural doctrine, with a special emphasis on Augustine and Hugh of St. Victor, this chapter turns to a consideration of the relation between natural law and scriptural divine law, as the scholastics understand it. Subsequent sections of the chapter turn to the scholastic discussions of moral reasoning and the application of moral norms, the status of natural law specifically considered as a law, and the relationship between natural and eternal law, as these are shaped by their distinctively theological concept of the natural law. Finally, the last section turns to a consideration of this concept as a way of drawing out the practical implications of the doctrine of creation, and defends it against those who would argue for an exclusively Christocentric approach to Christian moral reflection.

■

The claim that the scholastic concept of the natural law is distinctively theological will seem paradoxical to many readers. Most modern and contemporary defenders of the natural law have emphasized the rational and universally binding character of its precepts. This observation applies just as much to those who defend the natural law from within a religious or theological perspective as it does to more secular advocates.[1] By the same token, theologically oriented critics question whether a natural law ethic, with its emphasis on universally known moral truths, can allow for the pervasive effects of human sinfulness or do justice to the properly theological character of Christian morality.[2]

In his *Permanence du Droit Naturel,* Philippe Delhaye speaks of the ambivalence of the medieval concept of the natural law, going on to explain that some medieval authors understand the natural law in scriptural terms, while others offer a more philosophical account.[3] Yet, as we saw in the last chapter, the philosophy of nature on which the scholastics drew in developing their concept of the natural law was itself motivated by specifically Christian concerns, and was developed in part through a process of scriptural interpretation. Moreover, natural philosophy in the twelfth and thirteenth centuries tended to see nature as an expression of a divine, transcendent wisdom. For both these reasons, we cannot draw a sharp line between the philosophical and theological aspects of the scholastic concept of the natural law; even its philosophical components are more theological than is generally realized.

Nor is this so paradoxical as it might appear to be. The natural law has nearly always been understood in theological terms by classical as well as Christian authors, in the sense that it has been seen as a reflection of a divine wisdom, however that might be spelled out more specifically. The scholastic concept of the natural law is thus in continuity with older traditions of natural law reflection, even as it also reflects the distinctively Christian concerns of the scholastics.

At the same time, we also saw that the scholastic concept of the natural law is compatible with more than one understanding of nature. For this reason, it might seem that we could reformulate this concept in terms of a more purely philosophical account of nature: philosophical, that is to say, in a modern sense which excludes any reference to specific religious beliefs. However, the scholastic concept of the natural law is theological in a further way, which both reinforces and specifies the theological interpretations of nature that it incorporates. The scholastics ground their concept of the natural law in a particular reading of Scripture, while at the same time interpreting specific scriptural texts in terms of that concept.

As a result, the scholastic concept of the natural law is distinctively Christian, not so much in its particular elements as in the overall shape given to those elements as synthesized through a particular reading of Scripture.[4] This distinctiveness is expressed in the particular aspects of human nature that are given normative priority, and also in the accounts of moral reasoning and law that stem from this concept. This does not mean that, for the scholastics, the natural law is not rational, but unlike most contemporary authors, the scholastics see no incongruity in affirming the rational character of the natural law while at the same time interpreting it in terms of a distinctively Christian theology. By the same token, most of them affirm that the natural law is in some sense the common possession of the human race, but again, this does not imply for them that it should be understood in non-theological terms.

The scriptural and distinctively Christian components of the scholastic concept of the natural law cannot be excised without drastically truncating it. It is difficult to see what interest this truncated concept would have, particularly from the standpoint of theological ethics. The fully theological scholastic concept, on the contrary, has much to offer to contemporary thought, in part just because it challenges our assumptions about the proper relationship between scriptural and rational elements in a theological ethics.

The scholastics were not the first to interpret the idea of natural law in the light of a particular interpretation of Scripture. On the contrary, scriptural and classical elements were inextricably linked in the natural law tradition as the scholastics received it. The scriptural and distinctively Christian aspects of natural law thought in the mid-twelfth century reflected the influence of patristic authors, Augustine above all, as well as theological reactions to the renewal of natural philosophy in the early twelfth century.

1. Scripture and the natural law: Theological antecedents

In the last chapter, we saw that natural law reflection emerged out of an eclectic philosophical matrix that incorporated Stoic, Cynic, and neo-Platonic elements. The same might be said of Christianity itself, and so it is not surprising that we find Christian authors both drawing on and contributing to the natural law tradition from an early period. Arguably, Paul himself makes use of an idea of natural law in his letter to the Romans, and this is certainly the way in which patristic and medieval theologians understand him.[5] By the third century of the Common Era, we find the Christian theologian Origen appropriating the same eclectic account of the natural law as we find in both Cicero and Philo. From this point, as Carlyle observes, the idea of a natural law becomes a commonplace in patristic thought.[6]

When we examine patristic writings on the natural law, we find themes, assertions, and even specific phrases that will be repeated throughout the scholastic discussion. Origen equates the law of nature, or alternatively the law of reason, with the law of God. Ambrosiaster identifies the natural law with the Mosaic law, arguing that the latter confirms and extends the former. We find a similar claim in Ambrose, who also identifies Paul's reference to the inner law of the Gentiles with the natural law. Jerome likewise identifies this inner law with the natural law, as do many others, and in addition, he offers the much-quoted comment that synderesis, or reason, cannot be extinguished even in Cain.[7]

To a considerable degree, scholastic appropriation of patristic thought was mediated through glosses on Scripture compiled from patristic writings, particulary the comprehensive gloss produced by the school of Anselm of Laon at the beginning of the twelfth century which came to be known as the Ordinary (that is, the standard) Gloss.[8] In addition, patristic views on the natural law were mediated through the digests of patristic writings that circulated throughout the Middle Ages, above all, through Peter Lombard's *Sentences*. As a result, the scholastics were not always cognizant of the wider context of the remarks on the natural law that they cited. However, in compensation, the natural law tradition was mediated to them as an integral part of a wider theological world-view that took its organizing framework from Scripture, even though it also incorporated classical texts and ideas.

The thought of Augustine of Hippo calls for special attention, both because of its depth and originality and because of Augustine's status as the pre-eminent patristic authority for Western Christians throughout the medieval period. Alois Schubert observes that the concepts of order and law are central to Augustine's thought.[9] We thus find reflections on God's eternal law, and the natural law that stems from it, throughout Augustine's writings, even though he never writes a systematic treatise on law. It would take us well beyond the scope of this book to attempt a textually grounded, synthetic analysis of Augustine's understanding of eternal law, natural law, and related topics. Nonetheless, even a brief summary of his remarks on these topics will serve to indicate just how deeply scholastic reflection on the natural law is indebted to him.

For Augustine, any intrinsic norm of existence or activity can be described as an order. Hence, the principles of operation intrinsic to a thing can be described as an order, as can the harmonious interrelationships among the different components of a complex reality. Understood in this way, "order" is equivalent to a natural ordering, and we can clearly see the affinities between this aspect of the concept of order and the concept of nature as it developed in the early twelfth century. Augustine also sometimes understands "order" in a more specifically moral sense, according to which the better members of society have ascendency over those who are worse.

All authentic orders of existence, together with the order of the universe taken as a whole, are grounded in the eternal law of God, which can be seen from one perspective as the creative and providential wisdom of God, and from another perspective as God's will for the existence and preservation of the created world. In a fundamental sense, the eternal law *is* God, seen under the aspect of providential wisdom and love.

At some points, Augustine speaks of the eternal law as the ultimate criterion of rationality informing the universe as a whole. In the early treatise *De libero arbitrio,* he defines the eternal law as "that by which the just state of affairs exists, so that all things might be in the best possible order ..." (*De lib. arb.* I 6.15). As such, it transcends the human mind and provides the ultimate criterion for human judgments and laws. More generally, it is the supreme rational principle informing creation and providence: "The eternal law is the law of all arts and the law of the omnipotent artificer ..." (*De vera religione* 30.56). At other points, Augustine emphasizes that the eternal law is an authoritative moral law. And so, further in the *De libero,* we read that "The eternal law is the highest reason, which is always to be obeyed, through which the wicked deserve misery, and the good deserve the good life, through which the temporal law is rightly administered and rightly modified ..." (*De lib. arb.* VI 15).

Since all things are created by God and fall under the ambit of divine providence, the eternal law extends to all creatures. Among non-rational creatures, it is expressed through *rationes seminales,* that is to say, intrinsic principles of operation, which are eternally contained in the Word of God but which work themselves out in time through the ordered movement of all creatures toward their appropriate ends. In this sense, all creatures may be said to be bound by the natural law. However, only the human person can consciously sin against the eternal law; non-rational creatures do not have sufficient freedom, whereas the angels, who enjoy the supreme happiness of union with God, cannot choose to reject that happiness through sin.

The natural law is a temporal expression of the eternal law, as are all just (and therefore authentic) human laws. Within the human person, the natural law is grounded in reason; as such, it is a reflection of the image of God within the human person, which Augustine equates with the rational soul. Hence, the natural law is innate, it is coeval with the creation of the first human beings, and it cannot be eradicated. In common with many other patristic authors, Augustine connects the natural law with the unwritten law of the Gentiles mentioned in Romans 2:14-15, and consequently he considers it to be universally binding even though he sometimes adds that it has been almost entirely obscured through sin.[10]

Elsewhere, he identifies the natural law with the Golden Rule and the Decalogue, a view that is also a patristic commonplace. The former, he says, is a basic moral norm that is known to all, and from this rule, it would theoretically be possible to derive at least the fundamental principles of morality. At the same time, given the pervasive effects of sin, our moral knowledge is at best limited and corrupt. For this reason, God has mercifully formulated the fundamental precepts of the natural law in the Mosaic law, particularly in the Decalogue. Hence, the latter can be considered to be a written formulation of the natural law.

Even this brief summary suggests the profound influence that Augustine had on later Christian thought on the natural law and related subjects. It is clear that his conceptions of order and law had a formative influence on the natural philosophy that emerged in the early twelfth century. By interpreting the natural law as an expression of the image of God, that is to say, the rational soul, Augustine connects the natural law to one of the most suggestive scriptural images of human nature. His comments on the relationship of natural law to the Golden Rule and the Decalogue reinforced the views of other patristic authors, and for medieval canonists and theologians, they placed the legitimacy of this line of interpretation beyond question. Finally, his account of the eternal law was incorporated into two of the most influential of the thirteenth-century theories of the natural law, namely the theory of Alexander of Hales and his collaborators, and that of Aquinas.

It would take us too far afield to attempt to trace the development of Christian natural law thought from the end of the fifth century to the beginning of the twelfth century. We have already remarked on the importance of Isidore of Seville, whose *Etymologies* transmitted some remnants of Roman jurisprudence to the medieval West. After that time, the most important theological reflections on the natural law before the period we are considering come in the decades immediately preceding: that is to say, in the early part of the twelfth century. At the beginning of that century, we find Anselm of Laon and his school developing Augustine's claim that knowledge of the natural law was obscured by sin and thus had to be reformulated through the Mosaic law.[11] Similarly, most of the central themes of patristic discussions of the natural law reappear in Abelard's treatments of it.[12]

Among the theologians of the early twelfth century, Hugh, the great theologian and prior of St. Victor in Paris (d. 1141) is particularly important as a bridge between patristic thought, particularly that of Augustine, and subsequent canonical and theological reflection on the natural law. In order to appreciate his influence, it is necessary to see his work in the context of the emergence of natural philosophy in the early twelfth century.

Although twelfth-century natural philosophy was theological in its assumptions and orientation, it was also criticized on theological grounds, both because it seemed to imply the existence of creative principles other than God and because it did not appear to do justice to the particularities of salvation history. This is hardly surprising; what is surprising, at least from our standpoint, is the fact that the critics of natural philosophy also had a formative impact on the scholastic concept of the natural law.

This is particularly true of Hugh of St. Victor, who offered, in Winthrop Wetherbee's words "the most interesting and penetrating critique of the presumptions of natural philosophy."[13] As Wetherbee goes on to explain, Hugh's criticisms are particularly telling because he shares so many of the presuppositions of men such as Thierry and William of Conches: "He was plainly well grounded in the Platonist tradition, and insists on the necessity of understanding natural justice, and the process by which 'each nature reproduces its essential form' as a stage in the ascent to truth. But for Hugh, such knowledge is important only insofar as it enables one to realize and penetrate the letter of Scripture."[14] Wetherbee is here speaking specifically of Hugh's views as developed in the *Didascalion,* but this provides the background against which to read his definition of the natural law in *De sacramentis:*

> Only those things, therefore, which are such that they can never licitly be done, are prohibited by the law of nature ... One precept concerning prohibitions is written in the human heart: That which you would not have done to you, do not do to another. Similarly, there is one [precept] concerning injunctions: Whatever you would wish that other persons would do for you, you also should do likewise for them. Thus the human person from consideration of these may clearly discern what kind of behavior

SCRIPTURE AND THE NATURAL LAW

he should exhibit to the neighbor (I, 11, 7, quoted in Weigand no. 220).

What we see here is an appropriation of patristic thought in defense of an alternative way of thinking about the natural law, according to which it is considered as a scriptural doctrine. Hugh's approach does not necessarily imply that an account of the natural law that grounds it in the innate tendencies and needs of human nature is wrong, any more than his overall theological approach to a Platonic philosophy of nature implies the outright rejection of the latter. Nonetheless, it does imply that any naturalistic or non-Christian account of the natural law must be justified and interpreted through Scripture if it is to be correctly understood. This approach, furthermore, implies an alternative conception of what the natural law fundamentally is, since on this view, the natural law in its primary sense is proper to the human person. This does not necessarily imply that Ulpian's definition of the natural law is wrong, but it does undermine the civilian distinction between the natural law, which we share with all animals, and the distinctively rational and human law of nations.

Thanks to Gratian's use of his work, Hugh's approach to the natural law became the standard approach for the canonists, and for obvious reasons the theologians also found it congenial. The influence of Hugh's account of the natural law will become apparent when we compare his remarks quoted above to the opening words of Gratian's *Decretum*. We now turn to that text.

2. Natural law and Scripture in scholastic thought

At the beginning of the *Decretum*, Gratian writes:

The human race is ruled by a twofold rule, namely, natural law and custom. The natural law is that which is contained in the law and the Gospel, by which each person is commanded to do to others what he would wish to be done to himself, and forbidden to render to others that which he would not have done to himself. Hence, Christ [says] in the Gospel, "All things whatever that you would wish other people to do to you, do the same also to them. For this is the law and the prophets" (D.1, introduction).[15]

These words have been regarded with dismay by even the most sympathetic commentators. Odon Lottin claims that Gratian's claim "underscores a regrettable confusion between the natural law and the divine law."[16] Similarly, according to Michael Crowe, Gratian's definition is "an embarrassment," and it reflects the fact that Gratian was not a systematic thinker.[17]

Such remarks as these reflect our own presuppositions concerning the natural law, rather than Gratian's clarity or lack of it. Because we assume that the natural law must be purely rational, in such a way as to be fully accessible to all reasonable persons, any effort to link natural law and Scripture is bound to seem confused. However, when we place Gratian in his own context, and take account of what it is that he is trying to do, it becomes apparent that his approach is neither confused nor unsophisticated.[18]

As we noted in the first chapter, Gratian was in all likelihood a practicing lawyer, and so we should not be surprised that he writes in the usual style of a lawyer rather than an academic. That is to say, he prefers to make his points through the selection and placement of legal texts, keeping his explicit commentary to a minimum. If we read the *Decretum* through the lens of the legal maxim that placement is the first rule of interpretation, the significance of its opening words becomes clear.

The *Decretum* is, after all, an analytic compilation of the decrees and enactments or, in other words, the canons relevant to church practice. As such, it invites comparison with Justinian's *Digest,* which also begins with a definition of the natural law, namely, Ulpian's definition according to which the natural law is "that which nature teaches all animals" (*Dig.* I 1, 1.3). By setting a theological definition, clearly indebted to Hugh of St. Victor, at the beginning of his *Decretum,* Gratian endorses Hugh's position that the natural law, at least as seen from the perspective of canon law, can adequately be understood only through Scripture. By implication, the civilians' understanding of the natural law derived from Ulpian does not provide a suitable starting point for a properly theological understanding of law.

At the same time, Gratian does not intend to exclude the more immediately naturalistic approach exemplified by Ulpian's definition, any more than Hugh simply rejects the neo-Platonic idea of natural justice. He indicates this when, after setting forth a threefold division of law as natural, civil, and the law of nations, he turns to Isidore of Seville for an account of the natural law:

> Natural law is common to all peoples, because it is everywhere present by an instinct of nature and not by decree: as, for example, the union of man and woman, the succession and education of children, the possession of all things in common, and the equal freedom of all persons; the acquisition of those things which are taken from the heavens, the earth, and the sea; also, the restitution of something deposited, or a deposit of money, and the repulsion of violence by force. For this, or if there is anything similar to this, is never unjust, but is held to be natural and equitable (D.1, C. 7; he is quoting Isidore's *Etymologies* V.4).

Clearly, Isidore's account of the natural law has been drawn from the same sources as Justinian's *Digest* and, for that reason, it also reflects the distinctively civilian approach to the natural law, which takes its starting points from the *Digest*.[19] Delhaye is thus wrong to say that Gratian ignores the civilian understanding of the natural law.[20] On the contrary, by incorporating Isidore's definition of the natural law into the *Decretum*, Gratian indicates the legitimacy of the civilians' understanding of the natural law. At the same time, by placing it in a subordinate and explanatory position, he indicates that this understanding should be subordinated to and interpreted in terms of the scriptural definition with which he begins.

As Gratian goes on to explain, Scripture contains the natural law, but that does not mean that the two are simply equivalent:

> The natural law is contained in the Law and the Gospel. However, it can be shown that not everything that is found in the Law and the Gospel belongs to the natural law. For there are certain moral precepts in the Law, such as "do not kill," and of course, there are certain mystical or sacrificial precepts, such as that concerning a lamb, and other similar precepts. The moral commands belong to the natural law, and therefore they can be

shown to be immutable. The mystical commands, however, with respect to their surface meaning, can be shown to be distinct from the law of nature; with respect to their moral significance, they are seen to be connected to it. And given this, although they seem to admit of change with respect to their surface meaning, still it can be shown that they are immutable with respect to their moral significance (D.6, 3.1).

This fundamental distinction provides the starting point for all subsequent canonical and theological reflection on the relationship between the natural law and the divine law, that is, God's law as revealed in Scripture. The natural law is said to be contained in the divine law; the latter includes other kinds of precepts, including the ceremonial precepts of the Old Law and (for Aquinas, at any rate) the articles of faith contained in the New Law.[21] More specifically, Scripture provides a normative formulation of the natural law in the form of the negative and positive formulations of the Golden Rule, and in addition it offers the paradigmatic statement of the immediate moral implications of the natural law, in the form of the Decalogue.

At the same time, a number of scholastics mention the divine law as one of the forms of natural law. This has led modern commentators to accuse Gratian and his followers of confusion, but in fact this usage is entirely consonant with the overall scholastic concept of the natural law. We have already noted that the organizing principle for that concept is provided by the classical distinction between the natural and the conventional, interpreted in such a way as to allow for a broad construal of the category of the natural. For the scholastics, the divine law contained in Scripture can itself be considered as pre-conventional; in this sense it is a natural starting point for human custom and positive legislation. That is why the divine law can be spoken of as a form of natural law, albeit (for some of the scholastics) in a derivative or improper sense.

More fundamentally, natural law and divine law are closely connected in scholastic thought, because Scripture and nature (the latter being understood in almost any of the ways then current) provide two complementary modes of access to God's wisdom and God's providential will for humanity. The knowledge of God and of God's law provided through nature is bound to be incomplete and even corrupt; that is why it was necessary for the basic precepts of the natural law to be formulated anew through the Mosaic law.[22] Nonetheless, there can be no fundamental contradiction between natural law and Scripture. These are two different yet mutually complementary ways in which God's will is expressed to human beings.

The canonist Huguccio expresses this view with his usual clarity and critical acumen:

> Likewise, in a fourth sense, the divine law, that is, what is contained in the law of Moses and the evangelical law, is said to be a natural law. Thus it is understood at the beginning [of the *Decretum*]. And this is said to be natural law, because the highest nature, that is, God, transmitted it to us and taught it through the law and the prophets and the gospel, or because natural reason leads and urges us even through extrinsic learning to those things which are contained in the divine law. Hence, if I may speak boldly, I say quite certainly that this law is called natural in an improper sense, namely, because the natural law, that is, reason, urges those things which are contained in it, and one is obliged by reason to [do] those things (Lottin 110).

Huguccio is nearer to our own way of thinking than Gratian in his reluctance to speak of scriptural precepts as natural law, although he is conscious of expressing a controversial view ("if I may speak boldly"). At the same time, his claims that Scripture proceeds from God, the author of all nature, and accords with natural reason, would have been generally accepted. Cardinal Laborans claims that Scripture, particularly the Decalogue, makes explicit what God implanted in humanity at creation through endowing us with reason (Weigand no. 312). Richard de Mores claims that scriptural law imitates nature, and the anonymous canonical *Et est sciendum* observes that Scripture, or divine law, is so called because it derives from God and imitates nature (Weigand no. 366, 332).[23] Still more succinctly, the anonymous author of the canonical *Paris Summa* remarks that "the natural law is called the will of God, revealed through inspiration, or in another way" (Weigand no. 259).

Turning to the theologians, we read in the *Summa fratris Alexandri* that Scripture contains the natural law of reason while at the same time going beyond it (III–II 2.2.1 *ad* 1). Bonaventure claims that we would not be able to understand the moral message of Scripture if it were not for the light of reason with which God has endowed us (*Collationes de decem praeceptis* I 2.2), and similarly, Albert says that the human person could not be morally upright if he did not have natural principles of justice implanted within him (*Ethica* V.3.3). Finally, according to Aquinas the divine law contains both precepts of the natural law, and precepts directing the human person to a supernatural end (*Summa theologiae* I-II 91.4).

Contemporary authors sometimes assume that the moral precepts of Scripture should be understood as positive law, rather than natural law, but this is emphatically not a scholastic view.[24] Even those scholastics who distinguish most sharply between natural and divine law (such as Huguccio) do not consider divine or scriptural law to be on a par with human legislation. The canonist Honorius, writing near the end of the twelfth century, refers to an argument, apparently common among other canonists at the time, to the effect that anything that can be said to be divine law cannot be described as positive law (Weigand no. 351). Aquinas is more specific: "Those things which are commanded by divine law are morally right not only because they are enjoined by law, but also because they are in accordance with nature" (*Summa contra gentiles* III 129; cf. III 121).

By locating the natural law within Scripture, the scholastics set the parameters within which other conceptions of the natural law, including classical and philosophical accounts, can be assessed and incorporated into an overall concept. Gratian himself clearly sets forth the negative criterion implied by the appeal to Scripture: "Since, therefore, nothing is commanded by the natural law except that which God wishes to be done, and nothing is forbidden except that which God forbids to be done, and finally since there is nothing in the canonical scriptures apart from what is found in divine laws; and the divine laws are consonant with nature; it is plain, that whatever can be shown to be contrary to the divine will or the canonical scriptures, the same is also found to be at odds with the natural law" (D. 9, C.11).

More positively, Gratian and his followers also appeal to Scripture to establish which of the traditional accounts of the natural law should be taken as primary, or at least as legitimate. Gratian himself reads Scripture as providing a definitive formulation of the natural law through the negative and positive formulations of the Golden Rule, as found in Tobit

4:15 and the gospels (Matthew 22:39-40 and parallels), respectively.[25] Moreover, this is the way in which Gratian is read by the canonists and theologians interpreting him, and they make his position their own. In addition, they appropriate Augustine's claim that the precepts of the Decalogue summarize the immediate implications of the Golden Rule.[26]

The identification of the natural law with the Golden Rule and the Decalogue, in turn, is interpreted in such a way as to justify other traditional interpretations of the natural law. As we observed in the last chapter, many of the scholastics consider the fundamental injunction against doing harm to stem from that natural law that we share with all other animals. The Golden Rule can also be understood as both Bonaventure and Aquinas understand it, as the first and most basic moral principle discerned by reason (see, respectively, *In II Sent.* 39.1.2 and the *Summa theologiae* I-II 100.3; note, however, that Aquinas refers specifically to the injunction to love the neighbor in Matthew 22). Understood in either way (and these are not mutually exclusive options), the Golden Rule as articulated in Scripture supports the scholastic tendency to understand the natural law primarily in terms of fundamental principles, rather than identifying it too closely with particular moral precepts or existing social arrangements.

Not only do the scholastics find confirmation for their general approach to the natural law in Scripture, they also find scriptural warrants for the most important of the traditional definitions of the natural law. Ulpian's definition finds support in the Genesis account of creation, particularly the injunction "Be fruitful and multiply" (Gen. 1:28) and in other scriptural texts celebrating the goodness of marriage and fertility.[27] It is also reinforced by Paul's condemnation of homosexual behavior as unnatural (Rom. 1:26-27), because the scholastics understand Paul to be saying that homosexual acts are contrary to an aspect of human nature that we share with the animals, namely the capacity for reproduction (see, for example, Aquinas, *Ad Romanos* Lect. 8, 149).

The interpretation of the natural law as reason, or as tantamount to the most fundamental principles of practical reason, is undergirded by even more impressive scriptural support. As we have already noted, this interpretation is supported by appealing to Paul's claim that the nations are given their own law through reason (Rom. 2.12-16) and to his more obscure reference to the law of the mind (identified with reason), which

wars with the law of the flesh (identified as human tendencies toward
sinfulness, which are innate, given our fallen condition; Rom. 7.23). Less
obviously, the scholastics also appeal to the statement in Genesis that God
created Adam and "breathed into him the breath of life," which is
interpreted as the power of rational judgement (Gen. 2:7).[28] This line of
interpretation is in turn connected to Augustine's claim that our knowledge of God is derived from, or at least reflects, the image and likeness
of God, which is nothing other than the rational soul:

> ..the Gloss says there [Rom. 2.14], that because the human person
> bears the image and likeness of God, "he has a law by which he
> understands and is conscious within himself of what is good and
> what is evil." For in that part of the human person which
> corresponds to the image of God, he has knowledge of the first
> truth, which is God, because according to Augustine, the image
> is associated with the power of knowing. And on account of that
> which corresponds to the likeness, he is able and obliged to love
> the highest good, since the likeness is associated with the power
> of loving, as Augustine says ... And on account of this, there is
> something in the law which in itself ordains the human person
> to God, and also to his neighbor ... (*Summa fratris Alexandri* III.
> II, 2.4.2.1).

Not only does Scripture offer warrants for various aspects of the
natural law tradition, it also, and more fundamentally, provides the scholastics with starting points for establishing the normative content of the
natural law. Indeed, the influence of Scripture in this regard is so fundamental that it is easily overlooked. As we noted in the last chapter, the
scholastics appeal to the natural law in order to provide a *prima facie*
justification for practices that might otherwise appear to be problematic.
However, when they identify specific moral norms as stemming from
the natural law, these are almost always derived from Scripture, including
the Golden Rule in its various formulations and the precepts of the
Decalogue, and the more specific norms that are thought to be specifications of these basic rules of morality. Even the prohibitions against
unnatural sexual behavior appear to be grounded in scriptural condemnations, rather than in a purely speculative analysis of sexuality. In this
way, Scripture provides the scholastics with their account of the core
normative content of the natural law.

SCRIPTURE AND THE NATURAL LAW

If this is so, then it might seem that the scholastic concept of the natural law is empty or, at most, serves as a supplement to what is fundamentally a scriptural morality. However, such a conclusion would overlook the fact that the interpretative process we are examining did not move in one direction only. Not only does Scripture set the parameters for the scholastic concept of the natural law, but it is also itself interpreted in the light of scholastic assumptions and beliefs about the natural law. These assumptions and beliefs, in turn, are not derived solely from Scripture, but incorporate diverse Christian, Jewish, and classical elements, as we have already seen. Of course, the scholastics consider Scripture to be supremely authoritative and inerrant, and there is therefore no question for them of judging a scriptural norm to be mistaken on the grounds that it contravenes the natural law. Nonetheless, they are also aware that Scripture must be interpreted in order to be understood, and they are open to saving the truth of difficult texts by means of symbolic readings, interpretations that supply context, and other similar moves.[29] It is within this context that the natural law provides the scholastics with a way of understanding the moral prescriptions of Scripture. More specifically, the scholastics draw on their concept of the natural law in order to determine which of the particular norms of Scripture should count as precepts of the natural law, and therefore as perpetually in force, and in addition, they make use of this concept in order to interpret specific norms.

At the most foundational level, the distinction between moral precepts and other kinds of precepts, such as ceremonial precepts, is an interpretative distinction that is not perspicuous in Scripture itself. Yet some such distinction was necessary if the scholastics were to acknowledge the Old Testament as inspired by God without committing themselves to the view that Christians are obliged to observe the whole of the Mosaic law as recorded there. For the scholastics, the concept of the natural law provides a framework within which to draw this critical distinction. At the same time, the scholastics are aware of the interpretative character of this distinction, as we see from the care with which they explain and justify it:

Of the things contained in the Law, some are moral, some symbolic. Those that are moral shape our conduct. Consequently, they are understood according to their literal meaning: for example, you shall love God; you shall not kill; honor your father

... Symbolic things should be taken as types signifying something
beyond the literal sense ... No explanation can be given for the
literal expression given to ritual commandments: for example,
you shall not plow with an ox and an ass together (John the
Teuton, gloss on the *Decretum* D.6, C.3; James Gordley, translator).[30]

As these remarks indicate, the scholastics read Scripture through a set
of assumptions about what a natural law principle is, and this in turn
determines which scriptural norms they consider to be expressions of the
natural law. Most fundamentally, if Scripture contains a natural law that
is accessible to reason, then it should be possible rationally to assess
scriptural norms in order to determine which of them are expressions of
a natural law and which are not. This does not mean that the scholastics
assess the norms of Scripture by reference to a purely philosophical
account of moral rationality, as some modern thinkers were later to do.
However, they do assume that if a given norm is an expression of the
natural law, it will be reasonable in the sense of being intelligible, considered in light of the basic conditions and needs of human life. Correlatively,
a norm that cannot be understood in these terms will most likely be
interpreted as conditional, ritual, or symbolic, as the preceding passage
illustrates. Similarly, the Golden Rule is plausible as a precept of the
natural law precisely because it is general enough to serve as a first principle
for moral reasoning, as Albert explains (*De bono* V 1.1). Furthermore, the
precepts of the second tablet of the Decalogue can plausibly be interpreted
along these lines as specifications of a general precept of non-maleficence
(that is, a precept forbidding harm), which are themselves still general
enough to claim universal validity.

The scholastics draw a further distinction among those scriptural
precepts that they take to be expressions of the natural law. Once again
following the lead of Hugh of St. Victor, who connects the negative and
positive forms of the Golden Rule with the prohibitions and positive
injunctions of the natural law, the scholastics distinguish between prohibitions and injunctions, and add a third category of indications: that is,
those precepts that indicate what is permissible or, for some authors, what
accords with an ideal state of affairs. This line of analysis is almost ubiquitous among the canonists and theologians; once again, Huguccio offers
a succinct summary:

This law [the divine law considered as natural law] consists in three, that is, in prescriptions, prohibitions, and indications: it prescribes that which is profitable, as, "you shall love the lord your God"; it prohibits that which is harmful, as, "you shall not steal"; it indicates what is appropriate and advantageous, namely, that all things should be held in common, and all persons should be equally free, and one should claim what is his own, or not claim it; the natural law did not prescribe or prohibit these and other similar things, but indicated that they are permissible. Hence, those laws by which the property of one is appropriated by another can be established contrary to this indication of the natural law; for there can be no modification of the natural law which is contained in the law and the gospel, with respect to its precepts and prohibitions, but with respect to its indications, there can be a partial modification (Lottin 110).

In addition, the scholastics sometimes interpret specific moral precepts in the light of a particular construal of what is natural to the human person. Here, for example, is Bonaventure's interpretation of the precept "Do not kill":

I say, therefore, that this mandate, "do not kill," prohibits anger breaking out in destructive injuries to natural, that is, substantial life, and to unmolested life, and to honorable life. For nature desires that which is better, and so it is not enough for someone that he should have life alone. Rather, he wishes in addition to have a life which is healthy and unmolested and honorable. Accordingly, the Legislator, in this mandate, "do not kill," prohibits firstly anger breaking out in destructive injuries to natural life; secondly, to unmolested life, namely, an injury done through words or through wounds; and thirdly, to honorable life, such as the injury which is done through open or hidden detraction indicated by some sign.

Hence the Gospel says, "You have heard it said of old, do not kill, and he who kills will be held guilty by judgement. But I say to you, that anyone who is angry with his brother will be held guilty by judgment. He who says to his brother, 'Fool!' will be held guilty by the council, and he who says 'Idiot!' will be liable to the fires of hell" [Mt. 5. 21-22]. So it is plain that the human person acts contrary to the commandment, "Do not kill" in three ways, namely, when someone is angry with his brother, or says to him, "Fool!" or says to him, "Idiot!" And when this is done from deliberation of soul, then he says, that he is worthy of the flames of hell. And because natural life is the foundation of the others, therefore in this way, "Do not kill," the Legislator expresses the commandment *(Collationes de decem praeceptis* VI. 4).

Here we see an account of what is natural functioning in a way that both draws out the meaning of a particular scriptural injunction and explains how seemingly inconsistent Old and New Testament injunctions can be harmonized. This latter point is especially important to Bonaventure, as we see from the fact that he goes on immediately to devote six articles to a refutation of the Cathars' claim that Scripture is inconsistent in its treatment of homicide *(de decem prae.* VI 5-11).

In short, the scholastics construe nature, reason, and Scripture as three mutually interpreting sources for moral norms. This way of proceeding may appear to be circular, and so it is, but not in a vicious sense. The scholastics begin with assumptions about nature and the moral order that are derived from many sources, including both Scripture and traditions of philosophical reflection. In the process of articulating those assumptions and subjecting them to rational critique, they find themselves confronted with inconsistencies or difficulties, which are sometimes corrected by adjusting their constructive arguments, and sometimes by revising their interpretation of Scripture. Always, they attempt to preserve the overall harmony of their sources.

Because the scholastic concept of the natural law is both justified and developed on the basis of a particular reading of Scripture, we may fairly describe it as a scriptural concept, although it also reflects its classical and more narrowly philosophical antecedents. (It is difficult to think of any theological concept that does not blend scriptural elements with what might broadly be described as secular components in this way.) The scriptural character of the scholastic concept of the natural law has been overlooked by many commentators because they interpret this concept through the lens of a distinctively modern assumption that the natural law, properly understood, must be grounded in pure – that is, non-religious – reason. Seen from this perspective, the scholastic synthesis of considerations grounded in nature, reason, and Scripture can only appear as confused. This attitude leads in turn to the ultimately fruitless attempt to separate a purely rational natural law from what are seen as its scriptural and theological accretions.[31]

This attempt is fruitless because the scholastic concept of the natural law presupposes a particular scripturally grounded account of what is normative in human nature, and any attempt to abstract a "purely rational" account from that concept will result in a fragmentary and unpersuasive account of the natural law. We are likely to overlook this point because we are the heirs of the scholastic concept of the natural law, and precisely for that reason, we share many of the scholastics' beliefs about the moral significance of human nature, even though the theological character of those beliefs is now largely hidden from our view.

In order to appreciate the distinctiveness of the scholastic concept of the natural law and the account of the moral significance of human nature that it implies, it is necessary to return to a point made at the end of the last chapter. We observed there that, while the moral significance of human nature is philosophically defensible, it is also the case that there are limits to the moral claims that can be justified through an appeal to nature. That is, the exigencies of human nature place constraints on acceptable moralities, and its pervasive tendencies may give rise to partic- ular elements of our moral codes, but there is no one moral system that can plausibly be presented as *the* morality that best accords with human nature. Even if we leave aside the further problem that some of our characteristic tendencies are morally problematic, it seems clear that morality is under-determined by human nature.

For better or worse, this problem does not arise for the scholastics. The reason is not that they are operating within a "classical world-view," as some critics have suggested.[32] On the contrary, it is the scholastics' reliance on Scripture as a source for moral reflection that leads them to consider some human inclinations as centrally important from a moral standpoint, and to interpret others accordingly. Because they take the Golden Rule as spelled out through the Decalogue to be the paradigmatic expression of the natural law, the scholastics place non-maleficence at the center of their concept of the natural law. This is so fundamental to them that some of them locate the tendency to avoid harm in that aspect of

our nature that we share with other animals (as we saw in the last chapter):
that is, in the most primeval and universal dimension of our humanity.
Even more significant, the Golden Rule, or alternatively, the injunction
to love the neighbor as oneself, is so obviously true for them that they
frequently assume that it is rationally self-evident.[33] Correlatively, the
scholastics privilege basic human inclinations to care and reciprocity while
giving a secondary place to other pervasive human tendencies, such as
pride, anger, and self-assertion.

Moreover, their emphasis on the reasonableness of the natural law,
as confirmed by both Old and New Testaments, prompts them to give
the greatest weight, morally speaking, to those aspects of human personality that are most directly connected to rationality and freedom, even
though they do not go as far in this direction as Kant was later to do.
This emphasis on reasonableness, together with a general commitment
to maintaining the responsibility of all persons before God, leads them to
affirm an ideal of equality grounded in shared humanity and moral agency,
even though they also qualify this ideal in important (and often regrettable)
ways.

It is true that the resultant concept of the natural law was anticipated
in various ways by the traditions of natural law reflection which the
scholastics received from their sources, non-Christian as well as patristic.
Nonetheless, the scholastic appropriation of this tradition is selective, and
their principles of selection are largely scriptural. After the recovery of
Aristotle's ethical and political writings, the scholastics might well have
taken the natural law tradition in a more distinctively Aristotelian direction, reading their Stoic and neo-Platonic sources in the light of Aristotle's
remarks on natural justice and natural inequality. But instead, they interpret Aristotle's comments on natural justice in terms of later Roman
natural law theories (taken either from Cicero or from the jurists), while
ignoring or repudiating Aristotle's theory of natural inequality.[34]

We are so familiar with the general ideas of non-maleficence and
equality that the scholastic commitment to these principles is likely to
strike us as obvious and uninteresting. To the contrary, there is nothing
obvious about the claim that our basic tendencies to care, reciprocity,
and non-maleficence should be given moral priority over other standing
tendencies, or that our capacities for rationality and responsible freedom
are morally the most significant aspects of our nature. Human beings are

also naturally inclined to form hierarchically arranged social groups, to compete with one another for material necessities and social status, to vent aggression, and to seek sensual and sexual gratification even at others' expense. These tendencies may be expressed in ways that are destructive and repugnant, but they can also take forms that are striking, attractive, even praiseworthy, and it is possible to envision a moral system that gives them priority over inclinations toward care and reciprocity. Such a morality would be an authentic natural morality, and yet it would look very different from the scholastic concept of the natural law.

Recently, a number of philosophers have called attention to the Christian antecedents, and therefore the historical contingency, of even our most pervasive moral assumptions. Consider these comments by John Casey:

> Christianity has disposed all of us, whether believing Christians or not, to assume that ultimate values must be internal, and to feel more or less scandalized by any ethic which elevates special strengths, rare gifts, and luck. We all inherit from Christianity, and from Kant, the assumption that there must be some set of principles of conduct which apply to all men simply as men. We further assume that if there is such a set of principles of conduct, they will have authority superior to other, more particular principles. Paganism does not seem for most of us a real option. To be interested in how far an ethic influenced by "paganism" can be taken seriously is to be interested in an ethic which does not rigorously exclude contingency.[35]

Casey goes on to defend this point through an extended reflection of what a "pagan" morality might look like (although he does not claim to be representing the actual views of pre-Christian societies). One of his primary sources for such an ethic is Friedrich Nietzsche's conception of a noble ethic:

> The chief outcome of the noble ethic is that the man of noble soul has reverence for himself and looks for honour from others. The respect which others feel for him is not directed at his good will but at all those dispositions which both make possible and are the outcome of his successful action upon the world. He "takes pleasure in willing" — but this must be not only because

of an inner power, but also because he objectifies this power in actual life. Nietzsche insists that the noble ethic concentrates upon action, what is achieved, rather than on motive.

This gives us a notion of human excellence that is deeply involved with contingency, in which the qualities we most admire in people are qualities of their being-in-the-world. They will include spiritedness, aggression, fierceness. For Nietzsche only the self-affirmation, pride, self-reverence that goes with these qualities can make *persons* the source of values, and can make values intelligible.[36]

From our standpoint, this vision of human excellence is likely to seem deeply problematic. It is profoundly inegalitarian, not only in its sharp preference for noble persons over others, but also in its clear preference for typically masculine qualities and activities.[37] It allows all sorts of seemingly non-moral traits and abilities into the realm of moral evaluation, and it gives a secondary place to that which we assume to be supremely valuable: namely, a good will. Above all, its exaltation of pride and aggression is likely to strike us as morally repugnant.

Yet there is also something attractive, even thrilling in this moral ideal. We do admire the man (or woman – but this ideal cannot easily accommodate such a possibility) who goes his own way, lives by his own rules, and demands respect, even fear, for his independence and power. There are whole genres of popular fiction that owe their enormous powers of generating revenue precisely to this ideal of the "noble man." This ideal is so attractive, I would suggest, precisely because it invites us to imagine strong men acting out of deeply rooted human tendencies towards aggression, domination, and courage. These tendencies are part of human nature, no less than tendencies toward empathy and cooperation, and for this reason Nietzsche's moral vision may be described as a natural morality.

But, of course, it is not a Christian ethic; it is offered precisely as the negation of Christian morality. (From Nietzsche's standpoint, it is Christianity that represents the sickly negation of a morality fit for noblemen.) The difference between Nietzsche's moral vision and Christian morality is not that the one is natural and the other is not. Both visions are grounded in natural human inclinations, but each one gives priority to a different set of inclinations and subordinates and directs the others in accordance with those it privileges. For this reason, Nietzsche presents us with an alternative construal of what is normative in human nature, in the light of which the distinctiveness of the scholastic account can more readily be appreciated.

To what extent are the scholastics themselves aware of the distinctiveness of their concept of the natural law? Certainly, they are aware that their scripturally governed approach to natural law reflection is not the only possible approach, and in that sense they see themselves as working within a particular framework of thought that is not shared by all rational persons. Yet this self-understanding does not necessarily carry the same implications for them as it would for us.[38] In the first place, it does not lead them to reject other sources for knowledge. Precisely because they consider Scripture to be the definitive revelation of God's wisdom and providential intentions, they expect to find a fundamental harmony between Scripture and other sources of knowledge and insight, and generally they do. Where these sources seem to conflict, they typically attempt to harmonize them in a way that allows independent (although not finally decisive) weight to non-scriptural sources. For them, fidelity to Scripture does not require, but on the contrary forbids, the dismissal of non-scriptural perspectives.

Second, even though the scholastics are aware of what we might describe as the tradition-situated particularity of their reflection (in the sense just described), that does not at all mean that they consider their concept of the natural law to apply only to Christians. They see themselves as offering a theologically grounded interpretation of universal principles of moral action, which therefore apply to all persons. At the same time, this does not mean that they emphasized the universality of the moral norms of the natural law to the extent that later natural law thinkers were to do. In the last chapter, we observed that for most of the scholastics we are studying, the natural law in its primary sense is understood as a capacity for moral judgment, or a set of fundamental principles by which such judgment takes place, rather than as a set of specific moral rules. Given this basic assumption, the scholastics' claim to offer a universally applicable theological concept of the natural law appears more plausible than would be the case if they understood the natural law as being primarily a collection of specific rules.

Yet for the scholastics, the natural law also gives rise to specific moral norms. Even at this level, the scholastics are aware of an element of historical and social contingency in the specific norms of the natural law, as we will see more clearly in the remainder of this study. However, I do not believe they ever considered the possibility of a challenge to their fundamental moral convictions as radical as that which Nietzsche poses. For this reason, the scholastic concept of the natural law, understood as implying specific moral commitments as well as an interpretation of morality, will be problematic for us in ways that it was not problematic for the scholastics themselves. The problem of moral relativism has been raised in sharper forms for us, not only by philosophers such as Nietzsche and his heirs, but also by experiences of moral disagreement in an increasingly pluralistic and international world. At this point, it is impossible to deny the reality of genuine, serious disagreement among different traditions even with respect to fundamental moral commitments.

Nonetheless, the particularity of the scholastic concept of the natural law does not invalidate it, even considered as a concept of *natural* law. This concept implies a certain moral construal of human nature that is defensible, in the sense that it is grounded in inclinations that are genuinely part of our nature. Yet, at the same time, it stands in need of defense, because our nature has other tendencies, in virtue of which other moral visions could also be developed and put into practice.

3. Natural law and moral norms

At the theoretical level, the scholastic concept of the natural law was shaped by a particular reading of Scripture, and it served in turn to provide an interpretative key for understanding the ethical content of Scripture. In practical terms, it was shaped by the exigencies of the society in which it was developed. The concept of the natural law provided a basis for interpreting and rationalizing social practices, and since these practices had to be legitimated within the framework of an overwhelmingly Christian society, this function reinforced and shaped the Christian theological character of the scholastic natural law.

We already touched on some of these applications in the last chapter. From a theological standpoint, perhaps the most far-reaching of these was the natural law defense of marriage and procreation. This appeal both presupposed and was meant to support the theological dictum that the world as a whole, and taken in all its aspects, is the good creation of a beneficent God. In effect, the scholastics, and more particularly the mendicant theologians, drew on the natural law in order to spell out the social consequences of the doctrine of the creation.

There is another aspect of the application of the natural law that was perhaps even more important in shaping the way the concept itself was understood. That is, the natural law provided a way of addressing a complex set of questions arising out of the penitential practices of the society of the twelfth and thirteenth centuries. As R.W. Southern points out, there were no agreed upon practices for assessing sins, allocating penances, and reincorporating sinners into the community at the beginning of the twelfth century.[39] Even more seriously, the standards by which actions are to be assessed were themselves unclear, and it was by no means always clear whether a problematic action should be considered as sinful or licit. These may seem to us to be marginal concerns, but they were central to the social organization of the time. Even more important, they raised a question that is fundamental for any account of morality: how are moral norms to be applied to individual cases?

The scholastics take it for granted, as did their forebears, that the moral principles by which men and women should conduct their lives comprise a kind of law. Yet this assumption by itself did not resolve the question of application. On the contrary, this presupposition itself helped to frame the question, because the traditions of natural law reflection that the scholastics inherited contained, broadly speaking, two understandings of law.

In the previous chapter, we noted that the scholastics tend to speak of law as a principle of order underlying a normative system, rather than equating it with specific rules or even a set of such rules. This tendency reflects an understanding of law as a rational order that the human person should attempt to observe. However, it is also possible to understand law in a way that stresses its authoritative character, as Augustine frequently does and, accordingly, to interpret the natural law as the decree of some divine reality. This reality might be understood in personal terms, and correlatively the precepts of the natural law would then be understood as commands or as divine legislation. It can also be understood in impersonal terms, and then the natural law would be equated with whatever actually happens. In this latter sense, which seems to have been the Stoic understanding of the natural law, obedience to the natural law would be equivalent to willing acceptance of one's fate. The equation of the natural law with fate is not taken up by the scholastics. However, the understanding of the natural law as the decree of a personal God and as the expression of divine wisdom were both congenial to Christian theology, and we find both incorporated into the scholastic concept of the natural law.

These two ways of understanding the natural law, in turn, suggest two approaches to the application of moral norms. To the extent that the scholastics emphasize the authoritative status of the natural law, they approach questions of application by asking whether the precepts of the natural law admit of dispensation. Yet the understanding of the natural law as an expression of divine wisdom or reason complicates this approach by raising questions of intelligibility and consistency. The scholastics do not doubt that God has the authority to grant dispensations from the natural law, at least in some cases, but they attempt to make sense of these dispensations and especially to defend God from any suspicion of arbitrariness. As a result, the idea of divine dispensation is transformed through their reflections into an account of rational application.

We see the main lines of this development anticipated in the *Decretum,* taken together with its standard Gloss. Near the beginning of the *Decretum,* we read that "No dispensation is allowed against the natural law, unless it happens that two evils are so pressing that it is necessary to choose one or the other" (D.13). In defense of this claim, Gratian cites the Eighth Council of Toledo, which teaches that "if an unavoidable danger compels one to perpetrate one of two evils, we ought to resolve to commit the one which obliges us to acknowledge the lesser debt" (D.13, C.1), and Gregory the Great, who recommends that "when the mind is caught between lesser and greater sins, if absolutely no path of escape lies open without sin, lesser sins are always to be chosen" (D.13, C.2).

Gratian notes these passages without in any way attempting to soften or mitigate their recommendations. To the contrary, by citing these texts in the introductory distinctions of the *Decretum,* in which he sets forth the fundamental sources of law, Gratian validates the principles set forth at Toledo and in Gregory's *Moralia in Job* as basic norms of interpretation.

These principles, it should be noted, go beyond a simple recommendation to choose the lesser evil, to include some explanation or rationale for this recommendation. According to the Council of Toledo, one should choose the course of action that involves fewer kinds of offense or harm; for example, a liar offends against God and stains himself, but someone who promises to commit a crime offends God, harms other people, and inflicts damage to himself. Gregory recommends that someone who is perplexed choose the lesser evil, on the grounds that such an evil, being chosen as it were unwillingly, will be mitigated or excused.

Gratian's treatment of the problem of moral perplexity or, to be exact, the treatment that he validates, was not satisfactory for many of his successors. The author of the canonical gloss on the *Decretum,* probably John the Teuton, is shocked into open disapproval: "The Master makes one exception [to the absolute binding force of the precepts of the natural law] in the case of doubt, but he does so badly" (Gloss on D.13 *ante* c.1; this and the following quotations from John are taken from James Gordley's translation).[40] If we examine the matter more closely, he goes on to say, we will see that there is really no such thing as moral perplexity:

> But it must be stated that no one can really be in doubt between two evils in this way. For it would then follow that necessity can make one do something evil. But the canons say that God will never punish anyone unless he has done wrong voluntarily. Furthermore, if necessity really required us to do something evil, then the ordinance that prohibited this would be impossible to obey. But every ordinance must be possible. Therefore, the person's doubt cannot arise from the matter itself, but it must arise in the mind and from foolish opinion (*ibid.*).[41]

It is all very well to dismiss moral perplexity as a "foolish opinion," but how does this help us to correct our misapprehensions in particular cases? John does not offer any overarching principle or method for doing so, but in the course of discussing specific cases raised in the main text, he does suggest that the process of applying moral rules must take account of the rationale for the rules themselves. Speaking of the case of someone who has promised to kill another, and must now decide between breaking a promise and committing a murder, John states:

> Do not understand it [Gratian's text] to mean that in the murder
> three sins are committed, and in the lie, two sins. Instead it says
> there that in the murder, offense is done in three ways, and in
> the lie, in two ways. One may argue, therefore, that whoever
> offends in more ways sins more. Again it may be argued from
> this that one should decide on the course of action for which
> more reasons can be given. Thus he that can show the greater
> right can prevail. So also the poorer case is the one against which
> more can be said. The contrary is indicated by C. 24 q.5 c.5,
> where it says that lying is greater than homicide, but the contra-
> diction is resolved there. (Gloss on D. 13, C.1; I have omitted
> the internal references within the text.)[42]

This line of analysis is uncomfortably close to Gratian's own recommendation to choose the lesser evil in such a case, and it reveals just how
difficult the problem of moral perplexity is. Nonetheless, we can see John
pressing toward a solution that emphasizes the rational character of the
natural law and downplays, without denying, its status as an authoritative
decree. He suggests that in a case of perplexity, we should analyze the
different precepts of the natural law in the light of the rationale informing
each one, so as to determine where "the greater right" lies. This can be
taken as an attempt to decide which course of action involves the lesser
evil, but it can also be understood as an effort to resolve a seeming conflict
of moral precepts through a more nuanced interpretation of the scope
and force of each one. On this view, what appears to be a conflict of
rules, forcing an exception to be made to one or the other, is actually a
case calling for discernment in the proper application of rules which,
correctly understood, cannot come into conflict. At the same time, John
does not explicitly draw this conclusion.

The question of applying moral norms arises in a different context
for the theologians in our period. For them this question arises in the
context of a problem in scriptural interpretation, a standard quandary
owing to its appearance in the *Sentences* of Peter Lombard (IV *Sent.* 33).[43]
This is the problem: at a number of points, holy men and women among
the Hebrews are said to have committed actions that would ordinarily
be considered to be violations of the natural law and that are condemned
by Scripture itself. For example, Abraham was on the point of killing his
son, and furthermore he and the other patriarchs took several wives; the

prophet Hosea married a prostitute; the Hebrews in Egypt took the property of their former captors. Not only were these scandalous acts committed by supposedly holy people, they were committed at the express command of God himself! How could this be? Even if we assume that God, as the author of the natural law, can grant dispensations from this law, is this not a case of inconsistency on God's part?

For the scholastic theologians, who lacked the comforts of the historical-critical method, this was a serious theological and moral problem. Yet their concept of the natural law provided them with the resources for a solution. The main lines of this solution are already present in the *Summa aurea* of William of Auxerre: "The Lord did not give a dispensation contrary to the natural law with respect to the essence of the virtue, namely chastity, but with respect to the work. For virtue is unchangeable, but its works are variable" (*Summa aurea* IV 17, 3.2 *ad* 1). In other words, William distinguishes between the act and the intention that it expresses, a distinction that can be traced back at least as far as the reforms of religious life and spirituality of the early twelfth century.[44] In some form or other, this distinction proves to be central to the subsequent discussion of this problem.

This way of resolving the problem of the so-called sins of the patriarchs quickly becomes the standard approach, and for good reason; it preserves the consistency and integrity of the scriptural message while at the same time introducing an element of flexibility into the natural law. However, taken by itself, William's solution is not fully satisfactory. If God can simply drive a wedge between actions and the intentions that animate them, does this not suggest a certain arbitrariness in the natural law itself? For these theologians, at least, the idea that God has established the fundamental norms of morality by sheer fiat was not finally acceptable. The Franciscan theologian John of la Rochelle suggests that God does sometimes give commands simply to test our obedience, but he carefully separates such commands from others, which reflect some intrinsic quality of the acts themselves:

> Concerning precepts, some are natural, others are disciplinary, and yet others are of the written law; and this division is in accordance with the rationale of the subject matter. For what is commanded is either expedient, and so it derives from nature,

or it is indifferent, and so it [is a matter of] discipline, or it concerns
rectitude, and so it derives from the written law, either according
to the letter, or according to the spirit ....

Now a disciplinary precept is generally given for testing, in
order that the human person may know that he owes obedience
to God, not only in what is expedient and upright, but also in
indifferent matters ... (Lottin 120).[45]

This implies that many other precepts concern what is not indifferent;
John goes on to explain the rationale of the precepts of the natural and
the written (that is, the scriptural) law at some length. And so, just as John
the Teuton suggests that seeming conflicts of moral duty can be resolved
by attending to the rationale of the precepts in question, so John of la
Rochelle attempts to resolve difficulties in scriptural interpretation in a
similar way.

The idea that the precepts of the natural law must be interpreted in
terms of their rationale is taken still further by the secular theologian
Philip the Chancellor. Philip's contribution to this discussion is twofold.
First, he clearly distinguishes between kinds of actions and particular acts,
in order to make the point that a particular action, seemingly problematic,
may be permissible if it does not fall under the scope of a general
prohibition of a given kind of action. Second, and related to the first
point, he brings together the analysis of moral prohibitions with the
distinction between levels of the natural law discussed in the second
chapter. That is, he analyzes the precepts of the natural law in terms of
the purposes of nature that they express, understanding nature in terms
of both the biological nature that we share with other animals and the
properly human attribute of reason. In this way he underscores the
complexity of purposes that underlies the precepts of the natural law.

On the strength of this analysis, he goes on to argue that we already
qualify precepts at the first level in terms of purposes discerned at the
second level. Thus, he interprets God's dispensations in the cases described
above in a way that obviates the concern that these were arbitrary acts
on God's part. While God alone has the authority to dispense from the
precepts of the natural law, nonetheless, in doing so God acts in accordance
with the logic of the natural law itself. Philip's argument deserves to be
quoted at some length:

To the next objection, that this [ie, the sacrifice of Isaac] is to kill the innocent, the response is that if it is said, "do not kill a person," or "do not kill an innocent person," this does not refer to a disposition with respect to the end, but only with respect to the subject matter, because "innocent" refers to a disposition concerning the subject matter. Since therefore it belongs to nature as nature to preserve the individual, to kill a person is said to be contrary to the natural law in this respect, insofar as nature as nature directs this. Nature as reason directs us not to kill an innocent person. However, since it is often the case that a person is evil and a malefactor, nature as reason directs concerning such a person that he should be killed. And so a judge kills a malefactor, insofar as the law is consonant with nature considered as reason, and in this case, to kill a person would not be contrary to the natural law understood in this way. However, to kill an innocent person knowingly would be contrary to the natural law, because it is contrary to that which nature, as reason, directs. But so far, a disposition with respect to the end is not implied, according to which [such an action] could not be done by the authority of a superior; the law, however, is a superior [authority], and God is [an authority] above [the law]. From this it follows that if a judge according to his conscience knows this person to be innocent, yet the proofs are to the contrary, he will judge in accordance with the proofs. And the judge himself does not kill that person, but the law, whose minister he is, according to which one who is innocent is held to be guilty. Much more, if God commands the killing of the innocent, as for example Isaac, would Abraham be obedient, since it is presumed that he [is acting] on account of a good reason (Lottin 114).

In other words, for Philip the precepts of the natural law must be analyzed in the light of the intrinsic complexity of the natural law. A precept that follows from the natural law understood on one level ("Do not kill") must be modified in the light of exigencies introduced at another level of the natural law ("Do not kill the innocent"). Even then, its application in a given case must take account of further complexities introduced by the particulars of a given situation, including in this case the special responsibilities attaching to particular roles. Philip casts his analysis in terms of the juridical category of dispensations, but it is clear that, for him, God's dispensations can be rendered intelligible through rational interpretations of the norms in question. These interpretations, in turn, reflect the conviction, fundamental to the scholastic concept of the natural law, that natural processes are intelligible in terms of their purposes.

None of this implies that human persons can dispense from the precepts of the natural law, but it does suggest a broad scope for the interpretation of those precepts. This suggestion is picked up by others, most notably Albert the Great, who begins his treatment of dispensations by observing that only God can dispense from the precepts of the natural law. However, the precepts of the natural law may be interpreted in order to determine their application to particular situations by those human persons who are vicars of God by virtue of their authority, wisdom, and moral goodness. As he goes on to explain, "interpretation is carried out in accordance with the application of general laws to particular cases and particular works, and this is done through reason," and while the reason of the multitude is frequently deceived, those with more wisdom are capable of this kind of interpretation (*De bono* V 1.4).

Albert's pupil Aquinas continues further along this line. Although he begins his discussion of this issue by flatly denying that the precepts of the natural law admit of dispensation *(Summa theologiae* I-II 100.8), it becomes apparent that this is a reformulation rather than a contradiction of his predecessors' views:

> ... killing a person is prohibited in the Decalogue insofar as it has the character of something unjustified; for the precept contains the very rationale of justice. And human law cannot grant this, that a person might licitly be killed without justification. But the killing of malefactors or enemies of the republic is not unjustified. Hence, this is not contrary to a precept of the Decalogue, nor is such a killing a murder, which the Decalogue prohibits ... And similarly, if something is taken from another, which was his own, if he is obliged to lose it, this is not theft or robbery, which are prohibited by a precept of the Decalogue ...
>
> So therefore, these precepts of the Decalogue, with respect to the rational character of justice which they contain, are

unchangeable. But with respect to some determination through application to individual acts, whether for example this or that is murder, theft or adultery, or not, this indeed is changeable; sometimes only by the divine authority, namely in those things which are instituted by God alone, as for example marriage and other things of this sort; and sometimes by human authority, with respect to those things which are committed to human jurisdiction. For with respect to those things, human persons act as the vicar of God, not however with respect to all things (I-II 100.8 ad 3).[46]

Here we see Aquinas explicitly stating what had been implicit in the treatment of this question at least as far back as John the Teuton's gloss on the *Decretum*. While the precepts of the natural law may be supreme and overriding in their authority, nonetheless they must be interpreted in order to be applied. In other words, in difficult cases what is in question is not the binding force of a particular precept, but its applicability to this or that specific instance. That applicability, in turn, must be determined in the light of one's best insights into the purposes of the natural law. This strategy preserves the authority of the natural law while at the same time reinforcing its rational character. Not only does it resolve the exegetical problem, it also offers a way of resolving moral perplexity through an analysis of the conflicting claims. We find an example of Aquinas' use of this strategy in his analysis of the differing claims of family and religious life (*Summa theologiae*, II-II 101.4, *ad* 3,4).

Because the scholastic theologians approach the problems of moral perplexity and the application of moral precepts through a particular reading of Scripture, we might expect them to resolve these problems by appealing to divine fiat. But, as we have just seen, their natural law orientation leads them in a quite different direction. Because they are disposed to read the moral precepts of Scripture within a framework of assumptions about the rational cogency of the natural law, the scholastics approach seemingly incongruous passages with the assumption that they must in some way reflect God's providential wisdom, as well as God's authoritative power. At the same time, the flexibility of the scholastic concept of the natural law allows them considerable space to develop interpretations which bear that assumption out. We see them exploiting this flexibility through reflection on what it means to dispense from a law, which leads them on to consider what it means to interpret a law in the light of its purposes. This line of reflection, in turn, reinforces their understanding of the natural law as rational, and provides them with resources to address the more general problem of apparent moral perplexity.

At the same time, their approach preserves a sense of the natural law as the law of a personal God, while avoiding a more extreme divine-command morality according to which moral rules need not be reasonable or even humane by our standards. The scholastics do hold that human moral reasoning must be purified and supplemented by God's revelation, and they also insist that the observance of a reasonable morality alone is not sufficient to attain salvation. Nonetheless, they refuse to drive a wedge between God's will and the reasonableness that is expressed in moral judgments. The claim that God's will might be wholly discontinuous from anything we would consider reasonable or good only comes later, when reason and will begin to be separated in later scholastic voluntarism.[47]

Even then, the scholastic link between authority and reason was never completely broken. It survived into the modern period, to find its most powerful articulation in the moral theory of Immanuel Kant.[48] We have noted that the scholastic conception of reason is not Kantian, but there is an affinity between the scholastics and Kant nonetheless. The latter's conception of reason as both authoritative and law-like reflects the influence of later scholastic writings on the natural law, and through him the scholastic idea of the intrinsic authority of reason is passed on to contemporary moral thought.

4. The natural law as law

We turn now to a further set of questions. What is implied by the fact that the scholastics speak of natural *law,* in contrast to other expressions they might have used, such as natural morality? The expression "natural law" invariably suggests an analogy with positive law, even though the scholastics insist on distinguishing between the two. How far should this analogy be pushed? More generally, what does it mean to speak of the natural law as a law?

These questions have been in the background throughout our examination of the scholastic concept of the natural law. However, it is particularly appropriate to consider them at this point, because they raise issues which can be fully appreciated only in light of the theological character of the natural law as the scholastics understand it.

It is often said that the natural law, as understood in medieval (or alternatively, Catholic) thought, stands over against the positive laws of particular communities, offering criteria by which the latter may be evaluated or even providing an alternative to positive legislation. This view, in turn, accounts for much of the opprobrium attaching to the natural law in legal circles while also explaining the attractiveness of the natural law tradition for others.[49] Similarly, historians sometimes contrast the theological view of law found in Aquinas and others with another, more secular view of law that began to develop together with the consolidation of royal authority in the thirteenth century.[50]

There are elements of the scholastic concept of the natural law that might seem to imply such a view, especially its emphasis on the reasonable character of the natural law. As we observed above, the scholastics identify reason with the most God-like aspect of human nature, in virtue of which we are said to be created in the divine image. This, in turn, gives credence to the view that the rational person is a participant in God's own dignity and authority. Seen in this light, the human person is not only a subject before the heavenly king, but also potentially a viceroy of that king – as Aquinas says, an active participant in divine providence, by virtue of the human capacity for self-governance (*Summa theologiae* I 22.2 *ad* 4, 5).

This is both a striking theological idea and a potentially powerful social and political claim. If reason is in some sense divine, if the rational person therefore shares in the dignity and authority of God, then this implies that the rational person should have authority within the community. And we do in fact find claims for authority based on rational judgment and expertise being lodged in the medieval period. However, it is not the canon lawyers and theologians who are most eager to make these claims. Rather, they are pressed by secular jurists, particularly during the later eleventh and twelfth centuries, when political and legal structures are still rudimentary. In this context, secular jurists are prepared to make strong claims for the authority of the judge, whose court was the main, and sometimes the only, institutional expression of the rule of law in a given community.

For many of the early secular jurists, not only is the judge responsible for trying cases in accordance with the laws, he is also said to be responsible for judging the laws themselves and rejecting those that are not in accordance with reason and equity. This claim is supported by the view that reason and its judicial expressions — that is, justice or equity — are divine in origin, so much so that the jurist Martin even says that equity *is* God (Weigand no. 34).[51] Furthermore, authority over the laws could also be claimed by the legal scholar, simply in virtue of his expertise and judgment; hence, we find the anonymous author of the *Petri exceptiones* in the second half of the eleventh century coolly announcing that "If anything useless, broken, or contrary to equity is found in the laws, we trample it underfoot" (Weigand no. 21).[52]

This is a program for judicial activism on a scale undreamed of in contemporary society, and it was thinkable only in a society that had no regular procedures for generating and modifying laws. Even at the end of the eleventh century and the beginning of the twelfth, when the consolidation of European society was just getting underway, the deficiencies in this view of reason as a self-sufficient authority were already beginning to be apparent. A complex society cannot function as an organized system solely on the basis of ad hoc judicial law-making. Legal ordinances must be established through some kind of authoritative decree if they are to have the necessary clarity, stability, and force. Once again, we find the ideas of reason and authority held together in a concept of law, this time for eminently practical reasons.

This is apparent in the writings of the father of secular jurisprudence, Irnerius, whose commentary on Justinian's *Digest* was written in the early decades of the twelfth century. He carefully distinguishes between the exercise of equity in the courtroom and the creation of law properly so called: "it is proper to equity simply to set forth that which is just. But it is proper to the law to set forth the same by an act of will, that is, relying on some authority" (Weigand no. 20). Similarly, the anonymous author of the juristic summa *Divinam voluntatem vocamus iustitiam* begins by saying, "Absolutely speaking, we say that justice is the will of God," but he then goes on to add an important qualification to this claim: "The law seems however to have relied on the authority of human persons, and indeed, in the case of the civil law, this is not in doubt" (Weigand no. 46).

In the last chapter, we observed that the canonists and theologians, in contrast to the civilians, generally consider the natural law in its primary sense to be distinctively rational and human. For this reason, the concept of the natural law is central to their moral and social analysis, in a way that it is not for the civilians, who tend to relegate this concept to the prolegomena of legal analysis. Furthermore, as we will see in more detail over the next two chapters, the canonists and theologians do consider the natural law to have immediate social consequences in a variety of ways.

Nonetheless, the canonists and theologians, like the civilians, are fully aware that the positive laws of a community can be established only through some form of authoritative enactment. Hence, they do not claim that the natural law taken by itself offers an actual legal code, any more than the civilians consider reason or equity alone to be a sufficient basis for civil law.

In this respect, as in so many others, Gratian's *Decretum* sets the direction for subsequent thought. The first twenty distinctions of the *Decretum* comprise a detailed discussion of the sources for the laws of the church, the ways in which church law can be established or abrogated, the relation between church law and secular law, and related matters, in addition to some rather entertaining digressions. Gratian is the first to state explicitly that a positive law must be promulgated in order to be valid, adding that it must subsequently be confirmed by community observance (D.4, C.3.1).[53]

The natural law sets constraints on what can count as a legitimate positive law, whether in the church or in civil society. Indeed, Gratian places the natural law on a par with Scripture in this respect: "Hence, whatever is considered to be less authoritative than the divine will, or the canonical scriptures or divine laws, the natural law must also be given precedence over it. Therefore, all decrees, whether ecclesiastical or secular, if they can be shown to be contrary to the natural law, are to be completely rejected" (D.9, C.11). At the same time, Gratian and his successors acknowledge that there is a sense in which the natural law may be said to be legitimately altered by positive law, as we will see in Chapter

5. At any rate, while the natural law sets constraints on the establishment of positive law, it does not itself comprise a system of positive laws.

Subsequently, the canonists are careful to distinguish canon law from natural or divine law, and while they admit that there is a sense in which canon law can be said to be divine law, they point out that this is a secondary and qualified usage.[54] The anonymous author of the canonical summa *Et est sciendum* finds it necessary to say that canon law proceeds from God in a more excellent way than does civil law, and yet he does not deny the divine status of the latter (Weigand no. 336).

The theologians also take up the topic of positive law. Albert is the first to offer a definition of positive law, or *lex,* which incorporates the traditional four kinds of law: the natural law, the law of Moses, the law of grace, and the law of the members (that is, the innate tendency to sin, which Paul mentions in Romans 7:23) (*De bono* V 2.1).[55] In order to do so, he synthesizes definitions of positive law drawn from Cicero, Augustine, and Gratian, all of which are interpreted in light of Aristotle's claim that the purpose of law is to make the members of a community good.

Aquinas once again follows the lead of his teacher in developing his own analytic definition of law, a definition, it should be noted, that is meant to comprehend every kind of law, from the eternal law to human legislation (*Summa theologiae* I-II 90). For him, however, the key to the definition of law is not provided by its purpose in making men and women good. Rather, Aquinas emphasizes the character of law as a norm of reason and its orientation toward the good of some community or collective entity (*ST* I-II 90.1,2). At the same time, he points out that not just any rational norm can count as a law; rather, a genuine law can be established only by the community as a whole, or by those individuals who have responsibility for a community (*ST* I-II 90.3).[56] Furthermore, he follows Gratian in saying that a law must be promulgated in order to have force within its community (*ST* I-II 90.4). This brings him to his much-quoted definition of law: "Law is an ordinance of reason directed towards the common good, instituted by one who has responsibility for the community, and promulgated" (*ST* I-II 90.4).

So far, we have been considering the implications of the scholastics' concept of the natural law for their understanding of positive law. After the middle of the thirteenth century, some of the scholastic theologians begin to reflect on the relation of the natural law to quite another kind of law: namely, the eternal law as Augustine understood it. Odon Lottin observes that, among the scholastics, the Franciscans appear to have been the first to develop a systematic account of the eternal law, which we find in the *Summa fratris Alexandri*.[57] A little later, the Dominican theologian Peter of Tarentaise brings together elements from Augustine and pseudo-Dionysus into a second, independent account of the eternal law. It is unclear whether Aquinas is familiar with Peter's account, but there is no doubt that he is familiar with the Franciscan account as set forth in the *Summa fratris Alexandri*.

In the first section, we observed that Augustine emphasizes the authority of the eternal law, while at other points he speaks of it as the ultimate criterion of rationality informing the universe as a whole. These two aspects of the eternal law are explicitly endorsed and brought together in an analytic framework in the *Summa fratris Alexandri*:

> The eternal law can be considered insofar as it concerns good and evil things, or insofar as it concerns good things only. And this latter in two ways, because it can be considered insofar as it concerns good things generally, or to those particular goods which are proper to rational creatures.
>
> With respect to the first rationale, this definition is appropriate: "That I might briefly set forth the idea of the eternal law, it is that by which the just state of affairs exists, so that all things might be in the best possible order." For the eternal law, insofar as it is a governing law, concerns good and evil things, since God both brings about and governs good things, while he does not bring about evil things, but he does govern them. Hence to govern is the general act of this law with respect to good and evil things, and so this is the concept of the law insofar as it concerns these things.
>
> Insofar as it concerns good things in general, whether these are goods of rational or of irrational creatures, this definition is appropriate: "The eternal law is the law of all arts and the law of the omnipotent artificer ..." For insofar as it is the art of an omnipotent artificer, it concerns the divine cause, which is the art and cause of all goods.

But insofar as it concerns the goods proper to the rational creature, this definition is appropriate: "The eternal law is the highest reason, which is always to be obeyed." For the rational creature should be governed by laws. The temporal law is administered by a human being over human beings, and so, since it is appropriate to this law to administer temporal laws, as the definition says, it is agreed that this definition concerns rational creatures. Similarly, by the fact that it says "which is always to be obeyed," it is appropriate for it to concern the rational creature, because this action, that is, "to obey," is proper to the rational creature alone (Summa fratris Alexandri III.II 1.1.3).[58]

The Summa of Alexander maintains the synthesis of authority and reason throughout its subsequent discussion of the eternal law. For example, we read that the eternal law is appropriated to each of the three persons of the Trinity: the Father, in virtue of its authoritative character; the Son, in virtue of its wisdom; and the Spirit, in virtue of its goodness (SFA III-II 1.4).

As Lottin observes, Aquinas' account of the eternal law in the Summa theologiae adopts the topics and the structure of the Franciscan account, almost point for point.[59] At the same time, Aquinas' account emphasizes God's providential reason, and the idea of authority is far less prominent: "Eternal law is nothing other than the reason of divine wisdom, insofar as it directs all acts and motions" (Summa theologiae I-II 93.1). Aquinas appropriates the eternal law to the Second Person of the Trinity, in virtue of the fact that this is the reason, or Word, by which the universe is created and governed; the authority and goodness of the eternal law are assumed, but Aquinas does not underscore them as the SFA does (ST I-II 93.1 ad 2). Temporal laws are derived from the eternal law insofar as they are reasonable and directed to genuinely good ends (ST I-II 93.3); in other words, human authority depends on conformity to God's wisdom, rather than being derived in a juridical fashion from God's authority.

As we have just seen, Aquinas is aware that an adequate theory of law must take account of the authoritative as well as the rational character of law. Indeed, he takes pains to explain how the eternal law may be said to be promulgated, since otherwise it would not be a genuine law by his definition of law (*ST* I-II 91.1 *ad* 2). Nonetheless, in developing his account of the eternal law, it is clear that he is primarily interested in its rational, rather than its authoritative, character.

Why should this be the case? When we place Aquinas' account of the eternal law into the wider context of his work, it becomes apparent that, for him, this account functions as a way of placing the different kinds of law within an overarching theological framework. Lottin observes that just as Aquinas interprets the divine ideas as God's knowledge of the specific forms of creatures, seen as forms of participation in the divine essence, so he understands the eternal law as God's knowledge of creatures seen in relation to God and to the good of the universe as a whole.[60] In other words, for Aquinas the eternal law is God's providential wisdom, directing all things toward their proper fulfilment in union with God, in the way appropriate to each kind of creature. He thus emphasizes Augustine's idea of the eternal law as the supreme ordering principle of the universe, while de-emphasizing Augustine's remarks on the authority of the divine law.

Correlatively, Aquinas understands the natural law to be one expression of the intrinsic principles of operation through which each creature expresses its specific form and arrives at its appropriate form of union with divine goodness. Consider this passage from Aquinas' commentary on pseudo-Dionysius' *The Divine Names,* which comes in the context of an explanation of how God may be said to govern the universe:

> It may happen, however, that some prince, who may be desirable in his own person, will nonetheless give onerous laws to his subjects, which he himself does not keep, and therefore his subjects are not effectively subjected to him. But since this is excluded from God, [Dionysius] adds that he sets *voluntary laws* over *all;* for the law of God is the proper natural inclination placed in every creature to do that which is appropriate to it, in accordance with nature. And therefore, since all things are held by divine desire, so all are held by his law ... (*De Divinis Nominibus* X, 1.1, 857).

Elsewhere, as we have seen, Aquinas claims that only the human person can be said to follow a natural law. Nonetheless, he continues to hold that the natural law represents the distinctively rational form of the

more general processes by which all creatures participate in God's providential wisdom: that is, God's eternal law:

> Hence, since all things which are subject to divine providence
> are governed and given measure by the eternal law, as is plain
> from what has been said, it is clear that all things participate in
> some way in the eternal law, insofar as they receive from it
> inclinations towards their own acts and ends. Among others,
> however, the rational creature is subjected to divine providence
> in a more excellent manner, insofar as he himself is also made a
> participant in providence, being provident for himself and others.
> Hence, in the rational creature there is also a participation in
> eternal reason, through which he has a natural inclination towards
> a due act and end. And this participation of the eternal law in
> the rational creature is called the natural law. (*Summa theologiae*
> I-II 91.2)

As this passage indicates, the claim that the natural law represents the
distinctively human mode of participation in the eternal law implies that
it is also an expression of the principles of action, or the natural inclinations,
proper to the human person. However, these must be pursued in a
properly human fashion: that is, in accordance with reason or virtue
(*Summa contra gentiles* III 129; *Summa theologiae* I-II 94.4 *ad* 3, II-II 108.2).
In this way, Aquinas underscores the connection between human reason
and the natural law while at the same time reminding us of the essential
continuity between the natural law and other forms of participation in
God's providential wisdom.

5. The theological significance
of the natural law

In the last chapter, we observed that the scholastic concept of the
natural law offers us a theology of morality according to which the moral
life is seen both as a natural human phenomenon and as an expression of
God's creative wisdom and goodness. In this chapter, we have extended
our sense of the theological character of this concept by examining the
ways in which it is justified by a particular reading of Scripture, and serves

in turn to provide an interpretative key for understanding Scripture as a moral document.

We are now in a position to appreciate the theological richness and value of the scholastic concept of the natural law. This concept offers us an account of the moral life that is grounded in a defensible interpretation of Scripture and that is therefore cogent as a Christian theology of the moral life. Furthermore, this concept implies distinctive normative commitments, in virtue of which it provides a moral theology, as well as a theology of morality. These include, centrally, commitments to non-maleficence and equality, together with an approach to moral norms that attempts to analyze and apply them in terms of their purposes, understood in terms of natural exigencies and inclinations.

Given the specifically Christian theological character of the scholastic concept of the natural law, at least one traditional theological criticism of natural law theories does not apply to it. That is, it cannot be said that this concept fails to take account of the distinctively scriptural character of Christian ethics. However, it might still be argued that the scholastic concept is not sufficiently scriptural or Christian, because it offers us a concept of morality that is not uniquely Christian. Even granting the distinctiveness of the scholastic concept of the natural law, it still implies a considerable degree of overlap between Christian ethics and secular morality.

It is true that the scholastic concept of the natural law incorporates elements that are not uniquely Christian. Nonetheless, the scholastics were not simply the passive recipients of non-Christian traditions. As we have just seen, they develop the concept of the natural law through a selective reading of the traditions that they received, while at the same time reinterpreting key ideas by placing them in the wider context of Christian doctrine.

Moreover, the question of the distinctiveness of this concept is further complicated by its pervasive influence on subsequent moral reflection. Moral commitments that are so basic to late-twentieth-century Western moral thinking that they now seem self-evident were in fact mediated to modernity through the scholastic concept of the natural law. Given this, it is hardly surprising that there is a considerable degree of overlap between the latter and the common morality of our own day. This fact, taken by itself, does not call the fundamentally Christian character of the scholastic concept of the natural law into question. It may be that our common secular morality is in fact more Christian than either its critics or its defenders are prepared to admit.[61]

Most fundamentally, this line of criticism reflects a potentially destructive confusion between a distinctively or uniquely Christian account of morality and a theologically sound and adequate account of morality. All too often, the two have been confused, as if distinctiveness and theological soundness come to one and the same thing. They do not. It is true that the scholastic concept of the natural law implies continuities and areas of overlap between Christian morality and different forms of secular morality. Yet it does so precisely on theological grounds, including a commitment to the doctrine of creation and correlatively an insistence on the essential unity of revelation in the two Testaments. It is difficult to see how someone could argue for the uniqueness of Christian ethics without falling into corresponding theological errors: that is, failing to take the doctrine of the creation with full seriousness and truncating the scriptural witness to God as the one who creates and sustains the natural world.

At the same time, the distinctively theological character of the natural law as the scholastics understand it does carry with it certain theological presuppositions and implications that not everyone will find acceptable. It presupposes a certain approach to Scripture as a moral document, and it implies a particular assessment of the moral life which is not so unconditionally positive as modern natural law thinking would suggest but that is still more positive than many Christian ethicists today would allow. In this section, I will attempt to draw out and defend these implications of the scholastic concept of the natural law.

In the first section of this chapter, we saw that the scholastic concept of the natural law incorporates a particular reading of Scripture. On this reading, Scripture itself refers to the natural law, most notably in the different formulations of the Golden Rule. At the same time, the concept of the natural law provides a key for dealing with difficult passages, particularly those referring to the so-called "sins of the patriarchs." More generally, the concept of the natural law provides a particular orientation toward the moral teachings of Scripture, on the basis of which some norms are taken as strictly binding commands, others are taken as indications of what is permissible or ideal, and still others are considered to be ceremonial or judicial prescriptions that bind only in a particular time and place.

The obvious objection to this reading of Scripture is that it is incongruent with contemporary biblical scholarship. On some points, this objection is certainly true. For example, the narratives of the sins of the patriarchs do not present the same theological problem for us as they did for the scholastics, because we are more likely to see them as narratives generated by specific cultural forces, whereas the scholastics took them to be straightforward histories. Nonetheless, the scholastic interpretation of Scripture undergirding their concept of natural law is not as inconsistent with contemporary biblical scholarship as one might suppose. Recently, the distinguished Old Testament scholar James Barr has argued that Scripture taken as a whole, including much of the Old Testament as well as some of the Pauline material, presupposes or explicitly commends the view that human beings have some knowledge of God apart from revelation, a view that is tantamount to a kind of natural theology.[62] Natural theology is not quite the same thing as natural law, but Barr's reading at least leaves open the possibility of appealing to Scripture in support of a concept of natural law, as he himself acknowledges.[63] While Barr's interpretation is controversial, at the very least he shows that the scholastic concept of the natural law is defensible as a scriptural concept within the framework of a contemporary reading of Scripture.

This being said, the fact remains that the scholastic interpretation of Scripture in accordance with a particular concept of the natural law is a theologically informed interpretation. The scholastics read the scriptural texts in accordance with a particular set of doctrinal and philosophical commitments, as a result of which certain passages are privileged and others are interpreted in the light of an overall conception of the scriptural message. These commitments include a set of general principles for scriptural interpretation, as well as the particular doctrinal and philosophical presuppositions associated with the concept of the natural law.

I do not intend to defend the scholastic approach to scriptural exegesis in its entirety. Nor do I want to claim that our contemporary understanding of Scripture, painfully developed through more than two centuries of historical-critical biblical scholarship, is invalid or irrelevant to theological reflection. Nonetheless, it does seem to me that any theologically oriented reading of the Scriptures will necessarily be guided by some doctrinal and philosophical presuppositions. As the New Testament scholar Richard Hays says, "The task of hermeneutical appropriation [of Scripture] requires an *integrative act of the imagination*. This is always so, even for those who would like to deny it: with fear and trembling we must work out a life of faithfulness to God through responsive and creative reappropriation of the New Testament in a world far removed from the world of the original writers and readers."[64] Correlatively, anyone who approaches Scripture with the aim of discerning its significance for her own life and the life of the Christian community is already an engaged reader who brings particular concerns and a sense of what is important and relevant to its texts.

These concerns and saliencies, in turn, will be rooted in some individual and communal sense of what is religiously important, together with ideas about how the world works — all of which will be grounded, explicitly or not, in some congeries of particular theological and philosophical views. Hence, the scholastics cannot be criticized simply for the fact that they approach the texts of Scripture from a particular theological and philosophical point of view.

Nor does it count against them that they find references to the natural law in scriptural texts that do not explicitly make any such reference. If we were to limit ourselves doctrinally to what is clearly stated in the texts of Scripture, much of the doctrinal structure of orthodox Christianity would go by the board, including the doctrines of creation *ex nihilo*, the Trinity, and the Incarnation. Moreover, the scholastic interpretation is at least plausible in this respect. The Golden Rule is not explicitly presented in Scripture as a summary of the natural law in any of its formulations, nor are the precepts of the Decalogue said to be a summary of its central precepts. Nonetheless, it makes sense to take these precepts as statements of fundamental moral norms that are both generally known and foundational in the sense that other norms can be derived from them. As Barr observes, "It was easier to exclude natural theology from theology than to exclude natural law from law. The laws of the Hebrew Bible gained some degree of legitimization from their relation to universal principles of morality and right."[65] This is true not only for the classical reformation theologians about whom Barr is speaking at this point, but also for many other interpreters, Jewish as well as Christian.[66]

The scholastic concept of the natural law cannot fairly be said to be non-scriptural, and the reading of Scripture that it implies is not ruled out by the texts themselves, at least not in any obvious way. It does presuppose specific doctrinal commitments, but the same may be said of any theological interpretation of Scripture. It is at this point, however, that a more fundamental objection may be raised. That is, it may be said that the doctrinal commitments that inform this reading of Scripture are themselves flawed.

This objection is implied in Karl Barth's well-known critique of natural theology, which implies a rejection of any version of a natural law theory.[67] On Barth's view, natural theology and natural law are fundamentally flawed for at least two reasons. The first of these is epistemological; we cannot attain reliable knowledge of God's creation, and for this reason, we cannot draw reliable ethical conclusions from our partial and flawed knowledge of the created world. Second, and correlatively, Barth raises a Christological objection: we know only creation, and the demand of God as Creator only in and through our knowledge of Christ. We cannot separate God's will as expressed in creation from his will as expressed in Christ without driving a fundamental wedge between God as Creator and God as Redeemer, and between the human person as created and as redeemed.

What are we to make of these criticisms? The first thing to be noted is that Barth's critique of a natural law ethic must be seen within the context of his wider critique of moral philosophy, seen as a self-contained human enterprise.[68] For Barth, any moral system (whether pre-reflective or philosophical) that claims to offer clear, systematic, and self-contained guidance on matters of good and evil is fundamentally an expression of pride. It presupposes a degree of independent discernment that the human person cannot attain, and it reflects the human desire to attain justification and security independently of God, over against God. And since the only way the human person can stand over against God is through the separation of sin, therefore, ethics is itself the fruit of sin — even, as Barth suggests at one point, the original sin.

These claims are likely to seem problematic to us because we are the heirs of a very different idea of morality, discussed in more detail in the previous chapter, according to which morality is intrinsically transcendent and a locus of human contact with the divine. Seen in the context of this high doctrine of morality, Barth's critique becomes comprehensible; taken as a theological response to this doctrine, I believe it is both profound and persuasive. Nonetheless, the scholastic concept of the natural law does not fall within the scope of this objection, because it is not presented as the deliverance of pure moral reason, nor is it intended as an alternative to religious belief. Rather, it is itself a theological concept, grounded in a particular reading of Scripture.

This brings us to Barth's epistemological critique of the idea of a natural law. It is true that our knowledge of the created world is imperfect. Furthermore, Barth might have also appealed to the fact that there is apparently more than one theory of morality consistent with human nature as we know it, although to my knowledge he did not do so. However, the scholastics do not claim that their account of the natural law can be derived directly from observations of the natural world. They are aware that the facts of human nature and experience must be interpreted in the light of our best theological and philosophical understandings in order to become morally significant. Some of them brought considerable sophistication to this interpretative task; recall, for example, Bonaventure's interpretation of the prohibition against killing in the light of the different aspects of human life, or Philip the Chancellor's analysis of the way considerations introduced at different levels of human nature lead us to reformulate and refine our understanding of the precepts of the natural law.

We have already noted that the scholastics probably did not realize the extent to which the basic moral commitments informing their concept of the natural law are contestable. To the extent that we do recognize this fact, however, we find that it supports the scholastic concept of the natural law over against Barth's criticisms, rather than undermining it. That is, we can see the extent to which the scholastic concept of the natural law represents a theologically informed construal of the moral significance of human nature, as opposed to the simple discovery of a pre-existing moral order. This interpretative construal does not amount to a sheer imposition of Christian morality on a recalcitrant humanity. It draws on elements of human nature that are genuinely there and that can be developed in accordance with a Christian vision of humanity. Nonetheless, the fact remains that the scholastic concept of the natural law depends on a theologically informed construal of human nature that is not the only possible construal of human nature, as we can now more fully appreciate.

Nonetheless, all of this amounts to only a partial answer to Barth's criticism. For him, the fundamental mistake behind any natural law theory, or indeed any attempt to establish a morality apart from theological considerations, lies in the fact that these theories of morality presuppose that it is possible to discern moral goodness apart from God's Word as revealed in Christ. In other words, for Barth, an adequate account of morality must be not only theological but specifically and distinctively Christological.

It is not so clear that the scholastic concept of the natural law meets this more specific criterion for theological adequacy. While the scholastics did situate this concept in an overall theology, for which the person and work of Christ are central, nonetheless it is fair to say that their Christology is not directly formative for their understanding of the natural law. The doctrine of creation has more direct relevance to their concept of natural law than do the Christological doctrines.

Nonetheless, it is worth repeating that this does not mean that the scholastic concept of the natural law is not theological, or even that it is not Christian. The claim that the world is the good creation of one God is hardly trivial; to the contrary, it is hard to think of another doctrine that has been the focus of comparable controversy. Nor should we be misled by the fact that Christians are not alone in affirming the doctrine of creation; a particular belief may be central to a belief-system without being unique to it. If we were to reject the doctrine of the creation, or relegate it to an unimportant prolegomenon to Christianity, we would find it hard to know how to understand those doctrines that are uniquely Christian.

Consider, more specifically, what it would mean to construct a Christology without a doctrine of the creation. What could it mean to speak of an incarnation if we have no sense of God's reality apart from Christ? How can we hope for Christ's redemption without some idea of human goodness to provide the starting points for that hope? Taken to its extreme, an emphasis on Christ without some reference to the doctrine of creation risks a view according to which Christ is a wholly unexpected emissary from an utterly unknowable God — in other words, risks becoming a version of Catharism.

In fact, Barth's emphatic rejection of any kind of moral appeal to nature was rejected by many of his own peers, and it is called into question by some leading theologians who are generally sympathetic to Barth. For example, consider these remarks by Oliver O'Donovan:

> The resurrection of Christ in isolation from mankind would not be a gospel message. The resurrection of mankind apart from creation would be a gospel of a sort, but of a purely gnostic and world-denying sort which is far from the gospel that the apostles actually preached. So the resurrection of Christ directs our attention back to the creation which it vindicates. But we must understand "creation" not merely as the raw material out of which the world as we know it is composed, but as the order and coherence *in* which it is composed. To speak of the resurrection of creation would be meaningless if creation were no more than so much undifferentiated energy. Such a proclamation can have point only as it assures us that the very thing which God has made will continue and flourish. It is not created energy as such that is vindicated in the resurrection of Christ, but the order in which created energy was disposed by the hand of the Creator.[69]

This is not tantamount to an affirmation of a natural ethic, as O'Donovan subsequently insists, nor is it equivalent to the scholastic concept of the natural law.[70] Nonetheless, O'Donovan does show that, even on Barthian terms, there is some place, and indeed some need, for a consideration of something like a natural ethic, precisely in order to safeguard a fully orthodox understanding of the person and work of Christ.

There is one further element of Barth's critique to be considered. That is, it might be said that, even granting the goodness of creation, nonetheless the pervasive realities of human sinfulness have corrupted our moral sense to such a degree that we cannot now arrive at any knowledge of moral truths apart from revelation. In other words, the effects of sin have obviated any appeal to a natural law, even if some such appeal might have been possible in an ideal state of human existence.

The first thing to be said in response to this objection is that the scholastics themselves recognize that human sinfulness has undermined the possibilities for knowledge of the natural law. Indeed, as we will see in Chapter 5, this acknowledgment was incorporated into the concept of the natural law itself, on the basis of which it could account for the ambiguities of human institutions. At the same time, the scholastics also consistently say that human depravity cannot destroy our knowledge of the natural law. Because the natural law is grounded in human nature, knowledge of it cannot be wholly lost so long as human beings continue to exist. If a human being could lose all knowledge of the natural law, he would be altogether alienated from his own humanity, and the scholastics are not prepared to admit that the corruption of sin can extend that far.

The question that remains, however, is just how far actual knowledge of the natural law extends on the scholastic view. It might be argued that the only remnants of that knowledge left to us, apart from revelation or the operations of grace, are so formal in character as to provide little or no actual moral guidance. After all, the scholastics themselves generally insist that, in its primary sense, the natural law consists not of precepts, but of some basic principle of order such as reason or conscience. It might be said that the natural law understood in this sense remains in sinful humanity, but its operations are so weakened and corrupted that they are altogether incapable of proper functioning.

Recently, this line of interpretation has been defended for Aquinas in particular. According to Eugene Rogers, Aquinas holds that sin has completely destroyed the natural law, in such a way that it can have no efficacy apart from grace.[71] The burden of his argument rests on a reading of Aquinas' *Ad Romanos,* but in support, he also cites Aquinas' remark in the prologue of *In duo praecepta caritatis et in decem legis praecepta* that the natural law has been destroyed through the law of concupiscence.[72] This is indeed one of the strongest statements denigrating the natural law that we find in Aquinas, or in the other scholastics we are considering. However, seen in context, even this comment is not so pessimistic as it would at first appear to be:

> The first [law] is called the law of nature, and this is nothing other than the light of the intellect placed in us by God, through which

we know what is to be done and what is to be avoided. God gave this light and this law to the human person at creation. But many believe themselves to be excused through ignorance, if they do not observe this law. But against these the Prophet [i.e., David] says, in Psalm 4.6: "Many say: Who shows us good things?" as if they did not know what is to be done. But he himself, in verse 7, responds, "the light of your countenance has been imprinted upon us" [Ps. 4.6,7]: that is to say, the light of the intellect, through which those things which are to be done are made known to us. For no one is ignorant that he should not do to another that which he does not wish to have done to himself, and other things of that sort.

But granting that God gave this law to the human person in creation, that is, the law of nature, the devil however has sowed another law over it, that is, the law of concupiscence. For so long as the soul in the first human being was subject to God, observing the divine precepts, so also the flesh was subject in all things to the soul, or rather, to reason. But after the devil through his insinuation drew the human person from the observance of the divine precepts, so also the flesh became disobedient to reason. And so it happens that although a person may wish for the good in accordance with reason, however he is inclined to the contrary through concupiscence. And this is what the Apostle says in Romans 7.23: "I see another law in my members, opposed to the law of my mind." And hence it is that frequently [*frequenter*] the law of concupiscence corrupts the law of nature and the order of reason. And therefore the Apostle adds in the same place, "...making me captive by a law of sin, which is in my members."

Because therefore the law of nature had been destroyed through the law of concupiscence, it was necessary that the human person should be brought back to the works of virtue, and withdrawn from the works of vice, and the law of Scripture was necessary for this (*In duo praecepta*, prologue 1).

When Aquinas' comment about the destruction of the natural law is put in its immediate context, we see that it is not as absolute as it might appear at first to be. It is preceded by the observation that the natural law is *frequently* destroyed by concupiscence, and the whole discussion is framed by Aquinas' remark that no one can excuse himself from sin by pleading ignorance of the natural law.

Subsequently, in the *Summa* Aquinas remarks that while the first principles of the natural law cannot be abolished from the human heart, their implications can be obscured by sin, and knowledge of the secondary precepts can be abolished through sin (I-II 94.6). Yet he does not say that this must necessarily happen in every instance, even without grace, or that the obscuring effects of sin will always be thoroughgoing and complete. In his discussion of the necessity for grace, he observes that in our present situation, the human person without grace can do some good, but cannot attain the complete good appropriate to human nature (I-II 109.2). Similarly, he says that under present conditions, a human person without grace cannot fulfill the precepts of the natural law completely, but he does not say that such a one cannot fulfill them at all (I-II 109.4). There is no doubt that Aquinas believes that original and actual sin have greatly damaged our capacities to know and to act upon the moral demands of the natural law, but he does not say that these capacities have been completely destroyed, such that the human person without grace is not capable of any moral knowledge or goodness at all. Indeed, he says that even without grace it is possible to acquire the cardinal virtues in a form suited to the capacities and needs of natural human life, and adds that many among the nations did in fact do so (I-II 65.2; cf. I-II 63.2 *ad* 2). Since the cardinal virtues include justice, which takes its basic normative content from the natural law principles of the Decalogue, this implies that even without grace it is possible to know and observe the natural law, at least in part (II-II 122.1).[73]

Nonetheless, even granting that Aquinas affirms the possibility of genuine moral knowledge and goodness apart from grace, this still leaves a question about the extent of this possibility, for Aquinas or for the scholastics more generally. Let us turn back to a consideration of the more general scholastic view on this question. How far were the scholastics prepared to go in the direction of affirming a universally accessible morality grounded in the natural law? In attempting to answer this question, we are brought up against the fact that the concerns that motivated the scholastics are not altogether congruous with our own. In developing their concept of the natural law, they were not primarily concerned with providing a basis for moral dialogue within a context of cultural pluralism. This is rightly a major concern for contemporary philosophers and theologians, since we are increasingly confronted with the necessity for moral dialogue with others who do not share our cultural presuppositions. For the scholastics, on the other hand, this is not a practical priority. Their main concern is to provide a basis for understanding and rationalizing the laws and customs of their communities since, unlike us, they could not presuppose the existence of a network of stable and comprehensive institutions within their society. When we speak of the natural law, we tend to think of it as a universally shared moral code; when they speak of the moral law, they first of all think in terms of the pre-conventional origins of their own existing laws and customs, understood in terms of universally shared capacities or very general principles of judgment.

Nonetheless, these are not two mutually exclusive approaches to the natural law. Although the scholastics are not primarily concerned with the universality of the natural law considered as a set of moral precepts, they do comment on its universality understood in this sense, and these comments allow us to gather how far they consider the knowledge of the natural law to extend.[74] In the first place, they believe that all human persons share certain fundamental aims and practices, including procreation and the rearing of children and the formation of political communities. Second, they believe that all persons recognize the validity of the basic precepts of the Decalogue, and while they realize that these sometimes call for reflective application, they assume that their practical meaning will be clear in most cases. Finally, they take it for granted that almost all peoples share certain basic legal rules and institutions, namely, the law of nations, although for obvious reasons the civil jurists are more interested in this than the canonists and theologians. All these together comprise a shared moral knowledge that goes beyond the purely formal, even though it still leaves room for considerable diversity in moral beliefs and practices.

Most significantly, the scholastics do not automatically consider the existing diversities among human communities to be the result of sinfulness. It is true that sometimes, a community becomes so corrupted as to pervert the natural law altogether in some particular respect. And so, for example, the scholastics sometimes refer to Caesar's remark that the

Germans of his time considered stealing to be a virtue, rather than a vice (see, for example, Aquinas, *Summa theolgiae* I-II 94.4; the reference is to Caesar's *De bello Gallico*, 6.23). However, it is perhaps significant that no scholastic (to my knowledge) claims that a community might be capable of perverting the natural law in every respect while still continuing to function as a community. At any rate, the example of the Germans is not treated as if it were typical. Usually the diversity of human laws and practices is explained by an appeal to different needs and preferences, with no suggestion that these are somehow sinful or corrupt. Hence, the scholastics are prepared to admit that the mores of other communities are expressions of the same natural law that undergirded the mores of their own society, even though they do not attempt to draw out the implications of this view.[75] In addition, the scriptural passages discussed under the rubric of the "sins of the patriarchs" made it clear that there has been some degree of change over time with respect to standards of acceptable sexual behavior.

For the scholastics, therefore, the diversity of practices found among the communities of humankind, both historically and in the present, cannot be dismissed just as expressions of sinfulness. Customs and laws may be sinful in specific cases, of course, but the scholastics do not assume the sinfulness of those ways of life different from their own. This may seem like a modest concession, but it is nonetheless important in principle. By acknowledging the legitimacy of diverse human practices, the scholastics affirm that human diversity is intelligible as an expression of an underlying nature, and for that very reason, it is good in principle.

Christian theology stands in need of a category of natural goodness apart from Christian revelation or grace. Without some such category, it is impossible to preserve the doctrine of the creation, except as a bare abstraction; this means that we cannot hold onto the idea of Christ as Redeemer either. The scholastic concept of the natural law is one way of giving social expression to that affirmation, and therefore to the fundamental doctrinal commitments of Christianity.

Notes to Chapter 3

1   As we noted in the last chapter, Germain Grisez, John Finnis, and their collaborators emphasize that our knowledge of the natural law depends on reason alone, and the same is true of most other Catholic defenders of a natural law ethic. At the same time, Grisez also says that revelation specifies the content of the natural law in ways that could not have been foreseen in advance, although the rational character of the resultant norms can be grasped *post factum*; see *The Way of The Lord Jesus, Vol. 10: Christian Moral Principles* (Chicago: Franciscan Herald Press, 1983), 599-626.

2   The most important statement of these classical Protestant criticisms in this century is undoubtedly that of Karl Barth, whose views will be considered in more detail below. Among our own contemporaries, the most influential critic of natural law theories along these lines is undoubtedly Stanley Hauerwas; see in particular his *The Peaceable Kingdom: A Primer in Christian Ethics* (Notre Dame, IN: University of Notre Dame Press, 1983), 50-71.

3   Philippe Delhaye, *Permanence du Droit Naturel* (Louvain: Editions Nauwelaerts, 1960), 66-84.

4   So far as I have been able to determine, most of the specific components of the scholastic concept of the natural law are anticipated in classical sources, even the motif of reason as a reflection of the divine image; see Richard Horsley, "The Law of Nature in Philo and Cicero," *Harvard Theological Review* 71 (1978), 35-59 at 55.

5   This is, of course, a controversial claim. In his *Biblical Faith and Natural Theology*, after surveying the preceding debate, James Barr argues that Paul draws on a distinctively Jewish natural theology which incorporates Stoic elements; see *Biblical Faith and Natural Theology* (Oxford: Clarendon Press, 1993), 21-57. Crowe comes to a similar conclusion; see *The Changing Profile of the Natural Law* (The Hague, Netherlands: Martinus Nijhoff, 1977), 52-56.

6   On Origen's continuity with Cicero and Philo, see "The Law of Nature in Philo and Cicero," 39; for the observation that the idea of natural law was a patristic commonplace, see R.W. and A.J. Carlyle, *A History of Medieval Political Theory in the West*, 6 volumes (Blackwood and Sons, 1903-36, repr. 1970), Vol. 1, 103. The following paragraph is dependent on *ibid.* 102-110, except where otherwise noted.

7   I owe the latter point to Odon Lottin, "Syndérèse et conscience aux XII et XIII siecles," in *Psychologie et Morale aux XII et XIII siècles, Vol. 2: Problèmes de Morale, Première Part*, (Louvain: Abbaye du Mont César, 1948; six volumes published between 1942-1960), 103-379 at 103-104.

8   This is the same Gloss that later came to be attributed, wrongly, to Walafrid Strabo (d. 849). For a comprehensive account of the formation of the Gloss and its later significance, see Beryl Smalley, *The Study of the Bible in the Middle Ages* (1952; repr. Notre Dame, IN: University of Notre Dame Press, 1964), 46-65.

9   P. Alois Schubert, S.V.D., *Augustins Lex-Aeterna-Lehre Nach Inhalt und Quellen, Beiträge sur Geschichte der Philosophie des Mittelalters*, 24, 2 (Munster, i.W., 1924), 3. My account of Augustine's doctrine of the eternal law and its relation to the natural law closely follows Schubert, *ibid.*, 1-20. In addition, see Delhaye, *Permanence du Droit Naturel*, 53-65; Crowe, *The Changing Profile of the Natural Law*, 62-66; and Marcia Colish, *The Stoic Tradition from Antiquity to the Early Middle Ages*, two volumes (Leiden: Brill, 1990), vol. 2, 159-165.

10   Delhaye places particular emphasis upon this latter point; see *Permanence du Droit Naturel*, 53-56.

11   As Lottin points out; see "Syndérèse et conscience," 105-106.

12   As Crowe observes; see *The Changing Profile of the Natural Law*, 113-114. John Marenbon offers an excellent discussion of Abelard's concept of the natural law in *The Philosophy of Peter Abelard* (Cambridge: Cambridge University Press, 1997), 267-272.

13   Winthrop Wetherbee, "Philosophy, Cosmology and the Twelfth-century Renaissance," 21-53 in Dronke, ed., *A History of Twelfth-Century Western Philosophy* (Cambridge: Cambridge University Press, 1988), 39.

14   *Ibid.*

15   All translations of Gratian are my own. However, I checked my translations against Augustine Thompson's; see *Gratian: The Treatise on Laws (Decretum DD. 1-20), with the Ordinary Gloss*, Augustine Thompson, translator of Gratian, and James Gordley, translator of the Gloss, with an introduction by Katherine Christensen (Washington, D.C.: Catholic University of America Press, 1993). I also consulted the vocabulary notes of Justinian's *Institutes*, Peter Birks and Grant McLeod, trans. (Ithaca, NY: Cornell University Press, 1987), 148-157, for guidance in translating some of Gratian's technical legal language.

16   Odon Lottin, *Le droit naturel chez saint Thomas d'Aquin et ses prédécesseurs*, 2nd ed. (Bruges: Beyart, 1931), 11.

17   Crowe, *The Changing Profile of the Natural Law*, 81. Compare Grabmann's disparaging comments in "Das Naturrecht der Scholastik von Gratian bis Thomas von Aquin," in Vol. I of *Mittelalterliches Geistesleben: Abhandlungen zur Geschichte der Scholastic und Mystik*. München: Hueber, three volumes, 1926), 65-103 at 69, and Brian Tierney's similar remarks in *The Idea of Natural Rights: Studies on Natural Rights, Natural Law and Church Law, 1150-1625* (Atlanta: Scholars Press, 1997), 58-60. D.E. Luscombe and G.R. Evans suggest that Gratian equates divine and natural law, because he equates God and nature; see "The Twelfth-Century Renaissance," 306-340 in *The Cambridge History of Medieval Political Thought, c. 350-c. 1450*, J.H. Burns, ed. (Cambridge: Cambridge University Press, 1988), 335. But Gratian does not appeal to the formula *natura id est Deus* in support of his definition. Yves Congar offers a more sympathetic and accurate appraisal in his "Jus divinum," in *Église et Papauté: Regards historiques* (Paris: Cerf, 1994), 65-80 at 66-67.

18   In my discussion of Gratian's work, I rely especially on James A. Brundage, *Medieval Canon Law* (London: Longman, 1995), 44-69; Katherine Christensen, "Introduction," in *Gratian: The Treatise on Laws*, ix-xxvii; and R. W. Southern, *Scholastic Humanism and the Unification of Europe, Vol. I: Foundations* (Oxford: Blackwell, 1995), 283-318.

19   This is so, even if we agree with Crowe that Isidore rejects Ulpian's definition of the natural law as that which nature teaches all animals. Certainly, Isidore does not follow Ulpian on this particular point; that is, he does not claim that the natural law is shared with the rest of the animal kingdom. However, this does not necessarily mean that he would have rejected Ulpian's definition *tout court*. At any rate, there is no doubt that Isidore draws on the same sources as the *Digest*, and may have been familiar with it directly, as Crowe points out. See *The Changing Profile of the Natural Law*, 69-70.

20   Delhaye, *Permanence du Droit Naturel*, 69.

21   See Congar, "Jus divinum," 65-70, on this point.

22   The canonist Rufin gives particular emphasis to this point; see Weigand no. 236-240. Others who point out the corrective function of the Mosaic law include the anonymous *Tractaturus magister*, Weigand no. 330, the anonymous author cited by Lottin 124, and Aquinas, *Summa theologiae* I-II 94.4.

     Delhaye claims that Rufin intends his analysis of the natural law to be a refutation of the civilian understanding; see *Permanence du Droit Naturel*, 69-70. But Rufin does not present it in this way. He prefaces his analysis with the remark that the natural law may be understood in a more general sense as that which nature teaches all animals, and then goes on to explain that he is concerned with the natural law understood in a distinctively human sense (Weigand no. 236). This was a commonplace distinction and does not imply that the more general understanding of the natural law is invalid.

23   Among the canonists, other examples of this general line of interpretation include Odo of Dover, Weigand no. 274, the *Summa reginensis*, Weigand no. 383, and Lawrence of Spain, Weigand no. 434.

24   See John F. Dedek, "Premarital Sex: The Theological Argument from Peter Lombard to Durand," *Theological Studies* 41 (1980), 643-667, for a good example of this viewpoint.

25   As Crowe points out in *The Changing Profile of the Natural Law*, 82-83.

26   Nearly every canonist and theologian that I have examined cites the Golden Rule as one of the possible meanings of the natural law, and most of them add the Decalogue as well. This interpretation is not as common among the civilians, but it may be found there too; examples include Henry of Balia, Weigand no. 60, Acursius, Weigand no. 87, and Azo, Weigand no. 82-83.

27   See Jeremy Cohen, *"Be Fertile and Increase, Fill the Earth and Master It": The Ancient and Medieval Career of a Biblical Text* (Ithaca, NY: Cornell University Press, 1989), 277-279.

28   We have already noted that William of Auxerre grounds knowledge of the natural law in the contemplation of the divine image within each human soul; see the *Summa aurea* III 18.4. For other examples of a connection between the natural law and the image of God motif, see John Faventinus, Weigand no. 254, the anonymous author of the *Summa tractaturus magister*, Weigand no. 338, Bonaventure, *De Per. Evan.* IV 1 *ad* 4, and Aquinas, *Summa theologiae* II-II 66.1.

29   For an overview of the scholastic approach to scriptural exegesis, see Smalley, *The Study of the Bible in the Middle Ages,* 264-355, and Southern, *Scholastic Humanism and the Unification of Europe,* 102-133.

30   The text cited may be found in *Gratian: The Treatise on Laws, with the Ordinary Gloss,* 21- 22. There are numerous examples of this approach among the canonists; see, for example, Rufin, Weigand no. 243, Odo of Dover, Weigand no. 274, and the summae *Inter cetera, Tractaturus magister,* and *Cologne* (Weigand no. 286, 321-2, and Lottin 105-106, respectively). Among the theologians see, for example, John of la Rochelle, Lottin 120-121.

31   Dedek's "Premarital Sex" offers a good example of this approach. We also find it in Crowe's treatment of the canonists; see *The Changing Profile of the Natural Law,* 72- 110; compare Crowe's remark that "despite the rationalism with which he is often credited, Abelard shared his contemporaries' inability to distinguish unequivocally between the natural law and the divine revealed law." *Ibid.,* 114.

32   For an influential example of this line of criticism, see Charles Curran, "Natural Law in Moral Theology," in Charles E. Curran and Richard McCormick, eds., *Readings in Moral Theology No. 7: Natural Law and Theology* (New York: Paulist Press, 1991), 247-295.

33   For example, we find this view in both Bonaventure (*In II Sent.* 39.1.2) and in Aquinas (*Summa theologiae* I-II 100.3).

34   More specifically, Albert claims in the *Super Ethica* (V 9 419.35ff) that Aristotle's natural justice is equivalent to the natural law as Cicero defines it, and Aquinas interprets it as being equivalent to the jurists' law (or right) of nature and the law of nations taken together, both in his *Ethicorum* (V 1.12, 1019) and in the *Summa theologiae* (II-II 57.3). For the latter's repudiation of Aristotle's doctrine of natural inequality, see the *Summa theologiae* II-II 47.12.

35   John Casey, *Pagan Virtue: An Essay in Ethics* (Oxford: Clarendon Press, 1990), 9. Other philosophers have also recently called attention to the contingency and the specifically religious or Christian character of what we usually take to be common morality, including Derek Parfit, *Reasons and Persons* (Oxford: Oxford University Press, 1984, repr. with corrections, 1984, 1986, 1987, 1989), 443-454, and Bernard Williams, *Ethics and the Limits of Philosophy* (Cambridge, MA: Harvard University Press, 1985), 174-196.

36   Casey, *Pagan Virtue*, 81-82, emphasis in the original. Casey quotes Nietzsche, *Beyond Good and Evil*, sect. 208.

37   Casey appears to recognize this; see *Pagan Virtue*, 91-93.

38   Once again, I rely on Smalley and especially Southern for my account of the scholastic approach to Scripture; see above, note 28.

39   Southern, *Scholastic Humanism and the Unification of Europe*, 152-162.

40   *Gratian: The Treatise on Laws with the Ordinary Gloss*, 48.

41   *Ibid.*, 49.

42   *Ibid.*, 49.

43   This discussion has been examined by John Dedek in two highly influential articles: "Moral Absolutes in the Predecessors of St. Thomas," *Theological Studies* 38 (1977), 654-80 and "Intrinsically Evil Acts: An Historical Study of the Mind of St. Thomas," *The Thomist* 43 (1979), 385-413. Dedek's overall aim in these articles is to show that the scholastics do not have the same understanding of intrinsically evil actions as we find in later Roman Catholic moral theology, and he succeeds in doing so. However, in my view he is too quick to assume that the same concerns are driving the scholastic and contemporary discussions.

44   We usually associate this distinction with Abelard, but as Giles Constable shows, he was far from the only twelfth-century theologian to stress the importance of intention and inwardness; see *The Reformation of the Twelfth Century* (Cambridge: Cambridge University Press, 1996), 257-295. Marenbon offers a good account of Abelard's doctrine of intention seen in this context in *The Philosophy of Peter Abelard*, 251-264.

45   Similar arguments are offered by Hugh of St. Cher, Lottin 116, and Bonaventure, *Brev.* II.11.

      How do we know that the reference to writing indicates scriptural natural law, as opposed to human positive law? Augustine contrasts the natural law written in the heart with its reformulation in the written law of Moses (see, for example, *Ennar in Ps. 57*, 1), and similarly, the scholastics appear to have used the expression, "written law" as a shorthand for the natural law as contained in the Old Testament. See, for example, the *Cologne summa*, Lottin 106, and Bonaventure, *de Per. Evan.* IV.1, conclusion.

46   It is interesting to compare Aquinas and Albert with the decretalist Raymond of Peñafort, who states that the precepts of the natural law can be interpreted by the Pope – a restriction that neither Albert nor Aquinas mentions. See Raymond's *Summa Juris* I.10.

47   The scope of this book does not permit a discussion of later scholastic voluntarism, but it should be noted that this is a more complex and nuanced position than is generally realized. See Bonnie Kent, *Virtues of the Will: The Transformation of Ethics in the Late Thirteenth Century* (Washington, D.C. : Catholic University Press, 1995),

94-149, for an illuminating discussion of this view, seen in relation to the positions of Aquinas, Bonaventure, and other authors considered in this study.

48   This is not simply a coincidence or the expression of a general cultural influence. As Jerome Schneewind shows, Kant was deeply influenced by the modern natural lawyers, and to a considerable degree he made their issues his own; see Schneewind's "Kant and Natural Law Ethics," *Ethics* 104 (October 1993), 53-74.

49   For a recent example of someone who commends the natural law tradition (as expressed by Aquinas) on these grounds, see Alasdair MacIntyre, "Natural Law as Subversive: The Case of Aquinas," *Journal of Medieval and Early Modern Studies* 26,1 (Winter, 1996), 61-83.

50   This is MacIntyre's central contention in "Natural Law as Subversive"; for another example, see Hendrik Spruyt, *The Sovereign State and Its Competitors: An Analysis of Systems Change* (Princeton, NJ: Princeton University Press, 1994), 103. I do not challenge MacIntyre's and Spruyt's interpretation of the royal conception of law; nonetheless, their contrasting view of Aquinas, and by implication other scholastics, is at best misleading.

51   The canonist William of Gascony says the same thing; see Weigand no. 398.

52   As Paul Vinogradoff points out, the *Exceptiones Petri* is interesting for more than one reason. It indicates that there was some systematic study of secular jurisprudence in southern France in the eleventh century independently of the great center for legal studies which emerged in Bologna towards the end of that century. It also reflects the practical significance of these studies, since it is dedicated to one Odilio, a magistrate of Valence in Dauphine, for the express purpose of guiding him in the exercise of his office. See *Roman Law in Medieval Europe*, 2nd ed. (Oxford: Clarendon Press, 1929), 44-48; the whole chapter, "Revival of Jurisprudence," 43-70, is indispensable for understanding the emergence and the social impact of secular jurisprudence in the late eleventh century.

53   I take the observation that Gratian was the first to make this claim from Lottin, "La loi en Général: La Définition Thomiste et ses Antécédents," 11-47 in *Psychologie et Morale aux XII et XIII siècles, Vol. 2: Problèmes de Morale, Première Part* (Louvain: Abbaye du Mont César, 1948), 13.

54   See, for example, the *Summa inter cetera*, Weigand no. 287-290, a and b, Sicard of Cremona, Weigand no. 316, Honorius, Weigand no. 351, and the *Cologne Summa*, Lottin 105-106.

55   As Lottin points out in "La Loi en général," 22.

56   MacIntyre is therefore at best seriously misleading when he says, in "Natural Law as Subversive," that for Aquinas, "authority as to what the law is, on fundamentals at least, rests with plain persons and that the most important things that lawyers and administrators know about law, they know as plain persons and not as lawyers and administrators ...," 69.

57 See Lottin, "La Loi éternelle chez saint Thomas d'Aquin et ses prédécesseurs," in *Psychologie et Morale, Vol. 2,* 51-67. For his discussion of Peter of Tarentaise, see 58-63.

58 The three definitions are all taken from Augustine's writings, namely, *De libero arbitrio* I 6.15; *De vere religione* 30.56; and *De lib. Arb.* VI 15. All three are cited and discussed above.

59 Lottin, "La Loi éternelle," 64.

60 Lottin, "La Loi en général," 35.

61 However, some contemporary philosophers do recognize this. For Casey, Parfit, and Williams, the distinctively Christian character of Western morality is a historical accident which can and should be left behind. On the other hand, Alan Donagan affirms the essential congruity between common morality and the "Judaeo-Christian ethic" in his *The Theory of Morality* (Chicago: University of Chicago Press, 1977), but he explains it by construing these as expressions of a universally valid practical reason.

62 James Barr, *Biblical Faith and Natural Theology* (Oxford: Clarendon Press, 1993); see in particular 21-102 and 156-173.

63 *Ibid.,* 101.

64 Richard Hays, *The Moral Vision of the New Testament: A Contemporary Introduction to New Testament Ethics* (San Francisco: HarperCollins, 1996), 6; emphasis in the original. However, I do not want to imply that Hays would agree with the specific interpretative strategy being suggested here; on the contrary, I suspect he would not. Compare his own discussion of non-violence as a Christian norm, 317-346.

65 *Ibid.* This remark culminates a discussion of the Hebrew Law of the Pentateuch which emphasizes its congruity with a natural law; see 95-101.

66 *Biblical Faith and Natural Theology,* 100-101.

67 Barth develops his criticisms of natural theology throughout his writings; for his critique of natural law in particular, see Karl Barth, *Church Dogmatics, Vol. II, Part 2,* G.W. Bromiley, *et al,* trans. (Edinburgh: T. and T. Clark, 1957), 528-535. In my summary of Barth's arguments, I rely on Nigel Biggar, *The Hastening That Waits: Karl Barth's Ethics,* paperback edition with new conclusion (Oxford: Clarendon Press, 1995), 53-56.

68 In what follows, I rely on Biggar, *The Hastening That Waits,* 7-45, for my understanding of Barth's rejection of ethics.

69 Oliver O'Donovan, *Resurrection and Moral Order: An Outline for Evangelical Ethics* (Grand Rapids, MI: Eerdmans, 1986), 31; emphasis in the original.

70 Oliver O'Donovan, *The Desire of the Nations: Rediscovering the Roots of Political Theology* (Cambridge: Cambridge University Press, 1996), 19. Actually, I believe that O'Donovan is too sanguine about discovering *the* moral order which God has

inscribed in creation; for example, note his statement that "The way the universe *is* determines how man *ought* to behave himself in it," *Resurrection and Moral Order* 17 (emphasis in original). The scholastics themselves would not have made a claim quite as strong as that.

71   Eugene F. Rogers, Jr., "The Narrative of Natural Law in Aquinas's Commentary on Romans 1," *Theological Studies* 59.2 (June, 1998), 254-276.

72   "The Narrative of Natural Law," 269.

73   This does not mean that they were able thereby to save themselves, but for Aquinas, the human person could not have attained salvation through moral action alone, without grace, even in a state of uncorrupted nature; see the *Summa theologiae* I-II 109.5.

74   For examples of the claim that the natural law is universally known, see Odo of Dover, Weigand no. 271; the *Summa inter cetera*, Weigand no. 284; and Cardinal Laborans, Weigand no. 312. Egidius, the *Summa tractaturus magister*, Richard de Mores, and Simon of Bisiano all point out that the natural law is not charity, since the former is found in all persons whereas the latter is found only in the good; see Weigand no. 298, 330, and 365 and Lottin 106. However, the canonical *Distinctio Est jus naturale* does include charity among the accepted meanings of "natural law"; see Weigand no. 345.

75   On this point see Ewart Lewis, "Natural Law and Expediency in Medieval Political Theory," *Ethics* 50 (1940), 144-63.

Chapter 4

Marriage
and Sexual Ethics

Summary: The test of any moral concept lies in its application. This chapter examines the way the scholastics applied their concept of the natural law to questions of sexual ethics, deferring a consideration of their social ethic to the next chapter. As is well known, the scholastics inherited and extended a tradition of thought that was deeply ambivalent toward sexuality; yet through the process of developing a sexual ethic out of their concept of the natural law, they were led to rethink their initial hostility toward sexual pleasure. Toward the end of the period we are considering, some of them at least affirmed the goodness of sexual pleasure in its appropriate context. They see marriage as a practice incorporating both natural and conventional elements, and they follow the lead of earlier church reformers in insisting that it provides the only morally legitimate context for sexual activity. At the same time, they strongly defend the freedom of all persons to marry, and they develop a limited yet socially efficacious doctrine of the equality of the sexes. The last two sections consider the contemporary implications of the scholastic sexual ethic. This consideration begins with a defense of the scholastic commitment to the goodness of creation, and more specifically to the goodness of marriage and procreation as practical implications of this commitment. However, it is argued that today, these commitments should be expressed in terms of communally affirmed ideals for sexual behavior, and not values that must necessarily be attained in every sexual relationship, or much less every sexual act. Finally, the last section applies this approach to questions having to do with contraception, artificially-assisted reproduction, and homosexuality.

■

The scholastic concept of the natural law is associated above all with a particular sexual ethic, and it cannot be said that this association has enhanced its appeal. As Mark Jordan remarks, for us the medieval view according to which sexual activity should be linked to a procreative purpose "seems at best quaint, at worse tyrannical."[1] Even those who are most sympathetic to medieval moral thought consider the scholastic sexual ethic an aberration to be explained away. Commentators on Aquinas routinely lament the fact that he did not develop an enlightened sexual ethic. This failure is blamed variously on the influence of Ulpian's definition of the natural law, on Augustine, or on Aquinas' own failure to follow through on the radical implications of his overall theology.[2] The sexual ethic of other scholastic authors is generally not discussed by contemporary theologians and philosophers, not even to be deplored.

This reaction to the sexual ethic proposed by the scholastics is understandable. Many (but not all) of the scholastics hold a view of sexuality according to which sexual pleasure is a corruption of nature and the pursuit of such pleasure is always more or less sinful. This pessimistic view is not balanced by a clear sense that sexuality might also provide a medium for interpersonal communication and love, even though we find tantalizing hints of such a claim in some authors in this period. Given their overall view of sexuality, it is no surprise to find that they condemn any form of sexual activity outside marriage. Even within marriage, sex for any purpose other than procreation is at least suspect for them. Although a closer examination will reveal unsuspected points of contact between the scholastic understanding of marriage and our own, the fact remains that their sexual ethic is strikingly different from that of the majority in the industrialized West.

Yet it would be a mistake to equate the scholastic concept of the natural law with this sexual ethic, as if the scholastics had no interest in social and political issues. On the contrary, as we will see in more detail in the next chapter, they developed a strikingly sophisticated analysis of social relations. Moreover, this analysis includes the institution of marriage, which is seen by the scholastics as incorporating both natural and conventional elements. To some extent, therefore, the scholastics present marriage itself as an expression of human rationality. This might seem to provide a basis for a retrieval of the scholastic concept of the natural law that avoids the more problematic elements of its sexual ethic.

A retrieval along these lines, however, would result in a truncated and finally uninteresting variant of the scholastic concept of the natural law. It would be truncated in much the same way as would be a version that excised the theological elements of the scholastic concept. That is, it would involve stripping away elements of the scholastic concept that are central for the scholastics themselves and that are thus necessary for its overall coherence. For the scholastics, human reason is grounded in those aspects of our nature that we share with the animals, and these pre-rational components of our nature place constraints on the legitimate exercise of human reason. More fundamentally, the pre-rational dimensions of human nature provide reason with its starting points and give it shape and direction. While it is true that the scholastic concept of the natural law gives a central place to reason, this must be interpreted in the light of the fact that for the scholastics, reason and nature are not set in opposition to one another.

Precisely because they are aware of the importance of the pre-rational in the overall constitution of human nature, the scholastics give a central place to an ethic of sexuality in developing their concept of the natural law. In addition, the sexual ethic developed by the scholastics is central to their theological interpretation of the natural law. Their interpretation of the purposes of sexuality, which now seems uncritical or arbitrary, is in fact a theological judgment, formulated and defended in the face of serious doctrinal challenges to Christian orthodoxy. Modern interpreters tend to overlook this fact, or to miss its significance, because we generally assume that any theory of the natural law must be non-theological in its basic structure.[3] We have already seen how far this is from the scholastic understanding of the natural law.

We must keep in mind the presuppositions and the point of the scholastic sexual ethic when we consider its relevance for contemporary

Christian ethics. It would be possible to reformulate this concept in terms of a purely rationalistic ethic, but this strategy would systematically eliminate those aspects of scholastic moral thought that are potentially of the greatest contemporary interest, including the scholastics' recognition of the moral significance of the pre-rational aspects of our nature and their transformation of the natural law tradition into a theologically sophisticated Christian ethic.

Does it follow that we should adopt scholastic sexual ethics in its entirety? As I will argue below, it is possible to develop a critical reappropriation of the natural law that preserves the central scholastic insights into the human and theological significance of sexuality while also allowing for subsequent developments in our understanding of what counts as natural and appropriate in sexual relations. In order to do so, however, it will first be necessary to arrive at a clearer sense of what those insights are.

1. Sexuality in the scholastic concept of the natural law

The scholastics' sexual ethic is fundamentally an ethic for marriage, since on their view marriage provides the only legitimate context for sexual expression. The scholastic understanding of marriage, in turn, is grounded in their concept of the natural law and follows a familiar pattern, according to which marriage incorporates both natural and conventional elements. More specifically, marriage is the distinctively human expression of a tendency that we share with the animals, namely, the inclination to reproduce one's kind. For this reason, it cannot be understood solely in terms of the exigencies of the reproductive process, nor is it only an expression of human sexuality more broadly considered. At the same time, the scholastics believe that sexuality is intrinsically purposeful, in such a way as to set limits on appropriate forms of sexual expression even within marriage.[4]

However, marriage and sexuality raise distinctive problems for the scholastic concept of the natural law. As we saw in Chapter 2, one of the basic assumptions informing this concept and giving it normative purchase is the goodness of nature, with its implication that any expression of a natural inclination is *prima facie* good. Yet at least some kinds of sexual sins, namely those involving the usual form of heterosexual intercourse, appear to be expressions of a natural impulse, and this raises a problem for the scholastics. As we will see, some of the scholastics address this problem by distinguishing between those aspects of human sexuality that are genuinely natural and those that are not. Yet this solution generates further difficulties of its own, and it is increasingly rejected in favor of an analysis that focuses on appropriate and inappropriate expressions of human sexuality.

In this way, the logic of their concept of the natural law draws the scholastics into reflection on human sexual experience, and this in turn informs their views on sexual ethics generally and on marriage in particular. Here we see an important counter-example to the criticism that the scholastics attempted to derive moral conclusions from a fixed account of human nature; with respect to sexuality, the scholastics are led through their moral reflections to modify their understanding of human nature, in a way that finally acknowledges the goodness of sexual desire.

At the same time, the scholastics do not undertake their analysis of sexuality *de novo*; rather, this analysis should be seen as a continuation of attitudes toward sexuality that were deeply ingrained in Western culture by the beginning of the twelfth century. These attitudes reflected a deep antipathy toward sexual pleasure, together with a sense that sexual activity is fundamentally incompatible with spirituality, and not a little misogyny.[5] This negative view of sex is pre-Christian in origin, and appears to be rooted in a Stoic view that the wise person will engage in sexual acts only for the sake of procreation. At the same time, many Christian thinkers in late antiquity were remarkably vehement in their denunciations of sexual vice and their suspicion of sexual activity even between spouses.

The generally negative view toward sexuality that prevailed throughout much of the patristic period is reinforced by the dualistic cosmologies prevalent at the time since, according to these cosmologies, the material world in all its manifestations is in the most literal sense God-forsaken. Yet, the attraction of dualism and its attendant rejection of marriage served, perhaps paradoxically, to preserve a sense of the fundamental goodness of marriage among Christians.[6] Because the dualistic world-views current in late antiquity implied a rejection of procreation, a positive view of marriage became a test of Christian orthodoxy. From this point, however deep the suspicion of sexuality might run in particular Christian theologians, it would not lead to a rejection of the married state as a legitimate (albeit flawed, or less perfect) form of the Christian life. The early Christian attitude toward marriage and sexuality thus combined a fundamental affirmation of the goodness of marriage with an antipathy toward sexual activity, even within marriage, much less outside it.

This general attitude deepened and hardened in the early medieval period, as moral reflection and pastoral care were increasingly taken over by monks. As John Noonan points out, the monastic authors of the penitential manuals translated the complex and nuanced patristic sexual ethic into a codified system of offenses and penances, in the process reinforcing its rigorism and obscuring the theological framework that had provided it with a context.[7]

In the latter part of the eleventh century, the institutional church sought to consolidate its control over marriage, and as a result theologians increasingly turned their attention to Augustine's claim that marriage is a sacrament, a means of grace. Clearly, this view lent support to the ecclesiastical control of marriage, but by the same token, it made it increasingly difficult to denigrate marriage as incompatible with the spiritual life. At the same time, theologians began to speak of the personal bond, or the love, between spouses as a positive value. Bonaventure goes so far as to say that the love between the spouses is a sacrament of the relationship between God and the soul (*In IV sent.* 33.1.2).[8] Nonetheless, this positive valuation of marriage did not lead to a reassessment of sexual activity, even within marriage, and in the early twelfth century only Peter Abelard defended the view that sexual pleasure is fully natural and innocent in itself.[9] A little later, Peter Lombard reaffirmed Augustine's view that sexual intercourse is evil except within marriage, together with his claim that marriage is justified by a threefold good: the faithfulness of the spouses, children, and the sacramental bond between the spouses (IV *Sentences* 26.2). Owing to Peter Lombard's authority, this view of sexuality and marriage was formative for subsequent scholastic theology.[10]

As we have already observed, European society in the later eleventh century also began to experience the resurgence of dualistic movements, particularly Catharism, which denied the goodness of marriage and especially of procreation.[11] In addition, adherents to these movements were widely believed, fairly or not, to engage in sexual license and homosexual practices. In response, Christian theologians insisted all the more strongly on the goodness of marriage and procreation, arguing at the same time that non–procreative sexual acts are unnatural in the pejorative sense. The movement for the establishment of clerical celibacy that began in the late eleventh century may also have reinforced a sense of the dangers of unnatural sexuality, meaning in this context primarily male masturbation and homosexuality.[12]

By the middle of the twelfth century, therefore, Christian attitudes toward marriage had begun to move in a more positive direction, but sexual activity even within marriage was still viewed with suspicion and the pursuit of sexual pleasure outside marriage was universally condemned. Given these views, it is hardly surprising that the scholastics unanimously condemn any form of sexual expression apart from heterosexual intercourse as unnatural, in a specifically pejorative sense. Masturbation, homosexual intercourse, bestiality, and even non–procreative practices between man and woman are all condemned by them as gravely sinful. Indeed, these are the most grievous of sexual sins, because they usurp the order of sexuality established by God.

On the other hand, sexual sins involving ordinary heterosexual intercourse do seem to be natural acts. The scholastics are divided in their approach to this problem. For most of the canonists and some of the theologians, the pursuit of sexual pleasure outside marriage is sinful because sexual pleasure itself is not part of nature, at least as originally constituted; rather, it reflects the distorting effects of sinfulness.[13] On this view, even seemingly natural sexual intercourse outside marriage is unnatural in the sense of contravening the purpose of sexuality:

To have sexual relations with another for the sake of the preservation of the species, and to have sexual relations with another on account of one's pleasure, are opposite ends; the first is in accordance with the intention of nature, and the second is against the intention of nature; and if the preservation of the species should come about by an act of this [latter] kind, nonetheless, it is not in accordance with the intention of nature, but of libidinous pleasure. Hence, to command that someone should fornicate is not appropriate to God, because there is an end contained in adultery which is opposed to the intention of nature (Philip the Chancellor, Lottin 113).

This analysis is consistent with the scholastic view that the operations of nature are to be both understood and valued in terms of their purposes. Since the early scholastics usually assume that sexual desire is sinful, they cannot consider it to be either intelligible or good, and so they are forced to conclude that it cannot be fully natural. Moreover, such a view has the advantage of analytic simplicity, since it implies that all sexual sins are unnatural in one way or another. Nonetheless, it comes uncomfortably close to the view of the Cathars and other dualists that sexual activity itself is inherently evil. For example, Huguccio, who holds that sexual pleasure even within marriage is a venial sin, finds it necessary to explain why this view is not heretical; according to the Cathars, sexual pleasure is always a mortal sin, he says, whereas, on his own view, it is a very slight venial sin.[14] Huguccio's argument saves the doctrinal point, since it keeps open the possibility that marriage is consistent with the Christian life, but it also reveals the vulnerability of the rigorist view that all sexual pleasure is to some degree sinful.

We have already seen that some scholastics, such as the anonymous author of the *Leipzig Summa,* are prepared to say that sexual sins involving heterosexual intercourse are natural considered as sexual acts, even though they involve a violation of the due order of human sexual relationships (Lottin 108-109). Although this appears to be a minority view, it reflects a more general tendency among the scholastics to move away from the claim that sexual pleasure is wrong in itself, toward a view according to which heterosexual sexual sins involve a misdirected or excessive exercise of the sexual function. Hence, they involve a violation of virtue *(Summa fratris Alexandri* II-II Inq. 3, tr.4, sec.2, 1.9.1,2) or of the reasonable order of human sexual relationships (*Summa theologiae* II-II 154.1). This line of analysis is consistent, at any rate, with a view of sexual pleasure as neutral or even as good in itself. Finally, Aquinas explicitly asserts that sexual pleasure is morally neutral in itself (*Summa theologiae* II-II 153.2; see especially *ad* 2). In his commentary on the *Sentences,* he even identifies the purpose that sexual desire serves, in terms of which it can be understood and valued as a part of nature; that is, according to Aquinas, pleasure offers an inducement to reproduce oneself through the sexual act (*In IV Sent.* 41.2.1 *ad* 3). Even this does not mean that it is legitimate to engage in sex within marriage for the sake of pleasure alone, but at least it removes the taint of sin from married Christians whose sex lives are otherwise irreproachable.

It is sometimes said that Aquinas' treatment of sexual pleasure reflects his appropriation of Aristotle, whose analysis he incorporates.[15] Certainly, Aristotle provides Aquinas with an argument for the moral neutrality of pleasure, but it is also the case that Aquinas' views reflect the trajectory of scholastic thought on sexual ethics. In fact, Aquinas is not the first scholastic theologian after Abelard at least to suggest that sexual pleasure is not necessarily sinful. In the generation prior to Aquinas, we find the secular theologian William of Auxerre asserting that sexual delight is natural and would have existed in Paradise even if our first parents had not sinned; thus, he concludes, sexual delight is not the same thing as lust, which is by definition sinful pleasure (*Summa aurea* IV 17. 1).

However, there is a further aspect to Aquinas' analysis of pleasure that opens up a new direction for the scholastic understanding of sexuality. I am referring to his distinction between natural and non-natural desires:

> Desire is two-fold: natural and non-natural. Natural desire cannot be actually infinite, for it is of that which nature requires, and nature always aims at something finite and definite ... But non-natural desire is altogether infinite. For it follows reason, as was said above [I-II 30.3], and reason is capable of proceeding to infinity. Hence, he who desires riches is able to desire them, not to any fixed limit, but simply to be rich, as much as possible (*Summa theologiae* I-II 30.4).[16]

Observe that non-natural desires are not *ipso facto* morally bad. However, because they have no natural limits, they must be brought under some kind of reasonable control if they are not to overwhelm the individual.

This distinction suggests a further rationale for the condemnation of unnatural sexual pleasures that Aquinas takes over from his tradition. That is, since sexual pleasure is the most intense of all pleasures (*ST* II-II 153.4), the desire for this pleasure is more likely to distort the individual's reason and will than any other desire (*ST* II-II 153.3). This, in turn, implies that sexual desire pursued outside of the limits set by the natural purposes of sexuality is more likely to destroy the balance of an individual's life than any other non-natural pleasure. Hence, on this view non-natural sexual pleasure would always be unnatural in the pejorative sense. Aquinas does not explicitly draw this conclusion, but it is consistent with his overall position. If this is a fair reading, then it is particularly interesting because it suggests a natural law analysis of sexual morality grounded in the psychology of sexual desire, as well as in an appeal to the purposes of sexuality.[17]

At any rate, neither Aquinas nor any other scholastic (to my knowledge) affirms that the pursuit of sexual pleasure for its own sake is morally legitimate, even within marriage. For the scholastics, there is only one unambiguously good purpose for sexual intercourse within marriage: procreation. In addition, most of the scholastics consider it morally justifiable for either spouse to initiate sexual relations in order to satiate the sexual drive, if his or her purpose in doing so is to forestall temptation to sexual sin.[18] Indeed, following the injunction of St. Paul, they hold that either the husband or the wife is morally required to accede to the sexual demands of the partner, an obligation charmingly described as the marital debt.

By the same token, the scholastics condemn any use of contraceptives even within marriage. This prohibition raises complex questions, however. The scholastics inherited a tradition on contraception that included two quite different rationales for the prohibition of the practice. According to the first of these, which seems to trace back to Jerome, contraception is a form of homicide.[19] It is difficult to say how far this claim is meant to be taken literally, by Jerome or by his followers. As Noonan shows, it is hard to reconcile this first claim with the view, also widespread in the early medieval period, that abortion is equivalent to homicide only after the point at which the fetus was thought to be capable of receiving a human soul; furthermore, the penalties prescribed for the use of contraceptives are not always consistent with the view that it is a form of homicide.[20]

At any rate, the equation of contraceptive practices with homicide is generally rejected by the scholastics in favor of Augustine's view that such a practice is properly a sexual sin: that is, a violation of the natural purposes of sexuality in pursuit of pleasure.[21] This is the rationale for the prohibition that we find in Gratian and in most of the decretists. Albert goes so far as to explicitly to repudiate the equation of contraceptive practice with homicide, observing that there is no guarantee that a given act of sexual intercourse would produce offspring anyway (*In IV Sent.* 31.1.8). In his early writings, Aquinas takes the same line (*In IV Sent.* 31.2.3). More tellingly, a number of scholastic theologians either do not mention the use of contraceptives at all or they discuss them only in their earlier works.[22]

Official Catholic teaching on the use of contraceptives, as definitively stated in the 1968 encyclical *Humanae vitae,* is based on an appeal to the structure of the sexual act and its inherent orientation toward procreation, as this is revealed by rational analysis prior to theological interpretation (*HV* para. 16). However, the scholastics do not typically argue in this way. Rather, they focus on the proper purposes of sexuality and marriage as these are revealed through theological reflection, and then they judge particular kinds of acts to be unnatural because they are not in accordance with those overall purposes. They do sometimes speak in terms that suggest that unnatural sexual practices violate the purposes of the sexual organs, but it is important to realize that this way of speaking itself presupposes a particular understanding of the purpose of sexuality. Aquinas makes this clear in the *Summa contra gentiles:*

> Nor should it be considered to be a light sin if someone procures the emission of semen apart from a justified purpose of generation and education, on account of the fact that it is either a light sin, or no sin at all, if someone should use a part of his body in some way other than that ordained by nature; for example, if someone should walk on his hands, or use his feet to carry out the operations of the hands. For through such inordinate activities as these, the good of the human person is not much hindered, but the inordinate emission of semen is inimical to the good of nature, that is, the conservation of the species. Hence after the sin of murder, through which human nature actually in existence is destroyed, this kind of sin, through which the generation of human nature is obstructed, would seem to have second place.(*SCG* III 122).[23]

There is probably no point at which we feel the distance between the scholastics and ourselves more sharply than in their evaluation of sexuality. Their almost unanimous conviction that sexual pleasure is morally problematic seems perverse to us, and their view of marriage seems chilly at best. As for the claim that procreation is the only fully legitimate purpose for sexual intercourse, even the most sympathetic observers regard this as critically insupportable; as Noonan says, "Because the sexual act might be generative, and because generation was an important function, the theologian intuited that generation was the normal function."[24]

The scholastic view of sexuality is too different from our own to be adopted *tout court*, even if that were desirable. However, the common judgment that it represents nothing better than the imposition of prejudices is unfounded. Modern commentators have come to this conclusion because they assume that a natural law argument must necessarily be couched in universally accessible terms of moral rationality. As we saw in the last chapter, this is not the scholastics' view. On the contrary, they see no incongruity in developing their understanding of the natural law through theological arguments.

In the present instance, we will misunderstand the claim that the proper purpose of sexual activity is procreation unless we realize that this is a theological judgment, grounded in the theologically informed philosophy of nature current at the time taken together with a particular reading of Scripture. It is not an unsupported intuition, as Noonan suggests, nor is it intended as an observational report or a scientific theory in the modern sense. Recall that the scholastics share the view, fundamental to the natural philosophy of their time, that nature is intelligible in its operations and tends toward what is good.[25] If this is so, then sexual activity, like any other natural phenomenon, can be rendered intelligible only in terms of the good toward which it aims. The scholastics, with their sharp sense of the ambiguities of sexual pleasure, do not share our sense that sexual intercourse can serve many legitimate human aims. However, they are convinced on scriptural and doctrinal grounds of the goodness of procreation. This leads them to conclude that sexual activity can be rendered intelligible by interpreting it in terms of its procreative purpose and, correlatively, that procreation is the primary purpose of sexual activity.

This line of argument is particularly persuasive to the early scholastics, of course, because they also consider sexual pleasure to be morally problematic or sinful. This, too, reflects a theological judgment on their part, but its antecedents are not so clearly scriptural. Rather, this view came to the scholastics from patristic authors whom they considered to be authoritative, including in particular Gregory the Great. It fit into a general pattern which was ultimately scriptural, of distinguishing nature as it was before the fall from nature as we now experience it. However, the actual negative evaluation of sexual desire seems to owe more to the Stoics than to Scripture. As we have just seen, the scholastics were increasingly led to reject it as inconsistent with their wider theological and moral commitments.

Once we let go of the view that sexual pleasure is itself morally problematic, we can consider the possibility that sexual activity has other purposes besides procreation. Nonetheless, as I will argue below, there are still good theological arguments for considering procreation to be a primary (albeit not the only) purpose for sexual activity, in the sense that it is one purpose that the Christian community is committed to acknowledging and fostering, whatever other purposes it may also acknowledge.

2. Marriage in scholastic thought

There are two perspectives from which to approach the scholastic doctrine of marriage. On the one hand, we can consider the legal doctrine developed by the canonists and theologians in response to the institutional reforms of the eleventh and early twelfth centuries; on the other hand, we can look at the more general scholastic analysis of marriage as an institution incorporating both natural and pre-conventional elements. Both are relevant to the scholastic concept of the natural law, but the latter is more basic and expresses the distinctive lines of scholastic natural law analysis more clearly. We will therefore begin with the basic theory, deferring consideration of their legal doctrine of marriage to the next section.

In the last section, we noted that some scholastic theologians characterize sexual sins involving heterosexual intercourse as sins against virtue or reason, in contrast to sins involving unnatural sexual acts which, it is said, violate the order of sexual activity established by God. This is a remarkable claim, because it implies that marriage itself, together with the structure of kinship relationships that it sustains, is at least partially conventional rather than natural. Yet this is what the scholastics consistently affirm.

More specifically, the scholastics analyze marriage as the appropriately human form for the general tendency of all living creatures to reproduce one's own kind. As such, it is the form of sexual union that is appropriate to rational creatures; otherwise, there would be no distinction between marriage and fornication. For this reason, the scholastics are not content to affirm the naturalness of marriage. They also analyze it in the light of its rational and religious purposes. This leads them to conclude that marriage as an institution incorporates elements of social custom and religious practice, as well as expressing inclinations that we share with other animals.[26] Huguccio offers an especially clear example of this line of interpretation:

[Marriage] is the natural law, that is, its effect, that is, it derives from it . . . But of what kind of union is it to be understood? Of souls, or of bodies? I respond: Of souls, because that is marriage. Hence, the jurist [Ulpian] says, "The union of husband and wife, which we call marriage, derives from this." But marriage is nothing else than a union of souls. But from which natural law does this union arise? From reason, which directs a man that he should be joined with a woman through marriage, either for the sake of offspring, or on account of incontinence. For by such a law, that is, led by reason, did Adam consent to take Eve in marriage, when he said, "this now is bone of my bones," and so on; and so does anyone consent, who now contracts marriage. Or from the divine law, that is the evangelical law, when in the writings of the apostle [Paul], each man is permitted to have his own wife. To me, however, it seems that this should rather be understood of the bodily union of marriage (not that of fornication, since sin cannot be derived from the natural law). And this latter union is derived both from that natural law which is said to be an instinct of nature, and from that which is said to be reason. For man is moved by a certain appetite of the natural sensuality, that he should be joined in the flesh to a woman, and immediately reason follows, directing him that he should not be joined with anyone except a wife, and in a legitimate way, that is, for the sake of children, or to pay his debt; for any other union, whether with the wife or with another woman is not derived from any natural law, but is contrary to it (Lottin 110-111).[27]

Huguccio's remarks reflect his own distinctive legal doctrine of marriage, according to which the consent of the partners is the necessary and sufficient condition for the validity of the marital bond ("Of what kind of union? ... of souls, for that is marriage"). Nonetheless, the distinctive elements in Huguccio's theory find their context in a wider consensus that he expresses well: that marriage represents the rational expression of a fundamental pre-rational inclination.

Compare this with the view of marriage that later came to dominate Roman Catholic thought, according to which marriage has been instituted by God in the form that is most familiar to us: that is, as an indissoluble union between one man and one woman. In the words of the encyclical *Casti Connubii*, "The nature of matrimony is entirely independent of the free will of man, so that if one has once contracted matrimony he is thereby subject to its divinely made laws and properties" (Paragraph 6).[28] The scholastics would certainly have agreed that marriage has been instituted by God, but they are not committed to the view that one and only one specific form of marriage is likewise instituted by God.[29] Indeed, by the logic of their concept of the natural law, there is no inconsistency in asserting the divine institution of marriage while also acknowledging that human custom and decree have legitimately shaped the development of the institution of marriage. God's institution can be seen in this context as one aspect of the pre-conventional nature that forms a basis for human design in the actual formation of the institution.

At the same time, the scholastics draw two other implications from the claim that God is the author of marriage, and the related claim that marriage is itself a sacrament, a means of grace. The first of these is that marriage is legitimately under the direct control of the institutional church. Even though the institution of marriage incorporates elements of human design as well as reflecting divine decree, it is resistant to human control in a way that other human institutions are not. More exactly, the institutional control of marriage belongs properly to that institution that is authorized to act directly on God's behalf in the administration of sacred realities, namely, the institutionalized church (Aquinas, *Summa theologiae* I-II 100.8 *ad* 3).

The second implication is by now familiar to us; that is, the scholastics appeal to the divine and sacramental status of marriage in order to defend the goodness of marriage and its legitimacy as a Christian way of life. Of course, this claim is partially motivated by the arguments of the Cathars and others who denied the goodness of marriage, but the scholastics also find themselves increasingly drawn to defend marriage against those orthodox Christians who considered the monastic life to be the only truly spiritual way to live. As C.H. Lawrence has shown, this is particularly true for the mendicant theologians, whose commitments to evangelization and intellectual work led them into an alliance with the lay middle class emerging in the cities (paradoxical though this may seem, in light of the mendicants' commitments to poverty).[30] This informal alliance was furthered by the fact that the mendicants' way of life was itself suspect from the standpoint of monasticism. We find a striking illustration of this alliance in Bonaventure's *De perfectione evangelium,* where an enthusiastic defense of the goodness and spiritual value of marriage comes in the midst of an extended argument in favor of the Franciscan way of life. At the same time, Bonaventure also provides us with a good example of the way the natural law is interpreted through the lens of Scripture; marriage, he explains, is

> ... in accordance with that very law of nature by reason of nature as [originally] constituted, which was formed in distinct sexes, according to the beginning of Genesis: "God created the human person in accordance with his image and likeness, male and female he created them." It is also in accordance with the law of nature remaining to this day by reason of a further precept, according to the beginning of Genesis: "God blessed them and said, 'Increase and multiply, fill the earth and subdue it,'" which indeed cannot legitimately be done except through the exercise of conjugal chastity. It is no less in accordance with the law of nature by reason of a revelation given from above. For Adam spoke prophetically after his sleep, when he said, "This then is bone of my bones and flesh of my flesh. For this reason, a man shall leave his father and mother and cleave to his wife, and the two shall be one flesh" ... From the first of these, the union of man and woman is natural, from the second, it is moral, and from the third, it is sacramental; and these are all consistent with one another in accordance with a determination of the law of nature, from which in the first instance the acts and practices of conjugal chastity are drawn. (*De Per Evan.* 3.1).

Because they are aware that marriage incorporates conventional as well as natural elements, the scholastics can allow for the possibility of other forms of marriage besides the familiar monogamous union. In fact, Scripture itself forces this possibility on them, since it speaks of the polygamous unions of the saints of the first covenant without any disapproval. Furthermore, they are aware that the Muslims also practiced polygamy, and they may have known that their own ancestors did so as well.[31] It is likely that Aquinas' extensive defense in the *Summa contra gentiles* of indissoluble and monogamous marriage as the optimal (but not the only legitimate) expression of natural law is written with Muslim practices in view, even if this treatise was not in fact written expressly for the use of Christian missionaries in Muslim lands (*SCG* 123-124).[32]

For scholastic theologians, the polygamy of the patriarchs, together with other dubious practices such as the resort to concubines, are discussed under the general rubric of the sins of the patriarchs. They deal with this problem in the same way as they deal with the other problematic activities of the holy men and women of the Old Testament; that is, they argue that God had granted a dispensation to these saints, in virtue of which their actions were justified. However, God's dispensations are not simply expressions of authoritative fiat; rather, they must be understood in terms of the purposes of marriage. In this way, the general theological approach to morally problematic aspects of Scripture was developed in a way that leads the theologians to reflect on the diversity of purposes for marriage.[33]

This is the context in which to place Aquinas' distinction between the primary and secondary ends of marriage, which proved to be so influential for later Catholic thought:

> ... the natural law is therefore nothing other than a concept naturally placed in the human person, by which he is directed to acting appropriately with respect to actions which are proper to him, whether these are proper to him in accordance with his generic nature, as to procreate, to eat, and others of this kind, or in accordance with his specific nature, as to deliberate, and similar acts. And anything which renders an act inappropriate to the end which nature intends for some activity is said to be contrary to the law of nature. It is possible, however, for an action to be inappropriate with respect to either a primary or a secondary end,

and in either case, this can happen in two ways. In one way, from something which altogether obstructs the attainment of an end ... In another way, from something which renders the attainment of either a primary or a secondary end difficult or less fitting ... If therefore an act should be inappropriate to an end in such a way as to completely foreclose the attainment of a primary end, it is prohibited by the natural law through the first precepts of the natural law, which stand in the same relation to things to be done as the first common conceptions have to speculative matters. If, however, it should be inappropriate to a secondary end in either way, or even to a primary end in such a way as to render its attainment difficult or less fitting, it is not prohibited by the primary precepts of the natural law, but by the secondary precepts, which are derived from the first precepts (*In IV Sent.* 33.1.1).

He goes on to explain that the primary end of marriage is the bringing forth and education of children, its second end is the common life enjoyed by the spouses, and the third is the sacramental sign given by the fidelity between one man and one woman, which is distinctively Christian. Of these three ends, only the third is altogether ruled out by polygamy, the second is rendered difficult but not impossible, and the primary end is not compromised at all. Hence, he concludes, the dispensation in favor of the polygamy of the patriarchs is reasonable, because this practice is not inconsistent with the attainment of the primary purpose of marriage.

Although the terms of the primary/secondary distinction appear to have originated with Aquinas, we can see that his argument is in continuity with the general scholastic analysis according to which God's dispensations can be understood in terms of the rationale of the precept in question.[34] Hence, even though Aquinas' terminology is distinctive, his distinction between ends that admit of dispensation and those that do not is also made by other scholastic theologians.[35] More specifically, Aquinas' analysis of dispensations in his *Sentences* commentary is very similar to the analysis of William of Auxerre (*Summa aurea* III 18.5, IV 17.3.1), and it is also reminiscent of Bonaventure's argument that God granted dispensations for polygamy and concubinage in view of the conditions at the time, which made it imperative to build up the community of believers (*In IV Sent.* 33.1.3).

The language of primary and secondary ends of marriage was later to play a central role in the Roman Catholic doctrine of marriage, and so it is worth underscoring that this distinction would not have had quite the same point for the scholastics as it was to have for later theologians. In modern Roman Catholic thought, the language of primary and secondary ends is used to distinguish among the different purposes that the institution of marriage serves in its ecclesiastically sanctioned form, which increasingly comes to be seen as the only legitimate form of marriage.[36] But for Aquinas, this distinction provides a framework for analyzing different forms of marriage and, as such, it supports a view that at least some forms of marriage that do not meet the Christian norm are nonetheless legitimate.

Given the scholastic view of sexuality, we would expect to find that the central or primary purpose that they assign to marriage is procreation. This needs to be qualified; if physical procreation alone were the primary purpose of marriage, there would be no point in distinguishing between marriage and heterosexual sex outside marriage.[37] Rather, they identify the primary purpose of marriage as the procreation of children in a fully human fashion, in accordance with the demands of reason as well as our pre-rational nature.[38] What this means, on closer examination, is that marriage exists in order to bring children into the world not only physically but as social beings, with a definite and appropriate place in the social structure. Hence, marriage provides a framework within which children can be educated. Some of the scholastics add that it also guarantees the legitimacy of a man's children, thus safeguarding the kinship structure on which society is based.[39] In short, for the scholastics the primary purpose of marriage comprises the maintenance of a social order through the bringing forth, educating, and socializing of the next generation.

This purpose can be fulfilled by forms of marriage other than the normative Christian form, including, specifically, polygamous marriages. Nonetheless, according to the scholastics, there are further purposes of marriage that cannot be fulfilled in polygamous unions, including especially the creation of a personal bond between husband and wife and the preservation of parity between them.[40] Hence, polygamy is judged to be an inadequate form of marriage, which should not be practiced in a Christian society. Yet this judgment allows for the recognition that polygamy is a valid form of marriage with its own integrity and value, even though from the Christian standpoint it appears flawed.

3. Marriage, women, and society: Legal and moral views

The immediate impetus for scholastic reflection on marriage and sexuality was provided by the church reform movement, which began in the late eleventh century and continued throughout the period we are considering.[41] There were two aspects of this reform movement that were particularly relevant to the formation of the scholastics' sexual ethic. The first of these was a movement to require celibacy of all clerics. The second, which was even more far-reaching in its social effects, was the effort on the part of church reformers to institutionalize and enforce what they saw as an appropriate Christian sexual morality for married Christians. In order to carry this program through, it was necessary for the institutional church to confirm and extend its legal jurisdiction over marriage, and the reformers were remarkably successful in attaining this goal.

These reforms called for a more comprehensive and legally precise doctrine of marriage than had yet been developed, and it fell to the canon lawyers and theologians to develop such a doctrine. This doctrine, or more exactly the relevant competing doctrines, reflected the scholastic concept of the natural law and served to reinforce certain aspects of that concept. For that reason, they call for some examination here, although it would take us too far afield to attempt to analyze them in detail.

In developing their theories of marriage, the scholastics took their starting points from the institutional agenda of the reformers, an agenda that James Brundage describes as follows:

> [In addition to clerical celibacy, the] sexual agenda of the reformers also included a strong commitment, not only to deny marriage to the clergy, but to reorganize marriage among the laity as well. The reformers were anxious, for one thing, to bring marriage under the exclusive control of Church courts and in so doing to replace customary marriage law with ecclesiastical law. The ecclesiastical model of marriage that the reformers so vigor- ously – and successfully – championed rested upon seven funda-

mental principles. First, marriage must be monogamous; second, marriage should be indissoluble; third, marital unions should be contracted freely by the parties themselves, not by their parents or families; fourth, marriage represents the only legally protected type of sexual relationship, and therefore concubinage must be eliminated, even among the laity; fifth, and as a corollary of the fourth principle, all sexual activity outside of marriage must be punished by legal sanctions; sixth, all sexual activity, marital and nonmarital, falls solely under ecclesiastical jurisdiction; and seventh, marriage must become exogamous, and intermarriage within related groups of families should therefore be eliminated.[42]

As Brundage goes on to note, this program was resisted at every point.[43] Yet it was remarkably successful, with far-reaching consequences for European social life. Not only did the reformers' programs challenge long-standing customs, but they undermined the control of families over the marriages of their individual members. The requirement that marriage be entered into only with the free consent of the man and woman concerned meant that persons could not be forced into marriage for the sake of family alliances.[44] As Duby points out, this requirement could easily be circumvented, particularly with young girls, but there were also serious efforts to enforce it throughout the period under consideration.[45] Similarly, the prohibition of divorce inhibited noble families from dissolving and reforming their children's marriages as a means of furthering their mutual alliances. And the prohibition of concubinage challenged long-standing customs according to which men of higher social rank formed sexual alliances with women of lower social class but entered into marriage only within their own social rank. As a result of this prohibition, concubinage was gradually assimilated to marriage, at least when it involved a stable and exclusive alliance. In this way, the prohibition had the effect of breaking down class barriers to marriage.

In order to rationalize and implement these reforms, scholastic canon lawyers develop an analysis of marriage in terms of which legally valid unions can be distinguished from failed attempts at marriage and conflicts among spouses and other interested parties can be adjudicated. Perhaps the most important aspect of this analysis is its appropriation of the Roman doctrine that consent makes marriage. We find two main schools of thought on this issue among scholastic canonists and theologians.[46]

According to the first of these, which traces back to Gratian, the legal validity of marriage requires both the consent of the partners and sexual intercourse. Hence, on this view, a marriage that has been solemnized but not consummated can be dissolved. However, this view raised difficulties, not least the theological difficulty that it calls into question the legitimacy of the marriage between Mary and Joseph. These difficulties led a growing number of canonists and theologians in the later twelfth and thirteenth centuries to adopt a variant of the view taken by Peter Lombard, that the validity of marriage depends solely on the present consent of the two parties. That is to say, if a man and a woman agree to enter into marriage in the present moment (in contrast to forming an agreement to marry at some future date), this is considered sufficient in itself to establish a valid marriage between them.

This is the point at which the control of the church over marriages reached its logical limits, and church authorities recognized the fact, albeit reluctantly.[47] If the existence of a marriage depends solely on the consent of the two parties involved, then not only is the formation of marriages taken out of the control of the families of the two parties, it is taken out of the direct control of the church as well. On this view, even a secret agreement between two parties, concluded without benefit of church ceremony, establishes a valid marriage that can claim ecclesiastical protection. Secret marriages were condemned as illicit: those who entered into them were held to be guilty of wrongful behavior by so doing. Nonetheless, the validity of secret marriages — their moral and legal status as true marriages — was recognized and enforced throughout this period.

From our standpoint, the significance of this doctrine of consent lies in the fact that it both expresses and reinforces a more general ideal of natural equality that is central to the scholastic concept of the natural law. The doctrine that the mutual consent of a couple is sufficient to establish a valid marriage functioned as a powerful safeguard for the right to marry; as such, it opened up a space in which people could act freely in a matter of fundamental importance, whatever their place in a social hierarchy. This implied ideal of natural equality was also defended in other ways: for example, by explicit assertions of the rights of those in a state of servitude to marry, as we find in Gratian's *Decretum* (C.29, q.2). Although this view was contested, it was subsequently incorporated into church law in 1155 by a decree of Hadrian IV, *Dignum est,* which unequivocally affirms the right of unfree persons to marry without the approval of their masters.[48] Near the end of the period we are considering, Aquinas explicitly grounds the right to marry in an appeal to natural equality. Because all persons are equal with respect to the possession and exercise of sexual capacities, he explains, these capacities comprise a natural constraint on the obligations of obedience that one person can place on another. For this reason, no one can be forced either to marry, or to forswear marriage (*Summa theologiae* II-II 104.5).[49]

Moreover, since the consent of both man and woman is necessary for contracting marriage, they stand as equal to one another with respect to the act of contracting marriage. Husband and wife are also equal as sexual partners; sexual infidelity is equally sinful for each of them, and each is obliged to meet the sexual demands of the other in rendering the marriage debt. As Duby points out, this theoretical equality was not necessarily respected in practice.[50] Nonetheless, the canonists seem to take it for granted that the wife, rather than the husband, is most likely to demand payment of the debt, and there are cases in which a woman's right to the debt was enforced by ecclesiastical courts.[51] It is a little startling to find church officials solemnly safeguarding the right of women to receive sexual gratification from their husbands, but the fact that such cases were brought before the courts indicates that the sexual equality between men and women was not simply a pious ideal.

Of course, it is a limited ideal, as is well known. Alongside their defense of the equality of man and woman as sexual partners, the scholastics also defend the subordination of the wife to the husband in all other matters. Furthermore, this subordination was thought to extend to the public sphere, particularly in the church, where women were barred from ordination and the exercise of public office.

There is no necessary inconsistency in holding up an ideal of equality in some respects while at the same time arguing for differential treatment or subordination in other respects. Even today, there are very few who defend the claim that all persons should be treated as equal in each and every respect.[52] Generally, a defense of equality is combined with an analysis of ways in which persons are genuinely unequal, and may legitimately be treated as such, for example on the basis of capacity or need. On such an analysis, normative equality is said, for example, to be consistent with the view that children are appropriately less autonomous than adults, or the view that the sick and disabled have greater claims on public resources than do the healthy.

Nonetheless, the scholastic defense of the legal subordination of women strikes us as particularly problematic because it is difficult to see it as anything other than an expression of misogyny. This is not entirely fair, since the subordination of women within marriage is supported by clear scriptural precepts, and the scholastics did not have the kind of historical/critical perspective on Scripture that would have enabled them to relativize these precepts. At the same time, it cannot be denied that the scholastics inherit a considerable amount of misogyny from their classical and Christian authorities, and they perpetuate it in their own discussions of the status of women.

It is also the case, as David Herlihy points out, that, beginning in the twelfth century, the status of women fell in some respects.[53] While this does not excuse the scholastic tendency to disparage women, it does suggest that to some degree, this tendency reflects the circumstances and attitudes of the time. Prior to that time, women in the aristocracy exercised important administrative functions within the household, and women in the lower classes contributed substantially to economic productivity, particularly through the different aspects of textile and clothing manu-facture. However, the economic expansion and the social reforms of the twelfth and thirteenth centuries curtailed both kinds of functions; the emergence of centralized bureaucracy reduced the role of noblewomen as administrators, although they never lost this function entirely, and the emergence of guilds limited women's access to manufacture and the trades. At the same time, however, the resurgence of lay spirituality during the twelfth and thirteenth centuries provided women as well as men with opportunities for religious activity and leadership, and we find women functioning as lay preachers, giving spiritual counsel and advice on a wide scale, and assuming leadership of loose associations of disciples.[54] The scholastics tend to view these phenomena with some suspicion because of the prominence of women in heretical movements, but they also acknowledge that at least some women are capable of intelligence, learning, holiness, and leadership.

As we would expect, the complexities of their inherited tradition and social conditions lead the scholastics to a complex view of women. While they do repeat old saws about the lesser intelligence and steadiness of women taken as a class, they do not go so far as to claim (as Aristotle does) that women are constitutively incapable of full moral virtue.[55] On the contrary, they affirm that men and women are fundamentally on a par with respect to the possession of rationality, free judgment, and the capacity for holiness. Though they tend to denigrate the abilities of women in comparison to men, they see these as differences of degree and not kind, and they recognize that some women are more intelligent and holier than most men.

This complexity is particularly apparent in scholastic discussions of the question of the ordination of women. Contrary to what is commonly assumed, the scholastics are aware that the church practice of denying ordination to women gives at least an appearance of injustice, and they attempt to justify this practice through an analysis of the different symbolic or social roles played by the two sexes.[56] Aquinas asserts that women and men are equal with respect to the possession of the image of God, understood in its primary sense as the capacity for reasoned self-govern-ance, and he repeats with approval the Augustinian dictum that in the mind "there is no distinction of sexes" (*Summa theologiae* I 93.6 *ad* 2; cf. I 93.4 *ad* 1). On this basis, he defends the propriety of women exercising the charism of prophecy or acting as teachers and counselors in a private capacity (*Summa theologiae* II-II 177.2). He defends the exclusion of women from public offices within the church, however, through a kind of gender analysis. Since women are subordinate to their husbands in marriage, he argues, the social status of women carries with it an impli-cation of subordination. For this reason, a woman cannot represent Christ, who holds authority within the church (*ibid.*; also see *ST* II-II 183.1 and *In IV Sent.* 25.2.1a). Bonaventure, for his part, argues that a woman cannot be ordained because she cannot be a natural sign of Christ, but he considers the opposite opinion to be credible (*In IV Sent.* 25.2.2). Like Aquinas, he insists that women and men are equally created in the image of God, but the image, he adds, pertains to the rational nature of the human person, whereas ordination concerns the bodily existence of the person as well (*In IV Sent.* 25.2.2 *ad* 3).

Furthermore, the scholastics are well aware that within secular society women do exercise political authority. In their respective commentaries on the *Sentiniae*, both Aquinas and Bonaventure note that this is entirely legitimate (*In IV Sent.* 25.2.1a, and *In IV Sent.* 25.2.2 *ad* 1, respectively).

In fact, one of Aquinas' treatises, *De regimine judaeorum,* is addressed to a woman ruler (traditionally identified as Marguerite, daughter of Louis IX of France and Countess of Flanders) who ruled from 1244 to 1286, and who had written asking for advice on problems associated with her rule.[57] In his response, he takes the legitimacy of her rule for granted.[58]

Duby remarks that "medieval Christianity gradually accepted, however reluctantly, that women could take part in religious life. This medieval trend constitutes, in my opinion, the major difference between Christianity and Islam or Judaism, which left women in a far more marginal position." [59] To the extent that this it true, it reflects the gradual application of an ideal of natural and spiritual equality, which was only imperfectly realized throughout this period but had some force nonetheless. From the standpoint of our contemporary struggles to secure the full social and religious equality of women to men, the scholastic affirmations of the spiritual equality of women and men appear painfully limited and flawed. Yet our own struggles rest, in part, on the foundations provided by those flawed affirmations.

4. Implications
for contemporary Christian ethics

In considering scholastic views on sexuality and marriage, there is indeed much that is bound to strike us as quaint or tyrannical. But the scholastics' analysis of marriage also reflects a degree of sophistication that is likely to surprise contemporary readers, and their commitments to fostering equity and sexual equality between spouses would be endorsed by nearly all Christians today. These positive elements suggest that it would be premature simply to dismiss scholastic reflections on sexual morality as irrelevant to our own sexual ethic. Certainly, any attempt to appropriate the scholastic concept of the natural law for contemporary Christian ethics will require considerable reformulation of this concept. Nonetheless, I want to argue that this reformulation must begin by retrieving the theological claims that are central to the scholastic sexual ethic.

The most fundamental of these is the claim that procreation is good, and the married life, understood as a way of life integrally connected to bringing forth and raising children, is a fully worthy way of life for the Christian. In our day, this claim is likely to seem banal, and so it is worth underscoring that the scholastics defend it out of the same fundamental theological convictions that lead them to embrace the idea of a natural law. That is, they see procreation as a centrally important expression of the goodness of creation and the material processes by which the created order is sustained. This view seems to me to be both true and fundamentally important. There is no aspect of ordinary human experience that more profoundly expresses our embodiment, our mortality, and our place in a succession of human generations than procreation. That is why dualist movements within Christianity have typically rejected the legitimacy of procreation. By the same token, that is why a theological defense of procreation is central to any orthodox Christian theology.

But is a defense of the goodness of procreation tantamount to a defense of marriage? The scholastics assumed that this is so, and their rationale brings us to a further point that deserves to be retrieved. That is, when the scholastics speak of procreation in a human context, what they have in mind is not simply biological reproduction but the extended process by which children are educated and prepared to take their place in the community. As we have seen, the scholastics emphasize the importance of social context in part for the sake of the child himself or herself, because they believe, reasonably enough, that a child is most likely to flourish within a secure family context. In addition, some of them suggest that, without a secure social framework, men will not have reliable guarantees of their paternity. We are less likely to be sympathetic to this claim, but even here there is an insight worth preserving. That is, given their social context, the scholastics' concern with paternity is not just a reflection of a perennial male anxiety; it also expresses a sense that kinship relations form the basis for social identity.

Hence, when the scholastics defend the goodness of procreation, they are not just defending the goodness of physical reproduction. They are also defending the maintenance and development of the orderly structures of society, in which individuals find their identity as social beings, and the culture and traditions of the community are developed and sustained. Because marriage provides the primary institutional setting for these processes, the scholastic defense of procreation implies a defense of marriage as well.

This understanding of procreation as partially a social process may appear to be inconsistent with the scholastics' overall concept of the natural law, unless we recall that for them, human nature can be understood in a number of ways, in accordance with their general procedure of contrasting specific norms and practices with whatever may be said to ground them. Hence, from their perspective, human nature might be understood in such a way as to identify it with the pre-rational aspects of the human person only, but it can also be construed in a way that takes in all dimensions of humanity, including rationality and the social world that stems from it. Seen from this latter perspective, a defense of the fundamental goodness of nature implies an affirmation of the fundamental goodness of culture and society, considered precisely as characteristic and proper expressions of human nature.[60]

At the same time, the social component in human procreation should be clearer to us than it was to the scholastics, since we are more conscious than they of the extent to which human identity is shaped by social relationships.[61] Indeed, some would claim that the human person is fundamentally relational, which would make it inappropriate to speak of a unified personal identity. The scholastics would not go so far, for what I believe are good theological reasons, but neither do we need to go that far in order to recognize that men and women are profoundly shaped by their social context. We take our identity as social beings from our place in a network of kinship and community relationships, and while the reality of a human person is not exhausted by that social identity, yet it is a constitutive part of individual identity.

I emphasize this point because, as we will see further in the next chapter, there is some tendency among Christian theologians today to denigrate the goodness of secular culture and society. The scholastic defense of the goodness of procreation, comprehensively understood to comprise our self-perpetuation as social beings, is particularly relevant for us as a counterweight to this tendency. Certainly, human societies are distorted in many ways by human limitations and outright sinfulness; the scholastics themselves would be the first to point this out. Nonetheless, these societies are themselves fundamental expressions of our human nature, and furthermore, they provide the basic matrix for the formation of the individual persons whom we are enjoined in charity to love as ourselves. On both counts, they possess a basic goodness that a Christian should acknowledge and cherish. I refer here to any society, whatever its specific characteristics or its moral failings. Of course, this does not mean that we should accept every aspect of our societies uncritically, or avoid working for social change where it is needed, but appropriate social critique should not become a pretext for a wholesale rejection of secular societies or of those societies that stem from different religious traditions.

To summarize what has been said so far, any adequate Christian sexual ethic must take its starting points from the goodness of procreation, comprehensively understood to include social as well as biological reproduction, together with the fundamental link between marriage and procreation. This does not necessarily mean that childless unions are not true marriages (a claim that the scholastics denied). It does not even mean that there can be no other legitimate purpose for entering into a marriage (which they acknowledged, albeit grudgingly). However, it does mean that, for Christians, marriage as a social institution is fundamentally linked to procreation in this inclusive sense. Christians are no longer in a position to institutionalize this vision of marriage in the wider society, nor would it be desirable to try to do so. Nonetheless, Christian communities can and should embody this vision of marriage in their moral teachings and their ritual practices. That, at least, is my claim.

What about the scholastics' further claim that procreation is the primary purpose of marriage, and the only fully legitimate purpose for sexual intercourse? Even here, I want to argue, there is a theological insight that should be retrieved, although not in the form in which the scholastics express it.

For most of our contemporaries, the claim that procreation is the purpose of sexual intercourse is likely to be rejected out of hand, for at least two reasons. In the first place, it appears that evolutionary biology has undermined any appeal to teleologies in natural processes. Second, following on the work of Michel Foucault, most social theorists today would reject the view that human sexuality has a clearly defined structure that exists and can be studied prior to social formation. For both of these reasons, it is important to note once again that the scholastic claim that procreation is the purpose of sexuality is a theological claim, grounded in a theologically informed interpretation of nature taken together with a particular interpretation of Scripture. It does not depend on the supposed discovery of a design inherent in natural processes or organs, as these are considered independently of a theological framework. Nor does it presuppose that human sexuality exists in a fully formed state prior to its social expression.

In the last chapter, we saw that the scholastic concept of the natural law implies a selective privileging of the tendencies inherent in human nature, in accordance with which some are given normative priority and others are de-emphasized or discouraged. Here we see an example of that approach. By affirming that procreation is the primary purpose of sexuality, the scholastics privilege one of the purposes that sexuality can serve, while stigmatizing or at least de-emphasizing others. By the same token, when this claim is expanded to include the institution of marriage, it need not imply that marriage serves no other purposes, but it does privilege a purpose judged on theological grounds to be primary or central. We are more aware than the scholastics were of the complexity of both sexuality and marriage, but that does not prevent us from appropriating their fundamental theological insights into the significance of the procreative purposes of sexuality and marriage.

Yet this insight would not be credible if there were nothing in the reality of human sexuality as we know it prior to theological reflection that might be said to correspond to a procreative purpose. Or at best, this claim would amount to an imposition of a theological doctrine on the formless matter of human life, in another variant of the widespread tendency to collapse natural law arguments into appeals to practical (or, in this case, theological) reason. What, then, can we say about the pre-conventional givens that undergird the theological view of procreation and marriage proposed here?

The first thing to be said, surely, is that there are such pre-conventional givens, and they include the manifold forms of sexual desire as well as the biological realities of the human reproductive process. Even Foucault admits the existence of some recurring features in human sexual experience, and very few social theorists writing subsequently have argued that human sexuality is radically and comprehensively a product of social construction.[62] Furthermore, there are complex but evident connections between human sexuality and the human reproductive process. As the theologian Lisa Cahill remarks, "when all is said and done, the idea that there is no such thing as 'sex,' or that sex in humans has no intrinsic connection to reproductive physiology, is more rhetorical than factual.

Such a claim could only be maintained on the basis of an abrupt break between humanity and other mammalian species."[63]

Cahill's comment brings us to a second point. As we saw in the first chapter, there is a growing body of scientific research and philosophical speculation that underscores the continuities of psychology and behavior between humans and other animals. This does not mean that we can or should imitate the other animals in our own behavior, nor does it mean that every human tendency that finds parallels among other animals is *ipso facto* good and worthy of emulation. What it does mean, however, is that the study of animal behavior offers us an excellent route to self-understanding. By reflecting on the ways in which perennially recurring tendencies among other kinds of animals fit into the overall shape of their lives, we can arrive at some insight into the ways in which analogous inclinations fit into the overall shape of our own lives. This line of thought, in turn, suggests powerfully that the sexual impulse has an intrinsic connection to reproduction, at least among other mammals, and perhaps among ourselves as well. One might almost say that it exists in order to guarantee the reproduction of the species.

But is this not the kind of teleological language that has been ruled out by Darwinian biology? As Ernst Mayr points out, in order to answer such a question it is necessary to distinguish among different senses of teleology as applied to biological processes.[64] If biological teleology is interpreted in a way that implies that the process of evolution is itself intrinsically directed toward some ultimate goal (such as ourselves), or else that specific features of living creatures are the direct products of conscious design, then this idea is indeed ruled out by Darwinian biology. However, if an appeal to teleology is meant to indicate that individual living beings characteristically act in certain ways that can best be interpreted as goal-directed behavior, then in that sense the idea of teleology is fundamental to biological science. Indeed, on Mayr's view (which he explicitly describes as a kind of Aristotelianism), the distinctive mark of living as opposed to inanimate creatures, is precisely that they engage in goal-directed behavior.

What about the further claim that a given tendency or process, such as sexual desire and reproduction, exists for a purpose, such as the reproduction of the species? A considerable number of biologists and philosophers would agree that many of the traits found in living creatures today are there because similar traits served some purpose for their ancestors, in virtue of which they enhanced the reproductive fitness of those ancestors. Rowland Stout goes further, arguing that we can adequately account for the possession of the characteristic traits of biological species only through an appeal to the purposes that those traits serve within a given kind of environment for the species considered as a class.[65] This does not imply conscious design, as Stout insists, but it does imply that when we speak of the purpose of a trait or tendency in the human species, we are referring to something that has an objective existence prior to our choice in the matter.

Both Mayr and Stout take pains to distinguish their views from traditional Christian arguments from design. Yet, as we observed in Chapter 2, the scholastics have no stake in the view that specific traits of living creatures result from conscious design.[66] Rather, for them the operations of nature are to be understood as far as possible as the expressions of intrinsic principles of action that are a constitutive part of the specific identities of creatures. Certainly, the scholastics do believe that these operations are teleological. Furthermore, they sometimes form their views on the purposes of nature on the basis of theological convictions, as we have seen. Nonetheless, that does not mean that they see these purposes as externally imposed on creatures. The purposes of nature are intrinsic to its processes, so much so that natural operations would not be what they are if they were detached from any intrinsic connection to their purposes. As such, they reflect God's creative wisdom, which we discern through revelation as well as through reflective observation.

By the same token, the late-twentieth-century Christian can appeal to an objective link between human sexuality and reproduction without being committed to a discredited doctrine of design. Yet the question that remains is, what moral and theological conclusions can we draw from this link? At this point, contemporary social theory can help us to appreciate something that is implicit in the scholastic concept of the natural law, but that the scholastics themselves could not clearly articulate. That is, while sexuality and reproduction are objective components of our animal existence, we do not experience and express our sexual impulses in the same way as do the other animals. Not only are we aware of sexual impulses, we are aware of them (sometimes) as sexual impulses, which we know to be connected to the processes of reproduction and to much else besides. This knowledge, and the feelings and attitudes toward sexuality that are inseparably connected with it, inform our sexual activities and give rise to social structures within which sexuality is channeled. These social structures, in turn, convey a set of attitudes and expectations toward sexuality that appear to us to be natural. And so they are, in the sense of reflecting a second nature supervening on the first nature of mammalian reproductive biology.[67]

What does it mean, then, to say that human sexuality is linked to a reproductive purpose? This claim is tethered in the objective realities of human reproductive biology, but it cannot be reduced to a claim about those realities. Procreation is grounded (although not completely subsumed) in physical and pre-rational aspects of our humanity, but that does not mean that we experience our fertility in a pre-rational way. To the contrary, we experience it, and generally we prize it, as a part of our human potential. What is more, our feelings and attitudes towards sex cannot help but be shaped by the fact that sexual activity is still normally the way in which we exercise that potential. For this reason, an orientation towards procreation is part of the human meaning of sexuality, its meaning for us precisely as animals who are also rational, whatever else we might say about the natural purposes of the sex act.

However, none of this implies that procreation is the only purpose that can be served by sexual activity, or even that it is the only theologically defensible purpose. The scholastics privileged the procreative purpose in their interpretation of sexuality and marriage, but they did so in part out of a deep conviction that sexual pleasure is sinful, or at best problematic. We are far more likely to regard sexual pleasure as good, and correlatively, we are more open to the possibility that sexual activity can serve other legitimate purposes besides procreation, including especially the expression and fostering of love between two individuals. Here again, we are not so far from the theological world-view of the scholastics as we might assume because, as we noted above, at least some of them recognize the value of marital love. However, for us, unlike the scholastics, sexual activity is itself a means to express and foster love, and for this reason we cannot easily accept the view that procreation is the only purpose of sexuality.

How, then, should the scholastic privileging of procreation as the central purpose of sexual activity be formulated in a Christian ethic today?

And more fundamentally, *why* should we even try to do so? The answers to these two questions are interconnected. Consider what is involved in promoting a Christian sexual morality. In order to do so, a Christian community will need to develop, affirm, and as far as possible institution-alize its best theological understanding of marriage and sexuality. In this way, marriage and sexuality will be construed as having certain meanings within the Christian community. Such a construal will not be a sheer imposition of meaning, but it does involve a selective privileging of some of the possible meanings of sexuality over others.

Here we come to the central point. In order to promote a marital/sexual morality at all, the Christian community necessarily has to make selective judgments about the possible purposes for marriage and sexual behavior which it will privilege, if only because its institutional forms for marriage and sexuality will necessarily embody some but not all possible meanings of sexuality. For this reason, any socially embodied sexual ethic will necessarily identify some of the purposes for sexuality as primary or central. The Christian community cannot practically give the same weight to every possible purpose for sexual activity or marriage in its sexual ethic. Since this is so, the community should privilege those purposes for sexuality that it has the strongest theological reasons for promoting. First among these, I would argue, is the basic purpose of procreation, under-stood comprehensively as including both physical and social reproduction.

Why should procreation, as opposed to (for example) the promotion of personal love between two individuals, be privileged in this way? I offer three reasons. The first is that, out of all the possible purposes for sexual activity or marriage, procreation is most closely tied to the basic doctrinal commitments of Christianity. I have already argued that the fundamental commitment to the doctrine of creation implies an acknowl-edgment of the goodness of procreation, and correlatively, when this doctrine has been challenged, the challenge has practically implied the rejection of procreative marriage as a legitimate Christian way of life. In this sense, marriage, understood traditionally as involving a procreative purpose, may be said to be the praxis corresponding to the theological doctrine of creation.

Secondly, by privileging procreation as the primary purpose for sexual activity, the Christian community thereby tethers it to concerns and values that extend beyond the sexual partners themselves. This tethering is important because it provides an important counterbalance to the exclusive and even narcissistic tendencies inherent in erotic love. As Stanley Hauerwas frequently reminds us, children are the paradigmatic strangers whom the Christian community is called upon to welcome.[68] In the process of making room for these strangers, a man and woman are challenged to transform their erotic relationship into a bond of mutual caring for a third party. Furthermore, this tethering serves to strengthen the sexual relationship itself. As Oliver O'Donovan says, the traditional Christian connection between sexual activity and procreation

> ... is good for the *man-woman relationship,* which is protected from debasement and triviality by the fact that it is fruitful for procreation. When erotic relationships between the sexes are conceived mainly as relationships – with no further implications, no "end" within the purposes of nature – then they lack the significance which they need if they are to be undertaken responsibly ... The honouring of each partner by the other must be founded on the honour which the relationship itself claims, by serving a fundamental good of the human race.[69]

Finally, by affirming the centrality of procreation for sexual ethics, the Christian community places itself in a position to affirm the value of forms of marriage that do not conform to the ideal of a companionate union held together by the love shared between the two parties. In my view, this is an authentically Christian ideal that should be fostered whenever possible. Nonetheless, it seems that specific social conditions are required for this ideal to flourish, conditions which do not exist in every society. On the other hand, nearly all societies institutionalize some kind of link between sexual relationships and procreation; if they did not, they would cease to exist. It should be possible for the Christian community to affirm the value of marriage in those societies that do not promote romantic love as a marital ideal, without denying the profound theological significance of the personal love between spouses, or denigrating the value of such love in those societies that do promote it.

None of this implies that procreation is the only legitimate purpose of sexual activity or marriage, or that it is the only purpose that can be defended on theological grounds, or much less that it is the only purpose that individual Christians can or should pursue in their sexual activities.

On the contrary, I do believe that other purposes, in particular the
fostering of interpersonal love, are also theologically valid aims for a sexual
relationship, and that in some cases these will legitimately be the primary
or only purposes for pursuing a sexual relationship. My point is rather
that the Christian community, functioning as a social unit, is committed
to promoting the procreative purpose of sexuality and marriage, whatever
else it recognizes and promotes as a value for sexual morality. This does
not imply that other purposes are illegitimate, or even that a commitment
to procreation should be primary for every individual Christian in his or
her sexual relationships. What it does imply, however, is the development
and promotion of a particular ideal of marriage and, following from that,
a set of guidelines for sexual morality, on the part of the Christian
community.

This brings us to a further point. It is undeniably true that our attitude
toward sexual transgressions is very different from that of the scholastics,
even apart from our differences with respect to specific moral questions.
The scholastic attitude is well expressed by Aquinas' remark, quoted
above, that sexual sins comprise the worst form of wrong-doing, next to
murder (*Summa contra gentiles* III 122). For most contemporary men and
women, such a view is incomprehensible. We tend to presuppose that
there are important differences between those kinds of actions that harm
other people, and sexual transgressions. Acts that harm others are strin-
gently prohibited, and those who carry them out are universally
condemned, and often punished through law as well. In contrast, we are
less comfortable drawing sharp lines between permissible and prohibited
forms of sexual behavior. While we do consider certain kinds of sexual
behavior to be wrong or shameful, we are too conscious of the complexity
of sexual relationships, and their incommunicable personal dimensions,
to be entirely comfortable with a highly stringent sexual morality.

In spite of the great difference between the scholastics and ourselves
in this respect, our own contrasting attitudes toward kinds of harm and
sexual transgressions reflect one aspect of scholastic thought: namely, their
claim that non-maleficence is a fundamental principle of the natural law.
When we add to this claim our own sense of the personal significance of
sexual relationships, our contemporary attitude toward sexual transgressions appears to be not only comprehensible but entirely appropriate. Yet
this line of thought might seem to suggest that we cannot formulate any

sexual morality at all beyond the level of the most general principles. And for those within the Christian community, at least, this has been an uncomfortable conclusion.

However, once we take full account of the communal character of Christian sexual ethics, we find a way out of this quandary. If it is in good order, Christian sexual ethics will give institutional form to our theological understanding of sexuality and the values and priorities stemming from that understanding. (The same can be said, *mutatis mutandis,* of the sexual ethics of any community.) Correlatively, in developing its sexual ethic, the Christian community will identify some kinds of actions and attitudes as exemplary expressions of its theological understanding of sexuality, while marking out others as inconsistent with that understanding. Hence, the sexual behavior of individuals within the Christian community will have a significance, for them and for the community as a whole, that goes beyond its immediate consequences and interpersonal meaning. Some actions will express and foster the institutionalized values of the community, while others will negate and undermine those values. And this dimension of sexual acts will matter, not only to the community, but to the individuals themselves, at least to the extent that they are committed to living a Christian life within a social context.

This does not mean that communal judgments of this sort can or should be decisive in every instance in evaluating sexual behavior. Sexual relationships have an irreducibly personal dimension that limits the scope of general judgments. Nonetheless, this insight needs to be balanced by the recognition that the theological commitments of the Christian community also have their claims. That is why Christians cannot be satisfied with a sexual ethic that simply applies the general principle of non-maleficence to sexual conduct; this is certainly a necessary starting point for a Christian sexual ethic, but there are other values that our sexual ethic should also affirm and promote.

Hence, a Christian sexual ethic should focus primarily on the ways in which the Christian community taken as a whole embodies a particular view of sexuality and marriage, while acknowledging the ambiguities and the need for subtle and discriminating judgment in the evaluation of individual actions. At the same time, no community can institutionalize anything without drawing boundaries, marking out some kinds of actions as incongruent with its ideals or incompatible with its common life. How might these boundaries be drawn in accordance with the view advocated here?

In order fully to address this question, it would be necessary to develop a complete sexual ethic, and that would take us well beyond the limits of the present study. In the next section, I will attempt the more modest task of indicating how this view of sexuality and marriage might be applied to some specific issues that are frequently discussed in terms of a natural law ethic, at least in Christian circles. By doing so, I hope to indicate more clearly what might be retrieved from the scholastic concept of the natural law, and what the concrete implications of such a retrieval might be. However, I make no claim to completeness or comprehensiveness in what follows.

5. Some specific issues

For the past thirty years, theological discussions of the natural law have been inextricably tied up with debates over the Roman Catholic prohibition of the use of contraceptives as set forth in the 1968 encyclical *Humanae vitae*. For many people both within and outside the Catholic community, the understanding of the natural law presented in this encyclical is *the* theory of the natural law or, at least, the distinctively Catholic theory of the natural law. Yet the traditions of natural law reflection that inform official Catholic teaching in this encyclical can also be developed in alternative ways.[70] Our examination of the scholastics' views on sexuality and marriage suggests one such alternative, which will preserve the central insight in the official Catholic view while avoiding its problematic formulation.

As is well known, *Humanae vitae* justifies the prohibition on the use of contraceptives by appealing to the structure of the sexual act and its intrinsic finality toward reproduction. The teaching that the use of contraceptives is always morally wrong, it explains,

> is founded upon the inseparable connection, willed by God and unable to be broken by man on his own initiative, between the two meanings of the conjugal act: the unitive meaning and the procreative meaning. Indeed, by its intimate structure, the conjugal act, while most closely uniting husband and wife, capac-

itates them for the generation of new lives, according to laws inscribed in the very being of man and woman. By safeguarding both these essential aspects, the unitive and the procreative, the conjugal act preserves in its fullness the sense of true mutual love and its ordination towards man's most high calling to parenthood. We believe that the men of our day are particularly capable of seizing the deeply reasonable and human character of this fundamental principle (*HV* para. 16).

Clearly, the encyclical affirms the theological value of procreation. At the same time, however, it also claims that the moral teaching being presented is universally accessible to all persons, in virtue of its "deeply reasonable and human character." It is perhaps for this reason that the encyclical argues on the basis of an analysis of the structure of the conjugal act, which is presumably objective and open to inspection by all.

Yet even the most sympathetic critics of *Humanae vitae* have found its focus on particular acts of sexual intercourse to be unpersuasive and even offensive. "To break marriage down into a series of disconnected sexual acts is to falsify its true nature"; in this remark, O'Donovan speaks for a considerable number of theologians, both Catholic and Protestant, who share the encyclical's view of the positive value of procreation but find its specific analysis unpersuasive.[71]

Nonetheless, the Christian understanding of marriage does imply that children are among the greatest blessings of the marriage relationship, and what is more, that they are a gift that should not be refused lightly. At the very least, there is something problematic, from the Christian standpoint, in the deliberate choice to remain childless throughout a marriage. Many of the critics of *Humanae vitae* would agree with the encyclical up to this point. And yet, why should this be so?

In part, these questions can be answered by drawing on the theological arguments for the goodness of procreation, as the scholastics developed them. While *Humanae vitae* arguably reflects similar theological convictions, they are obscured by the encyclical's concern to present its arguments in terms of a universally accessible moral rationality. For the scholastics, on the other hand, the defense of procreation and marriage follows from a doctrinal commitment to the goodness of creation. Many Christians of all denominations share the view that the Christian community should be "pro-family," and the scholastic defense of procreation helps us to see that this sentiment reflects a deep and sound doctrinal instinct. This need not imply that other possible values are unimportant, or much less illegitimate, but it does reflect a sense that a commitment to procreation should have a central place in the public witness of the church.

Given such a public stance, we would expect the Christian community to discourage the use of contraceptives. We as a community cannot celebrate human procreation as a centrally important way of expressing our faith in the goodness of God's creation without also implying that the deliberate frustration of human fertility is at best regrettable. It does not follow that the use of contraceptives is never morally justified. Nor does it imply that the Christian community should attempt to formulate the circumstances in which contraceptives may or may not be used; this is the sort of judgment that can best be made by particular couples, in view of their own circumstances and personal needs. Yet we need not say that the use of contraceptives is unjustifiable in all circumstances in order to acknowledge that, seen from the Christian standpoint, this practice involves a genuine loss, a sacrifice of a precious human capacity.

For the past several decades, we have been aware of the fact that a deliberate policy of family limitation may be necessary if we as a species are not to outstrip the earth's capacity to sustain human life. At the same time, there has been considerable debate over whether birth control is either necessary to keep human population in check, or the best means for achieving this goal. Without attempting to resolve this debate, we can at least say that a collective policy of family limitation is expedient, and may be necessary, in light of the risk of global overpopulation. Nonetheless, the Christian community does have a stake in attempting to influence the way in which such a policy is carried out: for example, by encouraging reliance on education and the expansion of economic opportunities to the greatest extent possible. At the same time, it is critically important, for the sake of the integrity of its own witness, that the Christian community not fall into the trap of regarding procreation itself as undesirable in view of our planet's limited resources. It may well be that the Christian witness to the goodness of procreation should place more emphasis on the social and communal dimensions of this process, but that should not take the form of denying the fundamental goodness, the natural joy and hopefulness, of pregnancy and birth.

By the same token, a deliberate refusal on the part of a married couple to have children at all is problematic from a Christian standpoint. Of course, such a choice may be practically necessary: for example, if the woman's life or health would be threatened by pregnancy, or the economic or social conditions of the couple rule out the possibility that they could properly raise any children of the marriage. In such cases as these, the Christian community should encourage couples to express the value of procreation in other ways, either through adoption or the care of foster children or else through committing themselves as a couple to fostering the life of the wider society.

What about the contrasting case, in which couples who are incapable of having children turn to medical technologies to help them conceive? Once again, many readers will be familiar with the arguments around this topic that have developed in Catholic circles. The official prohibition against the use of most reproductive technologies rests on two arguments. The first of these appeals to the structure of the human act and its intrinsic orientation toward reproduction (*Donum vitae* sec.4; although I cannot argue the point here, I believe that the appeal to the structure of the human act, and the immediately subsequent appeal to the "language of the body," are in fact two variants of the same argument). A number of theologians, myself included, have found this line of analysis unpersuasive, just as it is unpersuasive as an argument against the use of contraceptives.[72] However, the second argument is in my view more telling:

> In reality, the origin of a human person is the result of an act of giving. The one conceived must be the fruit of his parents' love. He cannot be desired or conceived as the product of an intervention of medical or biological techniques; that would be equivalent to reducing him to an object of scientific technology. No one may subject the coming of a child into the world to conditions of technical efficiency which are to be evaluated according to standards of control and dominion (*Donum vitae,* sec. 4).

I do not want in any way to minimize the pain suffered by those who are unable to have children, or to deny the good faith and compassion of those who wish to use all the resources of medical technology in order to help them. Those children who are conceived by artificial reproductive technologies are certainly wanted children, as their parents' desperate efforts make clear. Yet once again we need to ask, what are the human meanings that are being institutionalized as we move toward the regular practice of artificial reproductive technologies? *Donum vitae* seems to me to be right on this point. In such a situation, the values embodied in our social practices do tend toward viewing children as potentially products of technology.[73] This, in turn, is problematic because it undermines the fundamental basis for equality in the shared biological givens of our lives. A child who is conceived and born in the normal way comes into the world as the result of biological processes that cannot be initiated simply at the parents' choice. In this respect, he or she comes into the world independently of the wishes of the parents, just as they themselves once did. On the other hand, a child who is conceived through biomedical technologies comes about as the foreseen product of a technical procedure, and it seems to me that this undermines the child's parity with its parents.

It does not follow that every form of biomedical technology should be discouraged. Various forms of genetic therapy, which involve manipulating the genetic code for the benefit of an individual or his or her progeny, are sometimes stigmatized as unnatural, but given the concept of the natural law defended here, there is no reason why this should be the case. There is nothing particularly sacred about the genetic code or its material substratum *per se,* although we would be well advised not to tinker with it unless we are very sure indeed about what we are doing. Even germ-line therapy, which involves manipulating the genetic material in reproductive cells, need not be considered in the same light as producing a child through artificial means of reproduction. Germ-line therapy is not aimed directly at producing a child; it is a therapeutic measure, aimed at curing a defect in the individual patient, with foreseen benefits for all that individual's future children.

What about the situation of those who cannot enter into procreative unions for another reason: namely, homosexuals? The scholastics are united in agreeing that the homosexual acts are gravely sinful violations of the natural order. Having examined their sexual ethic, we can appreciate why they make this claim. Not only are there explicit scriptural condemnations of homosexual practices, but the unnaturalness of homosexuality also follows from the scholastic understanding of the purposes of sexuality. Furthermore, the relevant scriptural texts and the classical sources, particularly Ulpian's definition of the natural law, reinforced each other on this point, in such a way as to foreclose the possibility of softening the scriptural prohibitions by interpreting them through an expanded concept of the natural law. Finally, their widespread consensus that sexual pleasure is inherently problematic made it impossible for the scholastics even to consider that acts that seemingly have no other purpose than pleasure could be morally licit.

Beginning (at least) in the early decades of the twentieth century, the condemnation of same-sex actions began to be challenged, within the Christian community as well as in the wider society. In part, this challenge stemmed from a growing conviction that homosexuality is itself a part of the natural human condition; more fundamentally, it reflected far-reaching changes in general attitudes toward sexuality itself. Increasingly, we have come to appreciate the ways in which sexuality can be a medium for the expression of love between two persons, a basis for self-development, and a source of joy and pleasure. None of these aims is necessarily linked to reproduction. Given this view of sexuality, it is difficult to expect someone to refrain from sexual expression simply because he or she is homosexual, particularly if homosexuality is seen as an irreversible orientation. Ironically, some Christians defend homosexual practices by appealing to a version of a natural law argument since, if homosexuality occurs spontaneously in some people, then it would appear to be *ipso facto* natural and good.

Even if it is the case that homosexuality is a constitutive part of human nature as it actually exists, however, that does not mean that it is good, at least not on the logic of the scholastic concept of the natural law. As we noted in Chapter 2, this concept can accommodate different understandings of nature, but not any understanding whatever. Specifically, the intrinsic tendencies of an individual cannot give rise to a natural law, because they are too general, and neither can recurring pathologies, even if characteristic of a species, because they are not directed toward some recognizable good. Hence alcoholism, for example, cannot be considered to be a naturally good tendency, even though it is natural in the sense of being proper to some individuals and appears to stem from a genetic defect typical of our species. I choose this example because it is so often put forward as a counter-example to the claim that homosexuality must be good because it is innate to some individuals or to the species as a whole.

Andrew Sullivan has recently responded to this counter-example. In the process of doing so, he develops a more persuasive theological argument for the moral licitness of homosexual acts:

> The real reason alcoholism does not work as an analogy [to homosexuality] is a deeper one. It is that alcoholism does not reach to the core of the human condition in the way that homosexuality, following the logic of the Church's arguments, does. If alcoholism is overcome, through a renunciation of alcoholic acts, it allows the human being to realize his or her full potential, a part of which, according to the Church, is the supreme act of self-giving in a life of matrimonial love. But if homosexuality is overcome, by the renunciation of homosexual acts, the opposite is the truth: the human being is liberated into sacrifice and pain, barred from the act of union with another that the Church holds to be intrinsic to the notion of human flourishing in the vast majority of human lives. Homosexuality is a structural condition which, even if allied to a renunciation of homosexual acts, disbars the human being from such a fully realized life. The gay or lesbian person is disordered at a far deeper level than the alcoholic: At the level of the human capacity to love and be loved by another human being, in a union based on fidelity and self-giving.[74]

As his subsequent argument indicates, Sullivan himself does not believe that the "gay or lesbian person is disordered at a far deeper level than the alcoholic"; rather, his point is that we should accept homosexuality as an alternative way of expressing the basic human good of interpersonal love.

Sullivan goes further; not only does homosexuality offer one form for the expression of interpersonal love, but it can serve as a kind of affirmation for the centrality of heterosexual love:

> In many animal species and almost all human cultures, there are some who seem to find their destiny in a similar but different sexual and emotional union. They do this not by subverting their own nature, or indeed human nature, but by fulfilling it in a way

that doesn't deny heterosexual primacy, but rather honors it by
its rare and distinct otherness ... the homosexual person might
be seen as a natural foil to the heterosexual norm, a variation that
does not eclipse the theme, but resonates with it. Extinguishing
– or prohibiting – homosexuality is, from this point of view, not
a virtuous necessity, but the real crime against nature, a refusal
to accept the variety of God's creation, a denial of the way in
which the other need not threaten, but may give depth and
contrast to the self.[75]

What we see here is an argument for the naturalness of homosexuality
precisely in terms of its intelligible purpose, seen from the standpoint of
a theological interpretation of human sexuality. As such, it is in accordance
with the basic logic of the scholastic concept of the natural law, although
Sullivan does not frame it in those terms. Furthermore, his argument
suggests a way in which the Christian community could incorporate a
positive affirmation of homosexuality into its corporate witness to the
goodness of procreation and marriage.

At the same time, we need to consider not only whether individual
homosexual acts might be morally permissible, or what forms a genuinely
Christian affirmation of homosexuality might take, but also how homosexuality is institutionalized in the wider society. In reflecting on this
issue, it is important to realize that there is as much diversity of lifestyles
among gays and lesbians as there is among straight men and women. Yet
there do appear to be some characteristically gay lifestyles, which are
cohesive enough to be considered as stable institutionalized social options
for expressing a homosexual orientation, and which are sustained through
a complex set of rituals, roles, and expectations. Generalizations in this
regard need to be offered with great caution, but it seems fair to say that
these lifestyles are typically characterized by a celebration of the erotic,
as expressed through a cult of personal beauty and the practice of widespread sexual activity.

What is wrong with any of this? Of course, the threat of AIDS has
led to modifications in gay sexual practices, but AIDS is not a necessary
concomitant of a gay lifestyle, nor is it by any means an exclusively "gay
disease." There is an element of misogyny in some sectors of the gay
community, and its celebration of personal beauty can have cruel conse-

quences for older persons. However, misogyny and the worship of youth and beauty are not unknown among heterosexuals, either. Over against these negative elements, these gay lifestyles offer much that is positive, in particular, a celebration of eroticism, humor, freedom, and play. A life devoted to the pursuit of such values can have its own integrity and goodness, even when it takes forms that shock the sensibilities of many others.[76]

Yet this does not mean that all of these lifestyles are necessarily compatible with Christianity, or that the church should try to incorporate them into its common life. In the last chapter, we observed that a way of life may be an expression of genuine natural goods but still be in tension with, or even incompatible with, Christianity. I would suggest that in some of its forms, contemporary gay culture offers examples of such a way of life. The privileging of the erotic and the affirmation of sexual freedom do reflect natural human tendencies and genuine goods. But such a construal of human sexuality, with its privileging of the value of the erotic and its concomitant de-emphasis of the value of procreation, stands in tension, at least, with a Christian sexual ethic. Hence, the difficulty with some forms of contemporary gay culture, seen from a theological standpoint, is not that they represent an evil or unnatural way of life. Rather, they are problematic because they represent an alternative construal of human nature that has its own value and integrity but that is nonetheless in tension with fundamental Christian commitments.

The tension does not stem from the fact that homosexual activity is non-procreative. Rather, it reflects a more basic tension between the values of erotic experience and procreation, when these are considered as potentially key values for a socially embodied sexual ethic. The bearing and raising of children is not particularly sexy, and more important, it requires a degree of stability in interpersonal relationships that is not readily compatible with a primary commitment to the pursuit of the erotic. I am not saying that the two values cannot be brought together, but it is difficult to see how individuals, or much less communities, could give equal weight to both. One or the other must be given priority, and it is here, in the choice of priorities, that a Christian sexual ethic will be in tension with some aspects of contemporary gay culture.

Of course, the gay community does not have a monopoly on the celebration of eroticism. Its privileging of the erotic reflects a more general

tendency to invest sexual experience with spiritual value and to celebrate
sensuality and immediacy over against the rational and historical, which
characterize romanticism. Seen in this light, gay culture in some of its
forms is only one expression, albeit an especially prominent and striking
expression, of a romantic strain that has been prominent in Western
cultures for at least two centuries. Romanticism, in turn, is partially rooted
in Christian beliefs and sensibilities, but that does not mean it is theologically unproblematic.[77] Christians should be wary of the high spiritual
value given to sexuality, not because of the carnality of sex, but because
this particular route to enlightenment is too easy. This does not mean
that romanticism is morally evil, but again, it reflects a privileging of
human goods that is in tension, at least, with a Christian construal of
human values. We Christians can acknowledge the goodness and integrity
of this strain of secular culture, while still promoting an alternative way
of life which is more congruent with our central doctrinal commitments.

Near the end of a survey of current Roman Catholic sexual ethics,
the theologian Lisa Cahill remarks:

In my view, the Catholic Church needs to develop a "credible
witness" on moral matters, including sexual morality. It needs to
speak to the situation of moral confusion in the larger cultures
in which it exists ... It needs the courage to hold up ideals in
sexual morality beyond personal fulfillment and individual
autonomy. It needs to be said that commitment and children are
somehow essentially connected to sexual relationships as important human meanings. There should be a bias in marriage in favor
of children; children are not a merely incidental outcome of the
marital relationship, to be excluded if spouses choose to be "child
free." Conversely, children are not a "right" of all adults, even
married ones, even though children are a great blessing. When
a couple faces infertility, they usually undergo considerable
suffering, and it is commendable to attempt its alleviation through
medical means. But there may be limits to means which are
acceptable.[78]

This is a good summary of the sexual ethic implied by a contemporary
appropriation of the scholastic concept of the natural law. While Cahill
does not propose it at such, it is no coincidence that she speaks from

within a moral tradition that has been shaped by that concept. In this way, it is not a sexual ethic for Catholics only (nor is that Cahill's intent).

Indeed, we would expect this ideal to take different forms in different churches. Some churches have theological and cultural traditions that are historically more open to recognizing a variety of purposes and forms for sexual expression, in addition to its primary procreative form; others are more austere in their construal of sexuality. By the same token, the churches have different resources for accommodating the complexities of individual experience through their official structures. For example, communities that emphasize the sacramental character of marriage will have less flexibility in recognizing alternative forms of partnership than those communities that have a "low" doctrine of marriage. However, these complexities must be left for another day.

Notes to Chapter 4

1   Mark D. Jordan, *The Invention of Sodomy in Christian Theology* (Chicago: University of Chicago Press, 1997), 156.

2   See, for example, John T. Noonan, *Contraception: A History of Its Treatment by the Catholic Theologians and Canonists* (1965; repr. New York: New American Library, 1997), 308; Charles E. Curran, "Natural Law in Moral Theology," in Charles E. Curran and Richard A. McCormick, S.J., eds., *Readings in Moral Theology No. 7: Natural Law and Theology* (Mahwah, NJ: Paulist Press, 1991), 247-295 at 254-261, and by implication, Michael Crowe, *The Changing Profile of the Natural Law* (The Hague: Martinus Nijhoff, 1977), 147-155; and Jordan, *The Invention of Sodomy*, 157-158.

3   For example, John Dedek argues that the scholastic theologians actually grounded their view that fornication is sinful in scriptural positive law, rather than the natural law; see John F. Dedek, "Premarital Sex: The Theological Argument from Peter Lombard to Durand," *Theological Studies* 41 (1980), 643-667.

4   This way of framing the scholastic view raises a question. Do the scholastics have a view of sexuality at all? Or is the very idea of a human sexuality that exists apart from sexual acts a modern invention, as Michel Foucault suggests in the first volume of his *Histoire de la sexualité* (Paris: NRF/Gallimard, 1976), 50-67?

It is true that "sexuality" is a modern term. As Pat Caplan points out, the first known citation dates from 1800; see her "Introduction" in *The Cultural Construction of Sexuality* (1987; repr. London: Routledge, 1996), 2. Furthermore, Foucault is right to say that the medieval sexual ethic is an ethic for marriage, although he is not correct on all the details of that ethic (*Histoire de la sexualité*, 51-52), and he is probably also right that the concept of a sexual orientation as an overall personal identity is a distinctively modern idea (59). Nonetheless, as Joan Cadden documents in some detail, during the period we are studying there was an extensive body of medical and philosophical work on the etiology of sex differences and their characteristic expressions, the biology of sexual desire, and related topics; see her *Meanings of Sex Difference in the Middle Ages: Medicine, Science, and Culture* (Cambridge: Cambridge University Press, 1993), particularly 105-166 and 279-282. The scholastics were aware of this work, and some of them, most notably Albert the Great, contributed to it. For this reason, it is not accurate to say that the scholastics were unaware of, or uninterested in, sexual desire and its effects on human life, apart from its expressions in particular acts. Furthermore, they did discuss the interrelationships between particular sexual tendencies and overall character and disposition, even though Foucault is right that they did not think of sexual orientation as a total personal identity. In short, the scholastics' discussions of sexual ethics are informed by an awareness that there is more to human sexual experience than sexual acts, and their moral reflections are informed by that awareness. In other words, they do have an idea of sexuality, even though they do not have any one term corresponding to the word "sexuality."

5   In this and the following two sections, I draw extensively on Noonan's *Contraception* and James A. Brundage, *Law, Sex, and Christian Society in Medieval Europe* (Chicago: University of Chicago Press, 1987), both to provide a background and context for scholastic thinking on sexuality and to supply details of their specific views not contained in the texts available to me. On the classical and patristic antecedents to the scholastic sexual ethic, see Noonan, *Contraception*, 66-136 and Brundage, *Law, Sex, and Christian Society*, 77-123.

6   Noonan, *Contraception*, 137-175; Noonan focuses here on Manicheeism and Augustine's reaction to it, but he also discusses the wider orthodox reaction to dualism.

7   *Ibid.*, 179.

8   Noonan attributes this view to Hugh of St. Victor (*Contraception*, 239), but so far as I can determine, Hugh only says that the agreement between the spouses is a sacrament of the love between God and the soul (*De sacramentis* I 8.13). At any rate, it is misleading to say, as Noonan does, that for Hugh the spiritual bond between the spouses is "the subject matter of the sacrament" (*ibid.*). It is a sacrament specifically of the relationship of God to the soul, while the bodily union between the spouses is a sacrament of the relationship of Christ to the church.

9   As Brundage points out, *Law, Sex, and Christian Society*, 203; cf. Peter Abelard's *Ethica*, with introduction and translation by D.E. Luscombe (Oxford: Oxford University Press, 1971), 18-24.

10   Noonan, *Contraception*, 237-288. As Brundage observes, the Augustinian analysis is also found in Gratian; see *Law, Sex, and Christian Society*, 235.

11   Noonan offers an especially helpful account of the influence of Catharism and similar movements on the sexual ethics of the twelfth and thirteenth centuries in *Contraception*, 211-244; also see Brundage, *Law, Sex, and Christian Society*, 429-431. According to Roger French and Andrew Cunningham, the polemic against homosexuals in Alan of Lille's *De Planctu Naturae* is motivated by the perceived homosexual practices of the Cathars; see *Before Science: The Invention of the Friars' Natural Philosophy* (Aldershot, U.K.: Scolar Press, 1996), 104-106.

12   According to John Boswell, clerical celibacy was frequently linked with homosexuality throughout the latter eleventh and twelfth centuries; see *Christianity, Social Tolerance, and Homosexuality* (Chicago: University of Chicago Press, 1980), 216-218. It is noteworthy that one of the most assiduous advocates of clerical celibacy in the eleventh century, Peter Damian, was also one of the most outspoken and vehement critics of homosexual practices in this period. His *Liber Gomorrhianus* reflects his fear that too many clerics are, so to speak, getting away with at least some such practices, and Mark Jordan suggests that he was also preoccupied with the possibility of homosexuality among monks; his *The Invention of Sodomy*, 45-66 and *Christianity, Social Tolerance and Homosexuality*, 210-214 offer good discussions of this treatise. At the same time, it is not clear that Peter Damian's contemporaries shared his strong views on this subject. Both Brundage and John Boswell believe that Pope Alexander II tried to have the *Liber Gomorrhianus* suppressed; see Brundage, *Law, Sex, and Chris-*

tian Society, 212-213, and Boswell, *Christianity, Social Tolerance, and Homosexuality*, 212-213. Jordan disagrees, citing only Boswell, but does not explain why; see *The Invention of Sodomy*, 45.

Boswell argues that the condemnations of homosexuality in the twelfth century were balanced by Christian authors in this period who affirmed "the positive value of homosexual relations ..." (*Christianity, Social Tolerance, and Homosexuality*, 210; the argument as a whole is developed in 207-242). However, the evidence which he offers here does not appear to me to support this claim. The authors he cites do not say that homosexual sexual relations are morally good or neutral; rather, they speak of their same-sex friendships in remarkably intense and erotic terms, which Boswell takes to be commendations of homosexual relations. Yet in the absence of more specific evidence, we cannot be sure that these authors would have understood their relations in sexual terms, or much less that they were actually sexual relationships and were being commended as such. What Boswell has shown, in my view, is that there was a marked strain of homoeroticism in twelfth-century culture, which should be seen in the context of a pronounced awareness of romantic love and sexuality in all its forms.

13   Brundage, *Law, Sex and Christian Society*. 262. Apparently, this view originated with Gregory the Great, in whom according to Noonan, "the Stoic distrust of pleasure was pushed to the limit." See Noonan, *Contraception*, 188 and, more generally, 187-190.

14   As we read in *Contraception*, 243.

15   See, for example, *Contraception*, 353-354; however, Noonan adds that Aquinas goes beyond Aristotle in his view that sexual pleasure serves a purpose, that is, providing an inducement to have sex; *Contraception*, 354.

16   The distinction between natural and non-natural desires goes back to the Epicureans; see Julia Annas, *The Morality of Happiness* (Oxford: Oxford University Press, 1993), 188-200 for a discussion of the Epicurean doctrine on this point. However, I am not able to trace Aquinas' direct sources for the distinction.

17   Similarly, Jordan observes that, for Aquinas, the pleasure connected with homosexual acts is "a kind of pleasure that cannot be divided without remainder into teleological sequences ... a pleasure without end" (*The Invention of Sodomy*, 156). He further asserts that Aquinas's account cannot make sense of this limitless pleasure, a view that in my opinion is incorrect precisely because Jordan ignores Aquinas's distinction between non-natural and natural desire.

18   On the doctrine of the marriage debt, see Noonan, *Contraception*, 343-345 and Brundage, *Law, Sex, and Christian Society*, 282-284.

19   Noonan sets out the patristic and early medieval development of this view in *Contraception*, 129-130 and 179-181.

20   *Ibid.*, 190-210.

21   As Noonan shows, the link between contraception and homicide continued to be affirmed throughout the twelfth and thirteenth centuries, but not firmly or consistently; *Contraception*, 282-288. In our own day, this analysis of contraception is once again being revived by Germain Grisez and John Finnis; see Germain Grisez, Joseph Boyle, John Finnis, and William May, "Every Marital Act Ought to Be Open to New Life: Towards a Clearer Understanding," *The Thomist* 52.3 (July 1988), 365-426. On the decretists, see *Contraception*, 212-221; on the views of Albert and Aquinas, see *Contraception*, 284-285.

Brundage claims, contrary to Noonan, that for Gratian the use of contraceptives is only venially sinful, on the basis of the *Decretum* D.25.3.7 and C.32.2.5; see *Law, Sex, and Christian Society*, 241. However, in neither place does Gratian say that the use of contraceptives is venially sinful; what he says (quoting Augustine, in the earlier passage) is that it is venially sinful to engage in sexual intercourse within marriage simply in order to satisfy sexual desire. At the same time, Gratian's condemnation of the use of contraceptives envisions a context in which the partners have entered into a relationship solely for the purpose of mutually satisfying their sexual desire; the question he is considering is whether such a relationship should count as a marriage, or not. This does not mean that he would have approved of the use of contraceptives within a full-fledged marriage, but it does suggest that, for him, the use of contraceptives per se is not a focus for concern. See C.32.2.7 for the relevant text.

22   On the views of the decretists, see Noonan, *Contraception*, 212-221; on the views of Albert and Aquinas, see *Contraception*, 284-285. I take the references just cited from Noonan.

23   Similarly, Bonaventure rejects a natural-law argument based on an appeal to the teleologies of organs, albeit not in a specifically sexual context; see *De Per. Evan.* II.3 *ad* 4.

24   Noonan, *Contraception*, 295; compare his remark at 293 on the appeal to animal behavior as a standard for rationality.

25   This would not apply to every sense of nature, but it would certainly apply to nature understood in the most relevant sense in this context, that is, to nature understood as the characteristic essence of a particular species of creature. In addition, for a discussion of twelfth-century natural philosophy as applied specifically to sexuality, see Cadden, *Meanings of Sex Difference*, 54-104.

26   In addition to Huguccio, most canonists and theologians, in addition to some of the civilians, analyze marriage in this way, of course with variations in detail. Civilians who provide or suggest such an understanding of marriage include Irnerius, Weigand no. 10; the *Summa Vindobonensis*, Weigand no. 27; and Azo, Weigand no. 81. Out of many possible examples among the canonists, see Rufin, Weigand 242; the *Summa Tractaturus Magister*, Weigand no. 322-323; the *Cologne Summa*, Lottin 106; Simon of Bisignano, Lottin 107; the *Leipzig summa*, Lottin 108; and Alan, Weigand no. 227-228. Examples of theologians who take this line include William of Auxerre, *Summa aurea* IV, 17, 3.2-3; Roland of Cremona, Lottin 1931, 115; the Fran-

ciscan William of Meliton, Lottin 121-122; Bonaventure, *In IV Sent.*, d.33, 1.1,2, and Aquinas, *Summa theologiae* II-II 153.2.

27 Brundage claims that Huguccio does not consider marriage to be a part of the nat-ural law because of his generally negative views on sexuality; see *Law, Sex, and Christian Society*, 261. However, as this quotation indicates, Huguccio does claim that the practice of marriage stems from sexual impulses grounded in the sensuality, since these are then directed by reason and divine law. In other words, he does recognize a natural law corresponding to our pre-rational sexual impulses, which he identifies as the basis for marriage. Nonetheless, he considers marriage itself to be an effect of the natural law because, as we have seen, he identifies the natural law with basic principles, not with the particular rules or practices stemming from those prin-ciples. Similarly, Azo, Weigand no. 81, the civilian *Summa Vindobonensis*, Weigand no. 27, and the canonist John Faventius, Weigand no. 252, all note that marriage is an effect of the natural law, rather than being itself part of the natural law.

28 Quoted by John Gallagher in "Magisterial Teaching from 1918 to the Present," in Charles E. Curran and Richard A. McCormick, eds., *Readings in Moral Theology No. 8: Dialogue about Catholic Sexual Teaching* (New York: Paulist Press, 1993), 71-92 at 73. Gallagher's essay offers a sympathetic and helpful overview of the development of official Roman Catholic sexual ethics in the twentieth century.

29 Albert explicitly says that, even though marriage was instituted by God, it has sub-sequently been shaped by both divine and human law; see *De Sacramentis* 9.6. The canonists held similar views; see for example the *Cologne summa*, Lottin 106.

30 C.H. Lawrence, *The Friars: The Impact of the Early Mendicant Movement on Western Society* (London: Longman, 1994), 102-126. In part, this alliance reflected the fact that the mendicants saw the urban societies of their time as a major field for their evangelical effort. It also reflected complex social and economic factors, which brought the mendicants and the urban middle classes into mutually beneficial rela-tionship of material and spiritual support. On this latter point, see in addition Lester K. Little, *Religious Poverty and the Property Economy in Medieval Europe* (Ithaca, NY: Cornell University Press, 1978), particularly 146-169.

31 In addition, as David Herlihy documents, not only was polygamy practiced until relatively late in parts of Western Europe, but it was mentioned in lives of the saints dating from the early Middle Ages; hence, the scholastics could have been aware that some Christians, as well as the saints of the old covenant, practiced polygamy. See Herlihy, *Medieval Households* (Cambridge, MA: Harvard University Press, 1985), 29-55.

32 The traditional view that the *Summa contra gentiles* was written for this purpose has been challenged, most recently by Thomas Hibbs, *Dialectic and Narrative in Aquinas: The Interpretation of the Summa contra gentiles* (Notre Dame, IN: University of Notre Dame Press, 1995). I find Hibbs's argument to be generally convincing. However, Aquinas need not have been writing a manual for missionaries in order to address

the moral beliefs of the Muslims at some points, and it seems likely that that is what he is doing in these texts.

33   In addition to Aquinas's treatment discussed below, we find discussions of the irregular sexual activities of the patriarchs in a number of theologians, including Philip the Chancelor, cited in Lottin 113; Roland of Cremona, Lottin 30; Bonaventure, *In IV Sent.* 22; and in Albert, *De Sacramentis* XI.3.1 and *In IV Sent.* 33.

34   For a discussion of specific antecedents to Aquinas's distinction, see Crowe, *The Changing Profile of the Natural Law,* 179-184.

35   Note, however, that Aquinas attempts to analyze the rationale in terms of the objective aims of the precept in question, and not in terms of distinguishing between licit and illicit motives, as most of his predecessors did.

36   See Gallagher, "Magisterial Teaching from 1918 to the Present," particularly 72-77, on this point.

37   As Noonan, at least, recognizes; see *Contraception,* 337-341.

38   See, for example, Albert, *In IV Sent.* 33.3; Aquinas, *In IV Sent.* 33.1.3, 2.2 and *Summa contra gentiles* III 121, 124; and Bonaventure, *De Per. Evan.* III.1, which describes the purpose of marriage as bringing forth children "for the cult of God."

39   For example, see Aquinas, *Summa contra gentiles* III 124, and Bonaventure, *In IV Sent.* 33.1.3 *ad* 2.

We may question whether a system for guaranteeing paternity is really essential to the maintenance of a social order, but the scholastics apparently did not. This assumption may reflect the fact that European society in the high Middle Ages moved increasingly from a cognatic system, which traces descent through both parents, to an agnatic system, which traces descent through the male line only; see Herlihy, *Medieval Households,* 82-88.

40   As we read in Bonaventure, *In IV Sent.* 33.1.1, and in Aquinas, *Summa contra gentiles* III 124.

41   In addition to the general background provided in Chapter 1, see Brundage, *Law, Sex, and Christian Society,* 176-228 and Herlihy, *Medieval Households,* 79-111 for a discussion of the impact of the church reform movement on sexual ethics in this period.

42   Brundage, *Law, Sex, and Christian Society,* 183.

43   *Ibid.*

44   As both Brundage and Herlihy point out; see *Law, Sex, and Christian Society,* 265 and *Medieval Households,* 81-82. It should be noted, however, that they are both referring to the more specific legal doctrine that present consent alone, that is to say, even without sexual intercourse, establishes a valid marriage.

45   Georges Duby, *Love and Marriage in the Middle Ages,* Jane Dunnett, trans. (Chicago: University of Chicago Press, 1994), 25-26; for a discussion of attempts to enforce this requirement, see Brundage, *Law, Sex, and Christian Society,* 331-336, 337-341.

46   For an extensive discussion of the different positions on the requirements for the validity of a marriage, see Brundage, *Law, Sex, and Christian Society,* 235-242 (on Gratian's view), 256-278 (on Peter Lombard and his followers), and 333-338, 430-443 on subsequent developments. In addition, see Herlihy, *Medieval Households,* 81-82 for a discussion of the social implications of Lombard's view.

47   As Brundage shows, secret marriages were discouraged and penalized but their legitimacy was nonetheless acknowledged in this period; see *Law, Sex, and Christian Society,* 189-190, 276-277, 335-336, 440-443.

48   On this and subsequent church legislation on the marriage of unfree persons, see Antonia Bocarius Sahaydachcy, "The Marriage of Unfree Persons: Twelfth Century Decretals and Letters," in *De Jure Canonico Medii: Festschrift fur Rudolf Weigand, Studia Gratiana* XXVII (1996), 483-506. As Sahaydachcy goes on to show, *Dignum est* was subsequently challenged, but the popes consistently upheld the validity of the marriages of unfree persons.

49   Compare Bonaventure's analysis of the limits of obedience, which is couched in more general terms but implies similar restrictions; see *De Per. Evan.* IV 4.1,2.

50   Duby, *Love and Marriage in the Middle Ages,* 28.

51   See, for example, the cases discussed in Noonan, *Contraception,* 357-358 and Brundage, *Law, Sex, and Christian Society,* 359-360, although we should be cautious about generalizing too far from them.

52   Bernard William's "The Idea of Equality," in his *Problems of the Self* (Cambridge: Cambridge University Press, 1973), 230-249, offers an early, highly influential analysis of the justification and meaning of normative equality. For an analysis of this ideal from the standpoint of recent work in theological ethics, see Gene Outka, *Agape: An Ethical Analysis* (New Haven, CT: Yale University Press, 1972), 260-274.

53   Herlihy, *Medieval Households,* 100-101. Compare his view to that of Duby, who believes that the position of women improved during the medieval period, but since the position of men improved still more, "it is debatable whether there was ever any appreciable change in the gulf between the two sexes"; *Love and Marriage,* 95. For a general overview of the legal and social position of women in the period between 1050 and 1250, see Edith Ennen, *The Medieval Woman,* Edmund Jephcott, trans. (Oxford: Blackwell, 1989), 97-147.

54   The roles played by women in this period as spiritual leaders, counselors, mystics, and even preachers has been well documented. Carolyn Walker Bynum's highly influential *Jesus as Mother: Studies in the Spirituality of the High Middle Ages* (Berkeley, CA: University of California Press, 1982), 110-262 shows how women in monastic communities drew on a fluid symbolism of gender to justify their exercise of author-

ity and power, just as men in these communities similarly drew on this symbolism to represent themselves as submissive to authority. For discussions of women's exercise of different forms of spiritual authority outside monastic communities, see Herlihy, *Medieval Households*, 120-130 and André Vauchez, *Les laïcs au Moyen Age: Pratiques et expériences religieuses* (Paris: Cerf, 1987), 189-250.

55   For Aristotle's view, see the *Politics* I 13, in particular 1260a 10-30.

56   See John Hilary Martin, "The Injustice of Not Ordaining Women: A Problem for Medieval Theologians," *Theological Studies* 48 (1987), 303-316.

57   The attribution of this letter has been challenged, but no one denies that it is addressed to a woman ruler; see Jean-Pierre Torrell, *Initiation à saint Thomas d'Aquin* (Fribourg: Cerf, 1993), 318-321, for a good summary of the relevant arguments.

58   Compare this to Gratian's remark that the exclusion of women from the office of judge is based on custom rather than nature, and more specifically, that it does not presuppose that women lack the power of judgment (*Decretum* C.3, q.7, 1.1).

59   Duby, *Love and Marriage in the Middle Ages*, 99.

60   We have seen a number of examples of this approach, including most recently Aquinas's distinction in *In IV Sent.* 33.1.1, cited above, between those natural ends that are proper to the human person generically, and those that are proper to the human person considered specifically.

61   This claim is made so often that it has assumed the status of a truism. For a theologically oriented defense, see Alistair I. McFadyen, *The Call to Personhood: A Christian Theory of the Individual in Social Relationships* (Cambridge: Cambridge University Press, 1991). More recently, Diana Fritz Cates has offered what is in my view a more satisfactory account of ways in which persons are and are not relational in her *Choosing to Feel: Virtue, Friendship, and Compassion for Friends* (Notre Dame, IN: University of Notre Dame Press, 1997).

62   For Foucault's remarks, see *Histoire de la sexualité*, 65-66; for a good general survey of work on the social construction of sexuality in the latter part of the twentieth century, see Caplan's "Introduction" in *The Cultural Construction of Sexuality*, 1-30.

63   Lisa Cahill, *Sex, Gender, and Christian Ethics* (Cambridge: Cambridge University Press, 1996), 111.

64   Ernst Mayr, "The Multiple Meanings of Teleological," in *Towards a New Philosophy of Biology: Observations of an Evolutionist* (Cambridge, MA: Harvard University Press, 1988), 38-66.

65   Rowland Stout, *Things That Happen Because They Should: A Teleological Approach to Action* (Oxford: Clarendon Press, 1996), 99-111. In addition to defending his own view, Stout provides a good summary of recent discussions on the place of teleology in evolutionary processes.

66   In my view, the real challenge posed by evolutionary biology to scholastic natural philosophy lies not in its repudiation of design but in its challenge to the neo-

Platonic view that the various kinds of creatures form an orderly and hierarchical array. I think that this challenge can be met, but it would take me well beyond the scope of this book to attempt to do so here.

67 According to some evolutionary psychologists, the process through which human nature is shaped by culture should be considered as itself a part of evolution; for a discussion of this claim and its theological implications, see Philip Hefner, *The Human Factor: Evolution, Culture, and Religion* (Minneapolis: Fortress Press, 1993), 28-31.

68 See, for example, Stanley Hauerwas, *A Community of Character: Towards a Constructive Christian Social Ethic* (Notre Dame, IN: University of Notre Dame Press, 1981), 212-229, and *Suffering Presence: Theological Reflections on Medicine, the Mentally Handicapped, and the Church* (Notre Dame, IN: University of Notre Dame Press, 1986), 189-210.

69 Oliver O'Donovan, *Begotten or Made?* (Oxford: Clarendon Press, 1984), 16-17; emphasis in the original.

70 Noonan argues this point specifically with respect to scholastic teachings on the use of contraceptives; see *Contraception*, 361-362. Of course, it does not follow that he would endorse the reformulation of scholastic natural law thought proposed here.

71 *Begotten or Made?* 77; O'Donovan's overall assessment of the official Catholic view on contraception comprises 76-79. Paul Ramsey offers a similar critique in *Fabricated Man* (New Haven, CT: Yale University Press, 1970), 41-43. Of course, this line of argument has also been put forth by many Catholics; for a good recent example, see Cahill, *Sex, Gender, and Christian Ethics*, 199-216.

72 See, for example, Cahill, *Sex, Gender, and Christian Ethics*, 231-232; Richard McCormick, "Document is Unpersuasive," in *Responses to the Vatican Document on Reproductive Technologies* (St. Louis, MO: Catholic Health Association, 1987), 8-10.

73 O'Donovan offers the same argument in *Begotten or Made?* 67-86. Likewise, William May, although his argument rests in part on a Kantian analysis of marriage which I find unpersuasive; see his "Donum Vitae: Catholic Teaching Concerning Homologous IVF," in Kevin W. Wildes, ed., *Infertility: A Crossroad of Faith, Medicine, and Technology* (Kluser Academic Publishers, 1997), 73-92. In addition, both Ramsey and Cahill raise similar concerns, although they do not pursue the same line of analysis; see *Fabricated Man*, 32-59 and *Sex, Gender, and Christian Ethics*, 243-246. For the record, I have changed my mind on this question; I express a different view in "Human Need and Natural Law," in Wildes, *Infertility*, 93-106.

74 Andrew Sullivan, *Virtually Normal: An Argument about Homosexuality*, 2nd edition with new afterword (London: Picador, 1996), 44-45.

75 *Ibid.*, 47.

76 I did not fully appreciate this until I read Oliver O'Donovan's "Homosexuality in the Church: Can There Be a Fruitful Theological Debate?" in Timothy Bradshaw,

ed., *The Way Forward: Christian Voices on Homosexuality and the Church* (London: Hodder and Stoughton, 1997), 20-36.

77   On this point, see Peter Gardella, *Innocent Ecstasy: How Christianity Gave America an Ethic of Sexual Pleasure* (Oxford: Oxford University Press, 1985), 150-161.

78   Lisa Cahill, "Current Teaching on Sexual Ethics," in *Dialogue about Catholic Sexual Teaching*, 525-535 at 533-534. Cahill has consistently defended this view; for a later and fuller statement of her position, see *Sex, Gender and Christian Ethics*, 108-120.

Chapter 5

Social Ethics

Summary: This chapter turns to the scholastic concept of the natural law considered as the basis for a social ethic. For the scholastics, the main institutions of society are conventional and not natural; even marriage is only a partial exception to this rule. Yet scholastic canonists and theologians, in contrast to most civilians, also insisted that there are some senses in which nature is directly normative for social practice. In particular, they developed a doctrine of natural equality, which was expressed through their support of the egalitarian tendencies in their society, and some of them at least went so far as to assert the existence of natural rights which have juridical effect. After considering the main lines of the social ethic that the scholastics derived from their concept of the natural law, this chapter turns to two hard questions: servitude and social persecution. In each case, it is argued, the scholastics did not succeed in applying their own principles as consistently as they should have done, and yet their concept of the natural law did enable some of them to recognize the problematic character of these practices and to protest against them. Finally, the last section of this chapter turns to contemporary theological implications of the scholastic social ethic. It is argued that this ethic offers a distinctive and theologically more satisfactory

alternative both to withdrawal into a Christian enclave and to Reinhold Niebuhr's Christian realism.

∎

As we saw in Chapter 2, the scholastic concept of the natural law is
grounded in a contrast between the natural, understood in any one of a
number of ways, and the conventional, which is established through
human custom or decree. Yet the scholastics are well aware that the major
institutions of society are conventional and not natural; even marriage is
only a partial exception. Does it follow, therefore, that social institutions
are immoral? This conclusion, which would be drawn by some later
natural law thinkers, was resisted by the scholastics.[1]

At the same time, they are aware that the conventional character of
society calls for some justification, given their fundamental concept of
the natural law. This is all the more important because, on their view, at
least some of the institutions of society are not only distinct from, but in
some sense contrary to, nature. We have already observed that after setting
forth his preferred definition of the natural law as the Golden Rule,
Gratian goes on to incorporate the Roman definition, as mediated
through Isidore. This includes, among other provisions, the claim that
the natural law includes "the possession [*possessio*] of all things in common,
[and] the equal freedom of all persons" (D.1, C.7.3). Gratian's authority
guarantees that most subsequent canonists and theologians will also
attempt to incorporate this understanding of the natural law. Clearly,
however, society is not structured in accordance with this radically egalitarian vision: "Yet there remains an objection to this: according to the
natural law, all persons would be equally free, and all things would be
possessed in common; this, however, is changed through the law of
nations" (*Cologne summa,* Lottin, 106).

Precisely because they are aware of these difficulties, the scholastics
are forced to think carefully about the various senses in which nature
might be said to be morally normative. As a result, they develop their
basic concept of the natural law into a framework for social analysis that
combines flexibility and real normative force. Seen from our own perspective, the scholastic treatment of the relationship between natural law and
the social order constitutes one of the most disturbing, and yet potentially
one of the most fruitful, aspects of their concept of the natural law.

Disturbing, because despite the radical implications of their analysis, the scholastics defend social practices that appear to us to be problematic or clearly unacceptable. Potentially fruitful, nonetheless, because the scholastic analysis of social institutions contains the seeds of its own revision while at the same time offering a nuanced and powerful vision of human society as seen from the perspective of Christian theology. In this chapter, we will accordingly examine the scholastic concept of the natural law as it was applied to social institutions, and the norms structuring them.

1. From natural inclination to social practice

By now, we are familiar with the scholastic view that nature can be understood on different levels, including both those aspects of our nature that we share with other animals and the distinctively human capacity for reason. For the scholastics, the pre-rational aspects of our nature are morally significant, and they never adopt the contemporary (or Stoic) view that morality can be derived from reason alone, without reference to these other dimensions of human nature. At the same time, however, they recognize that the human person is constituted in such a way that he cannot consistently live at this level of his nature. Because the human person is a rational creature, he can only act on the basis of rational judgments. Hence, the judgments of reason, which can be contrasted to the natural in one sense, are supremely natural in another sense, that is, as expressions of that which is proper or natural for an individual of the human species.[2]

It is a truism that medieval political thinkers believed that society is natural to the human person, whereas the moderns broke with this tradition by proclaiming that society is established through agreements. Like most truisms, this contains elements of truth. The scholastics do not believe that society is grounded in a social contract in the Lockean sense. Yet neither do they speak of human society as if it were on a par with procreation: that is, an expression of an inclination that we pursue in common with the rest of the animal kingdom. Rather, society is natural to the human person precisely as an expression of the distinctively human capacity for rational self-direction.[3]

We have already observed that for the civilians, the law of nature that we share with other animals is contrasted with the law of nations, which stems from reason or equity and is thus distinctively human. The canonists and theologians, in contrast, typically identify one or more distinctively human forms of the natural law. Yet they would agree that society develops through a process of rational reflection. Rufin, the first major commentator on the *Decretum,* makes this explicit:

> Since, therefore, the natural power within the human person had not been entirely extinguished [that is to say, through the sin of the first parents], undoubtedly he began to strive that he should be distinct from the beasts by his law of life, just as he is distinct from them by the prerogative of knowledge. And while the human person resolved to live with his neighbor, the traces of justice, that is, the precepts of modesty and shame emerged, which taught him to turn the rustic and wild ways of humankind into decorous and honorable ways of living, and to subject himself to agreements of concord and to enter into certain pacts. These indeed are called the law of nations, insofar as practically all nations observe them, as for example the laws of selling, of leasing and the exchange of goods, and other similar laws (Rufin, Weigand no. 238-239).

According to Philippe Delhaye, Rufin intends his analysis of the natural law to be a refutation of the civilian account of the law of nations.[4] It is true that Rufin goes on to say that the law of nations was subsequently vitiated by sin, with the result that it was then supplemented by the divine law given to Moses (Weigand no. 240). Nonetheless, Rufin does not appear to reject the civilian conception of the law of nations; on the contrary, in the text just quoted, he affirms it. Rather, he develops a theological interpretation of the law of nations by relating it to Gratian's account of the natural law as that which is revealed through the law and the prophets. More specifically, he harmonizes the two by means of a historical reconstruction of the way human society emerges through a process of rational reflection, which in turn is supplemented and corrected by the divine law revealed in Scripture. In this way, he acknowledges the rational origins of human society, even while insisting that reason alone is not sufficient to maintain society in good order.

In part, human society is grounded in rationality because it expresses fundamental tendencies that can arise only in rational creatures. Moreover, even those inclinations that we share with non-rational creatures can be expressed in human society only through a process of rational reflection. To put the matter in our terms, there is no realm of unmediated biological nature in human society. From the very beginning, whether understood logically or temporally, nature in the biological sense is mediated through culture, through the practices and institutions generated through rational reflection.[5]

This leads to a further point. To a considerable degree, the duties and claims that comprise the order of justice, which individuals can assert and defend over against one another in a public forum, presuppose a rationally generated civic order. As Richard Tuck observes, referring to the passage from Gratian quoted at the beginning of this chapter, "Isidore and Gratian's use of the term *possessio* is crucial; they understood by it something which was *not dominion*. Under classical law, of course, *possessio* and *dominium* were necessarily contrasted; to possess something was to occupy it and use it but not to have private property rights in it."[6] So understood, the natural law authorizes the free movement and unrestricted use of material resources that emerge spontaneously out of the animal life of the human person, whereas mutual obligations and the claims of justice emerge only with the law of nations. This interpretation is further confirmed by Gratian's earlier remark, again quoting Isidore, that "To pass through the field of another is licit [*fas*], but it is not right [*jus*]" (D.1, C.1.3), which he glosses by explaining that "the term, 'divine or natural law,' is taken to be whatever is licit, while the term 'human law' is understood of customs drawn up in writing and passed on as law" (*ibid.*).

We find a striking illustration of this point in the scholastic discussions of the inclination to resist injury with force. This would seem to offer a parade example of an inclination that we share with other animals, and as we saw in Chapter 2, at least some of the scholastics do indeed identify it with an inclination to vengeance, which we share with other animals.[7] Yet others distinguish between the distinctively human inclination to resist injury and the more general pre-rational inclination to defend oneself against attack on the grounds that the former presupposes a rational order of justice together with individual claims to respect that can be violated, and likewise publicly vindicated. This, as Johannes Faventius explains, is why the civilians do not consider resistance to injury to be a part of the natural law:

> ...since the jurists take the law of nature in a general sense, as that which is attributed to all animals in common, and our distinctive law to be that which is attributed to the human person alone, therefore since they know that such resistance to violence and injury is not held in common with the brute animals, who cannot suffer injury, they do not say that it ought to be associated with the natural law, but with the law of nations (Weigand no. 253).

This might seem to imply that the natural law has no normative implications for society as it actually exists, or else that the natural law has normative force only to the extent that it is identified in a straight-forward way with rational judgment. The civilians do seem to hold this view, although even they are prepared to defend some specific social practices as expressions of a natural law.[8] For the canonists and theologians, on the other hand, matters are more complex. Because they are committed to a tradition according to which the natural law is vindicated by and interpreted through Scripture, they cannot simply relegate this concept to the prolegomena of legal analysis, as the civilians tend to do. Moreover, according to this tradition there are specific precepts that stem from the natural law, including the Golden Rule and the Decalogue. Finally, the canonists and theologians also had to deal with authoritative claims that the natural law is supremely authoritative and cannot be abrogated; these and similar claims prevent them from simply dismissing the normative implications of the natural law as irrelevant to civil society.

These considerations help to explain what we have already seen to be the case; that is, the canonists and theologians do consider the natural law to have direct moral and social implications, even in human society as it now exists. It is true that for them, as well as for the civilians, the natural law must be expressed through human conventions in order to have practical force in the present historical order. Nonetheless, they also believe that the natural law places definite moral constraints on the legitimate forms of institutional life, and repeatedly they attempt to say what those constraints are.

In the first place, the moral implications of the natural law, including especially the precepts of the Decalogue, obtain in every human society and set constraints on acceptable forms of social institutions. No doubt the civilians would not have disagreed with this basic claim, but it plays a central role in the social thought of the canonists and theologians. Moreover, they insist that there is one centrally important social practice – marriage – that should be regulated by the church rather than by secular authorities. This extraordinary claim rests on the view that marriage is a sacrament, rather than on its origins in the natural law. Nonetheless, once this claim had been accepted in the society as a whole, it justified appeals to the natural law that were intended to have, and actually did have, immediate practical force.

Finally, appeals to the natural law or to general considerations of naturalness were offered in defense of the new religious practices of the mendicants, particularly Franciscan poverty. This line of argument presupposes and reinforces the general view that the church has a special insight into the normative implications of the natural law. Furthermore, it implies that, within the Christian community, it is possible to live in accordance with a more integral, less compromised version of the natural law; this is a radical idea, although its full implications were not yet recognized in the period we are considering.

For all these reasons, the canonists and theologians are committed to the view that there is a form of the natural law which is properly human, and moreover that it has direct and immediate social consequences. Yet, like the civilians, they also accept the moral legitimacy of some institutions that are conventional and not natural, including some, particularly property and servitude, that are in some sense contrary to the natural law. At the very least, this implies that there is no neat fit between what is natural and what is morally normative. Precisely because they are committed to defending the social relevance of the natural law, this recognition creates a problem for them, as it does not for the civilians. They are forced to consider carefully just what it means to say that nature is normative. If the institutions of human society are not derived directly from a natural order, then in what sense can they be said to be consonant with a natural law?

Up to a point, the scholastics are able to interpret the conventions of human society as rational elaborations or specifications of tendencies that we share with non-rational creatures. Marriage accommodates itself most readily to this kind of treatment, since it is understood by the scholastics as the appropriate distinctively human form of a more general tendency toward procreation. However, marriage is not the only social practice interpreted in this way. For example, the practice of vengeance (that is, retributive justice) can likewise be understood as the distinctively human form of a tendency that we share with other animals, as we have already seen. Similarly, the laws and customs surrounding inheritance can be so interpreted:

> Here there is a discussion of the succession of heirs, which is introduced either from the natural law or the evangelical law, since it is written that "children should not lay up treasure for their parents, but parents for their children." Or from the law of reason: for reason directs the human person that it is better to designate one's child as the heir of one's property, than a stranger. Or from the law of sensuality: for a parent is moved by carnal affection more strongly towards his own children, than towards strangers (*Summa Reginensis,* Weigand no. 385).

It is more difficult to explain other institutions in this way, as being institutionalized expressions of natural inclinations. As we have already noted, the scholastics inherit a tradition according to which the fundamental institutions of society, that is, property and servitude, are not only conventional in origin but in some sense opposed to the natural law. On this view, the foundational institutions of human society are at least problematic, and this is so not only for European society but for every society, as far as the scholastics would have known. Moreover, by the same token the practices of the church itself are likewise suspect: "By the law of nature, all things are held in common. Yet the highest pontiffs have sanctioned 'this is mine, that is yours' through canons and constitutions; also, this is what the church holds today. It would seem, therefore, that the natural law can be modified by positive law" (*Muenster Summa,* Lottin 107).[9]

None of the canonists or theologians is prepared to say flatly that the natural law can be abrogated by custom or positive law, yet neither do they call for the social revolution that the logic of their analysis would seem to demand. From our perspective, this is likely to appear as a too-easy accommodation to the powerful and comfortable, particularly when we remember the close ties between the scholastics and the urban and mercantile sectors of society. No doubt the scholastics' views do reflect a degree of accommodation, as well as a more positive desire to speak to the concerns and needs of the urban middle class with whom they were allied.

At the same time, the scholastic defense of these institutions cannot be dismissed as nothing more than a tendentious defense of the status quo. Their positive evaluations of property and servitude are congruent with, if not required by, their overall approach to the natural law. When we examine the details of the scholastic rationales for the legitimacy of property and servitude, it becomes apparent that these rationales take their starting points from Scripture.[10] In this way, they offer one of the most striking examples of the general scholastic tendency to develop the concept of the natural law through the medium of scriptural interpretation. At the same time, they render the scholastic defenses of property and servitude intelligible, given their overall concept of the natural law. That is, if Scripture provides the key to understanding the requirements of the natural law, then it follows that property and servitude cannot be condemned out of hand, if only because there are clear scriptural warrants for both institutions.[11]

Turning to the specifics of the scholastic analysis of property and servitude, we first see a number of authors for whom these institutions are considered to be the results of human sinfulness. This line of interpretation, perhaps surprisingly, is not uniquely Christian; we also find classical natural law thinkers arguing that the present state of society reflects the degeneration of the human race from the perfect state of a golden age.[12] At the same time, the scholastics place their distinctive mark on this interpretation by formulating it in terms of the specifics of the scriptural narrative.[13]

In addition to, or in place of, this kind of historical explanation for the emergence of property and servitude, the scholastics also attempt to explain how these institutions are justified, given a fully adequate understanding of the natural law. Although the details of these arguments differ, most of them fall under one of two general approaches. Either they rest on an analysis of the ways in which the natural law may be said to generate precepts, or they depend on a distinction between general principles and particular applications. In each case, the argument depends on a scripturally-based interpretation of the natural law.

This is particularly evident when we examine the first line of argument, which turns on a distinction between the natural law as a ubiquitous principle for judgment and action, and the natural law in its written, that is, its scriptural, form: "However, there still remains an objection; for according to the natural law, liberty would be the same for all, and all things would be possessed in common; these however are changed through the law of nations. To this we should respond that the natural law, to the extent that it is put in writing, is unchangeable ..." (*Cologne Summa*, Lottin 106).

This line of argument is further spelled out in terms of an analysis (already mentioned in Chapter 3) of the different senses in which scriptural divine law, considered as a form of natural law, may be said to exercise normative force. In one way, it is said to prohibit some things, and in another way, it commands that some things be done. There is a third sense in which the natural law is normative, however, which is more relevant to the problem at hand; with regard to some matters, it indicates what would be best, or ideal, or even just what is permitted: "The divine law consists of three [kinds of precepts], that is, prescriptions, prohibitions and indications. It commands what is beneficial, as to love God; it prohibits what is harmful, as forbidding us to kill; and it indicates what is appropriate, as that all persons should be free" (*Summa Tractaturus Magister*, Weigand no. 321).[14] This last category of prescriptions, usually referred to as indications, does not have the same absolute force as the first two, and therefore these prescriptions can be changed: "The law of nature which is contained in [divine] law cannot be modified with respect to its prohibitions and prescriptions, but it is modified in part with respect to the indications" (*Summa Reginensis*, Weigand no. 382).[15]

This appears to have been the most common way of addressing the difficulty raised by the existence of property and servitude, at least among the canonists.[16] By this argument, neither property nor servitude is contrary to the strict commands and prohibitions contained in Scripture, and so we may conclude that they are at least permissible. Taken by itself, this argument does not address the further question of the positive justification for these institutions, and some authors in this period did not attempt to deal with this issue. Others, however, do offer explanations for these deviations from the ideals of the natural law, either by identifying the "indications" with the domain of the morally indifferent, or else by appealing to the effects of sin, which renders conformity with the highest ideals of the natural law impossible. Once again, Huguccio presents the relevant arguments in an especially cogent way:

> Since, therefore, the natural law is understood in these different ways, how is it [to be] taken, when it is said that by the natural law, all things are [held in] common? Some understand it thus: By the natural, that is to say, the divine law, namely, that which is called permissible or licit, that which is neither commanded nor prohibited, by this law all things are common, in that it is neither commanded nor forbidden that all things should be in common, nor that something should be private property ... Or, by natural law, that is, an approving judgment of reason, all things are, or [that is to say] they would be common, if it were not for sin; for on account of sin, [private property] has been inflicted on the human person as a penalty ... Or better, when it is said that all things are common by the natural law, private property is not excluded, nor is "common" said in contrast to "private," but this is the sense: By the natural law, that is, by an approving judgment of reason, all things are common, that is to say, they are to be given to the poor in time of necessity. For led by natural reason, we appropriate to ourselves only that which it is necessary to retain, letting go of what we ought to distribute to our needy neighbor (Lottin 110).[17]

A second line of analysis depends rather on the idea that the general principles of the natural law admit of various applications in view of changing historical and social conditions, a view that goes back to Augustine. For example, in an anonymous text closely followed by Alexander's *Summa,* we find that the author retains the idea that property and servitude are the results of sin, but he rejects the standard division of the precepts of the natural law in favor of a more substantive analysis:

> Some want to say that in the natural law, there are prescriptions and prohibitions, and also indications...
>
> It can be expressed in another and better way, following Augustine, who says that the medical art is immutable, yet

according to this art, the doctor changes his prescriptions for those who are sick; and so there is no change with respect to the art, which remains the same with respect to its principles, but a change does take place with respect to the sick person. So he says that the natural law is immutable with respect to the rationale of its precepts, because the rationale of the precepts is not changed; it is not, however, unchangeable with respect to the effect of all its healings. Hence by the natural law, all things are held in common, and all things are not held in common; it directs that all things should be held in common, in accordance with nature as well-arranged, and it directs that all things should not be held in common, in accordance with nature as corrupted. Just as the art of medicine allows wine in a time of health, and denies it at a time of sickness, and for the same reason, the preservation of health, so the law of nature allows all things to be held in common in accordance with a sound [state of] nature, but not in a corrupt [state of] nature, on account of the consequent danger, for there would follow loss of goods and mutual deception. The rationale of health does not change, even though the precept changes ... (Lottin 124; cf. *Summa fratris Alexandri* III–II, Inq. 2, 3.2).[18]

The scriptural antecedents for this line of argument are not so apparent. However, it is noteworthy that, when we turn to Augustine himself, we find him using this argument in order to defend the consistency and moral decency of Scripture against Manichean claims to the contrary.[19] While the distinction between general principles and specific applications is not necessarily scriptural or theological, it did in fact emerge within the tradition the scholastics inherit as a way of dealing with seeming inconsistencies among scriptural texts.

It is, of course, possible to combine these two lines of analysis. We find an example of this approach in the theologian William of Auxerre, who claims that the indications do have a limited binding force in accordance with the exigencies of a particular time and set of circumstances, but by the same token they cease to oblige under other circumstances. He goes on to apply this line of analysis to explain the justification of property. The community of possessions, he says, falls under an indication, since it was not a precept of the natural law simply speaking, but only in accordance with some qualification; for it was a precept in the state of innocence, or in the state of nature as well organized; but in the state of greed and corrupted nature it is not a precept, nor should it be, since if it were, public order would be dissolved, and the human race would destroy itself by mutual slaughter. It is nonetheless true that all things should be held in common in a time of extreme necessity, since natural reason directs that the well being of the neighbor is to be cherished in preference to one's worldly goods (*Summa aurea* III 18.1).

Moreover, William of Auxerre here implies what some other theologians say explicitly; that is, property is not altogether contrary to the natural law, if the complexity of the latter is taken into account. Consider Albert's analysis:

The common possession of all things and the ownership of some things are both derived from the natural law, because the principles of the law are not the same, as we have already said. Hence according to that state in which there is neither robbery nor usurpation of that which is given over to common use, conscience and reason directed that nothing should be private property, but [the material world] should be handed over to the common possession of everyone, as it was created in common. But with changing conditions, and the increase of malice and robbery and rancor, nature employs another principle, namely, that private property should be legitimated, for the provision of oneself and of the poor. And so from that point it is not contrary to the law of nature to have something of one's own, but this is to be shared in time of necessity. And so the law according to which unowned property is granted to the occupant is established, as are other similar edicts ... (*De bono* V, 1.3 *ad* 6).

At the same time, Albert is hesitant to apply this line of analysis to servitude:

It follows from the natural law that all should be equally free, and the fact that this is not so is a punishment of sin. And so servitude as such does not have a justification in nature, but only insofar as it is a penalty for sin, insofar as nature has a principle of law that the sinner should be punished, and he should be punished in that very thing with respect to which he committed a crime. Thus, if someone has sinned against the father from whom he was born free, he should be punished in the freedom of those sons born from him. And thus servitude, in a accidental sense, is brought back to nature (*ibid.*, 1.3 *ad* 6).[20]

Aquinas takes Albert's analysis of property one step further, arguing that there is in some sense a natural right to private property:

> ...exterior things can be considered in two ways. In one way, with respect to their nature, which is not subject to human power, but only to the divine power, which all things obey straightaway. In another way, with respect to the use of the thing itself. And so the human person has natural ownership [*dominium*] of exterior things, because through his reason and will he is able to make use of them for his benefit, as if they were made for him, for more imperfect things always exist for the sake of more perfect things ... And by this argument, the Philosopher proves in the first book of the *Politics* that the possession [*possessio*] of exterior things is natural to the human person. Furthermore, this natural ownership [*dominium*] over other creatures, which is appropriate to the human person on account of reason, in which consists the image of God, is manifested in the very creation of the human person, where it is said, "Let us make the human person to our image and likeness, and let him have authority over the fishes of the sea," etc. [Gen. 1.26] (*Summa theologiae* II-II 66.1).

This passage was later taken as the starting point for an argument against the Franciscan claim that it is possible to live in absolute poverty, without owning anything (that is, having *dominium* over it), even while respecting the natural necessity to make use of some things to sustain life (thus, exercising *possessio* over them). If natural possession itself gives rise to *dominium*, that is, ownership, then clearly this dichotomy cannot be sustained. At the same time, this was probably not Aquinas' own intention since, as we will see farther on, he does not believe that individuals as such would have had a natural right to ownership in a pre-lapsarian world.[21]

Seen from our own standpoint, Aquinas' argument raises a more general question: To what extent do we find a doctrine of natural rights, either in Aquinas himself or in the scholastic concept of the natural law more generally? In addition to its obvious historical importance, this question helps to focus the normative implications of the scholastic concept of the natural law.

In order to address this question, it will first be necessary to look more closely at the central moral and social values that inform the scholastic concept of the natural law, and to ask how these values were both shaped by and expressed in the social conditions of the twelfth and thirteenth centuries. In this case, it will be particularly important to hold these two considerations together, because the central social ideal informing the scholastic concept of the natural law can only be fully understood in the context of the social conditions that gave it saliency and concrete meaning.

2. The ideal of equality
and its social expressions

We can best appreciate the scholastics' social ideals by examining what they took to be the most problematic aspects of society as it actually exists, namely, property and servitude. These are by no means obvious as a focus for reflecting on the theologically problematic dimensions of human society. For many theologians today (at least in the industrialized West), the foundational Christian ideal is peace, and the most problematic aspect of human society is its propensity toward violence. The scholastics are likewise concerned with the theological and moral problems associated with the use of violent force, and they draw on natural law arguments as one way of addressing those problems.[22] Nonetheless, in their theoretical discussions of the natural law, the scholastics consistently refer to property and servitude, rather than the use of violent force, as the most problematic aspects of human society. These institutions are problematic, moreover, because they are inconsistent with the ideal of natural equality that is central to the scholastic concept of the natural law.[23]

It is obvious that servitude is incompatible with natural equality, but why should property also be problematic in this respect? The difficulty with property, seen from the standpoint of an ideal of natural equality, is not simply that it is unequally distributed. More fundamentally, as Anabell Brett points out, during the later medieval period property was increasingly associated with personal freedom and the exercise of dominion over others, and correlatively, poverty carried connotations of servitude:

> "Poverty" was seen not merely to involve the absence of *divitiae*, riches (although this was certainly one of the senses of the term). It had in addition a sense as an antonym of *potentia* or *potestas*. The *pauper* was the *servus* or the *subditus*, the subject of the *dominus* or *potens*, the person of superior might. He was also the impotent, the socially insignificant or less significant, he who required protection against the power of the lords. Poverty thus came to have in addition a juridical dimension in the sense of absence of legal standing. It was the opposite of *dominium*, which signified the relation of power over other objects and persons, defensible in law and consequently yielding standing in law.[24]

Given this, we can better appreciate the significance of the conjunction of community of possessions with universal liberty in the tradition that is mediated to the scholastics through Gratian. These are closely related, if not equivalent, conditions for the attainment of personal equality, and correlatively, the idea of equality carries connotations of freedom from another's authority and the liberty to act as one wishes. Hence, equality implies something more than mutuality of respect or shared immunity from harm; it also implies a degree of positive freedom.

At this point, we should consider a possible objection to what has been said so far. That is, perhaps it is a mistake to give too much weight to the scholastics' repeated efforts to address the problems raised by property and servitude. After all, the naturalness of universal liberty and community of possessions was affirmed by the tradition of natural law reflection that they inherited and that was confirmed for subsequent scholastic reflection through the authority of Gratian. It may be that their repeated efforts to come to terms with property and servitude reflect their devotion to tradition rather than any special commitment to equality as a social ideal.

As we saw in Chapter 1, the scholastics are indeed committed to preserving the integrity of the traditions that they take to be authoritative.

Yet this does not mean that their defense of these traditions is uncritical or thoughtless. To the contrary, they attempt to preserve the integrity of their sources through creative interpretation, which involves both selective retrieval and constructive reflection on what they received. Hence, while it is certainly the case that a norm of equality is mediated to the scholastics through the tradition which they received, this does not necessarily mean that their own commitment to this ideal is superficial or uncritical. In order to assess the depth and character of the scholastic commitment to an ideal of equality, we need to examine the way they made use of the traditions they inherited.

Of course, an ideal of equality had long been a part of Christian thought, and it was mediated to the scholastics by a number of sources, classical as well as Christian.[25] The most fundamental such source was, of course, Scripture itself, where we find Paul's claim that Christ has done away with all divisions between human persons.[26] In addition, this same claim was amplified by patristic authors, and it was reinforced by those non-Christian philosophers, particularly the Stoics and those influenced by Stoicism, who argued for equality of moral capacity and responsibility for all persons, women and slaves included.

At the same time, in late antiquity and the earlier Middle Ages, these affirmations of equality were understood in a way that rendered them compatible with a very considerable degree of social inequality. The most ancient forms of inequality, between men and women and between masters and slaves, were not eliminated or even directly challenged in early Christianity, although Christian practices had the effect of increasing the autonomy of women in particular.[27] Scripture itself included affirmations of the dominion of men and masters over women and slaves, and this was taken to imply that the equality that Paul associated with the coming of Christ should be understood as spiritual rather than social or practical.

Throughout the early Middle Ages, conditions were not propitious for rethinking the implications of normative equality. Chattel slavery was gradually replaced by serfdom, which involved fewer restrictions on personal freedom than did outright slavery but was still a form of servitude.[28] As social institutions disintegrated in the aftermath of the collapse of the Western Roman empire, individuals came together in new relationships of dominion and subordination, constituting what most histo-

rians would call feudalism. The status of women in marriage continued
to be unfree, although the right of women to refuse marriage or to choose
a marriage partner was acknowledged, at least in theory, and religious life
provided opportunities for self-direction, at least for women within the
aristocracy.

The dominant paradigms for social thought in this early period
reflected and reinforced the realities of social stratification while at the
same time fostering the idea that equality should be understood primarily
in spiritual terms. The images of the three orders of society, and of society
as a body, reinforced the idea that social stratification is both necessary
and salutary.[29] However, the extensive social changes that marked the
late eleventh and twelfth centuries quickly rendered these paradigms
problematic.[30] While the effect of these social changes was not automatically to render society more equal, they did tend to break down previously
existing structures. New classes and forms of community membership
emerged as the economy became mercantile and money-based and society
became more urban. Above all, society became more mobile. The newly
emergent middle class found opportunities for advancement in the
expanding apparatus of secular governments and the church; even the
children of the poor could sometimes follow these routes. The expansion
of authorities and governing structures among secular and ecclesiastical
authorities had the further effect of creating administrative bureaucracies.
As Max Weber has shown, the creation of extensive bureaucracies exerts
a pressure toward social equality, since a bureaucracy places a premium
on ability and tends to regard its workers as interchangeable function-
aries.[31] This pressure was felt within both ecclesiastical and secular
contexts.

In addition, the church reforms pertaining to marriage had the effect
of breaking down class divisions and fostering a real, albeit limited, equality
between the sexes, as we observed in Chapter 4. Moreover, the reform
of canon law was itself a force for social equality, since, as James Brundage
points out, in principle its rules applied equally to everyone, men and
women, the powerful and wealthy as well as the unfree, the marginalized,
and the poor. As he goes on to say, "The canonical legal system, like any
other, often – perhaps too often – fell short of its ideals. What was
remarkable, however, was that impartial equality was a canonical ideal at
all."[32]

Given these conditions of social ferment, the ideal of equality began to take on new relevance and force. As Georges Duby has shown, a number of radical lay and spiritual movements aspired in this period to create a community of radical equality among themselves, and some of them advocated the same for society as a whole.[33] Significantly, many of these movements were associated with penitential practices. One of the defenses of social inequality had long been the claim that such conditions are a result of human sinfulness, either as penalty or as a necessary check on further destruction. So, if sinfulness can be eliminated through penitence and spiritual practices, then it would seem to follow that social inequality can also be eliminated; that at least was the claim.

In the first chapter, we observed that the newly emergent universities served to provide intellectual workers for the expanding apparatus of secular authority and the church. Consequently, the scholastics were intimately involved in these processes of social change, and more particularly in the development of social mobility and the concomitant breakdown of social hierarchy. Furthermore, the newly emergent universities were themselves agents of social change, since they provided a means of social advancement for young men of modest background and limited means, as well as training the sons of the aristocracy and the new monied classes.[34]

It is true that even the relatively fluid society of the twelfth and thirteenth centuries remained stratified and much of the population was still unfree. Nor did the scholastics question the need for structures of dominion; unlike those in the more radical lay movements, they did not believe that sin could be eradicated anytime before the coming of Christ, and so they accepted the necessity for social structures that reflect our fallen condition. Nonetheless, the scholastics, particularly the theologians of the thirteenth century, do defend the possibilities of social mobility, in the process lending support to egalitarian tendencies within their society.[35] As they develop their analysis of states of perfection and grades, or offices, within the church, they also develop a set of critical distinctions between personal holiness and state of life, and between person and office, which open up the possibility of separating the requirements of church offices from personal characteristics, at least to a considerable extent. Nor do they consider high birth, or even free status, to be absolutely necessary conditions for ordination, and hence to the exercise of authority within the church community. Only the most fundamental distinction of gender was thought to set up an absolute barrier against holding church office.

Furthermore, when the mendicant orders began to dominate the universities in the thirteenth century, the link between scholasticism and social change was rendered even stronger. The mendicant orders emerged out of the spiritualist movements of the twelfth century; thus, they emerged out of the same milieu that was generating an ideal of radical egalitarianism. Moreover, they considered themselves to have a special mission to members of the heretical lay movements. While this "mission" could take coercive forms, it also took the form of preaching and attempts at persuasion, through which the mendicants would have been exposed to egalitarian ideals. More generally, the sympathy between the mendicant movements and the emergent middle class led theologians from these movements to defend the independent value of marriage and of lay spiritualities, as we have already noted. Such defenses were not explicitly defenses of equality, but they did have the effect of equalizing a social situation in which the vast majority of lay men and women had been marginalized within the Christian community.

Similarly, the Franciscan defense of the ideal of radical poverty had the effect, whether intentional or not, of reinforcing the tendencies toward social mobility and greater equality within medieval society. As is well known, Francis' vision for the community that grew up around him included an ideal of absolute poverty which, as we have seen, carried connotations of humility and surrender of power as well as asceticism. Of course, this did not mean that the Franciscans renounced all use of material goods, since to do so would have been suicidal. Nonetheless, they appealed to the now-familiar distinction between possession and ownership in order to claim that they could take possession of external things, in the sense of making use of them, while leaving ownership in the hands of others, usually a patron or the church itself.

At first glance, this may seem to be a parochial argument of little general interest. However, it had far-reaching implications. The Franciscans defend their position (in part) by claiming that they are simply recapturing the way of life appropriate to the natural human being, at least to the extent of renouncing ownership. Understood in this way, the Franciscan ideal of radical poverty can be construed as an effort to live in accordance with the primeval natural law. This line of thought is evident in Bonaventure:

> Nature itself, whether as originally constituted or as lapsed, provides this way [the counsel of poverty] in a distinctive fashion. For the human person was made naked, and if he had remained in that state [that is, unfallen], he would not have appropriated anything at all to himself; and indeed, the human person as fallen is born naked, and dies naked. And therefore this is the most upright way, that, not turning away from the limit to which nature is able to endure, one goes about poor and naked (*De Per Evan.* 2.1).[36]

As Richard Tuck points out, the fact that the Franciscan defense of poverty was couched in these terms meant that its implications went well beyond the internal affairs of a particular mendicant order: "If it was possible for some men to live in an innocent way, then it should be possible for all men to do so."[37] The full implications of the Franciscan ideal may not have been apparent during the thirteenth century, but they were certainly apparent shortly thereafter. Because he recognized these implications, Pope John XXII began distancing the church from the Franciscans in the early fourteenth century.[38]

The scholastics are thus writing in a society in which traditional social divisions and the practices that sustain them are in flux. Moreover, they themselves are participants in, and often defenders of, these social changes. In this context, the egalitarian components of the natural law tradition have particular saliency for them, and in the course of developing their concept of the natural law they emphasize and expand upon those components.

There are a number of aspects of the scholastic concept of the natural law that reflect the emphasis on equality. Most fundamentally, this concept gives central moral weight to those aspects of humanity that are shared among all persons and even among the non-rational creation, and this at least suggests that social differences among persons are of secondary importance. Similarly, the fundamental contrast between the natural and the conventional tends to minimize the importance of social differences by emphasizing their contingent and provisional character.

In addition, because the scholastics take the Golden Rule to be a fundamental precept of the natural law, they emphasize the importance of mutuality within a framework of shared obligations: "The precepts of the law are these: To live uprightly in relation to those who are connected to you; not to harm another, not doing to him what you do not wish done to yourself; to render to each what is his own, with respect to those things which pertain to the right [*jus*], doing what you are obliged to do" (*Summa "Sicut vetus testamentum,"* Weigand no. 235). Taken by itself, such an appeal to the Golden Rule is not a charter for social equality. However, by emphasizing the importance of the claims of others, and especially by building on empathy for another as the basis for social morality, this approach gives relatively greater weight to our commonalities while de-emphasizing the moral importance of our differences.

Most significant, in developing their concept of the natural law, the canonists and theologians emphasize the connection between knowledge of the natural law on the one hand, and capacities for reason, judgment, or free action which all persons share, on the other.[39] Understood in this way, the natural law is one fundamental expression of the equality of moral capacity that the scholastics believe to be shared by all normal adults. Hence, just as every mentally normal adult, man or woman, good or bad, naturally possesses some capacities for moral discernment and action, so every human being necessarily possesses some capacity for moral discernment, or alternatively, some inclination toward moral goodness, which is tantamount to the natural law. While this knowledge (or inclination) has been dimmed and distorted by sin, it cannot be extinguished, as we are frequently reminded, not even in Cain himself.[40] Furthermore, we are explicitly told that the natural law is not equivalent to charity, since charity is the fount of true goodness, which is found only in those who have grace, whereas the natural law is innate in all persons.[41] This might seem like a devaluing of the natural law, and in one sense it is. Nonetheless, this claim makes the very important point that the natural law is grounded in aspects of our shared humanity so fundamental that nothing, not even the distorting effects of sin, can completely eradicate it.

This moral vision that gives central place to reason and free judgment does not originate with Christianity, but in the period we are considering, it is reinforced and given theological depth through its association with the *imagio Dei* motif. As we saw in Chapter 3, the scholastics identify the image of God with the human capacity for rational self-direction. And since this capacity is integrally connected to the natural law, it follows that the natural law is also an expression of the divine image in which we are created. In this way, the scholastics appeal to the doctrine that we are created in the image of God in order to justify and develop the claim that we are equal in virtue of a shared humanity. We have already observed several times that the scholastic concept of a natural law is distinctive because it offers a theologically informed account of which aspects of our nature should be given normative priority. Here we see a particularly telling example of this point. We are by now familiar with the claim that capacities for reason and free judgment are central to the human person, considered as a moral agent, and yet, this claim is not obvious. Given a different set of values, it might be said that a capacity for depth of feeling, or courageous and spirited self-assertion, is central to moral agency and forms the basis for the respect we owe to others.[42]

If the analysis of this section is sound, we may conclude that the egalitarian strains of the natural law tradition are particularly important to the scholastics because of their involvement with egalitarian movements in their own society. For this reason, they develop their concept of the natural law in a way that emphasizes those egalitarian strands and places them within a theological context. The question that remains is, what were the practical implications of this line of development?

We have already noted that on some issues, the scholastics appeal to natural law arguments in defense of policies that at the very least had the effect of breaking down social barriers and fostering egalitarian ideals. As we saw in the last chapter, they draw on natural law arguments in order to defend the goodness of marriage, the right to marry regardless of status, and the limited but real equality of husband and wife. Furthermore, as we have just noted, the Franciscans defended their radical vision of poverty on the basis of an appeal to what is most appropriate to the natural state of the human person.

However, these particular arguments, important though they were, do not convey the full social implications of the scholastic concept of the natural law. In order to draw these out, it will be helpful to return to a question raised at the end of the last section: to what extent does this concept give rise to a doctrine of natural human rights?

3. From natural law to natural rights

The origins of natural rights theories have been vigorously debated for the past several decades. On one side there are those, from Michel Villey to Alasdair MacIntyre, who have argued that the idea of natural rights is a late medieval or modern innovation that would have been unknown to the scholastics in the period we are considering.[43] Although they are not so prepared to see the doctrine of natural rights as a radical innovation, both Richard Tuck and Annabel Brett also date the emergence of this doctrine from the fourteenth century.[44]

On the other side, a number of influential scholars have argued throughout this century that the medieval concept of the natural law does contain or imply a doctrine of natural rights. Writing near the middle of the twentieth century, Jacques Maritain developed the argument that the medieval idea of the natural law implies a doctrine of human rights, which are seen as following from the claims and duties implied by the transcendent nature of the human person.[45] More recently, David Hollenbach has claimed that the natural law tradition forms the basis for the modern Catholic doctrine of human rights, a doctrine that he goes on to elaborate and defend, and John Finnis has argued that Aquinas' doctrine of the natural law (but not the medieval concept more widely considered) can be expressed equally well in terms of the modern language of human rights.[46] Finally, the medievalist Brian Tierney has recently argued that we can identify claims for the existence of natural rights among some scholastics as early as the beginning of the thirteenth century.[47]

What are we to make of this debate? In the first place, contrary to the claims of Villey and MacIntyre, it is difficult to deny some connection between the scholastic concept of the natural law and modern doctrines of human rights. According to Richard Tuck (who would agree that the early scholastics did not have a doctrine of human rights), the first human rights theory emerged out of fourteenth-century debates over the Franciscan ideal of radical poverty, debates which drew heavily on the natural law thinking of the preceding century.[48] Later work has challenged the specifics of Tuck's analysis.[49] Nonetheless, it appears very probable that medieval speculation on the natural law had some influence on the subsequent emergence of doctrines of natural or universal human rights, if only because the most important figures in this development, including

Hugo Grotius, Thomas Hobbes, and John Locke, frame their arguments in terms that are recognizably drawn from medieval discussions of the natural law.[50]

Second, it should be noted that this question cannot be settled on purely linguistic grounds. In support of his claim that the doctrine of natural rights is a late medieval innovation, MacIntyre asserts that "there is no expression in any ancient or medieval language correctly translated by our expression 'a right' until near the close of the middle ages," which he goes on to date at about 1400.[51] But as Tierney points out, this claim is incorrect.[52] As he goes on to observe, medieval society in the twelfth and thirteenth centuries was preoccupied with establishing the rights of various groups and individuals over against one another, and they had a perfectly adequate language in which to do so. Central to this rights discourse was the expression *jus* and its declensions, which should sometimes clearly be translated as "law" but which in other contexts should just as clearly be translated as "right," in the sense of an individual or group right. (Most of the authors we are considering, but not Alexander of Hales and his editors or Aquinas, use the term *jus* when referring to the natural law.) As an example of the latter usage, Tierney offers Gratian's assertion of a papal claim to "the rights of heavenly and earthly empire" *(terreni simul et celestis imperii iura, Decretum D.22, C.1; Tierney's translation).*[53] In this context and in most other examples of a similar usage, the rights asserted are not natural rights, as Tierney recognizes, since they are understood to presuppose specific social arrangements. Nonetheless, the fact remains that the scholastics in the period we are considering did have the linguistic and conceptual resources to develop a doctrine of natural rights.

More positively, it is clear that at the very least, the scholastics we have been considering have much in common with most modern and contemporary defenders of theories of natural rights. Most fundamentally, they believe that there is an objective moral order that places normative constraints on social practices, as we have already noted. In addition, they share many substantive views with later rights theorists, including a commitment to non-maleficence as the basis for morality, and a conviction that rational self-direction is central to moral agency.

Are these points of agreement sufficient to establish that the scholastic concept of the natural law implies a doctrine of natural rights? At least some of the contemporary authors mentioned above, including both Maritain and Finnis, would agree that they are.[54] For these authors, natural rights should be seen as expressions of the claims and duties that persons have over against one another by virtue of their mutual participation in an objective moral order. Because this order is seen as both supremely authoritative and universal in scope, it gives rise to claims and duties which are not dependent on any particular social arrangement, and which all communities are bound to respect. Furthermore, on this view the rights of one individual are generally correlated with duties that are incumbent on someone else. Indeed, someone may be said to have a right because another person has a duty that affects her (although it may not be a duty toward her specifically); for example, my right to life is grounded in the duty that everyone else has not to kill people, including me.

This last point raises a difficulty because, as Tuck points out, it seems to imply that the language of rights is nugatory:

> If any right can be completely expressed as a more or less complete set of duties on other people towards the possessor of the right, and those duties can in turn be explained in terms of some higher-order moral principle, then the point of a separate language of rights seems to have been lost, and with it the explanatory or justificatory force possessed by references to rights. This result has been acceptable to many political philosophers, but others have been worried by it, feeling ... that the point of attributing rights to people is to attribute to them some kind of "sovereignty" over the moral world. According to this view, to have a right to something is more than to be in a position where one's expressed or understood want is the occasion for the operation of a duty imposed upon someone else; it is actually in some way to impose that duty upon them, and to determine how they ought to act towards the possessor of the right.[55]

Tuck is not aiming here to legislate usage; if someone wishes to describe the claims arising out of a shared morality as rights, there is no reason why she should not do so. However, this way of speaking obscures an important theoretical issue, and by the same token, it trivializes the historical question before us. For, if a rights theory amounts to nothing more nor less than the view that there is an objective morality that imposes other-regarding duties, then of course medieval natural law authors had a theory of rights – and so did both Jeremy Bentham and Immanuel Kant, to name only two others.

However, when modern and contemporary theorists refer to natural rights, they frequently mean something more than the claims arising within a moral order. On such a view, a natural right properly so-called attaches to a person; it is, so to speak, one of the individual's moral properties. In the terms of contemporary political theory, it is a subjective rather than an objective right. Furthermore, the duties correlative to such a right arise *in virtue of* the right. The right is itself the ground of the duty. Finally, on this view natural rights exist prior to particular social arrangements, even though their effective exercise may require the existence of specific institutions, such as law courts.

Does the scholastic concept of the natural law contain or imply a doctrine of natural rights in this stronger sense? It would be too much to say that this concept is equivalent to, or necessarily implies, a strong doctrine of natural rights. While the scholastics we have been examining do believe that men and women have claims over against one another for certain kinds of aid and forbearance, they do not ground these in subjective individual rights; rather, these claims follow from fundamental obligations of non-maleficence that are thought to be apparent to all.

At the same time, this observation needs to be qualified. Even though the scholastic concept of the natural law does not necessarily imply a strong theory of natural rights, it is worth underscoring the point that the canonists and theologians do believe that human nature gives rise to moral claims that any just society must somehow acknowledge. This does not commit them to a theory of natural rights, but it does offer an important point of contact between them and later rights theorists. Moreover, there are some aspects of the scholastic concept that do come very close to a strong natural rights theory, and some scholastic authors in the thirteenth century do in fact speak explicitly of natural rights, even though they do not develop a full theory of rights. Hence, while the scholastic concept of the natural law does not necessarily imply a strong theory of natural rights, it is not inconsistent with such a theory, and some of the scholastics in the period we are considering do indeed move towards developing such a theory.

Let me offer two examples of aspects of scholastic natural law thought that come close to a strong theory of subjective natural rights without necessarily articulating such a theory in so many words. The first is taken from scholastic doctrines of marriage discussed in the last chapter. Marriage is significant in this context because it is the most important example of an institution that is grounded more or less directly in nature, in the sense of being a distinctively human expression of tendencies shared by the other animals. To be sure, marriage is thought to incorporate conventional as well as natural and divine elements, but it is also thought to involve claims that are prior to human laws and customs and can override them. Even more telling, these claims are considered to override church law as well, at least in some cases. In particular, the freedom to marry, which is defended even for those of servile status, functions very much like a subjective right is supposed to function. That is, it is attached to the person and may be exercised or not, as the individual chooses. Once it is claimed, it gives rise to duties in others, and it overrides most of the contrary claims that might be lodged against the individual, whether civil or ecclesiastical in origin. Similarly, the claim to sexual gratification that each spouse has against the other is held to be overriding and to generate a duty that can be defended at law.

I take my second example from an individual author, Thomas Aquinas. Both Maritain and Finnis claim that Aquinas offers a doctrine of natural rights, but as a number of other scholars have pointed out, this is so only if we assume that natural rights are equivalent to natural duties.[56] Aquinas has a concept of the natural right, or *jus,* as an objective order of equity established by nature, but he does not speak in terms of rights inhering in individuals, which give rise to duties in others (*Summa theologiae* II-II 57.1,2). With respect to the question of ownership of property discussed above, Aquinas considers the natural *dominium* over created things to be proper to the human person as a species; elsewhere, he explicitly says that private ownership by individuals is introduced by human ingenuity in view of the needs of life, just as Albert does (*ST* II-II 66.1,2 *ad* 2). Elsewhere, he explicitly endorses Gratian's claim that community of possessions and universal liberty pertain to the natural law, whereas property and servitude are introduced by human reason on the grounds of expediency (*ST* I-II 94.5). As Tuck notes, this aligns him with the more general scholastic view that persons can only lay claim to private ownership or to the services of others on the basis of specific social arrangements, which give rise to obligations and claims not specifically grounded in the natural law.[57]

Yet at some points, Aquinas does come close to articulating a doctrine of natural rights, although not in so many words. The most striking such example occurs in his discussion of the obligations of obedience, which for him include the obligations of servants to masters as well as the obligations of those under religious vows to their superiors, and in general, every sort of obligation of a subordinate to a superior (ST II-II 104.5).

As we would expect, Aquinas is quite prepared to defend the general institutions of subordination and superiority that structure his society. What may be surprising is that he places strict limits on the extent of this obedience. For him, there is no such thing as an obligation of *unlimited* obedience between one person and another. The requirements of obedience are limited by the point of the relationship, for one thing (ST II-II 104.5 *ad* 2). More important, there are limits on the sorts of obedience that can be exacted of anybody, under any circumstances. These limits are set by the fundamental inclinations of human life, which all persons share, and with respect to which all are equal: "However, one person is held to obey another with respect to those things which are to be done externally through the body. Nevertheless, in things which pertain to the nature of the body, one person is not held to obey another, but only God, since all persons are equal in nature" (ST II-II 104.5; cf. I 96.4). Thus, he goes on to explain, no one can command another either to marry or not to marry, for example, because marriage stems from an aspect of human existence that is common to all persons.

In this passage, Aquinas does not say explicitly that individuals have a right to freedom, which can be asserted over against others and defended as such in a court of law. However, he offers what many would consider to be the next best thing; that is, he defends human freedom in terms of an immunity from the interference of others with respect to the pursuit of certain basic human goals. If we agree with Tuck that for a defender of a strong subjective rights theory, "to attribute rights to someone *is* to attribute some kind of liberty to them," then it would appear that Aquinas at least comes very close to asserting a limited but definite right to freedom here.[58]

Similarly, in his discussion of the obligation of the rich to share their surplus wealth with the poor, Aquinas does not say that a poor individual has a right to the goods of a rich person (*Summa theologiae* II–II 66.7). But he does say that a poor person who takes from another what is necessary to sustain life is not guilty of robbery or theft; and this is equivalent to saying that someone is free to take from another in such circumstances, in the sense of enjoying immunity from guilt or punishment. This is not equivalent to saying that the poor person has a right which could be claimed against the rich person and defended at law, but it does imply that the rich individual cannot lodge a claim against the poor individual for the return of what the latter has taken. In other words, the poor individual cannot defend a claim against the rich, but neither can the rich individual defend an accusation of robbery or theft against the poor person in such a case. This is at least a subjective immunity, if not a full-fledged subjective right.

These examples are instructive because they show how much affinity there is between natural rights theorists and the scholastics we are considering, even when the latter stop short of explicitly asserting the existence of subjective rights. In his recent study of the emergence of a doctrine of subjective rights, Tierney argues that at least some thirteenth-century authors went still further in the direction of developing a theory of human rights.[59] As is well known, the scholastics in the twelfth and thirteenth centuries defended the view that the rich have an obligation to share their goods with the poor in time of need. We have just noted that Aquinas interprets this to mean that a poor individual who takes from another what is necessary to sustain life does not sin, but he does not actually say that the poor individual has a right to the superfluous goods of the wealthy. However, other thirteenth-century scholastics do say this explicitly. For example, the canonist Laurentius, who says that when the poor person takes from another under press of necessity, it is "as if he used his own right and his own thing."[60] Moreover, as Tierney goes on to show, this came to be recognized as a right which could be adjudicated at law:

> Alongside the formal judicial procedures inherited from Roman law the canonists had developed an alternative, more simple, equitable process known as "evangelical denunciation." By virtue of the authority inhering in his office as judge, a bishop could hear any complaint involving an alleged sin and could

provide a remedy without the plaintiff bringing a formal action. From about 1200 onward several canonists argued that this procedure was available to the poor person in extreme need. He could assert a rightful claim by an "appeal to the office of the judge." The bishop could then compel an intransigent rich man to give alms from his superfluities, by excommunication if necessary. The argument gained general currency when it was assimilated into the *Ordinary Gloss* to the *Decretum*.[61]

Those scholastics who speak of a right on the part of the poor to the superfluities of the rich do so on the basis of more general natural law considerations, and do not go on to develop a comprehensive theory of natural subjective rights. Nonetheless, it would be captious to deny that the authors whom Tierney cites do assert the existence of an individual right, explicitly referred to as a *jus*, which is grounded in the natural law rather than in specific social conventions, and which gives rise to claims that can be legally enforced. It is not clear that the obligation of the rich person in such a case would be seen as arising from the right of the poor person (as opposed to the more general obligation of the rich to share with those in need), but at the very least, general obligations are seen as giving rise to claims which function as subjective rights.

Hence, we have seen that even though the scholastic concept of the natural law does not necessarily imply a doctrine of subjective natural rights, there are some generally recognized natural law claims which do function much like subjective rights, and some scholastics in the latter part of this period do speak in terms of individual rights grounded in the natural law. Most importantly, these claims are seen as having juridical effect, and the scholastics attempt to devise mechanisms (marriage tribunals, evangelical denunciation) through which these claims can be publicly defended and enforced. Seen from this perspective, later natural rights theories appear as a natural (so to speak) development of the earlier scholastic concept of the natural law, even though they do not represent the only possible way in which that concept could be developed.

In particular, later rights theories represent a further expression of a central concern that was shared by the canonists and theologians in this period: namely, to find ways of giving social expression to the divine will as expressed through the exigencies of human nature. Seen in this context, an assertion of the existence of subjective natural rights is a particular development of more general theological concerns, a development that places particular emphasis on the authority of the individual as a participant in the divine attributes of reason or will. This is an important point, because it helps us to see what is at stake in affirming a doctrine of subjective natural rights that goes beyond an assertion of mutual duties.

All the canonists and theologians whom we are considering would agree that the natural law gives rise to claims and duties stemming from the dignity of the human person, considered as a bearer of the divine image and a potential participant in salvation. Furthermore, they would agree that these claims and duties have social implications, at least insofar as any truly just society is bound to respect them. The incipient accounts of subjective rights we have just considered go beyond this consensus, to assert the existence of individual claims that have juridical effect, and to assert further that a just society will necessarily give legal expression to these claims. In this way, a strong theory of rights places at least some of the responsibility for enforcing claims of non-maleficence on (potential or actual) victims themselves, and by doing so, it also gives individuals the opportunity to assert their own sense of dignity, and where necessary, their own sense of injury before society as a whole.[62] In this way, they are both an expression of and a safeguard for the autonomy and the dignity of the individual.

It is sometimes said that rights theories express a negative kind of individualism and serve as a vehicle for self-assertion and contentiousness. Of course they have often done so, but that does not mean that every rights theory will necessarily do so. Tierney offers a good assessment of the positive value of rights theories, seen from the perspective of the theological commitments that underlie the scholastic concept of the natural law:

> By around 1200 many canonists were coming to realize that the old language of *jus naturale* could be used to define both a faculty or force of the human person and a "neutral sphere of personal choice," "a zone of human autonomy." But they did not, like some modern critics of rights theories, expect such language to justify a moral universe in which each individual would ruthlessly pursue his own advantage. Like most of the

classical rights theorists down to Locke and Wolff they envisaged a sphere of natural rights bounded by a natural moral law. The first natural rights theories were not based on an apotheosis of simple greed or self-serving egotism; rather, they derived from a view of individual human persons as free, endowed with reason, capable of moral discernment, and from a consideration of the ties of justice and charity that bound individuals to one another.[63]

4. Two hard cases:
Servitude and social persecution

The scholastic concept of the natural law offers a sophisticated and theologically cogent analysis of social institutions and, in addition, it provides us with a basis for a persuasive social ethic. At least, that has been the argument so far. However, the scholastics' views on certain issues would seem to call this optimistic assessment into question. When we examine their views on gender and servitude it is apparent that, at best, they were not able or willing to draw out the full implications of their own commitments. What is more, these aspects of their thought raise the possibility that there is something intrinsic to their concept of the natural law that lends itself to social oppression. Can we still take this concept as a starting point for our own moral reflections, in the light of these ambiguities?

In my view, these problematic aspects of scholastic social thought are not necessary consequences of their concept of the natural law. In the process of appropriating the central scholastic commitment to natural equality, we will find ourselves repudiating many of the specific views that the scholastics held on the issues before us, but we can do so in accordance with principles that they themselves recognized. Or at least, that will be the argument of this section. In Chapter 4, we examined scholastic views on gender in some detail. In this section, we will consider their views on servitude, as well as examine the implications of their concept of the natural law for political persecution.

What is the scholastic view on servitude and, more particularly, what is their view on slavery? In order to answer this question, it is not sufficient to consult what they have to say on the topic, because our translation of key terms depends in part on whether we believe they mean servitude or, more specifically, chattel slavery, when they refer to *servitus* (from *servus,* servant or slave).

Most scholars agree that chattel slavery as a widespread, economically significant institution had come to an end by the beginning of the eleventh century, to be replaced by various forms of serfdom. According to Janet Coleman, the meaning of the terms *dominus/servus,* which would have been translated as "master/slave" in classical Latin, is transformed in the later medieval period to reflect this change:

> The vocabulary of the social categories used by canonists and moralists in the thirteenth century reveals perhaps the most funda-mental of contemporary oppositions in the pair *dominus/servus.* The *servus* is a part of society, he submits to a certain number of obligations and possesses rights limited by those who act as master or *dominus.* The *dominus* is the proprietor, the possessor of land and of *servi* attached to the property, and he draws revenues from the exploitation of both. This *dominus* possesses *dominium,* which is essentially an economic capacity ... The *dominus* was also he who possessed jurisdiction, authority to govern, to establish justice, to levy taxes in return for maintaining the security of his *subditi,* and to wage war within established limits.[64]

At the same time, chattel slavery did persist in some areas throughout the medieval period, and we must assume that the scholastics were aware of this fact.[65] Furthermore, while the serf did not suffer from all the disadvantages of the slave of antiquity, he was nonetheless not free. Out of the three characteristics that distinguished the slave according to Orlando Patterson – personal powerlessness, natal alienation (that is, "the loss of ties of birth in both ascending and descending generations"), and lack of honor within the society – the serf under feudalism retained two of them.[66] He suffered from a lack of social honor, and his personal power was strictly limited; like the slave of antiquity, he could be bought and sold.[67]

In my view, there is no good justification for limiting the meaning of *servitus,* as the scholastics use the term, to chattel slavery. As Coleman points out, by the thirteenth century this term has taken on new conno-tations given a changed economic and social context, and at any rate, there are too many forms of servitude by this time to limit the meaning of the term to slavery alone. This does not imply that the scholastics would have opposed the practice of chattel slavery, particularly given the fact that they never (to my knowledge) condemn the practice outright. Moreover, they do support the maintenance of a servile condition, however precisely that is to be understood.

At the same time, the scholastics do attempt to protect a space for some degree of personal freedom and equality even within the institutions of servitude. As we noted in the last chapter, they defend the right of those in a servile condition to marry, and these marriages are recognized as valid within canon law, as are marriages between free and non-free persons. This is particularly significant because it protects the serf's ties to both his family of origin and his own children, thus obviating that natal alienation which, according to Patterson, is "critical to the slave's forced alienation."[68] Someone of servile status cannot be ordained without the permission of his master. However, this is not an absolute prohibition, since if a man of servile status is ordained to the priesthood or diaconate in spite of the law, he can remain in orders if he compensates his master in some way (Gratian, *Decretum* D.54, C.1, 8). Furthermore, as we have just seen, Aquinas appeals to natural equality to circumscribe the obligations of obedience within the context of any social relationship, thus giving limited but real practical expression to the idea that we are all equal in virtue of sharing one common nature. While these liberties and protections do not amount to free status, neither are they consistent with chattel slavery as it would have been understood in antiquity, or as it once again prevailed in the modern period.

There is another aspect of scholastic social thought that is, if anything, more troubling in its implications than the scholastic defense of servitude. The social reforms of the late eleventh and twelfth centuries came with a price: namely, the identification of certain social groups as dangerous outsiders. As R.I. Moore points out,

> the eleventh and twelfth centuries saw what has turned out to be a permanent change in Western society. Persecution became habitual. That is to say not simply that individuals were subject to violence, but that violence began to be directed, *through established governmental, judicial and social institutions,* against groups

of people defined by general characteristics such as race, religion or way of life; and that membership of such groups in itself came to be regarded as justifying these attacks.[69]

This is a very serious claim indeed, particularly when we take the subsequent history of racial and religious persecution into account. From our standpoint, it raises a further question: Does the scholastic concept of the natural law lead necessarily to such an outcome?

There are some critics of the natural law tradition who do believe that a natural law approach to morality leads ineluctably to violence. For example, according to Stanley Hauerwas, "When Christians assume that their particular moral convictions are independent of narrative, that they are justified by some universal standpoint free from history, they are tempted to imagine that those who do not share such an ethic must be particularly perverse and should be coerced to do what we know on universal grounds they really should want to do." In this way, he continues, "violence and coercion become conceptually intelligible from a natural law standpoint."[70]

Hauerwas is right that a thoroughgoing moral universalism can be transformed into a rationale for violence, but as we have seen, the scholastic concept of the natural law does not imply this kind of moral universalism. Moreover, there are many routes to violence and persecution. When we examine the tragic history of violent conflicts, even in the twentieth century, it is apparent that devotion to a particular, historically embedded, narrative-specific way of life has led to violent persecution of the other at least as often as a commitment to an a-historical moral universalism. Hauerwas offers a salutary reminder that adherence to a (supposedly) universally valid morality is not, by itself, a safeguard against violence, persecution, or oppression of the other, but his claim that such a commitment is uniquely oriented toward violence is not convincing. More to the point, it is not plausible that the men and women of the eleventh and twelfth centuries were particularly prone to violent persecution *because* they adhered to a concept of the natural law (nor is this Moore's point). Rather, these persecutions result from a complex array of causes, as Moore himself notes.[71]

Furthermore, we cannot just assume that the different persecutions Moore discusses can all be reduced to examples of one general phenom-

enon. At least some of the heretical movements of the twelfth and
thirteenth centuries represented far-reaching social and intellectual challenges to Christianity. While this does not in any way excuse the violent
responses to these movements, it does help to explain why church and
secular leaders felt that they had to respond in drastic ways.[72] Medieval
efforts to exclude homosexuals and lepers from the social community are
harder to understand. It is worth noting, however, that on Moore's own
showing, lepers were not subject to violent persecution as a class, although
their social isolation left them vulnerable to sporadic violence.[73] In
contrast, male homosexuality became a capital crime in Spain, France,
and many Italian cities in the mid-thirteenth century. However, as Moore
points out, "The real impetus of the attack on homosexuality ... did not
come from the Church; the Fourth Lateran Council actually reduced the
penalties prescribed by its predecessor."[74] The persecutions of both lepers
and homosexuals seem to have arisen from complex social factors and
cannot be traced to religious beliefs and sensibilities alone.

The most troubling development in this period is the sharp increase
of attacks on the Jews, who up until the early twelfth century had lived
on the margins of Western Europe in relative security, albeit in conditions
of isolation and legal disability.[75] The causes for this ominous development
are subject to much debate. According to Anna Sapir Abulafia, the rise
in anti-Semitism in the twelfth century was due, at least in part, to the
growing popularity of natural law reasoning in that same period.[76] Jeremy
Cohen argues that the rise in anti-Semitism should be traced to a slightly
later development: the rise of the mendicant orders and their growing
familiarity with medieval rabbinic literature.[77] Moore suggests, with some
hesitation, that perhaps the educated and cultured Jews offered too much
competition to the educated Christian elite that began to emerge in the
twelfth century, with the result that educated Jews were pushed to the
margins of social life or excluded from the community altogether.[78] Other
authors, including both Lester Little and John Hood, argue that the rise
in anti-Jewish persecution is not so much the result of new theological
developments as an expression of ancient Christian anxieties and hostilities
in changing social and economic circumstances.[79]

Abulafia's argument offers the most direct challenge to the positive
assessment of the scholastic concept of the natural law developed here.
On her view, the Christian humanism of the twelfth century, and the

concept of the natural law that it generated, were both grounded in a profound reverence for reason, an attitude that was largely (not exclusively) Stoic in origin. This reverence for reason led to the conviction that the truths of Christianity are capable of rational defense, and by the same token, it led to the suspicion that anyone who fails to accept these truths is irrational. And since rationality was seen as the defining characteristic of the human person, it is only a short step to the conclusion that those who fail to accept Christianity's claims are less than fully human.

What are we to make of this argument? As an explanation for the rise of anti-Semitism, it is not convincing. Reason was critically important for Christian thinkers in this period, but that does not mean that they ignored the importance of other aspects of human life, as we have already noted. Nor did theologians in the twelfth century, or much less the thirteenth, typically believe that the truths of faith can be derived from reason alone. More to the point, Abulafia is only able to offer two examples of twelfth-century Christian authors who actually say that the Jews are not fully human because they do not accept rational arguments for Christian belief: Odo of Cambrai and Peter the Venerable. In Peter's case, she admits that he is well aware that the Jews are human and endowed with reason.[80] In my view, Abulafia places too much weight on the rhetorical excesses of these two authors.

At the same time, she makes an important point: in a climate of anxiety and hostility, a reverence for reason can easily be transformed into a rationale for dehumanizing those who do not accept one's views. By making this point she, like Hauerwas, calls attention to a danger that we should keep in mind in attempting to appropriate the scholastic concept of the natural law. Nonetheless, we can accept this caution without being forced to the conclusion that a high evaluation of rationality must necessarily lead us to dehumanizing the other.

At any rate, the rise of anti-Jewish persecutions in the twelfth and thirteenth centuries appears to have resulted from a complex set of factors. Certainly, theological ambivalence towards the Jews played a necessary role in this process, although I am inclined to agree with Hood that what we see in this period is not so much a new departure in Christian theology as a shift in emphasis from a relatively tolerant attitude to a more repressive stance. The tensions generated by the rise in heretical movements and the fervor generated by the Crusades also undoubtedly played a role, as did economic anxieties that were projected onto the Jews.

To a considerable extent, the scholastics were complicit in the rise of anti-Semitism and anti-Jewish persecutions, although this is more true in the later thirteenth and fourteenth centuries than in the period we are considering. However, over against this, we should set the fact that the scholastic concept of the natural law offered resources for defending the possibility of a moral community not dependent on shared Christian faith.

Aquinas is particularly noteworthy for his willingness to make explicit appeals to the natural law in this context. He argues on natural law grounds that Christians do have obligations of loyalty and obedience toward non-Christian rulers, except when the latter actively persecute the Christian faith or are themselves apostates from Christianity (*Summa theologiae* II-II 10.10). Moreover, he argues that Jewish children cannot be baptized against their parents' will, because such an act would be a violation of natural justice, which prescribes that the spiritual formation of children should be left to their parents until they reach the age of reason (*ST* II-II 10.12). As Hood points out, this argument reflects "the astonishing depth of [Aquinas'] commitment to the natural law," because on Aquinas' view, unbaptized children are at the very least at grave risk of eternal damnation.[81] Yet, for Aquinas, even this cannot justify us in overriding the demands of natural justice, because these demands are themselves expressions of God's wisdom and will.

Seen from our standpoint, such arguments are likely to seem inadequate. Yet they express a fundamental conviction that is still valid and, indeed, crucial: it is possible to live together in a moral community on the basis of an acknowledgment of shared humanity and the mutual claims that that recognition generates without necessarily sharing common views on even the most fundamental matters. We may well wish that the men and women of the middle ages had taken this insight more seriously; it is critical that we ourselves take it seriously in our own time.

5. Towards a theology of social life

From the perspective of contemporary theology, there are (at least) two criticisms that might be directed against the social ethic implied by the scholastic concept of the natural law. On the one hand, the substantive commitments that inform that ethic may seem to be problematic, given the widespread, very different assessment of the central values of modern Christian social ethics. On the other hand, the scholastics are likely to be criticized for being insufficiently radical in following through on the commitments that they do affirm.

I have already attempted to address the second criticism. It is certainly true that the scholastics were not always as consistent or far-reaching in applying their own principles as we might have wished. At the same time, it would be misleading to say that they simply provided a rationale for the existing institutions of their society since, as we have already seen, those institutions were themselves undergoing rapid development and change. They did not call for far-reaching social changes in part because they were the immediate heirs of social changes that they attempted to consolidate and defend. We can recognize and build on the foundations that they laid for further reform, even while acknowledging that they did not go as far on some questions as their own principles would require.

The more fundamental challenge is posed by the scholastics' commitment to equality as a central value for a Christian social ethic. Until fairly recently, this would not have seemed problematic to most Christian theologians. It was widely assumed that Christianity and secular Western societies were in general accord in their affirmation of the basic value of equality. This assumption was reinforced by a widespread view that the fundamental Christian moral value is a distinctive kind of love, which was readily associated with the philosophical principle of equal regard.

Beginning in the 1970s, however, this view began to be challenged by a number of theologians, including John Yoder, Stanley Hauerwas, and more recently John Milbank, who argue that the foundational Christian value is not equality but non-violence.[82] On this view, the Christian should renounce the use of violence under any circumstances whatever, even in defense of third parties. To the charge that this stance would rule out any sort of radical challenge to social injustices, these authors would reply that, even if this is true, social action as it is normally understood in secular society is not the primary Christian vocation. Rather, Christians are called to preserve the integrity of their fundamental commitments through the formation of communities in which non-violence can be put into practice. Such communities would have a greater effect on society than any direct social or political engagement, because they would serve as a form of witness that another way of life is possible.

What is at stake theologically in the affirmation of non-violence as the central Christian value? Although a full answer to this question would call for a detailed examination of several contemporary authors, John Yoder indicates the basic lines of such an answer through his account of the kind of Christian ethics that he himself opposes:

> [Social ethics] will derive its guidance from common sense and the nature of things. We will measure what is "fitting" and what is "adequate": what is "relevant" and what is "effective." We shall be "realistic" and "responsible." All these slogans point to an epistemology for which the classic label is the *theology of the natural:* the nature of things is held to be adequately perceived in their basic givenness; the right is that which respects or tends towards the realization of the essentially given. It is by studying the realities around us, not by hearing a proclamation from God, that we discern the right.[83]

In the last sentence, we find a key to what is at stake theologically in contemporary theologies of non-violence. That is, these theologies reflect a conviction that any adequate Christian ethic must be grounded in what is distinctively Christian and, more specifically, in the uniqueness of Jesus' person and message as revealed in the New Testament. In this, they reflect the influence of Karl Barth, even though these theologians break with Barth on the specific issue of the legitimacy of the use of violence for the Christian. Yoder confirms this elsewhere; the ethic of non-violence, he says, "has the peculiar disadvantage – or advantage, depending upon one's point of view – of being meaningful only if Christ be he who Christians claim him to be, the Master. Almost every other kind of ethical approach espoused by Christians, pacifist or otherwise, will continue to make sense to the non-Christian as well."[84] Correlatively, Yoder's ethic emphasizes the discontinuity between human nature and the meaning of humanity as revealed by God in Christ; the Incarnation, he says, does not mean "that God took all of human nature as it was, put his seal of approval on it, and thereby ratified nature as revelation. The point is just the opposite; that God broke through the borders of our standard definition of what is human and gave a new, formative definition in Jesus."[85]

It is in this context that we should understand the remarkably negative attitude toward secular society and especially political life that marks the writings of Yoder, Hauerwas, and Milbank. In part, this attitude follows from the commitment to non-violence itself, since the maintenance of a civil society is inextricably bound up with the threat, and sometimes the use, of coercive force. A Christian commitment to non-violence would not necessarily lead to a wholesale rejection of secular society. Yet all three of these authors insist on the alien and hostile character of secular society. For Yoder, secular society is dominated by the Powers, quasi-personal, hostile forces that Jesus has definitively overcome. Hauerwas is scathing in his denunciations of secular liberalism, and of those theologians who equate Christian morality with liberalism. Milbank goes even further; Christianity is unique, or very nearly unique, he says, because only Christianity (and perhaps Judaism) rests on a foundational myth that does not place violence at the foundation of reality: "Christianity is unique in refusing ultimate reality to all conflictual phenomena. For this reason, I shall argue, it is the true 'opposite' of Nietzschean postmodernism, and also able to deny it in a more than merely despairing, Manichean fashion. By comparison, all other myths, or narrative traditions, affirm or barely conceal an original primordial violence, which a sacral order merely restrains."[86]

Given all this, we can better appreciate what is at stake in the implicit conflict between the scholastic concept of the natural law and the theologies of non-violence proposed by Yoder, Hauerwas, Milbank, and others. The differences between the scholastics and our own contemporaries go well beyond the fact that the scholastics are prepared to justify the use of violent force; they reflect two different ways of interpreting the moral significance of Scripture and, correlatively, two profoundly different attitudes toward all those aspects of natural and human life that do not readily fit within a Christian world-view.

This brings us to a point that has already been made several times and that should be emphasized again in this context. It would be a mistake to assume that the difference between the scholastic defenders of the natural law and the defenders of Christian pacifism lies in the fact that, for the scholastics, Christian ethics is derived from reason and nature, whereas pacifist theologians derive their morality from the Bible. Rather, what is at stake here are two alternative ways of interpreting the moral significance of Scripture. We have already seen that, for the scholastics, the concept of the natural law is explicitly presented as a scriptural concept, and they find both warrants and interpretative guidance for their appropriation of the earlier natural law tradition in their reading of Scripture. It is true that they also interpret Scripture at some points on the basis of their concept of the natural law. But this is not a matter of reading Scripture through the lens of an alien philosophical doctrine, because their concept of the natural law cannot be equated with its pre-Christian antecedents. It is a theological concept grounded in a scripturally informed interpretation of earlier traditions of natural law reflection. In this sense, when the scholastics use their concept of the natural law to interpret specific scriptural texts, they are interpreting Scripture (as represented by a particular text) by Scripture (taken as a whole, through the medium of theological reflection).

The fundamental difference between the scholastics and contemporary pacifist theologians is a doctrinal difference. For the latter, Christian ethics can rest only on Jesus Christ, whether he is seen in more or less orthodox terms or is considered as the central figure in the foundational Christian narratives and practices. Correlatively, for these theologians, distinctiveness is a (perhaps, *the*) criterion for adequacy in Christian ethics. In this respect, all of them reflect the influence of Karl Barth, even though they break with Barth in their insistence on pacifism as the paradigmatic Christian commitment. In contrast, the scholastics give priority to preserving the integrity of Christian doctrine taken as a whole, and given the context within which they wrote, they give particular weight to the doctrine of creation. As a consequence, they have no theological stake in the uniqueness or distinctiveness of Christian morality. Indeed, they would expect on theological grounds that there should be some continuities between Christian morality and the moralities of other societies, since these would be further expressions of God's creative wisdom and goodness.

In Chapter 2, I argued that distinctiveness is inadequate and misleading as a primary criterion for an adequate Christian ethic. It seems to me that the theologians of non-violence whom we have been considering confirm this point. In saying this, I do not at all want to deny the value of their cautions against a too-easy accommodation with values of the secular order, or the integrity and power of their witness to the pacifist alternative. Yet this witness comes at a high price: namely, the rejection of whatever does not fit neatly into a Christian conceptual framework as alien and evil.

This stance of rejection is suggested by Yoder's claim that through the incarnation of Christ, God "breaks through the boundaries" of our understanding of what it is to be human. Both Hauerwas and Milbank go further in this direction than Yoder does, but Yoder provides a helpful focus for considering how the scholastics might have responded to the theologies of non-violence, since he is closest to them in his explicit theological views.

For Christians, certainly, our understanding of what it is to be human is inextricably tied up with our beliefs about the person and work of Christ, but what is implied by Yoder's contrast between this claim and the view that God ratifies human nature in the Incarnation? Are we to understand that God is indifferent or hostile to human nature as it exists apart from the redemptive work of Christ? It is hard to see how this view can be reconciled with our faith in God as the Creator of nature. Indeed, it is hard to see how it can be reconciled with a faith in the Incarnation. If human nature apart from redemption has no goodness or integrity of its own, then how could the Word of God take on this nature as the mode of God's definitive existence in time?

It might be said that it is precisely through the Incarnation that Christ transforms the meaning of humanity or, at least, in Yoder's words, radically alters our concept of humanity. Yet this does not appear to be the case. The Jesus of the gospels is clearly human and can be recognized as such in terms of our ordinary common notions about what it is to be human. Jesus is presented as "one of us," someone whose life is in continuity with human experience everywhere, and that is precisely why his extraordinary authority and claims are so scandalous (see, for example, Mt. 13:53-58).

Theologically, it is more satisfactory to say with O'Donovan that Christ's resurrection is "God's final and decisive word on the life of his creature, Adam."[87] Through this final word, God affirms human nature, itself God's good creation. Of course, our faith in that affirmation changes our perspective on human nature, and it also transforms our understanding of what is central and normative in human nature. Nonetheless, the life of Christ, culminating in the Resurrection, represents God's definitive affirmation of humanity, the final proof that "God so loved the world."

And if God so loved the world, then we as Christians are likewise called to love the world; not in the sense of being worldly, but in the sense of making common cause with humanity as a whole. What does this mean? At the very least, we are called upon to acknowledge the bonds of common humanity that bind us to one another, and to affirm and cherish whatever is good in the society around us. The demands of Christian charity go beyond this, but we can never do less than this.

As we saw in the last chapter, we cannot preserve a stance of loving charity toward men and women without also acknowledging the goodness to be found within the communities that shape them. This does not mean that we are called on to embrace uncritically every aspect of secular culture. Nonetheless, it does imply a willingness to accept the inevitable ambiguities that are present in every human society, including (we must keep reminding ourselves) Christian societies and the churches themselves. In his gloss on the traditional prayer known as the "serenity prayer," Reinhold Niebuhr prays for the willingness to take, "as Christ did, the world as it is, not as I would have it." This, it seems to me, is a concise expression of a fundamental Christian attitude.

There can be no question about the ambiguities to be found in the "world as it is." This ambiguity is not just a reflection of the mixed character of human experience, the fact that we find violence, oppression, and squalor occurring together with tenderness, peace, and plenty. More fundamentally, the ambiguity results from the fact that good and evil, virtue and sin, are inextricably tied together in human experience. Near the end of his *Freedom in the Making of Western Culture*, Orlando Patterson remarks on "the tragic interdependence of good and evil," going on to observe that, "To its great credit, Western culture has never tried to conceal this terrible truth, although it is one our present era is all too eager to shun."[88]

For the contemporary theologians whom we have been considering, the ambiguities of human society are interpreted as the results of sinfulness, without remainder. Correlatively, they believe that it is possible to create a social order — that is, a church community — in which no such ambiguities will occur. Yet it is questionable whether this interpretation of Christian theology is adequate, even considered on its own terms. It is true that, according to the classical Christian doctrine, God is a complete and self-sufficient being, "without any shadow of variation or change." There is neither violence nor ambiguity in the Triune life of God. Nonetheless, it does not follow that created existence can attain the perfection of God's life. Simply because we are finite creatures, with limited capacities and conflicting needs, we can expect to experience some degree of privation and conflict, even apart from the mutual hostility and oppression that is the direct result of our sinfulness.[89]

The greatest merit of the scholastic concept of the natural law considered as a social doctrine lies in the fact that it provides us with resources for addressing this ambiguity. The scholastics recognize that the fundamental institutions of their society are problematic, yet they are also prepared to accept them as necessary conditions for the attainment of social goods. In this way, they provide a theological framework for affirming the limited but real goodness of human societies, while also keeping open possibilities for social critique and reform.

In their awareness of the inevitable ambiguities of social life, and their willingness to embrace it nonetheless, the scholastics are surprisingly similar to Reinhold Niebuhr. Nonetheless, their social ethic is also different in important aspects from his Christian realism.

For Niebuhr, God's love as revealed in Christ is a purely self-sacrificial love, which by its very nature cannot be given social embodiment:

> Though the relation between the divine and human in Christ is not contradictory, it is paradoxical. The final majesty, the ultimate freedom, and the perfect disinterestedness of the divine love can have a counterpart in history only in a life which ends tragically, because it refuses to participate in the claims and counterclaims of human existence. It portrays a love "which seeketh not its own." But a love which seeketh not its own is not able to maintain itself in historical society. Not only may it fall victim to excessive forms of the self-assertion of others; but even the most perfectly balanced system of justice in history is a balance of competing wills and interests, and must therefore worst anyone who does not participate in the balance.[90]

As this passage indicates, Niebuhr gives as much weight to the uniqueness of Christ, the discontinuity between the ideal of humanity that he reveals and our own expectations, as do Yoder, Hauerwas, and Milbank. However, he draws very different practical conclusions from this view. According to him, we are obliged by Christian charity itself to work for justice and peace, insofar as these can be secured through the "balance of competing wills and interests" intrinsic to all human institutions. This will require us to participate in activities and forms of life that are not consonant with the ideal of Christian love as revealed in the cross of Christ. We must nonetheless assume our responsibilities in human society, trusting in the mercy of God finally to overcome "the sinful corruption in which man is involved on every level of moral achievement by reason of his false and abortive efforts to complete his own life and history."[91]

Contrast Niebuhr's view with that of William of Auxerre:

> Indications are those [precepts] which are given for a particular time and oblige conditionally, so that the opposite may licitly be done on account of some consideration which may emerge. For example, according to the law of nature it is legitimate to resist force by force, since vengeance derives from the natural law, as Cicero says in the first book of the *Rhetoric*. However, our Lord commands the opposite to the apostles, saying, "He who strikes you on the cheek, give him the other one, and he who would take your tunic, give him your cloak as well," so that in that time and place they should so offer themselves, in order that through their unaccustomed mildness men and women might be drawn to God (*Summa aurea* III.18, 1).

From the standpoint of Niebuhr, no less than the theologians of non-violence whom we have been considering, this passage is likely to appear as a shocking dilution of the gospel. Yet by now, we can see it in another light.

In this passage, what William offers is not a dilution of Scripture but an interpretation through which the meaning of a particular imperative is discerned in the light of its likely purpose, seen in the context of one's overall theological commitments. His appeal to Cicero should not be allowed to obscure this fact, because Cicero is taken here as a classical spokesman for a tradition that by William's time has been thoroughly incorporated into a theological framework. Moreover, William does not claim that Jesus' command represents an impossible ideal; on the contrary, he presents it as representing a real, practical imperative that can readily be understood and put into practice once the scope of the command has been delineated.

Most fundamentally, William here expresses the fundamental scholastic view that human nature reflects the goodness and wisdom of its Creator. This view gives rise to the presupposition that if there is an apparent conflict between the natural law and the gospel, it is possible to reconcile them dialectically. That is what William does. In the process, he does limit the scope of the evangelical prescription, but he does not relegate it to an impossible ideal that cannot be fulfilled in history. Yet he also leaves room for the expression of fundamental human tendencies toward self-protection and the vindication of justice, even within a Christian community.

It might appear that William is too quick to accept the traditional view that these tendencies are in fact part of the natural law. After all, the scholastics themselves were in doubt about whether sexual desire is an authentic part of human nature or a corruption introduced by sin. Perhaps the same thing should be said of our tendencies toward retaliation and vindication, which are by their very nature self-concerned and violent. Perhaps we should place anger in the same category as the early scholastics placed lust: that is, a pervasive human tendency that is nonetheless sinful and corrupt.

But this will not do. Anger and a self-protective instinct are clear examples of tendencies that we share with other animals, even though in our case they are transformed through rational reflection into something distinctively human. This does not prove that these tendencies can be understood as components of human well-being, but it does at least suggest that we look for purposes that they serve for the individual or the community, in terms of which they can be rendered intelligible. And, in fact, it is not difficult to identify such purposes. These tendencies serve the basic aims, which we share with all other animals, of self-protection and survival; it is difficult to imagine any human being, even a small child, surviving and flourishing without some tendencies to lash out at what hurts or frustrates. Moreover, when transformed through rational judgment, these tendencies are fundamental to the preservation of a just society. All societies need some structures for adjudicating claims and protecting individual members from one another. More fundamentally, an inclination to resist unfairness is necessary for developing a sense of justice at all, and, in addition, we depend on this sense of indignation to alert us to forms of injustice to which we might otherwise be blind.[92]

Hence, our inclinations toward self-defense and retaliation can be understood in terms of the authentic human goods that they serve. Given the scholastic concept of the natural law, this implies that they reflect the goodness of human nature and the wisdom and love of its Creator. It may well be that other aspects of human nature should be given normative priority (as we and the scholastics would agree), but the appropriate expression of these tendencies cannot be considered to be contrary to the will of God.

Of course, none of this implies that the Christian can simply disregard scriptural imperatives whenever they seem to conflict with natural inclinations. At the same time, neither can we ignore or dismiss our best insights into the exigencies of our nature on the basis of an unconsidered or partial appeal to scriptural imperatives. Rather, we must strive to bring together our understanding of Scripture and our own nature through a dialectical process of mutual interpretation that harmonizes the two while respecting the integrity of each, as far as we can do so. This process, it should be emphasized, will also involve an element of reflectively shaping our nature to bring it into accordance with our best theological insights, through community formation and the education of children and converts. These ongoing efforts of self-development, in turn, will have much to teach us about the inclinations and limits of our nature, if we are attentive to the lessons they offer.

Notes to Chapter Five

1   See, for example, Gerard Winstanley, "The True Levelers Standard Advanced" (1649), in *Gerard Winstanley: Selected Writings*, Andrew Hopton, ed. (London: Aporia Press, 1989), 7-23.

2   This is documented at some length in Chapter 2; for an explicit statement of the distinction, see Aquinas, *Summa theologiae* I-II 31.7.

3   I have not found any example of a scholastic thinker who believes that human society emerges spontaneously, without some element of rational reflection. Albert's account of the natural law, while it lacks the historical dimension we find in Rufin, is similar in its emphasis on the necessity for rational reflection in order to express even the most basic pre-rational tendencies. For other examples of similar lines of analysis, see Stephen of Tournai, Weigand no. 246-249, William of Gascony, Weigand no. 400, and Philip the Chancellor, Lottin 112-113.

4   Philippe Delhaye, *Permanence du Droit Naturel* (Louvain: Editions Nauwelaerts, 1960), 66-84.

5   Albert is especially clear on this point, as the passage cited in Chapter 2 indicates. In addition, among the jurists, see Cyprianus, Weigand no. 70; among the canonists and theologians, see Stephen of Tournai, Weigand no. 246-249; Cardinal Laborens, Weigand no. 311; William of Gascony, Weigand no. 400; Simon of Bisiniano, Lottin 106-107; Philip the Chancellor, Lottin 112-113, and Aquinas, *Summa theologiae* I-II 94.2.

6   Richard Tuck, *Natural Rights Theories: Their Origin and Development* (Cambridge: Cambridge University Press, 1979), 18; emphasis in the original.

7   See, for example, the *Summa reverentia sacrorum canonum*, Weigand no. 324-327, cited in Chapter 2.

8   For example, according to Walter Ullmann, the civilians defend the enforcement of the mutual obligations between superiors and subordinates generated through the feudal system as an expression of the natural law; see *The Individual and Society in the Middle Ages* (Baltimore, MD: John Hopkins University Press, 1966), 82-84.

9   The *Summa Monacensis*; I am grateful to my colleague Albert Wimmer for identifying the place name for me.

10   For a more detailed and very helpful analysis of the specifics of this analysis, at least among the canonists, see Rudolf Weigand, *Die Naturrechtslehre der Legisten und Dekretisten von Irnerius bis Accursius und von Gratian bis Johannes Teutonicus* (Munich, Germany: Max Hueber, 1967), 259-282, 307-360.

11   This point is sometimes made explicitly; see, for example, the *Summa Jus aliud divinum*,Weigand no. 443-4.

12   See R.W. and A.J. Carlyle, *A History of Medieval Political Theory in the West*, 6 vols. (Edinburgh: Blackwood and Sons, 1903-36, repr. 1970), 1: 23-24 for a discussion

of the motif of the Golden Age in Seneca; as they go on to observe, this motif is
adopted by patristic authors generally (117) and emphasized by Lactantius (134).

13 On this point, see Weigand's discussion in *Die Naturrechtslehre*, 259-282, including
the examples collected there.

14 Earlier in this treatise, the divine law is identified as a natural law; see Weigand no.
285-286.

15 This line of analysis is exceedingly common among the canonists. For other examples, see Roland Bandinelli, Weigand no. 229; Rufin, Weigand no. 241; the *Summa*
"*inter cetera*," Weigand no. 291; Honorius, Weigand no. 350; the distinction "*Est jus
naturalae*," Weigand no. 362-363; Alan, Weigand no. 389; William of Gascony,
Weigand no.401; the *Summa Duacensis*, Weigand no. 408; the *Cologne Summa*, Lottin 106; Simon of Bisigianio, Lottin 107; the *Muenster Summa, ibid.*; Huguccio, Lottin 110. Most of these link this division explicitly with the natural law as expressed
in Scripture, but some link it with the natural law understood as reason, for example,
the *Summa Duacensis*.

16 On the other hand, it does not seem to have been at all popular among the civilians.
Among the theologians, William of Auxerre (cited below) makes the most extensive
use of this schema, but we also find Bonaventure interpreting the divine will in
terms of a similar threefold distinction; see the *Breveloquium* I.9.

17 John of La Rochelle offers a similar argument; see Lottin 120-121.

18 Lottin does not attempt to determine whether this anonymous text is the source for
the parallel passage in the *Summa fratris Alexandri*, or conversely. This part of the *SFA*
is widely believed to be the work of John of La Rochelle, and the passage cited may
well be his. See Odon Lottin, *Le droit natural chez saint Thomas d'Aquin et ses prédécesseurs*, 2nd ed. (Bruges, Belgium: Charles Beyaert, 1931), 53-57. At any rate, I cite
this text instead of the parallel in the *Summa fratris Alexandri* because it is more
explicit in its preference for Augustine's approach; the latter simply offers Augustine's solution as an alternative, without indicating any preference for it.

19 See, for example, the *Confessions* III, 7-10.

20 The reference to the child who sins against his father is almost certainly meant to
apply to Ham, the son of Noah; cf. the *Munester Summa*, Weigand no. 461. This
argument was, of course, to have an unhappy afterlife in defenses of American slavery. However, so far as I can determine, the scholastics did not identify the descendants of Ham with any identifiable ethnic group; for them, this argument was simply
a way of accounting for servitude in accordance with the historical narratives of
Scripture, similar to the argument that property began with Nimrod.

21 See Tuck, *Natural Rights Theories*, 20-31, for a fuller discussion of this point.

22 See Frederick H. Russell, *The Just War in the Middle Ages* (Cambridge: Cambridge
University Press, 1975), 42-43, 102-103, 132-4.

23   This is argued at length in R.W. and A.J. Caryle, *History of Medieaval Political Theory in the West*. The views of the Carlyles have since been challenged, particularly by Walter Ullman. Nonetheless, without wanting to commit myself to every detail of their analysis, and recognizing that they overstate their claims, I am still convinced that they are right about the importance of equality to medieval political thought. For a helpful assessment of this book and its critics, see J.H. Burns, "Introduction," in Burns, ed., *The Cambridge History of Medieval Political Thought: c. 350 - c. 1450* (Cambridge: Cambridge University Press, 1988), 1-10.

     In *Freedom, Volume I: Freedom in the Making of Western Culture* (Basic Books/ Harper Collins, 1991), 347-401, Orlando Patterson argues that freedom is the central moral and social ideal in the Middle Ages. However, since the ideas of equality and free-dom are closely linked for the scholastics, this interpretation is not inconsistent with the view being offered here.

24   Annabel S. Brett, *Liberty, Right and Nature: Individual Rights in Later Scholastic Thought* (Cambridge: Cambridge University Press, 1997), 12; more generally, see 10-48 for an extended discussion of this point. It should be noted that Brett is particularly concerned with developments in the thirteenth and subsequent centuries; but the equation of property and individual power seems to have been in place by the early thirteenth century, since we find it shaping the thought of the earliest mendicants, and so it seems likely that it was already emerging in the latter part of the twelfth century.

25   For a detailed and helpful discussion of the classical and early Christian roots of the medieval Christian ideal of equality, see R.W. and A.J. Caryle, *History of Mediaeval Political Theory in the West*, 1: *passim.*; the discussion of Cicero's political thought, 1-18, and patristic thought on natural equality, slavery, and property, 102-146, are especially germane.

26   There is an enormous literature on the egalitarian strain in Paul's thought, and its subsequent influence; for an insightful discussion, which is particularly useful from the standpoint of the issues discussed in this chapter, see Patterson, *Freedom in the Making of Western Culture*, 325-344.

27   This appears to be the current scholarly consensus, at any rate; for a good summary of the relevant arguments, see Pierre Bonnassie, *From Slavery to Feudalism in South-Western Europe*, Jean Birrell, trans. (Cambridge: Cambridge University Press, 1991), 25-32.

28   Over the past century, there has been considerable debate over when, and indeed whether, chattel slavery was eliminated in Western Europe. The most likely view appears to be that chattel slavery as a widespread, economically significant system was eliminated by the beginning of the eleventh century; see Bonnassie, *From Slavery to Feudalism*, 1-59, for a defense of this view, together with a helpful survey of the preceding debate. At the same time, Bonnassie acknowledges that chattel slavery continued to exist in some parts of Europe throughout the medieval period, and

according to some scholars, it was more widespread than he would allow; see, for example, Patterson, *Freedom in the Making of Western Culture*, 347-352.

29   On the image of the three orders of society, see Georges Duby, *The Three Orders: Feudal Society Imagined*, Arthur Goldhammer, trans. (Chicago: The University of Chicago Press, 1980); the image of society as a body is discussed in more detail in the first section of Chapter 2.

30   Throughout the remainder of this section, I draw on the authors cited in Chapter 1, note 30, particularly C.H. Lawrence, *The Friars: The Impact of the Early Mendicant Movement on Western Society* (Essex: Longman, 1994), and Lester K. Little, *Religious Poverty and the Profit Economy in Medieval Europe* (Ithaca, NY: Cornell University Press, 1978, paperback ed. 1983). In addition, Alexander Murray offers an illuminating analysis of the egalitarian effects of rationalism in the eleventh and subsequent centuries in his *Reason and Society in the Middle Ages* (Oxford: Oxford University Press, 1985), 81-116.

31   Max Weber, *Economy and Society*, Two volumes, Guenther Ross and Claus Wittich, eds., (Berkeley, CA: University of California Press, 1968/1978), Volume 1, 223-226.

32   James A. Brundage, *Medieval Canon Law* (London: Longman, 1995), 3.

33   Georges Duby, *The Three Orders*, 138-139.

34   On this point, see R.W. Southern, *Scholastic Humanism and the Unification of Europe, Volume I: Foundations* (Oxford: Blackwell, 1995), 163-197.

35   Scholastic discussions of order and status within the church take their starting points from Gratian's *Decretum* D.54 and Peter Lombard's *Sentiniae* IV 24 and 25. See in particular Albert, *In IV Sent.* 24.7; Bonaventure, *In IV Sent.* 24.1.2.1, 25.2.2,4; and Aquinas, *In IV Sent.* 24.1, 25.2.1. It is noteworthy that, while all three theologians emphasize the contingency of social or ecclesiastical status, only Aquinas explicitly appeals to natural equality in order to make this point; see *In IV Sent.* IV 2.1.

36   Similarly, in this treatise Bonaventure defends radical humility (1.1 *ad* 1), the diversity of vocations among mendicants (2.3 *ad* 1), marriage (3.1), and servitude and obedience (4.1) as being in accordance with the natural law; however servitude, unlike filial obedience, is only conditionally such (*ibid.*).

37   Tuck, *Natural Rights Theories*, 22; the whole chapter, 5-31, offers an illuminating history of this debate. For further discussion of the background of this debate, see Lawrence, *The Friars*, 43-64 and especially Little, *Religious Poverty and the Profit Economy*, 158-169; for a more recent discussion of the debate and its relevance for later human rights theories, see Brett, *Liberty, Right and Nature*, 10-48.

38   At any rate, this is Tuck's view; see *Natural Rights Theories*. What Pope John XXII did, specifically, was to renounce church ownership of Franciscan property, thus forcing them in 1322 to claim ownership as well as use of the goods necessary for their survival; then in 1323, he followed this with the bull *Cum inter nonnullos*, which declared the view that Christ and his apostles renounced all proprietary rights (like

the Franciscans) to be heretical. On these events and their aftermath, see Lawrence, *The Friars*, 62-64.

39   This point is particularly stressed by Brian Tierney, who sees this as a central pre-supposition for the emergence of a doctrine of natural rights; see *The Idea of Natural Rights: Studies on Natural Rights, Natural Law and Church Law, 1150-1625* (Atlanta: Scholars Press, 1997), 43-77. Particularly noteworthy examples among the canonists include Stephen of Tournai, Weigand no. 246; Odo of Dover, Weigand no. 271, and Richard de Mores, Wiegand no. 365. As for the theologians, Aquinas expresses a general consensus when he says that knowledge of the natural law cannot be alto-gether extirpated from the human soul, although it can be distorted or obscured; see the *ST* I-II 94.6.

40   This appears to have been a truism; for an example, see Simon of Bisiniano, Lottin 107.

41   See, for example, Egidius, Weigand no. 298; the *Summa "Tractaturus Magister,"* Weigand no. 330, the *Summa "Et est sciendum,"* Weigand no. 338, Richard de Mores, Weigand no. 365, and Simon de Bisiniano, Lottin 106. However, Weigand does include an example of a canonical treatise which does take the identification of the natural law with charity to be an acceptable interpretation of the natural law; see the *Dist. "Est jus naturalae,"* Wiegand no. 354.

42   John Casey makes this point in some detail in his *Pagan Virtue: An Essay in Ethics* (Oxford: Oxford University Press, 1990); see in particular 51-103.

43   For my information on Michel Villey, and the earlier debate more generally, I am dependent on Brian Tierney, *The Idea of Natural Rights*, 13-42. For MacIntyre's comments on this issue, see Alasdair MacIntyre, *After Virtue*, 2nd ed. (Notre Dame, IN: University of Notre Dame Press, 1984), 68-70.

44   See Tuck, *Natural Rights Theories*, 7-31; Brett, *Liberty, Right and Nature*, 49-87.

45   See in particular Jacques Maritain, *Man and the State* (Chicago: University of Chicago Press, 1951), 76-107; in addition, Thomas A. Fay, "Maritain on Rights and Natural Law," *The Thomist* 55 (1991), 439-448, offers a helpful summary of Marit-ain's views.

46   David Hollenbach, *Claims in Conflict: Retrieving and Renewing the Catholic Human Rights Tradition* (Mahwah, NJ: Paulist, 1979), in particular 41, 108-18; John Finnis, *Natural Law and Natural Rights* (Oxford: Clarendon Press, 1980), 198-230. It should be noted, however, that Hollenbach's analysis is focused on the social encyclicals from Leo XIII's *Rerum novarum* through the statement of the 1971 Synod of Bishops; he discusses the medieval view of natural law and natural rights only tangentially.

47   Tierney, *The Idea of Natural Rights*, 69-77. Furthermore, Tierney argues that we find an appeal to a natural right to life in a quodlibetal question of the theologian Henry of Ghent, dated probably 1289, and therefore just outside the terminus of my study; see *ibid.*, 83-89.

48   Tuck, *Natural Rights Theories*, 5-31.

49 For an alternative interpretation of relevant developments in the later Middle Ages, including a helpful summary of scholarship since Tuck's book appeared, see Brett, *Liberty, Right and Nature*, 10-87.

50 Exactly how deep the allegiance of any given author to an idea of the natural law may have been is, of course, very much a matter of dispute. At any rate, it is not my purpose here to offer an analysis of modern political theory.

51 MacIntyre, *After Virtue*, 69.

52 Tierney, *The Idea of Natural Rights*, 44; for his subsequent discussion of the uses of the term *jus*, see 54-69. This discussion, in turn, occurs in the context of a more far-reaching investigation of the linguistic and conceptual origins of the idea of natural rights from 1150 to 1250; see *ibid.*, 43-77.

53 Tierney, *The Idea of Natural Rights*, 54.

54 Maritian does not say explicitly that rights claims can be translated without remainder into claims about mutual obligations, but his discussion seems to imply this; see in particular *Man and the State*, 97-107. Finnis does say this explicitly in *Natural Law and Natural Rights*, note 12 at 209-210; I first noticed this reference through its citation by Michael J. Perry in *The Idea of Human Rights: Four Inquiries* (New York: Oxford, 1998), 56, who himself goes on to say that "What really matters - what we should take seriously - is not human rights talk but the claims such talk is meant to express: the claims about what ought not be done to or about what ought to be done for human beings" (*Ibid.*).

55 Tuck, *Natural Rights Theories*, 6.

56 See Maritain, *Man and the State*, 84-85, and Finnis, *Natural Law and Natural Rights*, 42-48. Brett offers a generally insightful discussion of Aquinas' concept of objective right, and I agree with her conclusion that Aquinas has a notion of objective, but not of subjective right; see *Liberty, Right and Nature*, 88-97. This is likewise the view of both Tuck and Tierney; see *Natural Rights Theories*, 19-20, and *The Idea of Natural Rights*, 45. However, Brett reads Aquinas through the lens of Grisez's interpretation, and for this reason (I suspect) she overlooks the extent to which Aquinas gives moral significance to pre-rational aspects of human nature.

57 Tuck, *Natural Rights Theories*, 19-20.

58 *Natural Rights Theories*, 7, emphasis in the original; note, however, that Tuck here speaks of active rights, rather than subjective rights.

59 Tierney, *The Idea of Natural Rights*, 69-76.

60 *The Idea of Natural Rights*, 73; I am quoting from Tierney and the translation is his. He offers here several examples of similar expressions, including some taken from decretalists as well as decretists.

61 Tierney, *The Idea of Natural Rights*, 74.

62 I came to realize the significance of this aspect of natural rights theories through reading Judith N. Shklar's *The Faces of Injustice* (New Haven: Yale University Press,

1990), even though natural rights theories as such are not her main focus of concern there.

63   Tierney, *The Idea of Natural Rights*, 77.

64   Janet Coleman, "Property and Poverty," in *The Cambridge History of Medieval Political Thought*, 607-648 at 626.

65   I am grateful to Joseph Capizzi for helping me to see the force of this point.

66   Orlando Patterson, *Slavery and Social Death: A Comparative Study* (Cambridge, MA: Harvard University Press, 1982), 7; note that this reference concerns the definition of slavery only.

67   Patterson, *Freedom in the Making of Western Culture*, 356-359; however, as Patterson points out in *Slavery and Social Death: A Comparative Study*, 24-25, liability to be bought and sold is by no means always an indication of servile status. See more generally 1-14 in this book for an illuminating discussion of the meaning of slavery seen in contrast to other forms of servitude.

68   Patterson, *Slavery and Social Death*, 7.

69   R.I. Moore, *The Formation of a Persecuting Society* (Oxford: Blackwell, 1987), 5; emphasis in the original.

70   Stanley Hauerwas, *The Peaceable Kingdom: A Primer in Christian Ethics* (Notre Dame, IN: Notre Dame University Press, 1983).

71   On his view, the increase in social persecution was inextricably connected with the rise of a literate bureaucracy, and he refuses to address the question of whether the latter could have taken place without the former; see Moore, *The Formation of a Persecuting Society*, 124-153.

72   On this point, see Malcolm Lambert, *Medieval Heresy: Popular Movements from the Gregorian Reform to the Reformation*, 2nd ed. (Oxford: Blackwell, 1992), 33-61, 105-146. Even Moore seems to recognize that the Cathars, at least, posed a real doctrinal and social challenge; see Moore, *The Formation of a Persecuting Society*, 19-23.

73   Moore, *The Formation of a Persecuting Society*, 88-91. Similarly, both Little and John Boswell emphasize the complexity of the factors leading to the rise of social persecution in this period; see *Religious Poverty and the Profit Economy in Medieval Europe*, 1-58, and John Boswell, *Christianity, Social Tolerance and Homosexuality: Gay People in Western Europe from the Beginning of the Christian Era to the Fourteenth Century* (Chicago: University of Chicago Press, 1980), 269-302.

74   Moore, *The Formation of a Persecuting Society*, 93; see more generally 91-94. Similarly, Boswell suggests that church practice, unlike church rhetoric, was less harsh than civil law in the twelfth and thirteenth centuries; see *Christianity, Social Tolerance and Homosexuality*, 293-294.

75   In the remainder of this section, I rely especially on Jeremy Cohen, *The Friars and the Jews: The Evolution of Medieval Anti-Judaism* (Ithaca, NY: Cornell University

Press, 1982); John Hood, *Aquinas and the Jews* (Philadelphia: University of Pennsylvania Press, 1995); Little, *Religious Poverty and the Profit Economy*, 42-57; and Moore, *The Formation of a Persecuting Society*, 27-44.

76 Anna Sapir Abulafia, *Christians and Jews in the Twelfth-Century Renaissance* (London: Routledge, 1995).

77 Cohen, *The Friars and the Jews*, *passim*; see 242-264 for his summary and his arguments.

78 Moore, *The Formation of a Persecuting Society*, 146-153.

79 Hood explicitly rejects Cohen's claim that the anti-Semitism of the high middle ages is due to a theological revolution; rather, he sees it as an expression of Christianity's fundamentally ambiguous attitude toward the Jews, an attitude that can support either toleration or repression. See *Aquinas and the Jews*, ix-xiv, for a summary of his arguments on this point. Little does not mention Cohen's work, but he does argue that the rise in anti-Jewish activity should be traced to anxieties over the rapidly changing economy of the twelfth century, rather than to any new departure in theology concerning the Jews; see *Religious Poverty and the Profit Economy*, 42-58.

80 For her discussion of Odo of Cambrai, see Abulafia, *Christians and Jews*, 83-85, and for her discussion of Peter the Venerable, see 87-88, 115-116.

81 Hood, *Aquinas and the Jews*, 90. However, Hood underestimates the cogency of Aquinas's argument, because he assumes that a natural law argument must be non-theological in character. For Hood's complete discussion of this text, see *Aquinas and the Jews*, 88-92.

82 In what follows, I rely especially on the following works: Stanley Hauerwas, *A Community of Character: Toward a Constructive Christian Social Ethic* (Notre Dame, IN: University of Notre Dame Press, 1981); *The Peaceable Kingdom: A Primer in Christian Ethics*; *Against the Nations: War and Survival in a Liberal Society* (Minneapolis: Seabury/Winston Press, 1985); and *After Christendom? How the Church Is to Behave if Freedom, Justice, and a Christian Nation Are Bad Ideas* (Nashville, TN: Abingdon, 1991); John Milbank, *Theology and Social Theory: Beyond Secular Reason* (Oxford: Blackwell, 1990); and John Howard Yoder, *The Politics of Jesus: Vicit Angus Noster*, 2nd ed. (Grand Rapids, MI: Eerdmans, 1994). With respect to Hauerwas and Yoder, I have also drawn on Richard Hays' insightful discussion in *The Moral Vision of the New Testament: A Contemporary Introduction to New Testament Ethics* (New York: HarperCollins, 1996), 239-265.

83 Yoder, *The Politics of Jesus*, 8-9; emphasis in the original.

84 *Ibid.*, 237.

85 *Ibid.*, 99.

86 Milbank, *Theology and Social Theory: Beyond Secular Reason*, 262. This seems to me to be a dubious claim. There are many forms of classical Hinduism, for example, to which it would not apply; see Ninian Smart, "Hinduism," in *A Companion to Phi-*

losophy of Religion, Philip L. Quinn and Charles Taliaferro, eds. (Oxford: Blackwell, 1997), 7-14. However, judging by the overall argument of the book, it may be that Milbank is referring here specifically to Western traditions.

87   Oliver O'Donovan, *Resurrection and Moral Order: An Outline for Evangelical Ethics* (Grand Rapids, MI: Eerdmans, 1986), 13.

88   Patterson, *Freedom in the Making of Western Culture,* 405.

89   Milbank is wrong to assert that, for the scholastics, evil exists only as a result of angelic or human sinfulness; see *Theology and Social Theory*, 124-125. On the contrary, Aquinas explicitly says that God is the cause of that evil which consists in the corruption of material things. The perfection of the universe requires that it include all the grades of being, including perishable and corruptible as well as incorruptible entities; hence, by bringing about the good order of the universe, God necessarily causes the corruption of some things (*Summa theologiae* I 49.2).

90   Reinhold Niebuhr, *The Nature and Destiny of Man, Volume II: Human Destiny* (1943; repr. Louisville, KY: Westminster/John Knox Press, 1996), 72; more generally, see 68-97.

91   *Ibid.,* 68.

92   This point is eloquently argued by Judith Shklar in her *The Faces of Injustice, passim.*

Conclusion

The Continuing Relevance of the Natural Law

There would be little point in undertaking a detailed study of the theological and moral thought of past generations if we did not believe that we could learn something from it today. In the case at hand, the scholastic concept of the natural law shows us that it is possible to bring together aspects of moral reflection that we have long considered to be essentially disparate, and to do so in an integrally united way. Because it is grounded in a scriptural interpretation of human nature, comprehensively understood to include rational as well as pre-rational components, this concept offers a framework for moral reflection that is authentically theological while remaining open to the best insights of the natural and social sciences. By the same token, it offers resources for affirming the goodness of human societies even while acknowledging their limitations and ambiguities. Moreover, the specific theological and moral commitments which are central to this concept – namely, the doctrine of creation and the ideal of natural equality – are as important today as they were in the twelfth and thirteenth centuries.

Of course, no medieval concept, however sophisticated or potentially fruitful, can be incorporated into contemporary theology without critical appropriation and revision. Our examination of the scholastic concept of the natural law has revealed unsuspected affinities between the scholastics and ourselves. Nonetheless, we cannot ignore the considerable differences between their religious, philosophical, and scientific beliefs, and our own. Just as importantly, we need to take account of the fact that our dominant concerns are different from theirs in important ways. For that reason, if for no other, we will need to develop their insights in ways they would not have anticipated.

It would call for another book to develop fully a revised concept of the natural law along these lines. My aim in this conclusion is more modest. I want to draw out those aspects of the scholastic concept of the natural law that are particularly relevant to our own moral reflections, and especially to the task of contemporary Christian ethics. Hence, I will be summarizing the main features of the scholastic concept of the natural law, with the aim of underscoring those aspects of the concept that are particularly relevant to contemporary reflection, and calling attention to points at which the scholastic concept calls for further development in the light of our own concerns.

What is the scholastic concept of the natural law, and what is its relevance for contemporary Christian ethics? This study has been directed toward answering that question; the time has now come to summarize the main lines of the answer that has emerged.

The scholastic concept of the natural law is first of all a way of approaching moral issues, which comprises both a fundamental orientation towards moral reflection, and inseparably from that, a set of specific normative commitments. As such, it is something less determinate than a fully developed theory, yet more coherent than a set of ad hoc appeals or fragments from earlier traditions. In this respect, it is comparable to other, more familiar approaches to morality, such as Kantianism or utilitarianism, both of which are rooted in specific theories but have now expanded into general orientations toward moral reflection.

At the same time, the scholastic concept of the natural law emerged out of a specific tradition of reflection, and was shaped by the presuppositions and concerns that informed that tradition. This point is worth emphasizing, because we tend to think of the natural law as stemming directly from natural or rational exigencies. In contrast, scholastic reflections on the moral significance of nature were grounded in a tradition of reflection, and the scholastics themselves were aware of this fact.

Although the tradition of natural law reflection received by the scholastics incorporated both classical and distinctively Christian voices, they understood it as being fundamentally a scriptural tradition that offered, for that very reason, a framework within which Scripture could be interpreted afresh in the light of new concerns. It also offered resources for incorporating the best of twelfth-century natural philosophy into Christian theological reflection. The resultant concept of the natural law thus reflected the best understandings of nature that were available at the time. Even more important, it represented an attitude of openness to natural philosophy that kept it from becoming rigid and unrealistic. At the same time, it was a theological concept in the distinctively Christian sense of reflecting a particular set of theological commitments, grounded in a particular, doctrinally informed reading of Scripture.

This brings us to a second and complementary way of understanding the scholastic concept of the natural law: in terms of the fundamental commitments that informed it. What were these commitments? They included, first of all, the goodness and integrity of the created world, as seen through the prism of the rich and complex medieval idea of nature. This was no mere theoretical affirmation, but a response to the resurgence of dualistic movements that considered the material world to be in the most literal sense God-forsaken. The scholastics recognized that these movements offered a profound challenge to Christian belief, and their concept of the natural law should be seen as one aspect – the praxis-oriented aspect, as it were – of their response to that challenge. Correlatively, the theological commitments underlying the scholastic concept of the natural law included the integrity and the revealed status of Scripture, and more particularly the Old Testament, which witnesses to God's work as Creator and provident Sustainer of the visible world. Finally, they included a limited yet real commitment to natural equality, seen as grounded in the commonalities of our shared human nature, especially our capacities for moral discernment and free action.

In my view, these commitments are still theologically valid, and just as important for us as they were for the scholastics themselves. Of course, the scholastic understanding of nature and, even more, the specifics of their moral conclusions, would call for considerable revision in order to be acceptable today. Nonetheless, the scholastic concept of the natural law offers us an affirmation of the goodness of nature, together with a framework for thinking through the practical implications of that affirmation, which is still sound in its main lines.

The affirmation of the goodness of nature implicit in the scholastic concept of the natural law is all the more important today because it is in tension with the prevailing direction of much contemporary theology, at least in the English-speaking world. Throughout this book, we have had occasion to compare the scholastics with contemporary theologians who emphasize the distinctiveness of Christian morality. This latter approach offers a valuable reminder of the radical demands of the gospel and the pervasive effects of human sinfulness. In addition, it provides a necessary corrective to the proud assumption that we can autonomously determine the meaning of human moral goodness. Yet, taken to its extreme, the current emphasis on the distinctiveness of Christian ethics leads to the attempt to create a self-referential, self-enclosed Christian moral community, within which the Christian neither needs to, nor can, engage in any alternative discourse.[1]

The difficulty with this approach is that it risks falling into another kind of pride, the pride of assuming that we can create our own world of meaning, within which we can take refuge from the ambiguities of human society and the stark inhumanity of the physical universe. Over against this, the scholastics remind us that we live in a world that we did not make, under the sovereignty of a Creator whose goodness we can trust but whose designs will always be to some extent opaque to us. Correlatively, they draw our attention to the fact that human social practice and moral reflection stem from natural givens that we did not put in place and that condition and constrain us even within the Christian community. We need not assume that we can distinguish with certainty between the natural and the conventional in any given instance, in order to acknowledge that pre-conventional constraints are operative in every social practice. What the scholastic concept of the natural law provides is not an absolutely reliable guide to determining what is natural, but a framework within which to reflect on the moral significance of the pre-conventional roots of human social practices, in accordance with our best efforts at any given point to discern what these are.

A contemporary appropriation of the scholastic concept of the natural law would undoubtedly go beyond the scholastics in recognizing the element of human construction in the development of social practices and mores. Even here, what is needed is not so much a break with the scholastics as an extension and development of certain lines of their thought. As we saw in the last chapter, the scholastics do not believe that the natural law gives rise to moral claims directly and immediately. Rather, the general imperatives of the natural law must be translated into social practices through the conventions of a particular society in order to be practically effective. These conventions are not themselves part of the natural law in a primary sense, and they stand in a complex relationship to it. At the same time, they can be described as natural law in a derivative sense, since they are expressions of the natural law properly so called, and are in some cases very nearly as universal as the natural law itself. (This would be generally said to be true for the civilians' law of nations, for example.) Moreover, even those precepts of the natural law that are revealed by God cannot be translated directly into social practices without a considerable degree of interpretation. In this sense, there is some room for human construction even with respect to the fundamental moral precepts that are confirmed by revelation.

The scholastics do not explicitly raise the question of whether the precepts of morality are discovered or constructed by human reason. If we ask what answer to this question is implied by their concept of the natural law we must conclude that, seen from this perspective, their concept is ambiguous. They emphasize the permanence, supremacy, and binding force of the natural law, considered as the pre-conventional origin of all laws and social practices. Yet they also recognize that there is considerable room for human construction at the level of formulating specific norms. At the same time, this process of construction itself operates within constraints, partly set by the exigencies of reason and pre-rational nature, and partly normative in character.

Yet this ambiguity need not be regretted; seen from our standpoint, it is potentially fruitful. To the extent that the scholastics recognize that there are some conventional elements even in the precepts of the natural law, they provide a point of entry for us, who are very conscious of the extent to which morality is a social construction. Yet their concept of the natural law also implies that there are practical and normative constraints on the social construction of morality. Correlatively, it implies that the status of morality as a human construct need not imply sheer moral relativism. For this reason, the scholastic concept of the natural law suggests a way to respond to contemporary challenges to the existence of an objective morality that does justice to what is valid in these challenges while avoiding the conclusion that morality is solely the product of contingent social forces or the expression of a collective will to power.

In short, what the scholastic concept of the natural law offers to contemporary Christian ethics is first of all a theology of morality: that is, a theological context within which to interpret and evaluate the natural phenomenon of human morality. Seen from this perspective, morality as such is neither transcendent nor a perspicuous expression of the divine will. It is essentially a mundane reality, and as such it is both flawed and limited. Yet it is also an expression of human nature and, as such, it reflects God's creative wisdom and expresses the fundamental goodness of the human person considered as a creature of God. Ultimately, this affirmation of the limited yet real validity of human morality implies the further affirmation of the doctrine of creation and of the correlative view that the visible world, including the structures of human life, reflects the goodness of its Creator. In Chapter 4, I suggested that marriage is the praxis corresponding to the doctrine of creation as theoria. We may extend the same observation to respect for human morality as a whole, considered as a reflection of the goodness of human life and therefore as an expression of God's creative wisdom and generous will.

Although the goodness of human nature, comprehensively under-stood, is the ground for the value of human morality, it is also the case that human nature under-determines morality. Correlatively, there can be more than one authentic natural morality. Indeed, there are many such, because every indigenous moral tradition should be considered as a distinctive form of a natural morality. This brings us to the second respect in which the scholastic concept of the natural law can contribute to contemporary Christian moral reflection. That is, this concept implies a particular set of normative commitments that should guide the ongoing development of Christian morality, as well as offering a starting point for assessing other moral traditions.

These commitments take the form of judgments about those aspects of human nature that should be privileged and, correlatively, those aspects that should be given secondary importance. More specifically, the scholastic concept of the natural law implies a privileging of our capacities for rational self-direction and, correlatively, it gives a secondary place to, without discounting, those temperamental and emotional capacities that are more clearly unevenly distributed. Moreover, because it incorporates commitments to non-maleficence and an ideal of natural equality, it implies that we should promote those capacities for empathy and cooperation, which foster those commitments, while de-emphasizing tendencies toward aggression and hierarchical organization, which tend to undermine them.

Thus, the scholastic concept of the natural law provides a set of criteria for interpreting specific social practices. In this way, the theology of morality offered by this concept of the natural law is transformed into a moral theology with definite normative implications. The specific moral content of this concept of the natural law will not be as comprehensive or unambiguous as the moral conclusions promised by many later versions of the natural law. Nonetheless, this concept does have specific normative implications; it is not merely formal or motivational.

As we assess the specific normative implications of the scholastic concept of the natural law, we should remember that the scholastics did not attempt to draw out moral conclusions by way of deducing them from a fixed and determinate human nature. In fact, the scholastics did believe that we have a species-specific nature (at least, they did in the period we have been considering), but that does not mean that they considered it to be sufficiently knowable to serve as a basis for a deductive system of moral rules. More important, they did not argue as if they believed that moral conclusions can be unambiguously established on the basis of our knowledge of human nature. Rather, their moral arguments moved dialectically between accepted moral precepts and practices, and their views on the natural and scriptural bases of those beliefs and customs, interpreting and reformulating each in the light of their best understanding of the other.

The development of scholastic thinking on sexuality and marriage offers one of the clearest examples of this. As we saw in chapter four, many of the early scholastics held the view that sexual desire is intrinsically sinful and, by implication, not a part of human nature. However, this view stood in tension, to say the least, with the affirmation of the goodness of marriage and procreation, an affirmation that not only reflected a widely accepted practice, but was seen as required by fundamental theological commitments. This tension led the scholastics to modify and then finally to reject the claim that sexual desire is intrinsically sinful; in the process, they drew on their concept of the natural law to develop a new interpretation of sexual desire, according to which it is rendered intelligible through the purpose it serves in human life, and thus acknowledged as a part of human nature.

Hence, what we have here is an example of a rethinking of the meaning of human nature, prompted by fundamental moral and theological commitments, and made possible through the framework of the scholastic concept of the natural law. When we in our turn rethink norms for sexual activity along the lines indicated in Chapter 4, we are not breaking with the scholastics, but continuing a process of dialectal interpretation of sexuality begun by the scholastics themselves.

This brings us to a second question. What can the scholastic concept of the natural law bring to the work of contemporary Christian ethics at the level of specific moral insights? Throughout this study, I have attempted to answer this question through a consideration of the implications of this concept for sexual and social ethics. Nonetheless, it may be helpful to offer a summary outline of the normative implications of this concept.

Modern and contemporary accounts of the natural law have accustomed us to associate natural law reasoning with definite, stringent prohibitions. The scholastics certainly gave a particular set of prohibitions a central place in their concept of the natural law, but as we have seen, this concept was not in the first instance negative and limiting. On the contrary, the concept of the natural law served most fundamentally as a positive and legitimating concept. Whatever can be construed as an expression of nature, in most of its generally accepted senses, was considered to be *prima facie* legitimate and good, even though this *prima facie* assumption could be overridden by other considerations. In order to prevent misunderstanding, it should be remembered that nature in this context is always understood in terms that admit of construal in terms of some general intelligible purpose. For this reason, not everything that emerges spontaneously in human beings as a class, or in a given individual, can serve as a basis for moral legitimation, since the human constitution includes some elements that are either accidental, or harmful, and the constitution of an individual is not sufficiently general to serve as a basis for moral conclusions. Nonetheless, this way of applying the natural law offered considerable flexibility, since it allowed for an appeal to nature in any sense that admits of its construal in the light of general intelligible purposes.

Applied to contemporary moral reflection, this aspect of the scholastic concept of the natural law offers a way of interpreting the moral beliefs and practices of other cultures, and even of different sub-cultures within our own society, in the light of the natural human purposes that they reflect and serve. Natural purposes, in this context, should be understood broadly to include the exigencies of human social life, as well as biological needs and the basic inclinations that we share with other animals, or with the other higher primates. If the seemingly arbitrary or even repugnant practices of other societies can be seen as expressions of natural purposes so understood, they can at least be rendered intelligible and accorded the value of expressions of a fundamentally good human nature, even if they still call for challenge on other grounds.

We have already noted that the scholastic concept of the natural law, precisely because of its specifically theological character, does not yield the universally valid moral code that modern and contemporary natural law theorists have attempted to provide. However, it offers us something that is perhaps of even greater value than the supposedly universal moral code associated with later natural law theorists. It provides a framework for what I believe is a more realistic recognition of the irreducible diversity of human moral beliefs and practices, together with resources for a more nuanced assessment of these diverse mores. This line of approach does not force us to judge ways of life different from our own as intrinsically iniquitous or sinful. Nor does it lead to the conclusion that any moral code that is incompatible with Christian ideals is ipso facto to be condemned. Rather, it allows for a positive theological assessment of diverse human mores, seen as expressions of human nature bearing their own integrity and value, even when they are not compatible with a Christian way of life.

Does it follow that we must give up any possibility of cross-cultural moral dialogue and critique? In my view, it does not. The moral and legal agreements and conventions that today serve as a framework for international relations are our contemporary equivalent of the ancient and medieval law of nations and, like the law of nations, they can themselves be considered as a kind of natural law. However, we must keep in mind that these agreements and conventions are not given perspicuously by nature or by reason; like the mores of particular societies, they are a determinate expression of human nature, arrived at through a complex process of negotiation, mutual accommodation, coercion, and unreflective practice among the nations and peoples of the world. We Christians are participants in this process, and have as much claim as anyone else to attempt to shape it in accordance with our best ideals, but we should not expect that ours will be the only, or even the dominant, voice in this process.

Within the Christian community, the scholastic concept of the natural law likewise offers a framework for acknowledging the value of diverse practices, but in this context, the assessment of these practices must also take account of a distinctively Christian vision of what is of primary value in human life. That is, within the Christian community we need to ask not only whether a given practice is intelligible in the light of the natural purposes it serves, but also whether it is compatible with a distinctively Christian construal of those purposes.

Here is an example. On December 14, 1998, Gustav Niebuhr, writing in the New York Times, reported that the Celestial Church of Christ, founded in Nigeria in 1947 by a Methodist layman, S.B.J. Oshoffa, had recently been denied admission to the World Council of Churches because of that church's policy on allowing clergy to have more than one wife.[2] Since 1986, according to the Reverend Alexander Bada, its current head, the Celestial Church of Christ has refused to ordain men who have more than one wife, but in order to avoid splitting the community and endorsing divorce, it has not required men ordained before that time to give up their additional wives. According to one senior clergyman, Olantunji Akande, the 1986 policy had "put the church back on to the path of rectitude." However, this was not enough for the WCC, which on December 10, 1998, voted to reject the church's application for membership by a 3-2 margin.

What are we to make of this judgment? It might be said that it does not take account of the distinctive practices of African societies. Yet almost no one would want to say that every traditional practice of every society should be accepted; otherwise, what basis would there be for a Christian critique of culture?

Consider this dilemma in the light of the scholastic concept of the natural law. In the first place, it is easy to construe polygamy as an expression of natural human purposes, if only because it reflects an efficient reproductive strategy. However, polygamy does seem vulnerable to the criticism that Aquinas lodged against it in the thirteenth century; that is, it undermines the equity that should exist between husband and wife, reducing the wife to a near-servile status (*Summa contra gentiles* III 124). As such it appears to be an intelligible expression of genuine human purposes, but one that is insufficiently responsive to a Christian construal of human nature according to which the ideal of natural equality is given a central place. Hence, the WCC would appear to be justified in challenging those churches that allow polygamy among their members to repudiate the practice.

Yet it is one thing to challenge a Christian community to reflect on the conformity of its practices with the ideals of the Gospel; it is something else to refuse to enter into association with it on the grounds that its practices are incompatible with the Christian profession. Seen from this perspective, the WCC judgment in this case appears to be excessively harsh. At the very least, the practice of polygamy is a legitimate expression of the natural law, albeit one that does not appear to be optimum from the perspective of Christian moral ideals. Given this, it is difficult to say that this practice is so fundamentally at odds with Christian ideals that it requires other churches to break off association with those churches that endorse or tolerate it. Furthermore, a natural law perspective invites us to consider how far the reaction of the WCC reflects distinctively Western sensibilities, rather than Christian commitments. I do not mean to say that equality between spouses is an exclusively Western sensibility. But is it so clear that polygamy is necessarily incompatible with equality and equity among the partners in a marriage in the specific cultural setting that is in question here? It is also worth noting that the Celestial Church of Christ is moving away from tolerating polygamy, but it has hesitated to require monogamy of all its clergy because to do so would imply an endorsement of divorce, and this, as they rightly point out, would also be problematic from a Christian standpoint. It appears to me that a more flexible practice with respect to divorce and remarriage is consistent with Christian morality (although that is an argument for another day); nonetheless, it is difficult indeed to claim that a church that gives great importance to the permanence of marriage, even at the expense of monogamy, is taking up a stance that is radically inconsistent with the ideals of the Gospel.

If the scholastic concept of the natural law amounted to nothing more than a framework for thinking through issues like this one, it would still offer a valuable contribution to contemporary Christian ethics. However, this concept also incorporates normative commitments and prohibitions that bring greater specificity to its moral content.

In order to appreciate the significance of these commitments and prohibitions, we must once again be on guard against reverting to a widespread assumption about what a natural law theory must involve. We commonly associate natural law reasoning with injunctions against seemingly unnatural practices. Yet, as we have seen, the idea of the unnatural plays a less central role in scholastic natural law reasoning than we might expect. The scholastics do stigmatize certain sexual practices as unnatural, but they have clearly been influenced in this judgment by Paul's claim that homosexual acts are contrary to nature. According to some scholastics, usury is also unnatural in a pejorative sense.[3] However, for Aquinas at least, it is unnatural in the sense of being irrational, not in the sense of violating some supposedly pre-conventional aspect of economic exchange (*Summa theologiae* II-II 78.1, especially 78.1 *ad* 3; he also observes that this view has scriptural justification, even though the practice is permitted in the Hebrew law, at II-II 78.1 *ad* 2). Yet these kinds of judgments do not appear to be central to scholastic natural law reasoning, however important they are in some specific contexts.

Given the interest among some contemporary theologians and philosophers in applying natural law reasoning to specific questions of biomedical ethics, this aspect of scholastic natural law thinking may be a disappointment. Yet the scholastics' reticence to characterize specific practices as unnatural reflects, once again, the distinctively theological and scriptural character of their concept of the natural law. As we saw in Chapter 5, this concept incorporates the complexity of traditional and scriptural judgments concerning the naturalness of social practices and institutions. For this very reason, it does not readily lend itself to condemnations of specific practices as unnatural. What is contrary to nature in one sense may well express natural purposes in another sense, as we saw with respect to property in particular. More fundamentally, the scholastics appear to be reluctant to condemn as unnatural what Scripture and the traditions of the church pass over in silence.

These considerations suggest that the scholastic concept of the natural law would function primarily as a legitimating, rather than a boundary-setting, concept in biomedical contexts. So far as I can determine, there is nothing in the scholastic concept of the natural law to suggest that interventions in the genetic code, or the enhancement of bodily functioning by technological or pharmacological means, is in itself unnatural in a pejorative sense. The scholastic concept of the natural law does not imply that there is anything morally normative about the biochemical and physical processes that comprise our bodily existence, considered in themselves. However, the proper functioning and flourishing of the organism does have a positive moral value within the framework of this concept, and this implies that interventions that enhance human health and well-being are at least prima facie good.

In contrast to prohibitions of unnatural behavior (at least outside of sexual contexts), the norms of non-maleficence implied by the Golden Rule and summarized in the Decalogue do play a central role in scholastic reflection on the natural law. This is critically important, because it had the effect of placing the notion of harm, rather than unnaturalness, at the center of the scholastic concept of the natural law. That is, in most instances the natural law was seen by the scholastics as prohibiting particular kinds of actions because they are harmful, to others or to the agent of the act, and not directly because they are unnatural, although of course they did appeal to their understanding of human nature in order to determine what counts as harming another and what sorts of harms might be permissible.

In Chapter 3, we observed that the scholastics drew on their concept of the natural law in such a way as to emphasize the rational and intelligible character of scriptural moral norms, without rejecting their status as expressions of God's authoritative will. Now we should add a further point. That is, they see the specific moral norms of Scripture as being intelligible precisely as expressions of the basic injunction to love one's neighbor as oneself. That means that they must be interpreted and applied with reference to fundamental human needs, vulnerabilities and desires. In this way, they reinforce the connection between morality and non-maleficence.

This brings us to a further point. The negative prohibitions associated with the natural law convey a positive meaning that goes beyond the specifics of the prohibitions themselves. That is, they come to function as expressions of a fundamental commitment to human dignity, which is safeguarded by prohibitions against harming others in fundamental ways. Aquinas remarks that anyone who harms another, contrary to the prohibitions against murder, wrongful injury, theft, or robbery, "dishonors him by depriving him of some excellence on account of which he has honor" – a general remark, it should be noted, that is not tied to any specific status apart from shared participation in a common humanity (*Summa theologiae* II–II 72.1). This aspect of the scholastic concept of the natural law is well captured by the encyclical *Veritatis splendor,* when, after observing that the norms of morality apply equally to all, it states:

> In this way moral norms, and primarily the negative ones, those prohibiting evil, manifest their meaning and force, both personal and social. By protecting the inviolable personal dignity of every human being they help to preserve the human social fabric and its proper and fruitful development. The commandments of the second tablet of the Decalogue in particular – those which Jesus quoted to the young man of the Gospel (cf. Mt. 19:19) – constitute the indispensable rules of all social life.[4]

At the same time, there is another aspect of the commitment to human dignity embodied in the scholastic concept of the natural law that this encyclical does not fully express, and that likewise merits recovery for contemporary ethical reflection: as we saw in Chapter 5, the scholastics grounded human dignity positively in the capacity for moral discernment and self-direction enjoyed by each rational adult. They are very far from claiming, as this encyclical at least suggests, that men and women must depend on their "bishops and pastors" for knowledge of the moral law.[5]

By the same token, they value human freedom, seen as the capacity for self-direction on the basis of the individual's own moral discernment, and some, although not all of them, express this through a defense of individual rights. Certainly they hold that human persons ought to make right use of their freedom through obedience to God's law, but they do not equate that freedom with right moral behavior, nor do they deny that even an abused freedom has value as a reflection of the divine image in the human person.[6]

This suggests that if the Christian community is to incorporate a respect for human dignity into its social life and communal witness, it must not only respect and promote human well-being, it must also find ways to honor and foster human autonomy and self-direction. The specific forms through which this is done will vary from church to church, but it seems to me that in any case, they will include some recognition, formal or implied, of the rights of individual Christians over against the institutional church, as well as a more general acknowledgment of the independent value of human freedom, apart from any consideration of the ways that freedom is used.

These are arguments for another time. However, they illustrate a more general point that is worth underscoring: precisely because it lies at the root of so much Christian moral reflection and practice, the scholastic concept of the natural law offers both a fresh perspective on familiar commitments and a valuable reminder of the forgotten or unfashionable implications of those values.

More generally, as I have tried to show throughout this study, the scholastic concept of the natural law is fundamentally sound and can still serve as a fruitful starting point for theological reflection. For both these reasons, it merits retrieval as a resource for Christian theological ethics. It is my hope that others will take up this retrieval by drawing on the insights of this concept of the natural law in their work on contemporary questions.

Notes to the conclusion

1 Among the authors we have considered, John Milbank goes the furthest in this direction; see his *Theology and Social Theory: Beyond Secular Reason* (Oxford: Blackwell, 1990), *passim*.

2 Gustav Niebuhr, "Polygamy Keeps a New African Church from World Council," *New York Times*, December 14, 1998.

3 On the development of a natural law argument against usury, see John Noonan, *The Scholastic Analysis of Usury* (Cambridge, MA: Harvard University Press, 1957), 38–81.

4 "The Splendor of Truth," (*Veritatis splendor*), promulgated on October 5, 1993, para. 97.

5 This phrase is taken from *Veritatis splendor* para. 117; compare paragraph 53, which states that the concrete meaning of the natural law in specific historical circumstances must be determined by the magisterium, although the latter is expected to draw on the reflections of laypersons and theologians in doing so. It is also worth noting that according to the encyclical, de-Christianization will necessarily lead to a decline or obscuring of the moral sense (para. 106), a claim that from the scholastic perspective would be overly simple, at best.

6 Again, compare *Veritatis splendor*, which comes very close to saying that authentic freedom consists in following the moral law in accordance with Christ's example (para. 85), and dwells at length on the "weakness" and the "tragic aspects" of human freedom (para. 86), while saying very little about its theological significance.

Bibliography

Primary sources

Albert the Great (1891). *Super ethica*, Vol. 7 in *Opera Omnia*, Parisiis apud Ludovicum Vives.

(1893-1894). *In librum IV Sententiarum*, in Vols. 25-30 of *Opera Omnia*, Parisiis apud Ludovicum Vives.

(1895-1896). *Summa de creaturis*, Vols. 34-35 in *Opera Omnia*, Parisiis apud Ludovicum Vives.

(1951). *De Bono*, Vol. 28 in *Alberti Magni Opera Omnia ad fidem codicum manuscriptorum*, Münster, Germany: Aschendorff.

(1958). *De Sacramentis*, Vol. 26 in *Alberti Magni Opera Omnia ad fidem codicum manuscriptorum*, Münster, Germany: Aschendorff.

Alexander of Hales (1924-1948). *Summa theologica*, also known as *Summa fratris Alexandri*, 1260, Florence: College of St. Bonaventure.

Aristotle (1932). *Politics*, Loeb Classical Library. Cambridge, Mass.: Harvard University Press.

Augustine (1956). *Enarrationis in psalmos*, Vols. 38-40 in *Corpus Christianorum*, Turnholti: Typographi Brepols.

(1962). *De vera religione*, Vol. 32 in *Corpus Christianorum*, Turnholti: Typographi Brepols.

(1970). *De libero arbitrio*, Vol. 29 in *Corpus Christianorum*, Turnholti: Typographi Brepols.

(1981). *Confessiones*, Vol. 32 in *Corpus Christianorum*, Turnholti: Typographi Brepols.

Bonaventure (1882-1889). *Commentaria in quatour libros sententiarum*, Vols. 1-4 in *Opera Omnia*, Florence: College of St. Bonaventure.

   (1891). Breviloquium in Vol. 5 in *Opera Omnia*, Florence: College of St. Bonaventure.

   (1891). *Collationes de decem praeceptis*, Vol. 5 in *Opera Omnia*, Florence: College of St. Bonaventure.

   (1891). *Quaestiones disputatae de perfectione evangelium*, Vol. 5 in *Opera Omnia*, Florence: College of St. Bonaventure.

Cicero (1940). *De Inventione*, Loeb Classical Library, Cambridge, Mass.: Harvard University Press.

Gratian of Bologna (1582). *Decretum Gratiani Emendum et Notationibus Illustratum una cum Glossis*, Rome: in aedibus Populi Romani.

   (1993). *Gratian: The Treatise on Laws (Decretum DD 1-20), with the Ordinary Gloss*, Augustine Thompson and James Gordley (trans.), Washington, D.C.: Catholic University of America Press.

Hugh of St. Victor (1800–1875), *De sacramentis*. Vol. 176 in *Patrologiae Latina*, J.-P. Migne, ed., Paris: Garneri Fratres.

Isidore (1911). *Etymologiarum sive originum*, Oxford: Oxford University Press.

Justinian (1888). *The Institutes of Justinian*, London: Longman's Green and Co.

   (1985). *The Digest of Justinian*, Philadelphia: University of Pennsylvania Press.

   (1987). *Institutes*, Peter Birks and Grant McLeod (trans.), Ithaca, N.Y.: Cornell University Press.

Peter Abelard (1971). *Peter Abelard's Ethics, an Edition with Introduction*, English Translation and Notes by D.E. Luscombe, Oxford: Clarendon Press.

Peter Lombard (1916). *Libri IV Sententiarum*, Florence: College of St. Bonaventure.

Raymond of Peñafort (1975-1978). *Summa de iure canonico*, Rome: Commentarium pro religiosis.

Thomas Aquinas (1871-1880). *In epistolam ad Romanos*, Vol. 20 in *Opera Omnia*, Parisiis apud Ludovicum Vives.

   (1871-1880). *Scriptum super libros IV Sententiarum*, Vol. 30 in *Opera Omnia*, Parisiis apud Ludovicum Vives.

   (1871-1880). *Super Librum Dionysii De divinis nominibus*, Vol. 29 in *Opera Omnia*, Parisiis apud Ludovicum Vives.

   (1885). *In duo praeceptis caritatis et in decem legis praeceptis*, Vol. 27 in *Opera Omnia*, Parisiis apud Ludovicum Vives.

   (1888-1906). *Summa theologica*, Vols. 4-12 in *Opera Omnia iussa edita Leonis XIII P.M.*, Rome: Ex Typographia Polyglotta S.C. de Propaganda Fide.

   (1918-1930). *Summa contra gentiles*, Vols. 13-15 in *Opera Omnia iussa edita Leonis XIII P.M.*, Rome: Ex Typographia Polyglotta S.C. de Propaganda Fide.

(1969). *Sententia libri Ethicorum*, Vol. 49 in *Opera Omnia iussa edita Leonis XIII P.M.*, Rome: Ex Typographia Polyglotta S.C. de Propaganda Fide.

(1970-1976). *De Veritate*, Vol. 22 in *Opera Omnia iussa edita Leonis XIII P.M.*, Rome: Ex Typographia Polyglotta S.C. de Propaganda Fide.

William of Auxerre (1985). *Summa Aurea, Liber Quartus*, c. 1220, Paris: Centre National de la Recherche Scientifique.

Secondary sources, articles

Benson, Robert L. and Giles Constable (1982). "Introduction," in Robert L. Benson and Giles Constable, with Carol D. Lanham (eds.) *Renaissance and Renewal in the Twelfth Century*, Reprint, Toronto: University of Toronto Press, pp. xvii-xxx.

Bresnahan, James F. (1981). "An Ethics of Faith," in Leo O'Donovan (ed.) *A World of Grace: An Introduction to the Themes and Foundations of Karl Rahner's Theology*, New York: Crossroad, pp. 169-184.

Bullough, Vern (1982). "The Sin Against Nature and Homosexuality," in Vern Bullough and James Brundage (eds.) *Sexual Practices and the Medieval Church*, Buffalo, N.Y.: Prometheus Books, pp. 55-71.

Burns, J.H. (1988). "Introduction," in J.H. Burns (ed.) *The Cambridge History of Medieval Political Thought: c.350-c.1450*, Cambridge: Cambridge University Press, pp. 1-10.

Cahill, Lisa (1993). "Current Teaching on Sexual Ethics," in Charles E. Curran and Richard A. McCormick (eds.) *Readings in Moral Theology No. 8: Dialogue About Catholic Sexual Teaching*, Mahwah, New Jersey: Paulist Press, pp. 525-535.

Caspar, Ruth (1985). "Natural Law: Before and Beyond Bifurcation," *Thought* 60:236.

Christensen, Katherine (1993). "Introduction," in Augustine Thompson and James Gordley (trans.) *Gratian: The Treatise on Laws (Decretum DD 1-20), with the Ordinary Gloss*, Washington, D.C.: Catholic University of America Press, pp. ix-xxvii.

Coleman, Janet (1988). "Property and Poverty," in J.H. Burns (ed.) *The Cambridge History of Medieval Political Thought: c.350-c.1450*, Cambridge: Cambridge University Press, pp. 306-340.

Congar, Yves (1994; originally 1978). "Jus Divinum," in Congar, *Eglise et Papaute: Regards historiques*, Paris: Cerf, pp. 65-80.

Cook, Martin (1988). "Ways of Thinking Naturally," *The Annual of the Society of Christian Ethics*, pp. 161-178.

Crysdale, Cynthia S.W. (1995). "Revisioning Natural Law: From the Classicist Paradigm to Emergent Probability," *Theological Studies* 56:464-484.

Curran, Charles (1991). "Natural Law in Moral Theology," in Charles E. Curran and Richard A. McCormick (eds.) *Readings in Moral Theology No.7: Natural Law and Theology*, Mahwah, New Jersey: Paulist Press, pp. 247-295.

Dedek, John (1977). "Moral Absolutes in the Predecessors of St. Thomas," *Theological Studies* 38:654-680.

(1979). "Intrinsically Evil Acts: An Historical Survey of the Mind of St. Thomas," *The Thomist* 43:385-413.

(1980). "Premarital Sex: The Theological Argument from Peter Lombard to Durand," *Theological Studies* 41:643-667.

Fay, Thomas A. (1991). "Maritain on Rights and Natural Law," *The Thomist* 55:439-448.

Flanagan, Owen J., Jr. (1982). "Quinean Ethics," *Ethics* 93:56-74.

Gallagher, John (1993). "Magisterial teaching from 1918 to the Present," in Charles E. Curran and Richard A. McCormick (eds.) *Readings in Moral Theology No. 8: Dialogue About Catholic Sexual Teaching*, Mahwah, New Jersey: Paulist Press, 71-92.

George, Robert (1997). "Natural Law Ethics," in Philip Quinn and Charles Taliaferro (eds.) *A Companion to the Philosophy of Religion*, London: Blackwell, pp. 460-465.

Gersh, Stephen (1982). "Platonism - Neoplatonism - Aristotelianism: A Twelfth-Century Metaphysical System and Its Sources," in Robert L. Benson and Giles Constable (eds.) *Renaissance and Renewal in the Twelfth Century*, Reprint, Toronto: University of Toronto Press, pp. 512-537.

Grabmann, M. (1926). "Das Naturrecht der Scholastik von Gratian bis Thomas von Aquin," in Vol. I of *Mittelalterliches Geistesleben: Abhandlungen zur Geschichte der Scholastic und Mystik*, 3 vols., München: Max Hueber, pp. 65-103.

Gregory, Tulio (1988). "The Platonic Inheritance," in Peter Dronke (ed.) *A History of Twelfth Century Western Philosophy*, Cambridge: Cambridge University Press, pp. 54-80.

Grisez, Germain (1965). "The First Principle of Practical Reason: A Commentary on the *Summa theologiae*, 1-2, Question 94, Article 2," *Natural Law Forum* 10:168-201.

Grisez, Germain, Joseph Boyle, John Finnis, and William May, (1987). "Practical Principles, Moral Truth, and Ultimate Ends," *American Journal of Jurisprudence* 32:99-151.

Grisez, Germain, Joseph Boyle, John Finnis, and William May (1988). "Every Marital Act Ought to Be Open to New Life: Towards a Clearer Understanding," *The Thomist* 52,3:365-426.

Gustafson, James (1982). "Nature: Its Status in Theological Ethics," *Logos* E:5-23.

Himes, Michael J. (1989). "The Human Person in Contemporary Theology: From Human Nature to Authentic Subjectivity," in Ronald R. Hamel and Kenneth R. Himes, O.F.M. (eds.) *Introduction to Christian Ethics: A Reader*, New York: Paulist Press, pp.49-62.

Horsley, Richard A. (1978). "The Law of Nature in Philo and Cicero," *Harvard Theological Review* 71:35-59.

Kekes, John (1985). "Human Nature and Moral Theories," *Inquiry* 28:231-245.

Kenny, Anthony and Jan Pinborg (1982). "Medieval Philosophical Literature," in Norman Kretzmann, Anthony Kenny, and Jan Pinborg (eds.) *The Cambridge History of Later Medieval Philosophy*, Cambridge: Cambridge University Press, pp. 11-42.

Koester, Helmut (1968). "NOMOS PHYSEOS: The Concept of Natural Law in Greek Thought," in Jacob Neusner (ed.) *Religions in Antiquity*, Leiden: Brill, pp. 521-541.

Kuttner, Stephan (1982). "The Revival of Jurisprudence," in Robert L. Benson and Giles Constable, with Carol D. Lanham (eds.) *Renaissance and Renewal in the Twelfth Century*, Reprint, Toronto: University of Toronto Press, pp. 299-323.

Ladner, Gerhart B. (1982). "Terms and Ideas of Renewal," in Robert L. Benson and Giles Constable, with Carol D. Lanham (eds.) *Renaissance and Renewal in the Twelfth Century*, Reprint, Toronto: University of Toronto Press, pp. 1-36.

Lapidge, Michael (1988). "The Stoic Inheritance," in Peter Dronke (ed.) *A History of Twelfth-Century Western Philosophy*, Cambridge: Cambridge University Press, pp. 81-112.

Leclercq, Jean (1982). "The Renewal of Theology," in Robert L. Benson and Giles Constable, with Carol D. Lanham (eds.) *Renaissance and Renewal in the Twelfth Century*, Reprint, Toronto: University of Toronto Press, pp. 68-87.

Lewis, Ewart (1940). "Natural Law and Expediency in Medieval Political Theory," in *Ethics* 50:144-163.

Luscombe, D.E. (1982). "Natural Morality and Natural Law," in Norman Kretzmann, Anthony Kenny, and Jan Pinborg (eds.) *The Cambridge History of Later Medieval Philosophy*, Cambridge: Cambridge University Press, pp. 705-719.

Luscombe, D.E. and G.R. Evans (1988). "The Twelfth Century Renaissance," in J.H. Burns (ed.) *The Cambridge History of Medieval Political Thought: c.350-c.1450*, Cambridge: Cambridge University Press, pp. 306-340.

MacIntyre, Alasdair (1996). "Natural Law as Subversive: The Case of Aquinas," *Journal of Medieval and Early Modern Studies* 26.1:61-83.

Martin, John Hilary (1987). "The Injustice of Not Ordaining Women: A Problem for Medieval Theologians," *Theological Studies* 48:303-316.

May, William (1997). "Donum Vitae: Catholic Teaching Concerning Homologous IVF," in Kevin W. Wildes (ed.) *Infertility: A Crossroad of Faith, Medicine, and Technology*, Dordrecht, The Netherlands: Kluwer Academic Publishers, pp. 32-59.

McCormick, Richard A. (1987). "Document is Unpersuasive," *Responses to the Vatican Document on Reproductive Technologies*, St. Louis: Catholic Health Association, pp. 8-10.

Najman, Hindy (1999). "The Law of Nature and the Authority of Mosaic Law," *Studia Philonica Annual* II.

Nederman, Cary J. (1991). "Aristotelianism and the Origins of 'Political Science' in the Twelfth Century," *Journal of the History of Ideas* 52:179-194.

Niebuhr, Gustav (1998). "Polygamy Keeps a New African Church from World Council," *New York Times*, December 14.

Niebuhr, Reinhold (1957). "Christian Faith and Natural Law," in D.B. Robertson (ed.) *Love and Justice: Selections from the Shorter Writings of Reinhold Niebuhr*, Louisville, Kentucky: Westminster/ John Knox Press, pp.46-54.

Norr, Kurt Wolfgang (1982). "Institutional Foundations of the New Jurisprudence," in Robert L. Benson and Giles Constable, with Carol D. Lanham (eds.) *Renaissance and Renewal in the Twelfth Century*, Reprint, Toronto: University of Toronto Press, pp. 324-338.

Nussbaum, Martha (1988). "Non-Relative Virtues: An Aristotelian Approach," in Peter French, Theodore E. Uehling, Jr., and Howard K. Wettstein (eds.) *Midwest Studies in Philosophy XIII: Ethical Theory: Character and Virtue*, Notre Dame: University of Notre Dame Press, pp. 32-53.

O'Donovan, Oliver (1997). "Can There Be a Fruitful Theological Debate?," in Timothy Bradshaw (ed.) *The Way Forward: Christian Voices on Homosexuality and the Church*, London: Hodder & Stoughton, pp. 20-36.

Pigden, Charles (1989). "Logic and the Autonomy of Ethics," *Australian Journal of Philosophy* 67.2:127-151.

(1993) "Naturalism," in Peter Singer (ed.) *A Companion to Ethics*, London: Blackwell, pp. 421-431.

Porter, Jean (1996). "Contested Categories: Reason, Nature, and Natural Order in Medieval Accounts of the Natural Law," *Journal of Religious Ethics* 24,2: 207-232.

(1997). "Human Need and Natural Law," in Kevin W. Wildes (ed.) *Infertility: A Crossroad of Faith, Medicine, and Technology*, Dordrecht, The Netherlands: Kluwer Academic Publishers, pp. 93-106.

(1999). "What the Wise Person Knows: Natural Law and Virtue in Aquinas' *Summa Theologiae*," in *Studies in Christian Ethics* 12.1:57-69.

Potts, Timothy (1982). "Conscience," in Norman Kretzmann, Anthony Kenny, and Jan Pinborg (eds.) *The Cambridge History of Later Medieval Philosophy*, Cambridge: Cambridge University Press, pp. 687-704.

Quinn, J.F. (1974). "St. Bonaventure's Fundamental Conception of Natural Law," in *S. Bonaventura* 1274-1974, Rome: College of St. Bonaventure.

Rogers, Eugene F., Jr. (1998). "The Narrative of Natural Law in Aquinas's Commentary on Romans 1," *Theological Studies* 59.2:254-276.

Rouse, Richard H. and Mary A. Rouse (1982). "*Statim invenire*: Schools, Preachers, and New Attitudes to the Page," in Robert L. Benson and Giles Constable, with Carol D. Lanham (eds.) *Renaissance and Renewal in the Twelfth Century*, Reprint, Toronto: University of Toronto Press, pp. 201-225.

Sahaydachcy, Bocarius (1996). "The Marriage of Unifree Persons: Twelfth-Century Decretals and Letters," in *De Jure Canonico Medii: Festschrift for Rudolf Weigand, Studia Gratiana* XXVII, LAS.

Schneewind, Jerome (1993). "Kant and Natural Law Ethics," *Ethics* 104:53-74.

Schubeck, Thomas L. (1992). "The Reconstruction of Natural Law Reasoning: Liberation Theology as a Case Study," *The Journal of Religious Ethics* 20,1:149-178.

Smart, Ninian (1997). "Hinduism," in Philip L. Quinn and Charles Taliaferro (eds.) *A Companion to Philosophy of Religion*, London: Blackwell, pp. 7-14.

Speer, Andreas (1994). "Reception – Mediation – Innovation: Philosophy and Theology in the Twelfth Century," in J. Mamesse (ed.) *Bilan et perspectives des études médiévales: Actes du premier congrès européen d'études médiévales*, Louvain: La Nevve, pp. 129-149.

Strawson, Galen (1996). "In Deepest Sympathy: Towards a Natural History of Virtue," *Times Literary Supplement*, 29 November:3-4.

Tierney, Brian (1963). "Natura id est Deus: A Case of Juristic Pantheism?," *Journal of the History of Ideas* 24:307-322.

Van Caenegem, R.C. (1988) "Government, Law and Society," in J.H. Burns (ed.) *The Cambridge History of Medieval Political Thought: c.350-c.1450,* Cambridge: Cambridge University Press, pp. 174-210.

Watson, Gerard (1971). "Natural Law and Stoicism," in A.A. Long (ed.) *Problems in Stoicism,* London: Athlone, pp. 216-238.

Wetherbee, Winthrop (1988). "Philosophy, Cosmology, and the Twelfth-Century Renaissance," in Peter Dronke (ed.) *A History of Twelfth-Century Western Philosophy,* Cambridge: Cambridge University Press, pp. 21-53.

Winstanley, Gerard (1989). "The True Levelers Standard Approach," in Andrew Hopton (ed.) *Gerard Winstanley: Selected Writings,* London: Aporia Press, pp. 7-23.

Secondary sources, books

Abulafia, Anna Sapir (1995). *Christians and Jews in the Twelfth-Century Renaissance,* London: Routledge.

Annas, Julia (1993). *The Morality of Happiness,* Oxford: Oxford University Press.

Barr, James (1993). *Biblical Faith and Natural Theology,* Oxford: Clarendon.

Barth, Karl (1957). *Church Dogmatics, II:2,* Edinburgh: T. and T. Clark.

Biggar, Nigel (1995). *The Hastening That Waits,* Oxford: Clarendon.

Bloch, Marc (1961). *Feudal Society,* 2 vols., Chicago: University of Chicago Press.

Bonnassie, Pierre (1991). *From Slavery to Feudalism in South-Western Europe,* Cambridge: Cambridge University Press.

Boswell, John (1980). *Christianity, Social Tolerance, and Homosexuality,* Chicago: University of Chicago Press.

Brett, Annabel S. (1997). *Liberty, Right and Nature: Individual Rights in Later Scholastic Thought,* Cambridge: Cambridge University Press.

Brundage, James A. (1987). *Law, Sex, and Christian Society in Medieval Europe,* Chicago: University of Chicago Press.

(1995). *Medieval Canon Law,* London: Longman.

Bynum, Carolyn Walker (1982). *Jesus as Mother: Studies in the Spirituality of the High Middle Ages,* Berkeley: University of California Press.

Cadden, Joan (1993). *Meanings of Sex Difference in the Middle Ages: Medicine, Science, and Culture,* Cambridge: Cambridge University Press.

Cahill, Lisa (1996). *Sex, Gender, and Christian Ethics,* Cambridge: Cambridge University Press.

Caplan, Pat (1996). *The Cultural Construction of Sexuality,* Reprint, London: Routledge.

Carlyle, R.W. and A.J. Carlyle (1970). *A History of Medieval Political Theory in the West,* 6 vols., Reprint, Edinburgh: Blackwood and Sons. Originally 1903–1936.

Casey, John (1990). *Pagan Virtue: An Essay in Ethics*, Oxford: Clarendon.

Cates, Diana Fritz (1997). *Choosing to Feel: Virtue, Friendship, and Compassion for Friends*, Notre Dame: University of Notre Dame Press.

Chenu, M.D. (1964). *Toward Understanding Saint Thomas*, Albert M. Landry and Dominic Hughes (trans.), Chicago: Henry Regnery Co.

(1968). *Nature, Man, and Society in the Twelfth Century*, Jerome Taylor and Lester K. Little (eds.), Chicago: University of Chicago Press.

Clark, Stephen R.L. (1997). *Animals and Their Moral Standing*, London: Routledge.

Cohen, Jeremy (1982). *The Friars and the Jews: Evolution of Medieval Anti-Judaism*, Ithaca, New York: Cornell University Press.

(1989). *"Be Fertile and Increase, Fill the Earth and Master It:" The Ancient and Medieval Career of a Biblical Text*, Ithaca, New York: Cornell University Press.

Colish, Marcia L. (1990). *The Stoic Tradition from Antiquity to the Early Middle Ages*, 2 vols., Leiden: Brill.

Congregation for the Doctrine of the Faith (1987). *Donum Vitae*, an Introduction promulgated on February 22, 1987.

Constable, Giles (1996). *The Reformation of the Twelfth Century*, Cambridge: Cambridge University Press.

Crowe, Michael (1977). *The Changing Profile of the Natural Law*, The Hague: Martinus Nijhoff.

Curran, Charles E. and Richard A. McCormick, eds. (1991). *Readings in Moral Theology No. 7: Natural Law and Theology*, New York: Paulist Press.

Delhaye, Philippe (1960). *Permanence du Droit Naturel*, Louvain: Editiones Nauwelaerts.

D'Entreves, A.P. (1970). *Natural Law: An Introduction to Legal Philosophy*, rev. edn., London: Hutchinson.

De Waal, Frans (1996). *Good Natured: The Origins of Right and Wrong in Human and Other Animals*, Cambridge, Mass.: Harvard University Press.

Donagan, Alan (1977). *The Theory of Morality*, Chicago: University of Chicago Press.

Douglas, Mary (1966). *Purity and Danger: An Analysis of the Concepts of Pollution and Taboo*, London: Routledge.

Duby, Georges (1980). *The Three Orders: Feudal Society Imagined*, Arthur Goldhammer (ed.), Chicago: University of Chicago Press.

(1994). *Love and Marriage in the Middle Ages*, Jane Dunnett (trans.), Chicago: University of Chicago Press.

Ennen, Edith (1989). *The Medieval Woman*, Oxford: Blackwell.

Evans, G.R. (1983). *Alan of Lille: the Frontiers of Theology in the Later Twelfth Century*, Cambridge: Cambridge University Press.

Finnis, John (1980). *Natural Law and Natural Rights*, Oxford: Clarendon Press.

(1998). *Aquinas: Moral, Political, and Legal Theory*, Oxford: Oxford University Press.

Flanagan, Owen J., Jr. (1991). *Varieties of Moral Personality: Ethics and Psychological Realism*, Cambridge, Mass.: Harvard University Press.

Foot, Philippa (1978). *Virtues and Vices*, Oxford: Blackwell.

Foucault, Michel (1976). *Histoire de la sexualité*, Paris: NRF / Gallimard.

French, Roger and Andrew Cunningham (1996). *Before Science: The Invention of the Friars' Natural Philosophy*, Aldershot, U.K.: Scholar Press.

Gadamer, Hans-Georg (1989). *Truth and Method*, rev. edn., New York: Crossroad.

Gardella, Peter (1985). *Innocent Ecstasy: How Christianity Gave America an Ethic of Sexual Pleasure*, Oxford: Oxford University Press.

Gilson, Etienne (1948). *L'Esprit de la Philosophie Medievale*, Paris: Vrin.

Grant, Edward (1996). *The Foundations of Modern Science in the Middle Ages: Their Religious Institutional, and Intellectual Contexts*, Cambridge: Cambridge University Press.

Grisez, Germain (1983). *The Way of the Lord Jesus 1: Christian Moral Principles*, Chicago: Franciscan Herald Press.

    (1993). *The Way of the Lord Jesus 2: Living a Christian Life*, Chicago: Franciscan Herald Press.

Gustafson, James (1981). *Ethics from a Theocentric Perspective, Volume One: Theology and Ethics*, Chicago: University of Chicago Press.

    (1984). *Ethics From a Theocentric Perspective, Volume Two: Ethics and Theology*, Chicago: University of Chicago Press.

Hart, H.L.A. (1961). *The Concept of Law*, London: Clarendon.

Haskins, Charles Homer (1957). *The Renaissance of the Twelfth Century*, Reprint, Meridian.

Hauerwas, Stanley (1981). *A Community of Character: Towards a Constructive Christian Social Ethic*, Notre Dame: University of Notre Dame Press.

    (1983). *The Peaceable Kingdom: A Primer in Christian Ethics*, Notre Dame: University of Notre Dame Press.

    (1985). *Against the Nations: War and Survival in a Liberal Society*, Minneapolis: Seabury/Winston Press.

    (1986). *Suffering Presence: Theological Reflections on Medicine, the Mentally Handicapped, and the Church*, Notre Dame: University of Notre Dame Press.

    (1991). *After Christendom: How the Church Is to Behave if Freedom, Justice, and a Christian Nation Are Bad Ideas*, Nashville: Abingdon.

Hays, Richard (1996). *The Moral Vision of the New Testament: A Contemporary Introduction to New Testament Ethics*, New York: Harper Collins.

Hefner, Philip (1993). *The Human Factor: Evolution, Culture, and Religion*, Minneapolis: Fortress Press.

Herlihy, David (1985). *Medieval Households*, Cambridge, Mass.: Harvard University Press.

Herrin, Judith (1987). *The Formation of Christendom*, Princeton: Princeton University Press.

Hibbs, Thomas (1995). *Dialectic and Narrative in Aquinas: The Interpretation of the Summa contra gentiles*, Notre Dame: University of Notre Dame Press.

Hollenbach, David (1979). *Claims in Conflict: Retrieving and Renewing the Catholic Human Rights Tradition*, Mahwah, New Jersey: Paulist Press.

Hood, John Y.B. (1995). *Aquinas and the Jews*, Philadelphia: University of Pennsylvania Press.

Hudson, W.D. (1969). *The Is/Ought Distinction*, London: Macmillan.

Hume, David (1888). *A Treatise on Human Nature*, L.A. Selby-Bigge (ed.), Oxford: Oxford University Press.

Hurka, Thomas (1993). *Perfectionism*, Oxford: Oxford University Press.

John Paul II, Pope (1993). *Veritatis Splendor*, encyclical letter promulgated on October 5, 1993.

Jordan, Mark (1997). *The Invention of Sodomy*, Chicago: University of Chicago Press.

Kass, Leon (1985). *Toward a More Natural Science: Biology and Human Affairs*, New York: Macmillan.

Kent, Bonnie (1995). *Virtues of the Will: The Transformation of Ethics in the Late Thirteenth Century*, Washington, D.C.: Catholic University of America Press.

Kovesi, Julius (1967). *Moral Notions*, London: Routledge and Kegan Paul.

Kuttner, Stephan (1937). *Repertorium der Kanonistk (1140-1234): Prodromus Corporis Glossarum I (Studi e Testi 71)*, Vatican City.

Lambert, Malcolm (1992). *Medieval Heresy: Popular Movements from the Gregorian Reform to the Reformation*, 2nd edn., London: Oxford: Blackwell.

Lawrence, C.H. (1994). *The Friars: The Impact of the Early Mendicant Movement on Western Society*, Essex: Longman.

Leo XIII, Pope (1891). *Rerum Novarum*, encyclical letter promulgated May 15, 1891.

Little, Lester K. (1978). *Religious Poverty and the Profit Economy in Medieval Europe*, Ithaca, New York: Cornell University Press.

Lottin, Odon (1931). *Le droit naturel chez saint Thomas d'Aquin et ses prédécesseurs*, 2nd edn., Bruges: Beyart.

 (1942-1960). *Psychologie et morale aux XIIe et XIIIe siècles*, 6 vols., Louvain: Abbaye du Mont César.

MacIntyre, Alasdair (1984). *After Virtue*, 2nd edn., Notre Dame: University of Notre Dame Press.

Marenbon, John (1997). *The Philosophy of Peter Abelard*, Cambridge: Cambridge University Press.

Maritain, Jacques (1947). *The Person and the Common Good*, University of Notre Dame Press.

 (1951). *Man and the State*, Chicago: University of Chicago Press.

Mayr, Ernst (1988). *Toward a New Philosophy of Biology: Observations of an Evolutionist*, Cambridge, Mass.: Harvard University Press.

McFadyen, Alistair (1991). *The Call to Personhood: A Christian Theory of the Individual in Social Relationships*, Cambridge: Cambridge University Press.

Midgley, Mary (1978). *Beast and Man: The Roots of Human Nature*, New York: Meridian.

(1994). *The Ethical Primate: Humans, Freedom, and Morality*, London: Routledge.

Milbank, John (1990). *Theology and Social Theory: Beyond Secular Reason*, London: Blackwell.

Moore, G.E. (1903). *Principia Ethica*, Cambridge: Cambridge University Press.

Moore, R.I. (1987). *The Formation of a Persecuting Society: Power and Deviance in Western Europe, 950-1250*, London: Oxford: Blackwell.

Murray, Alexander (1985). *Reason and Society in the Middle Ages*, Oxford: Oxford University Press.

Murray, John Courtney (1960). *We Hold These Truths*, New York: Sheed and Ward.

Nelson, Daniel Mark (1992). *The Priority of Prudence: Virtue and Natural Law in Thomas Aquinas and Its Implications for Modern Ethics*, University Park, Penn.: Pennsylvania State University Press.

Niebuhr, Reinhold (1996). *The Nature and Destiny of Man, Vol. II: Human Destiny*, Reprint, Louisville, Kentucky: Westminster/John Knox Press.

Noonan, John, T. *The Scholastic Analysis of Usury*, Harvard University Press.

(1965). *Contraception: A History of Its Treatment by the Catholic Theologians and Canonists*, Cambridge, Mass.: Harvard University Press.

Northcott, Michael S. (1996). *The Environment and Christian Ethics*, Cambridge: Cambridge University Press.

Nussbaum, Martha (1994). *The Therapy of Desire: Theory and Practice in Hellenistic Ethics*, Princeton: Princeton University Press.

O'Donovan, Oliver (1984). *Begotten or Made?*, Oxford: Clarendon.

(1986). *Resurrection and Moral Order: An Outline for Evangelical Ethics*, Grand Rapids, Michigan: Eerdmans.

(1996). *The Desire of the Nations: Rediscovering the Roots of Political Theology*, Cambridge: Cambridge University Press.

Outka, Gene (1972). *Agape: An Ethical Analysis*, New Haven, Conn.: Yale University Press.

Parfit, Derek (1989). *Reasons and Persons*, Reprint, Oxford: Oxford University Press.

Paul VI, Pope (1968), *Humanae Vitae*, an encyclical letter promulgated on July 25, 1968.

Patterson, Orlando (1982). *Slavery and Social Death: A Comparative Study*, Cambridge, Mass.: Harvard University Press.

(1991). *Freedom in the Making of Western Culture*, San Francisco: Basic Books.

Perry, Michael J. (1998). *The Idea of Human Rights: Four Inquiries*, New York: Oxford University Press.

Pope, Stephen J. (1994). *The Evolution of Altruism and the Ordering of Love*, Washington, D.C.: Georgetown University Press.

Prior, A.N. (1949). *Logic and the Basis of Ethics*, Oxford: Oxford University Press.

Ramsey, Paul (1970). *Fabricated Man*, New Haven, Conn.: Yale University Press.

Reynolds, Barbara (1994). *Fiefs and Vassals: The Medieval Evidence Reinterpreted*, Oxford: Oxford University Press.

Rhonheimer, Martin (1987). *Natur als Grundlage der Moral*, Innsbruck: Tyrolia Verlag.

Runia, David T. (1993). *Philo in Early Christian Literature: A Survey*, Assen, The Netherlands: Van Gorcum.

Russell, Frederick H. (1975). *The Just War in the Middle Ages*, Cambridge: Cambridge University Press.

Salisbury, Joyce (1994). *The Beast Within: Animals in the Middle Ages*, London: Routledge.

Schubert, Alois (1924). *Augustins lex-aeterna-Lehre nach Inhalt und Quellen, Beiträge sur Geschicte der Philosophie des Mittelalters 24*:2, Münster: i.W. Aschendorff.

Shklar, Judith N. (1990). *The Faces of Injustice*, New Haven, Conn.: Yale University Press.

Smalley, Beryl (1952). *The Study of the Bible in the Middle Ages*, London: Blackwell.

Southern, R.W. (1953). *The Making of the Middle Ages*, New Haven, CT: Yale University Press.

(1995) *Scholastic Humanism and the Unification of Europe, Volume One: Foundations*, London: Blackwell.

Spruyt, Hendrik (1994). *The Sovereign State and Its Competitors: An Analysis of Systems Change*, Princeton: Princeton University Press.

Stout, Rowland (1996). *Things That Happen Because They Should: A Teleological Approach to Action*, London: Clarendon.

Sullivan, Andrew (1996). *Virtually Normal: An Argument about Homosexuality*, London: Picador.

Tellenbach, Gerd (1991). *Church, State and Christian Society at the Time of the Investiture Contest*, Reprint, Toronto: University of Toronto Press, originally 1940.

Tierney, Brian (1997). *The Idea of Natural Rights: Studies on Natural Rights, Natural Law and Church Law, 1150-1625*, Atlanta: Scholars Press.

Torrell, Jean-Pierre (1993). *Initiation à saint Thomas d'Aquin*, Fribourg: Cerf.

Tuck, Richard (1979). *Natural Rights Theories: Their Origin and Development*, Cambridge: Cambridge University Press.

Ullman, Walter (1966). *The Individual in the Middle Ages*, Baltimore: The John Hopkins Press.

Van Caenegem, R.C. (1992). *An Historical Introduction to Private Law*, D.E.L. Johnston (trans.), Cambridge: Cambridge University Press.

Vauchez, Andre (1987). *Les laïcs au Moyen Age: pratiques et expériences religieuses*, Paris: Cerf.

Vinogradoff, Paul (1929). *Roman Law in Medieval Europe*, 2nd edn., London: Clarendon.

Weber, Max (1968/1978). *Economy and Society*, 2 vols., Berkeley: University of California Press.

Weigand, Rudolf (1967). *Die Naturrechtslehre der Legisten und Dekretisten von Irnerius bis Accursius und von Gratian bis Johannes Teutonicus*, München: Max Hueber.

Williams Bernard (1973). *Problems of the Self*, Cambridge: Cambridge University Press.

(1985). *Ethics and the Limits of Philosophy*, Cambridge, Mass.: Harvard University Press.

Wilson, Edward (1978). *On Human Nature*, Cambridge, Mass.: Harvard University Press.

Yoder, John Howard (1994). *The Politics of Jesus: Vicit Agnus Noster*, 2nd edn., Grand Rapids, Mich.: Eerdmans.

Index

Proper Names: Classical and Medieval

(Names are listed in accordance with the spelling given in the text.
Names of works are not listed except in the case of works
with no known author.)

Proper Names: Modern and Contemporary

Subjects

Scriptural References

Printed in the United States
69784LV00004B/192